"Rosetree is a renowned aura and face r[...] are open-minded." — *NAPRA Review*

"Rose Rosetree can spot a potential fibber a mile away. Or, in this case, 2,400 miles away." — Las Vegas Sun

"It's like she's known you forever…but that's crazy, because you just met. Still, she has described you perfectly, and not just your surface traits."
— *The Washington Post*

"She flutters with enthusiasm for her work, eager to share her zest and her skills. She makes sure, even when sharing a negative reading, to tell how a person can use that trait to his or her benefit."
— The Washington Times

Students "sat in rapt attention — despite white molded plastic chairs — for almost two hours, listening to her describe her craft and watching her read the faces and auras of audience members…Her basic belief that we worry too much about our faces and not enough about our souls is difficult to argue with."
— *The Los Angeles Times*

"I decided to send her a picture of myself…with the caveat that my wife would 'check' her report for accuracy. 'She's got your number,' was my wife's simple response." — The Catholic Standard

"Your readings for *The Kalamazoo Gazette* were the most amazing thing I've ever seen in a newspaper. I'm in politics myself. I know these people."
— *Politician from Kalamazoo, Michigan*

"You have more credibility with me as an aura reader than any others I've interviewed."
— Rob McConnell (Paranormal research broadcaster since 1995),
"XZone Radio," internationally syndicated

"You haven't been reading my face, you've been checking with my Mum."
— *John Maytham, "Capetalk Radio," Capetown, So. Africa*

"Usually I debunk anything spiritual but…You really didn't know me before seeing my photo? Your reading was like listening to my mother."
— Brendan O'Connor, "Tony and Julie," BBC radio, England

Online Supplement

To enrich your experience of this book,
visit its "Online Supplement"
at the home page of www.co-createwithGod.com.
The website, itself, is an enrichment
to one I've offered for several years:
www.rose-rosetree.com,
where you can find a wealth of articles and FAQs
plus my previous books and other resources
about deeper perception.

What will this new website offer?
I can't give you the definitive answer yet.
My big project lately
has been getting *this* book to press.

Still, I do have some dreams for this website.
So far, I can tell you for sure that it will include
a detailed "Contents" section for this book
plus the "Index."
You will be invited to contribute, too.
Together we'll co-create this website with God.
See you online!

— Rose Rosetree, October 2005

Let today be a Holiday

365 WAYS TO CO-CREATE WITH GOD

ROSE ROSETREE

Let Today Be a Holiday:
365 Ways to Co-Create with God

Editors: Teresa Kramer, Liane McCabe and Mitch Weber for Women's Intuition Worldwide, L.L.C.
Cover Design: Melanie Matheson, Rolling Rhino Communications, www.rollingrhino.com
Book Design Consultant: Eda Warren, Desktop Publishing Services, Inc., www.go-training.com
Typesetting: Rose Rosetree
Printed in the United States of America
10 9 8 7 6 5 4 3 2 1

Contribute to a website for people like you who are learning more, day by day,
about how to consciously co-create with God,
for service to the world, for human fulfillment:
www.co-createwithGod.com

For Rose Rosetree's books, personal sessions, workshops, monthly e-zine:
www.rose-rosetree.com

Please direct all inquiries about this book
(including requests for quantity discounts and library sales) to the publisher:
Women's Intuition Worldwide, L.L.C.,
703-404-4357, 116 Hillsdale Dr., Sterling, VA 20164-1201.

Dedication

Dedicated to the gift
that only you
can give God,
complete acceptance of who you are,
however human, quirky, uniquely wonderful.

To your love!
To your light!
To your power!

Foreword

In Japan, spirituality has traditionally been at the core of daily life, even in business. Gradually, however, the emphasis has shifted. Rather than simply honoring an abstract, metaphysical dimension, people are demanding results. Spirituality has become accountable.

I consider this a positive development. For generations, spiritual seeking has subtly influenced every aspect of life, from physical health to material success, from casual friendships to the most intimate relationships. Yet spiritual matters were seldom discussed. Inadvertently they were diminished by being held so high, beyond human comprehension.

We're no longer satisfied with having the source and essence of life be abstract, mysterious or unknowable. People actively seek to understand. Throughout Asia, this search is evident in the best of our books, movies and TV. Seekers demand a kind of spirituality that combines depth with tangible results.

No longer is spirituality a fantasy. It has become something to live more fully 365 days a year. This is why I'm so delighted with Rose's new book. Turn to any page and you'll find ideas to inspire you.

Besides the range of topics and the depth Rose brings to them, I'm enthusiastic about the sheer practicality of this book. It is packed with techniques that you won't find elsewhere, techniques that really can make a difference.

Through my company, VOICE, I've sponsored teachers for 16 years. I've seen Rose in action here in Japan, both teaching and doing personal sessions. From this perspective, I can assure you that she is outstanding. What Rose teaches is in alignment with who she is as a person. What she writes about, she lives.

May this important book influence seekers of God throughout the world and uplift all who desire to go beyond merely seeking. It's time to co-create!

Masumi Hori
President, VOICE, Inc.
Tokyo, Japan
November 2005

Introduction

Though ever-present as your helper and creator, God has made a sanctuary of free will where only you are in control. It's your *consciousness*. However you choose to wake up that truth-seeking awareness within, God will support you. Hasn't this happened so far?

- What if you seek God by means of beliefs? God will illuminate the truth within those beliefs.
- What if you ask God to live within your heart? No problem. It has always been so.
- What if you resolve to honor your body as God's temple? You can do it through athletics, yoga or dance; through health food or pleasure food, celibacy or sex. Whatever your choice, sooner or later, the result will be a stronger version of God's presence coursing through your blood.
- What if you pursue God through religion? Depending on the beliefs within your beliefs, God will participate just as you've requested.

But uh-oh! Despite always being successful as a co-creator with God, you may encounter one problem. Whether you're involved in organized religion or what I call "disorganized religion," whether you're an Olympic athlete, a sophisticated theologian or a world-class lover of humanity, good intentions can bring you God knowledge. But that doesn't guarantee a life where you *actively* co-create with God.

For this to happen, it is important to learn about yourself, not just some far-away Almighty Being. How were you designed for knowledge and service? Quick, glib answers won't do. They won't satisfy the longing to experience those gifts directly, all the way from the surface of life to the deepest part of you.

One reason to fully own your gifts is that they can help you experience God more clearly. Over time, your consciousness wakes up more. Thus, you earn the standing to do more than simply have conversations with God. Together you can co-create.

Fingerprints are an outward symbol that you are one of a kind. But that uniqueness goes way beyond the whorls built into your thumbs.

Uniqueness includes your gifts for *deeper perception.* Techniques to activate this can bring you to the level of angels, of auras, of deep human secrets.

Deeper perception turns theories about living with God into direct experience. You discover yourself in a love story — awe-inspiring, tender and extremely private. No human words are adequate to describe it.

Personally, I know something (not everything, just something) about this kind of love story. Like you, I'm on a spiritual pilgrimage, learning day by day. In that spirit of fellowship, I offer you 365 ideas that have helped me to move forward. Sure, you can start using them on January 1, but it's just as powerful to resolve that *today* will initiate your best year yet, consciously co-creating with God.

1. Co-Create or Pray?

Prayer is the traditional way to ask for God's help. In this book I favor a more contemporary method: *Co-creation.* How do they differ?

Prayer is done at church or a quiet place at home. Sure, sometimes you might pray in your car — and prevent a crash, too. Still, the more classic setting is *contemplative.* Whatever the size of your prayer group, you move one step back from your surroundings and ask to receive God's blessing.

Co-creation is mostly done *actively.* Although you're alone at first, the team soon becomes you plus God's presence, consciously connected. Together, you join forces to improve real-life situations.

Another difference: For prayer, *spiritual awareness* is optional. Millions of believers say the right words but achieve haphazard results because they haven't yet learned to engage their consciousness. Co-creation requires that you wake up this most intimate, sacred component of who you are.

Creativity won't win you points with traditional prayer. Religious instruction gives you the right words; afterwards you can throw in some personal requests. By contrast, co-creation doesn't demand that you follow set rules. Although you can learn ways to start things rolling (this book, in fact, being chock full of them) co-creation invites you to improvise.

In prayer we ask God for what we want. In meditation, we listen. Beautiful! But, if you think about it, defining prayer and meditation like this turns people into passive supplicants. Many of us have been taught not only to ask but to beg. If a prayer doesn't bring what we wish, it's considered a test of faith. Soon, we may feel more unworthy than ever. Then, more than before, we beg. Even a conversation with God can involve beseeching, imploring.

Co-creation is NOT about begging. Consciously connected to God, with mutual respect, you make things happen. In this collaboration, you participate as an adult, no longer a supplicating child.

Remember when you graduated from being a kid? Not legally, inwardly. Something changed inside. Starting now, you would insist on your money, your rules, your choices.

Long before, you had made a similar choice to stop crawling. Starting now, you would walk. The choice to co-create is another milestone in your personal evolution. You dare to seek a new kind of spiritual maturity. Today, think about your relationship to God. You have always been God's beloved child. Are you interested in becoming God's grownup?

2. Beauty, the Sneaky Resource

You happen to live in a culture with way too many images of beauty. Even if you didn't watch TV, you'd see these images in stores and newspaper ads, on the Internet. Spiritually empty, these images are inflicted upon you, usually with the ulterior motive of making you buy things. Call it *coercive beauty*.

But beauty is best enjoyed when you make the choice to seek it. This kind could be called *soul-awakening beauty*.

A third type is *customary beauty*. Even an exquisite painting becomes a mere possession if you habitually see it the same way. How can you make it come alive again? Be willing to look long enough, differently enough. When you find something new, joy will be your signal. You have rediscovered soul-awakening beauty.

All three kinds of beauty are part of a Beauty Scale. It ranges from coercive through customary to distinctively lovely. Once you understand this, you can choose where to position yourself along the continuum. Intention can move you from a low-end beauty experience to the kind that thrills your soul.

Each day you start toward the low end because familiar surroundings (no matter how gorgeous) are dulled by habit. But you can easily re-position yourself.

Start by choosing one sense. Which will delight you most — a sound, a sight, a touch, a smell, a taste? Decide, then pick your beauty object. It could be something you never noticed before, like one square inch of a table. Stay with it long enough to find its lotus-like heart of splendor.

Or begin with something you already find beautiful and deepen your senses by adding something new. Put on a favorite shirt or fragrance, then ask inside for an original idea to link with it, for example, "Through this I explore a new quality of God's tenderness."

A person can be undernourished though fat. Similarly, though bombarded by images, you can long for real beauty. What will happen when you switch it on, full and strong, early in your day?

With experience, moving up high on the Beauty Scale can be done in seconds. All it takes is practice. Whenever you seek and find *soul-awakening beauty*, the process changes you, opening up a channel to beauty's Source.

Each channel works in two directions, both to and from Source. So your game of hide-and-seek for beauty creates new ways for the joy of God to find YOU. Sneaky, huh?

3. Sounds of Delight

All around you, heavenly choirs sing. The trick is to hear them through *human* ears.

Whether auditory or otherwise, beauty for humans registers only when we are willing to receive it. This is one way to distinguish a beauty experience from a pain experience.

If you're walking down the street and a piano falls on your foot, you'll notice. Pain grabs attention. Real music, however, is never inflicted upon you. To hear really beautiful music (the kind that awakens your soul) you must meet it halfway.

Background music may rightfully make you snooze. Dispassionately you recognize what's playing, but so what? To open up delight, you must open the ears within your ears. Inwardly you must say, "Let the concert begin!"

Your role as listener is so instrumental, you can even attend a concert where no official music plays at all. Right where you are now, for instance, you can breathe deeply, close your eyes and investigate what you hear.

Postmodern life may be treating you to layers of electronic buzz from half a dozen gadgets. Can you hear car rhythms or the wordless chant of an air conditioner? Nature adds harmonious sounds, like wind and rain. Listen closely enough and your own body will play music. Have you ever appreciated the quiet roar of your breath? If you were to listen intently enough, could you hear your heart beat?

One extra sound of delight is available no matter where you are. Silence underlies everything. In silence, God's voice speaks with majesty. Listen for That comfort, That wisdom, variations on the theme of love.

Could there be more to the heavenly concert? Sure. As you develop deeper perception, you open up mystical layers of hearing. Next time you hold a flower, listen for its song. At every layer of creation, you can eavesdrop on sounds of delight.

4. Munch Into That New Day

Yum, a new day!

Perhaps that isn't how you greet each morning…yet. But how long has it been since you took in your minimum daily requirement for flavors?

According to the ancient healing science of Ayurveda, you need six different flavors each day. Unless you taste them all, you'll feel incomplete. Here's the lineup:

- Start with *sweet* — or perhaps end with it. Sweetness doesn't come only from desserts. It's the subtle essence of many vegetables, from asparagus to zucchini.
- *Sour* provides the obvious contrast. Citrus fruits, unsweetened yogurt, vinegars or pickles will get you there.
- *Bitter* isn't necessarily bad, or folks would never crave coffee and chocolate.
- *Salty* can come from celery, olives or sea vegetables (like those that wrap sushi), not only snack food like pretzels.
- *Astringent* tastes make you pucker, such as the apple a day that keeps the doctor away or oh-so-mighty spinach.
- Putting *pungent* flavors into your diet requires just a twirl of your pepper grinder, a dollop of hot salsa, a smidge of Tabasco sauce or a wink of chutney.

So there you have it, six highly distinctive and necessary flavors. All it takes is one bite of each to balance your buds, and multiple tastes can combine in one dish. One salad, for instance, could score you the flavor equivalent of bingo.

Ideally it's best to sample all six at each meal. Doing this might help you to lose weight. It's definitely guaranteed to help you lose boredom.

Has anything been left out from our discussion of the six flavors? Only the best part: Your own moods may need to go through the full sequence, too. Let all your emotions — not just the sweet ones — be welcome as you savor this day.

5. Snuff for the Soul

When I finally tried snuff, I was shocked, shocked! Powder that you put in your nose to make yourself sneeze? And this ridiculous stuff was once all the rage in genteel social circles? Well, sneezing does clear your brain temporarily. Even better, with each sneeze your consciousness transcends to a higher vibration, just for a second. It's like a mini-orgasm for your face, causing you to forget all lesser pleasures.

Etiquette acknowledges sneezing, after a fashion. After someone sneezes, a person might say "God Bless You," but not after other bodily functions that we could mention. Why? Perhaps the distinction is a tiny acknowledgment that sneezing is, in its way, a trip. Sneezing takes you on a tiny voyage in consciousness. Enough sneezes might make you slightly (ever so slightly) high.

Better than tripping by means of snuff, you can hitchhike onto any good smell. Contrast between one fragrance and another will enhance your pleasure. And, frankly, *there may be no better snuff for your soul than the weather.* Take your nose outdoors. Go for contrast. Until you've explored at least three fragrances, you haven't given yourself enough nasal space to get high.

Contrast isn't merely a matter of clean vs. dirty, or you could inspire yourself olfactorily by breathing in essence of garbage pail, then eau de soap. Better contrasts await you outdoors. Country air has soul. In suburbia, even look-alike housing developments can reveal quirks to an inquiring nostril. Cities provide innumerable odors of interest. You can find them even without walking a dog!

All you need do is go outside and let your nose lead you. Smell the temperature. Each season has a fragrance, ripe with local variations. Let your discerning nose explore how much moisture is in the air. Savor the way fresh air enhances plain soil plus any plants growing on it. With trees, don't forget to stand near enough for your nose to hear a bark.

You can even smell the direction of wind. Close your eyes and turn your head until your nose gets into it, the flow of purity, subtle but satisfying. How amazing, the things you can do with your nose, once you give it a chance!

As a pre-schooler, my son loved to play the kazoo through his nose. Who knows what extraordinary specialties will be *yours* when you set your nose to them? And the great outdoors can always inspire your spirit to soar. That's where you transcend indoor civilization and encounter something bigger, freer, untamable...something wild.

So walk your nose outdoors. Plunge in deep. God has written His signature in the wind just for you. There may be no better snuff for your soul.

6. Touched by Joy

Joy can be as close as your fingertips. This secret is known by every toddler, forgotten by most adults. Seniors rediscover it, however. Long after other senses fade, touch remains a source of joy — perennially juicy.

But why wait until old age to cherish your amazing sense of touch? Use it today to replenish your *inner fountain of youth.*

Once I dined at a restaurant with a wonderful dessert buffet. Imagine elegant bowls of cream puffs, strawberries, miniature fudge cakes and fruit kebabs. Then picture something even better…a chocolate fountain. Yes, some food genius designed a three-foot sculpture of milk chocolate. Who knew chocolate could flow like that: Warm, silken, cascading in sheets, swirls and ribbons. At this restaurant, you're encouraged to skewer already scrumptious desserts, then drench them in chocolate.

If you're like me, a fountain like this is the stuff of dreams. But a simpler version lies right at your fingertips. Simply touch something new. And, please, don't cheat by touching with your eyes only. Move those sensitive finger pads directly onto something you haven't explored lately, like a doorknob, the edge of a table or your own highly fascinating knee.

Once you've found your touch object, jump in with both hands, every finger. What a treat, to compare the over- and under-sides of sticky tape! Discoveries are intensified if you'll do two things more: Close your eyes and breathe generously.

Then go touch-hunting again. Since each hand has five fingers, it seems fair that you treat each hand to five different textures. You'll find marvelous nuances to things you supposedly already knew(to the point of boredom) like the bristles on your toothbrush.

Could novelty be why kids laugh so much? Whatever your age, you can make life new. It takes such a small shift of attention. And after you take the initiative to peek around one corner of life, around the very next corner you may find a new face of God peeking right back at you.

7. Hide and Seek

Do troubles weigh on you? Feel frightened, angry or sad? Here's a little game to rearrange unwelcome emotions, maybe even laugh some of them out of town.

Write a little love note to yourself, praising some of your finer attributes. Fold up the paper and hide it someplace where you live.

Then forget about your note.

Later, when you feel ready for inspiration, do a treasure hunt. Find that note. Only before you read it, pretend that it is a love letter from God. Whether you read silently or aloud, speak in an imitation of God's own voice.

Maybe you'll laugh, maybe you'll cry. Guaranteed you'll move some emotions around, which is the point.

Some of us unintentionally play a game like this as we grow older. Spacing out, we lose little things or forget why we came into a room. Typically, we criticize ourselves for it.

Re-interpret that tired old game. Voluntary hide and seek can help keep life fresh. When you finally locate any object, consider it a message from God. Behold the Divine symbol that has popped into your reality. Wow, keys!

8. 10,000 Ways to Make it a Good Day

What will you make today? Your creation need not be on the scale of designing an Adam or an atom. It could be music, with or without any recognizable scale. It could be pulling scales off fish or waxing a piano that someone else plays.

All day, all night, you have the chance to make things. Every problem you solve counts as a creation. So does every problem-solving experiment, even if it apparently fails.

Re-creating yourself counts, too, although self-creation can be the toughest form of creativity. Did you know that someone who tries a diet or other lifestyle change usually succeeds? But the catch is, it could take seven or more separate attempts. The day we *stop* making an effort, that's the day we fail.

As grownups, too often we ignore our creativity. It's different for children because teachers present them with structured activities. Consequently, the kids come home all excited about their drawings and songs. By contrast, we school-free adults must structure our own activities.

Once upon a time, even counting was a thrill, remember? If you pretended you were making a counting book for a kid, maybe numbers could become fun again. When was the last time you sat in a waiting room and made sport of counting things?

Instead of thinking about *creation*, we silly grownups often emphasize *obligation*. Yet, even with the most dutiful chore, each project can become a one-of-a-kind. Something as dull as dishwater can contain your prayers or songs. Maybe you'll stir up appreciation for the elegant design of a spoon. How about experimenting with a new way to stack the bowls you're washing? At my kitchen sink, three elegant glass carafes hold different colors of dish soap. Cleaning will never be my favorite activity but at least this way I don't always have to settle for same old, same old.

Activities you actually *like* offer extra scope to be creative. You can play with refinements that other people won't even notice until you show them. Take breathing, for instance. It offers an ocean of in and out and roundabout, as any yoga teacher knows.

Creativity isn't optional. You were born to create. If you don't make something good, you'll create anyway. Only it will be troubles.

So enjoy how this marvelous world sets you up to make things all day long. Nobody but you can force you to do the same thing twice in the same boring way. Keep the routines that bring comfort but otherwise — play, play, play.

9. Make a New Wish

Make a new wish.
The old ones either
already appeared or they can't be spared,
not for a while yet.

So blow off those sorrows.
Beneath each despair
is only an old wish in poor repair.
And you can find something else good.

This wondrous day isn't
used up yet. Neither
is your creative skill nor your fire.
Depend on them, friend.

Dream now, from your heart
through your passionate soul.
Especially dream if old wounding says "No."
This particular season of miracles might
demand just that hard-to-make, very first spark.

The best wishes of light can be made in the dark.

10. Deeper Perception

Worlds within this world can open up to you. Each holds more delight, a progressively deeper truth and a subtly unique way of knowing. How could this be? And if these inner worlds really exist, how come nobody told you about them before?

Disneyland helps to explain it. Think of the best amusement park you've ever seen. The big rides and smells of fun food, the excited crowds — how intoxicating the very air! Entertainment experiences like Disneyland symbolize *earth reality*. Human life fascinates us, sticky as flypaper.

Deeper perception doesn't happen physically, not at first anyway. It starts in the opposite direction. If you wish, refer to non-physical reality as "The inner" to distinguish it from "The outer."

To explore either direction, your tool is *consciousness*, just being awake. That simple awareness you've had your whole life can become your new best friend. Abstract though it may seem at first, conciousness is your tool for deeper knowledge. At its most glorious, consciousness brings you deeper perception.

To understand how, picture *matryoshka*. Bet you've seen these traditional nesting dolls, even if you didn't know the Russian name for them. First, the doll simply looks like a big, smiling woman. She has eyes, nose, mouth…but, unlike you or me, she's made of wood. Plus, her head unscrews.

Inside lies a hidden version of that same doll. Eventually, you can extract a whole series of smaller dolls. Just twirl their heads back on, line them up, and voila! You have an entire row of dolls, exactly the same except for being different sizes. The ultimate doll, deepest within, is solid wood, seemingly indestructible.

What an inspired symbol of *spiritual reality*! When you only pay attention to the surface of life, that's like mistaking the biggest doll for the whole set. Exploring with consciousness takes you to subtler levels that correspond to the inner dolls.

Corresponding to the most miniature, indestructible doll, there's the best part of deeper perception: Crystal-clear experience of auras, angels and deep human secrets. Your destiny is to be conscious here, at will, whenever you wish. And when you can co-create with God at that level, imagine!

To make it happen, take some time today to connect with God in silence. Then ask to learn more about the areas in life where you naturally slip into deeper perception. (For me it's writing, cooking, singing; you have your special areas, too.) Later in this book, various techniques will strengthen your access to deeper perception. Unlike Disneyland, it won't be a matter of tickets and rides. It's portable, convenient and free, with God running all the attractions. Best of all, never once will you have to wait in line.

11. Speedy You

Do you have any idea how fast you can move? Olympic athletes can't compare to how speedy you are — and always have been — with consciousness. And strong? Omigosh, to say that you can lift weights! By comparison, the most muscle-bound athlete you've ever seen is some puny weakling.

Instead of being a weightlifter, you're a light-lifter. You do it with consciousness. Quick as thought, your consciousness travels in, out and back again, landing inside your body to rest a while. Unless pretty awake inside, you'll only notice that last part. So you'll develop a sense of self that defines you as a separate individual, unconnected to anyone else and far away from God. Ha, such an illusion!

Faster than a candle flickers, you travel in consciousness. Sheer effortlessness can keep you from paying attention, yet these quick journeys still happen often.

Maybe you'll flash on an insight that solves a tough problem. Or you'll experience what it's like to be your pet dog. Or, for one inspired meal, you'll cook the most delicious food in the world because — consciously or not — your Big Consciousness has joined with the food's own intelligence. (Talk about the ultimate recipe!)

Sex is another example. It can bring both physical pleasure, stronger emotional connection and…an adventure in consciousness. Has your awareness ever shot into space, released after your body had all that fun? Or perhaps your consciousness went inward, so you spiritually merged with your partner. No wonder some folks want to smoke afterwards — cigarettes may not be good for one's lungs but they sure help a person's consciousness snap back into the body.

Usually, when you take stock of yourself, body and all, you may be tempted to rush on to the next self-improvement project. Whether it's New Year's resolutions or exercise or breaking that smoking habit, you can team up consciousness with free will, working to become the person you most wish to be.

Still, just for today, how about making this your only self-improvement project? *Do nothing.* Don't change one iota about your consciousness.

Oh, all right, if you must do something, give yourself credit. Acknowledge your brilliant, Olympic-caliber consciousness. No amount of effort can improve its shining light. It's that fast, that strong, that effortless, that magnificent.

How could such an effortless part of yourself be all that and more? Bring awareness within, to stillness and silence. When you no longer meet with speed or muscles, effort or effortlessness, you will be in the presence of That full magnificence.

12. Fill Up and Give

Not yet fully convinced of your spiritual magnificence? Then it's time to become even more conscious of your consciousness.

Which is what? Your sense of "Here I am" comes so naturally and gently, it's easy to take for granted. To find it, use *intention* plus *attention*. Intend to experience your consciousness. Then close your eyes, slow down and notice the quality of silence within. Recognize that simple experience of just being? Voila!

Right after you wake up in the morning can be the easiest time to notice your consciousness. Sleep clears away and you think the equivalent of, "Woo-hoo! Here I am for another day." Deep down, you're conscious of guess what?

Abstract as consciousness is, it's the basis for all experience. Yet being so prevalent, consciousness is tricky to isolate. Avoid trying to focus on it while engaged in everyday activities. You'll divide your mind and become less efficient at what people (jokingly or not) call "real life."

With regular spiritual practice, you will discover a *silent witness* inside you, always able to be conscious of consciousness. But this comes through grace, not struggle. When ready to receive this gift, you'll find that witnessing life with big consciousness takes about as much effort as having a nose.

How can you get there? Every day, do 15 minutes of FILL UP, 10 minutes of GIVE.

- For FILL UP, use a spiritual practice to bring your awareness to God, such as prayer, meditation, visualization or yoga. Any deep experience will wake up your consciousness.
- How about the GIVE part? Use a technique to read people deeper (like face reading, aura reading, empathic reading) or simply do a favor for someone you love. Any kind of authentic giving is fine.

Give by any means you like, so long as it involves service, devotion, learning. What, there's nobody in your life you are all that crazy about, much less devoted to? Psssst. Any person you choose is, spiritually, just a stand-in for God.

Giving will *move* the extra consciousness gained from your spiritual practice, opening channels for it to flow directly through your senses. Spread the joy around. FILL UP and GIVE.

13. Feet of Champions

Take a tip from champion runners, cyclists, swimmers and other top-performing athletes. Much as they want to win, they'll only do it by paying attention here and now, one foot at a time.

When I taught writing at a community college, I discovered many students who wanted to be writers, not to write. Doing the actual job left them cold. Similarly, you'll meet many aspiring movie stars, rock stars, and so forth. Some follow a deep calling. Most just hope to leap into fame. Understandable though these yearnings are, success usually comes when you're actively doing your best, not merely seeking rewards.

Consider two writers. One was born with an open channel for inspiration; he honors it by developing solid technique and then pours his life into each paragraph. Another writer has grand ambitions; he types out words while looking over his shoulder for the cheering multitude. Which writer's work would you rather read?

Better to simply do whatever work lies before you. Pour your yearnings into it. Any task, however humble, can be done in a way that leaves you open to inspiration.

But what if the work you do for a livelihood really doesn't thrill your soul? Unfortunately, starving won't either. I recommend that you make the sacrifice while you must and, somehow, squeeze in time each day for something you do love.

Whatever you're doing, you can make it spiritually glorious by being fully present to it. And, to improve your work even more, sprinkle in spiritual practice.

How much? You'll find the balance that's perfect for you. Usually, it's like seasoning your food. A few well-chosen spices can brighten up your dish of broccoli. But you wouldn't serve a bowl of curry powder sprinkled with just a few flecks of brocc. So don't do spiritual practices constantly, just enough to start and end your day deliciously.

Otherwise, remember that results come when you do your best in the moment. To some degree, you co-create with God 24/7. But some times you'll do it more actively, which is what really counts as co-creation. As for the rest of the time, you'll emphasize just being you. *Both* choices are sacred.

So move through this day confidently, blending soul evolution with human intelligence, spirituality with reality. Alternate creating as yourself and asking God for help. All this is moving you somewhere great. So, Champ, don't forget to bring your feet.

14. How Big?

Your body is way bigger than you thought. Actually, this is good news. No need to fear a new, horrifying form of stealth obesity, I'm talking spiritual dimensions here. Take a few minutes to explore *the size of your aura.* Neither a scale nor a tape measure will be needed, just your own consciousness.

One of my students told me, "There I was, just sitting on the couch, when I got it. I am so much more than my physical body. I'm huge, with this big energy body that radiates out from my regular body." Smiling, she added, "Life will never be the same again."

How big is *your* energy body? To explore it, sit comfortably (eyes open or closed, as you prefer). Know that directly in front of your face, splat!, there's your aura. And you can explore it through deeper perception.

What is meant by the term "aura"? It's an overlapping set of bodies, surrounding your physical body and just as real, only made of electro-magnetic energy rather than the fleshy stuff that is so familiar.

This metaphysical (rather than physical) part of you continues outward for quite some distance. Although you could get fancy, exploring its various layers and the doodads within your chakras, etc., let's keep things simple for now and refer to it all as "your aura" or "your energy body." And, yes, for now let's focus on pure size.

Your balloon-like aura happens to be pretty big. Why didn't you notice before? As a baby you probably did. But in order for Earth School to work, certain illusions are needed. Parents pass along the traditional belief that "You are your physical body." Since few parents give their child permission to have an aura, let alone words to describe it, eventually most of us play along and stop reaching for our own edges.

Now having mastered this illusion, you're ready to transcend it. Yes, you're hereby given permission to *experience* what you've had all along.

Just how big are you, aura included? To put it bluntly, you're huge. (But, remember, this a good thing.) Take some deep breaths and set the intention to explore your size. Does your aura fill the room? Or might you extend still farther, clear around the building? Maybe you reach out even farther.

Feel it now, not trying to change a thing. Excellent stuff indeed! And yes, for real, this is you.

15. Accordion World

Learning about yourself as an energy body is just the beginning. Many discoveries await you, including first-hand experience of why our planet could be called "Accordion World."

You've seen how accordions whoosh in and out, playing their music. With consciousness, you do the same — more or less silently, more or less unconsciously. Prove this to yourself by shifting your aura's size *on purpose*.

Sit quietly, eyes open or closed, with the intention to explore the size of your complete aura. Breathe and be, without effort. That soft, vibrating experience of you can be perceived in all sorts of ways, including feelings located off-physical-body, sounds or shifts of silence, colors or images, fragrances, even shifting light or space.

Please, avoid any shoulds or supposed-to's. You'll get what you get, in terms of the gifts God has given you from birth for experiencing deeper perception.

Once you've made contact with your aura, you can play with its size. Stretch it. Shrink it. Such a game! Draw your aura close around or shoot it out toward the stars. As long as you're gentle, you won't hurt a thing, so feel free to explore.

But what if you worry, "I'm imagining this"? Go ahead, imagine. Imagination does many things well. One of these is to move the kind of consciousness that makes up your aura.

Once you start moving your aura, there's so much to learn. With a meditation, for instance, check in with your size at the start or middle or end of your practice.

Or, just for fun, scope out your size randomly during everyday life. In a crowd, you may feel yourself shrink up. With a lover, you might merge. Can you keep track? Hey, you can if you want to. It's your body.

Until you know how big you really are, you'll often underestimate yourself. In other situations, you'll also over-estimate yourself.

And unless you wake up to this level of life, it's easy to assume that everyone you meet vibrates to your own frequencies, as if your particular quality of light could color the entire known universe. Actually, every person, animal and plant has a moveable aura. Each of us plays that accordion, with skill or without.

How big are you really? What about the size of other players in your life? Play away.

16. Habitual Honest Person

Are you familiar with the term "Habitual liar"? Sadly the term is more common than its opposite.

"Habitual honest person" — it even sounds awkward. But don't let that deter you, because habitual honesty won't merely help in a court of law. Nor will honesty just give you a good reputation for business. Honesty can clear the way for authentic intimacy in your relationships. That includes helping you tell when *someone else* is honest with you.

- *Genuine honesty,* or its lack, clearly shows in an aura. All that electro-magnetic energy around your physical body is full of information. Mostly inspiring, this information includes problems too. People who deceive themselves or others may think that lying is their clever little secret. To an aura reader, however, any chronic pattern of deception sticks out like a stiff, sore thumb.
- *Brutal honesty* also shows in auras. Glad to say, there's plenty of difference between being honest versus being just plain nasty.
- *Balanced honesty* is required for spiritual growth. Balanced honesty means that you let yourself notice what's going on within you. Some denials and self-deceptions go so deep, it takes enormous courage to explore them. But after the first few inward journeys, you'll know that you can survive any dive.

Refusing to be anything but honest with yourself brings an extra benefit. This habit makes it easier for you to recognize God. Surely you've heard that one of His or Her names is *I Am that I Am.* What if, instead, God were more like *I Am Me When Convenient, Especially When Forced Not to Lie*? Ugh, who'd want to co-create with that?

This is God's world, after all, a place where truth can always be found. In fact, finding spiritual truth can be simple. Calm down, remembering that — whatever your circumstances, however difficult or complicated — this is always God's world. So don't be afraid to ask inside, "What is my part of the truth here?"

17. Only Human?

Higher Self or human self? Many a spiritual seeker believes that the two must compete. Eventually the Higher Self can win, if only you try hard enough.

Ironically, when struggle is involved, neither side may win any time soon. Why? First some definitions: *Higher Self* is the enlightened, God-centered version of who you are; all clarity, charity, kindness and grace. *Human self* makes itself known in likes and dislikes, personal ego and, sometimes, a vexing lack of control. Human time seems light years away from the Higher Self's eternal bliss.

After an experience of Higher Self, we sigh, "May it never end." Whether making big resolutions on New Year's Eve or small prayers on a typical day, you probably turn toward That. If you have a favorite spiritual practice, doesn't it aim to make your Higher Self your everyday self?

But in contrast to what? "Human" means dealing with such delights as work, transportation, necessary but numbing routines. Sometimes we must even muddle through the hideous false eternities of fear, isolation, poverty, fatigue or illness.

What, you don't always adore this human identity? What, you're not thrilled with all those problems, everything from serious disease to tiny torn cuticles? Once we become aware of the big and bountiful Higher Self, only a fool wouldn't prefer to live exclusively as That. But it won't happen by *renouncing* your human self, which would only deepen its shadows. No, the way to ennoble your human self is to live with it.

Try this. Start today, as usual, with a spiritual exercise to awaken Higher Self — any method will work if it dips your soul into eternity. Then put your human self in charge for the rest of your day. Now comes the tricky part: Live as though every human like and dislike exists for good reason. Even anger serves a purpose.

So long as you live on earth, your human self must be the basis for co-creating with God. Granted, sometimes you may feel so discouraged that it's as if you never once knew your Higher Self existed. Good! Sooner or later you'll learn that no day is bad enough to destroy that Higher Self. Can you blot out the moon merely by covering it up with your thumb?

Loving your human self today will pay off tomorrow. Laugh at your limitations, if you can. Just keep on steadily alternating both modes of being each day: One peek at Higher Self, then a day of human self.

Here's what will happen. Each day you'll clear obstacles from your path, moving forward faster than you know. So let them last as long as they can…those seemingly endless days without eternity.

18. I Came Here to Be Me

Okay, I admit it.
I'm stuck here as me.
All the twirling around like a weather vane, seeking approval?
Over.

Why seek my soul through somebody else?
All those volunteer tastemakers
also are twirling, awaiting permission.
Of course, each of us is allowed to be here.
And whose nod of approval weighs so much as a feather,
or one bite of good chocolate?

Glorious God made us each an "I am."
So a simple perfection shines out
in my looks, through my heart, with these hands.
My soul walks around in such comfortable shoes,
crinkled from having been worn just so,
even stylish, after their own fashion.

No matter who sneers at my walk through life
or honks at my confidence,
I'll remember this concept, clear as a bell:
I am just one person, just one, just one.
Humble but mighty, I can walk tall.
In my peace of this world, all is well.

19. Call Out My Name

Here's the chorus of one of my favorite rock n' roll songs:

> You just call out my name
> And you know wherever I am
> I'll come runnin' to see you again
> Winter, spring, summer or fall
> All you have to do is call
> And I'll be there
> You've got a friend....

Sure, this is a great friendship song, but it's not just about being friends with people. Such great spiritual wisdom is tucked into these lyrics! No accident — the songwriter is Carole King, who studied with the great spiritual teacher Swami Satchidananda.

Her advice works whatever your spiritual path. When calling on a Divine Being, it's enough to think the name. No mystical inner calling is required. Imagine, you can co-create with St. Francis, Archangel Raphael or Kwan Yin, whomever you chose. You're not making a lifetime commitment, like marriage. Think of it instead more like a date...or even a one-night stand.

No strong bond is required for permission to call on any Divine Being. (Without having the Divine Being in your life, how would you form that strong bond in the first place?) Special relationships develop over time.

Archangels are high-vibrational angels for the whole planet. Archangel Michael removes what doesn't belong; Archangel Raphael brings healing; Archangel Gabriel helps with communication.

Ascended Masters are enshrined in world religions but not defined by them. If you were raised Christian or Buddhist, you owe it to yourself to experience your spiritual teacher directly. *Countless versions* of Jesus and Buddha are real — each one appropriate to a community at its particular vibration. But when you personally call on Him, you'll get the version to fit *your* vibration.

Now I've given *my* definition of "Divine Beings," but in such an intensely personal matter, *you* must find your own definition. You might prefer to ask for your guardian angel, a favorite spirit guide or an extra-terrestrial helper; all these loving beings are dedicated to your service, regardless of whether you're familiar with their individual names. "My Guardian Angel" works just as well as "Francine."

What matters is that you ask. Call out His or Her name. Instantly That presence will join you, helping and healing, co-creating with no strings attached. Winter, spring, summer, or fall, call on That friend.

20. Birthday Darshan

Your eyes always express your soul: Yearnings, triumphs, emotions, physical health, the specialties of your intelligence. One day each year, however, your eyes carry an extra light within their light. That's *birthday darshan*.

Darshan (DAR-shaan) is a special kind of contact high. It comes from a person with great spiritual wisdom. On your birthday especially, that's you.

When you made your entrance this lifetime, both you and your mother noticed something special was happening. Yet the circumstances may not have been entirely pleasant. In case you don't remember your side of things clearly, here's a hint — that little matter of terror.

For welcome contrast, compare how you are today: More or less adjusted to the light, the air, the rules here. Each year they become more familiar because you are evolving into mastery here at earth's mystery school.

On this birthday, do you still have a long list of unfulfilled goals? Do any problems worry you? Just for today, let them go. Celebrate the glory of your life as it is right now. God is willing for you to do that, so why not you?

Wherever you look today, you'll bring a special blessing. That birthday light within your eyes is the spiritual equivalent of throwing golden coins at the multitudes. So wherever you go, feel the grace of God move through you. Enjoy being generous with it. Look at many people. Fling out copious blessings of love, light and power.

Incidentally, don't forget to look in the mirror. You know how you can angle together a couple of mirrors to make innumerable reflections? In that same surprising manner, and more easily than on non-birthdays, when you look in the mirror today you just might catch a glimpse of God smiling back at you.

21. Unique

Here's one of your under-recognized but amazing tricks. *With any friend you know and love, you can recognize his energy presence instantly.* Wherever that friend is, far or near, you make a connection so fast, it's as though you have him on speed dial.

Why is it so easy to attune to a friend's unique energy? Because this is a friend, you have a heart connection, something you can activate at will.

Even without this, you can connect with anybody's energy. Try this technique. All you'll need are a few minutes of time and your undivided attention.

- First, center yourself in your favorite way. (Mine is to close my eyes, take a few deep breaths, and have the intention to notice what it is like being myself. Then, I pay attention to whatever happens for the next few seconds.)
- Now think a particular person's name or imagine how that person looks, whichever you prefer.
- Whatever experience comes to you next, consider it valid as information about your friend.

This simple tune-in technique has amplified an energy connection that you have already established. Therefore, results are automatic, effortless, even inevitable.

Often people do energy readings casually. We pick up vibes from tone of voice, body language or an underlying feeling. Alas, some casual energy quickies are sadly incomplete. Problems, limitations or pain cause one to turn away. Sometimes you even can tell that (for whatever reason) the person who's giving *you* the quickie doesn't especially like you.

But next time you're tempted to give someone else that kind of quickie, don't. Stick around energetically long enough to connect with that person's magnificence.

Until you make contact with that, you haven't read far enough. Sure, you'll find a few sick puppies, from whose energy you'll instinctively (and wisely) recoil. But for every one of those, you'll find hundreds of people who are like you: Beautiful, distinctive souls, with loving hearts and good intentions despite, perhaps, a little stuff in the way.

What would happen if, each day, you would connect deeply with one other person's unique energy? As experience increases your perceptiveness, what will happen when your intention is to read the energy of God?

22. Handling Problems

Inner healing versus outer healing — which is wiser to attempt first? If, for example, there's chronic knee pain, the cure may require removing resentment more than disposing of unneeded cartilage. Yet when you suffer from a problem, you can't deny its obvious level. Each problem has a context, be it work, money, relationships, physical health, psychology or spirituality.

To solve a problem, action will be required at the level of that problem. Even if you care far more for spirituality than anything else, each level of life is real and requires its due.

Your relationship with one annoying relative, the elegance of your manners, how fashionably you dress, matters like these may never be important in the grand scheme for your life…unless you ignore them completely. Then the grand scheme will bombard you with problems. It's a kindness, really. Otherwise, what would motivate a person to pay attention?

Denial means not paying attention to something both real and important. Denied problems can feel too scary to touch until pain grabs attention. At such times, we're forced to deal with a problem right at its level, even if we're not overly fond of that aspect of life.

Still, we can also use our Divine allotment of wiggle room: Go to the level of spirit and ask for help *before* returning to your responsibilities at problem level.

How strong will the spiritual connection feel? Irrelevant question! Maybe you'll feel so bad that your so-called "Spiritual Interlude" feels just as lousy as the rest of your problems. Well, count that as wildly successful anyhow. Almighty God isn't limited by your moods.

What matters is that you've called on a Divine Being, poured out your heart, asked for help. Regardless of your mood at the time, you've placed the problem-solving project in God's hands. Will large fingers have to drop out of the sky for you to believe that help is coming?

Meanwhile, use your own hands, your heart and will. That's your share of co-creation. Return to the level of the problem, figure out one specific action you can take, then do it.

Above all, trust that the spiritual help you have set in motion will come. In retrospect, as a spiritual detective, you may find God's fingerprints all over it.

23. Freedom of Religion

For religion, intention makes a bigger difference than anything else. Let's say, for example, that the faith of your fathers has 10 major tenets. You believe strongly in 3, sort-of believe 3 more, and toss the rest into a subconscious closet of denial (the spiritual equivalent of mothballs). Can you still be a member in good standing? Of course. Every thinking person in your group does a similar version of pick-and-choose.

But this is religion, not just some book club. Whether conscious or subconscious, all your beliefs shape how you co-create with God. So today you're invited to go through your religion's credo, point by point. Invite the founder of your religion to keep you company, if you like. *Tell God directly what you don't and do believe, and why.* Then announce your intention to co-create on that basis from now on. Listen for God's response.

- Choose to be saved from Hell? Sure, God can do that. With this belief, however, you'll always be looking over one shoulder, sniffing for brimstone. Might you prefer a God of love to a God of fear? You do get to choose, you know.
- Will you believe that only those who are "born again" in a particular way can really know God? That's excellent, provided you don't expect everyone else to make your same choice. Alternatively, what if you believe you have always been connected to God and don't require any particular experience of being "born again" to bring you closer? Omnipotent God will respect that, too.
- If you believe in no god at all, that presence will honor your choice by staying clear out of the way for as long as you like. Go forth and create all by yourself!

Deeper perception can help you to release outgrown expectations. Sure, believe that your path is the greatest. That's like thinking one's child is the best and the brightest. Love like this makes the world go around, inspires us to keep on twirling along with it. Still, you'll find that auras contain no equivalent of a price tag, no assurance that one believer's forehead counts for more than anyone else's.

Instead, you'll find something far more interesting. In any group, some members have magnificent auras. Others may wear fear on their foreheads, thick as mud. Yet anyone can ask God to help remove fear, then bring in trust and truth.

Bottom line: If your religion requires that you be a missionary, do it. But don't neglect your day job, which is being human. How well you do that, plus the degree to which you connect to God, shines out unmistakably. And everybody's aura can be glorious.

24. Beyond Belief

Regarding organized religion, it's often possible to find a group of more-or-less like-minded believers. But if you haven't found a group of kindred spirits, you still can connect with God perfectly well one-on-one.

You can, for instance, take on this project for today: Let love deepen your perception so that you can *learn directly through a compassionate heart.* Here's one way to do it.

- Early in your day, connect your own heart to God.
- Then ask for help in exploring the hearts of others — without judgment or pushing, simply to learn. Also take this precaution: Ask to be protected from taking on anyone else's problems.
- Afterwards, when you're with people today, choose sometimes to go into your heart space and dip into the heart of another person. Ask inside how *that* person connects to God. What will you find? Hmmm.

Before ending your day, let God know what you learned. And just in case you became enmeshed in other people's difficulties (despite your precautions) ask God to free you from all that does not belong to you. No laundry list is needed. Simply ask God to handle it, then fill you with unconditional love.

Whether your particular brand of religion is organized or disorganized, your way to God is an open door through which you are always welcome to walk. Beliefs may come, beliefs may go, but this particular door welcomes you forever. Today's exercise in walking through *other* people's doors can remind you that each person has a distinctive way to connect with God. For instance, one man grows through solving problems while another evolves through acts of devotion.

Beyond that, a minority of people have a deep calling to work with a specific Divine Being. How can you tell? Right in that person's heart or aura, you'll find someone like St. Germain or Mother Mary. Hindus can have Ishwara (rows of assembled gods adding up to one holy presence). Some Buddhists sport a pristine silence, the immaculate footprint of their teacher. Muslims sometimes carry the presence of Muhammad (no idol but the real thing) while some Jews chime out an electrical presence of the "I am" Jehovah.

Intention being the driving force of religious life, don't be shy about asking any Divine Being to help you grow spiritually. If you love the faith of your fathers and mothers, ask that it keep growing with you. Whatever you ask, the response to any sincere request will take you beyond...mere belief.

25. Flying Bummers

Far back as you can remember, you've had many spiritual Agreements with the Universe. These Agreements define who you think you are, what you expect from other people, how successful you can be.

Positive Agreements make life glorious. Even without joining Boy Scouts, you may have agreed to be forever trustworthy, loyal, helpful, friendly, courteous, kind, obedient, cheerful, thrifty, brave, clean and reverent.

Yet all Agreements are not as positive as they first seem. How healthy is it, for instance, to be perpetually cheerful?

Bummer Agreements are even worse. These are patterns you'd never choose consciously…unless including them as part of your Life Contract, back when you were on the Other Side planning out this hilarious lifetime.

Bummers are negative programming — often subconscious — and definitely contradicting common sense. When will you spot these loathsome things so that you can dump them? Make it a project for today to choose at least one. Tomorrow we'll go into removal procedures.

Which are the Bummers? Often, they're connected with your most familiar patterns of pain.

- To find yours, make this mental note: The next time a Bummer flies by, you'll catch it with the spiritual equivalent of a butterfly net. Ask yourself, "So, I feel bad right now. What's the worst part?"
- Another strategy is to take advantage of the next time you're tired or grumpy. Certain defenses will be down. Excellent! Take pen in hand and write down the story of "What always happens to me."
- *Always* and *never* are excellent tip-offs that you're in the presence of a Bummer Agreement. Be brave as you inquire, "Always what?" You might find a pattern like "I always give without receiving anything back in return."
- When you catch one of these flying Bummers, you may feel a strong emotion, like embarrassment, helplessness or despair. Good! You're really onto something.

God can help you change that Bummer Agreement. Tomorrow you'll learn one technique for doing this.

However you decide to remove old Agreements that don't serve you now, the results can be profound. Your life may re-align until inwardly you fly as free as a butterfly…but way stronger.

26. Tasty Pudding

Here's a recipe for cooking up a delicious new Agreement with the Universe. You'll need no food, no money. No dishwashers or lawyers. No human witnesses whatsoever. Maybe a piece of paper and a pen. Mostly you'll need two ideas: What do you wish to release? And what would you like to receive?

You'll need to know both. Since the new Agreement may be with you for the rest of your life, it's worth fussing a bit to get the words right. Hence the paper. Write or draw a pair of *Release and Receive Statements* until you like how they make you feel. Then edit from a practical perspective. Sure this new Agreement feels good, but does it also make sense?

Now, don't fuss too much with the editing. You can always make an even more improved Agreement later. Besides, if you avoid struggling now you won't have to make any extra Agreement later…about not being fussy when cooking up your Agreements. Here is an example of Release and Receive Statements:

- "I am always cheerful," can claim a certain appeal as an Agreement. But it might make an even better *Release Statement:* "I release the old Agreement, that I must always be cheerful."
- How can you follow this up with a *Receive Statement?* Well, how about, "I am cheerful when this will improve my life. But if I have problems, my *main* job is to co-create a solution with God, not just to seem cheerful. So I have the wisdom to know the difference between situations where cheerfulness helps and situations where too much cheerfulness would be a distraction."

After writing your pair of Agreements, turn the occasion into a ceremony. *Invoke God,* e.g., "God, I'm talking to you now." Next, *bring in a Divine Being to witness,* as simple as saying, "Mary, be here now." Say you're changing what you believe to be an old Bummer Agreement. Speak out your pair of Statements. Like a marriage, your Agreement Ceremony needs just one set of "I do's," spoken aloud.

With this new Agreement in place, your life will reinforce it. What remains is to inform your *subconscious* mind, that hidden assortment of expectations, beliefs, memories and stories that define your reality. Post a copy of the words on your bulletin board or, if you're high-tech enough, use it as a screen saver. Perhaps you'd prefer to program your new Agreement into a crystal or place your script under your pillow and sleep on it.

The proof of the pudding is in the eating, and this dish will taste mighty good, far better than what you've been in the habit of eating.

27. Volunteer Gold

If only every day could stretch
like an accordion,
I'd volunteer to help so many ways:
Huge checks, plus giving labor every week.
Each worthy cause would find a friend in me
and I could easily afford to give
enough to turn my wrinkled conscience smooth.

But I am caught in human time. Right now
because of obligations, work routines,
the time and money that I give are less
than I would wish, which makes
my struggling life seem smaller every day.

Yet there is one way I can volunteer,
by taking time apart
within heart beats.
While stuck in traffic or a dawdling line
I'll reach into my soul, from there pull out
a shiny coin of charity to give.

A smile or helping hand, though meager things,
are tokens I can easily afford.
Symbols of wealth and love, God's plenitude,
contagious as a yawn, This I can share.
So opening a pocket into space,
I'll pluck out one new coin of friendliness.
And, once again, I'll get to spend
as God's enormously rich volunteer.

28. Surrender

Surrender to God is sweet. Surrender means a lifestyle of gratitude, stretching yourself to find meaning, no matter what happens. With surrender, you choose to accept the will of God... even if you don't always like it.

When I work with students, it's easy to tell which ones are committed *exclusively* to spiritual surrender. Typically, when I ask them to call on a Divine Being, they'll say, "Sure. I'll be grateful whoever shows up."

But sweet as surrender is, it's also passive. What if the first volunteer to help with your spiritual quest is the spirit of your slightly disreputable uncle, now dead? What if a newly deceased bum happens to be in the neighborhood, all too willing to step through your open door? Sure he's an angel now, but is that the highest and best you deserve? I don't think so. And in no scripture that I've seen are God's humble servants commanded to be content with leftovers.

Your guardian angel is wonderful, as are all the guides whom your soul has chosen to help you. Notice, however, that they were assigned to help with life *at your present level of consciousness*. Where's the stretch in that?

Regardless of how advanced they are on the astral plane, personal angels don't vibrate at the super-high frequency of etheric beings. That privilege belongs to Ascended Masters and Archangels. These Divine Beings, the most evolved beings with an individual form, are sometimes worshipped as *personal* versions of God, while God Everywhere Now is the *impersonal* version.

Another way to distinguish personal from impersonal aspects of God is to give them names like Inner Teacher (for personal God) in contrast to the Holy Spirit (for impersonal God). Whatever terms you prefer, it's important to use something, because these two aspects of God can help you in different ways.

Co-creating, you'll often get best results by calling on a personal version of God, a Divine Being. If you telephoned someone, which way would you receive results faster, by calling a specific phone number or by simply listening to a dial tone?

Discover the differences for yourself by co-creating with both the impersonal and personal aspects of God, sometimes one, sometimes the other. Please, don't be shy about introducing yourself to the personal crew. You can ask for whomever you like. Get help directly from Archangel Gabriel, Moses, Hestia or Brigid. Through co-creation, make your wishes known. Acting on the best knowledge available, take action. Then, if what you strive for doesn't show up, by all means, use your surrender.

29. Dating God

Sure you can go on a date with God. Just sign up for the Cosmic Dating Service. It's free, in more ways than you might first imagine.

To get started, list all your requirements for The One, e.g., Generous, loyal, kind, good looking, gives you thrills. Date it all...scaled up to God-size.

For instance, regarding generosity, you can depend on God to give you exactly what you want. It may take a while since the result must obey earth's complex laws of cause and effect. But surely somewhere between your sense of urgent need and God's sense of eternity, the two of you can work something out. Don't all couples have to negotiate sometimes?

As when signing up with a regular dating service, you'll also think about what *you* have to offer. Well yes, plenty! And you can be sure that God notices all those good things about you (and more).

Boldly put in your request to the Cosmic Dating Service. Results will be instantaneous. God will stick to your desires faster than a meter maid can write out a ticket.

To notice God's response, just slow down. Take your attention off the cars parked out on the street and look within. Notice? It's subtle but real. After you call up your Date...instantly...a very fine, abstract kind of consciousness will show up more strongly within you. That loving presence has become one chunk brighter.

"Chunk," now there's a technical term.

Hey, feel free to substitute whatever word you prefer.

And what if you find That presence difficult to notice at all? It's only because That was with you all along. It's as if you stood knee-deep in a blizzard and asked for the novelty of something called "Snow." Expect that to seem like a refreshing contrast to your usual experience? Then you might have to wait quite some time to feel those flurries.

God's enormity and omnipresence make for mysterious dating. Keep that in mind as you co-create.

For concrete help with specific problems, you may get clearer results by calling on a personal form of God rather than the His or Her nature as unbounded Dazzling-Colorless, Dancing-Motionless Infinity. But however you hold God in prayer today, choose *something*, not just a vague or wistful blank. Before you fall asleep, you may notice the divine equivalent of a good night kiss.

30. *Image Consulting*

Have you heard the rumors? They're as ancient as the Old Testament: *You were created in the image and likeness of God.*

On the face of things, this seems absurd. Why would the Almighty Creator need nostrils or ear wax? Taking a broader perspective, when there are so many worlds in the universe — some of which surely contain sentient life — why would humans be singled out as winners of the God look-alike contest?

Then there's the not entirely silly matter of sex. Would the inventor of female and male look like…which?

Having puzzled over this mystery, I've had this thought: How does any human being look exactly like God? In *consciousness.*

Transcending the illusions of earth experience, your vibration of consciousness is unique. Even when not wearing a human form, you're fingerprinted better than anyone could be with mere fingerprints. Before and after this incarnation, you exist as a pulsating, patterned and highly distinctive puddle of awareness.

As this unique pattern of consciousness, you've been given a complete set of God-like abilities. Granted, they're scaled-down versions. Still, they're awesome. Consider:

- God is *omniscient*. When you use the full power of your consciousness, you too can know anything you choose — only just one thing at a time.
- God is *endlessly creative*. Have you run out of creativity yet?
- God is *love*. To the relief of everyone who knows you (self included) deep down you are That.

Give yourself some time today to give thanks for your various scaled-down, God-like attributes. Not to worry, this wouldn't be delusions of grandeur, just acknowledging your heritage.

31. Spiritual or Psychological?

Inner healing can be spiritual or psychological, or both. Without understanding their differences, you'll lose out on their very distinctive benefits.

Therapists aren't the only ones who facilitate *psychological* healing. You'll find it in books and magazine articles, support groups, workshops — even many activities connected with religion and spirituality. Today, most popular methods of self-help involve this mode of healing.

Psychological healing improves thinking, altering conscious and subconscious patterns. *Work* is the signature quality. You must work on yourself, and work hard. Even with help from a skilled therapist, you're the one who will have to confront shame, fear, guilt or other difficult emotions.

And then the *big* work begins, examining memories, dreams, habits, patterns both functional and dysfunctional, present and past. Before this psychological inquiry can produce results, still more work will be demanded of you: Behavior must be rigorously monitored, then changed one day at a time.

Sometimes this slow and painful approach is the only one that will work. Other times it doesn't seem to help much at all. Think of people you know who have been "Working on my issues" for decades. Although a meaningful hobby, it may produce no visible results whatsoever.

Spiritual transformation, by contrast, requires no work at all. Even when painful patterns change, the emotional undercurrent is *joy*. Results come instantaneously, understood through Aha! experiences. And this healing is permanent.

How could something so good be so easy? Spiritual healing is done through co-creation. A Divine Being does the heavy lifting. Granted, spiritual healing succeeds best when the facilitator is clear enough to distinguish between wishful thinking and a genuine spiritual connection. Then real changes work through your aura, making it relatively easy for you to re-pattern thoughts and actions.

Another advantage of spiritual healing is that, once you've apprenticed with a skilled facilitator, you won't need elaborate training. The main thing is to set up the healing request, then get completely out of the way. Once you understand how to do this at depth, *you* can become a facilitator, helping yourself and others.

Is it better to solve a problem psychologically or spiritually? Case by case, you'll know.

Besides, you can always supplement your first choice with the second, as needed. If you'll pay attention to the difference between both methods of healing, you'll become more resourceful. Today, for instance, are there situations where you could stop working quite so hard and, in your way, let in some spiritual light?

32. Oops, It's The Other One

Still sorting out the difference between spiritual transformation vs. psychological healing? The choice is complex. So if you're somewhat puzzled about which works when, that can be a good thing, part of your learning curve.

Take a tip from the ancient Chinese classic, the *I Ching*. This book of changes is used like an oracle, where you throw coins or yarrow stalks, creating tri-grams (sequences of three tosses in a row). Results can be *yang* or *yin*, masculine or feminine energy. Looking up the meaning of each tri-gram can give you practical advice. But even without looking up one single tri-gram, you can find a brilliant insight from a basic principle that underlies all *I Ching* interpretations.

To build a tri-gram, *2 out of 3* throws will form a more stable balance than 3 out of 3. For example, you'd count 2 yang + 1 yin as yang. By contrast, *3 out of 3* yang goes so strongly in one direction that it's ready to turn into its opposite. The *I Ching* instructs you to interpret such excess accordingly.

Extreme yang is preparing to turn into yin, and vice versa. This is like having kids caught up in a rowdy game. A wise parent says, "Sure you're laughing now. But if you don't settle down, soon one of you will be crying."

Now let's apply this principle of balance to psychology and spirituality. At a certain point, so much can be done in a psychological direction that it becomes time for a spiritual lift, when you supplement personal responsibility with Divine co-creation. Or sometimes the opposite happens. Spiritual transformation is stuck, so it's time for human effort. Go forth and tweak some psyche.

Can you think of one life area where you've worked inwardly for years, yet still feel stuck? Which approach have you favored, psychological or spiritual? Maybe it's time to try the other one. Consider it a chance to complete things from the opposite direction.

Unless a person is willing to let go of the favored modality and switch to its opposite, progress can slow to a crawl. How human it is to become attached to the path we're on, forgetting the destination. Probably you can think of several people who have gotten stuck that way. But could this also, in some small way, apply to you?

Correcting that overbalance of yang or yin can be easy. Bet you can manage it without having to toss a single yarrow stalk.

33. Holy Spirit, The Movie Star

Today you're invited to investigate God as the ultimate character actor. He or She works constantly, so you're sure to have seen Him or Her in loads of movies. I'm especially fond of His or Her starring role in the film called "The Holy Spirit."

You've seen that one, haven't you? It's a prequel to some incredible blockbusters: "Earth," "Air," "Fire," "Water" and "Pure Space." You could go throughout your whole day in love with any of those movies, watching it for the umpteenth time and finding it ever fresh.

Okay, all this isn't as obvious as movies that you'd find in a theater. But the show is everywhere. It's called spiritual life. When you contemplate any of earth's sacred elements, you can find the Holy Spirit within. And this super-subtle God-impulse goes by many names.

- In *Autobiography of a Yogi*, Paramahansa Yogananda referred to It as *Lifetrons*.
- A physicist might call It *elementary particles*, with a hidden identity as wave patterns.
- A musician might hear It as *vibrating silence* while an artist (admittedly, a fanciful one) could call It tiny *God-sparkles*.
- A child might spend hours watching it, like *enchanting particles of dust* dancing in a beam of sunlight.
- Lovers might stroll through it at night, sharing the joy that seeps through their skin, calling it *the romance of moonlight* or, simply Love itself.

As for you, you may already have a secret collection of names for The Holy Spirit. It's never too late to find some new ones, either.

As quick as thought — deep within the texture of any thought — on every surface you see — within what connects all surfaces — in any one place where you can put your awareness, there! Exactly there you can find The Holy Spirit. It is the Great Comforter. And with patience, That presence will only grow dearer, a movie in endless reruns.

34. Attributes

Which is it to be for you, a God of power, of love or of light?

Really you don't have to choose. Whatever your definition of God, That will show forth in your experience.

But theoretical definitions of God's greatness aren't enough. Your gut-level expectations may be smaller, even contradictory. And it's the sum total of your expectations that will shape what you manifest in life.

Take *power*, for example. It's easy to believe in a God with the driving force of a hurricane, the electricity of a lightning bolt, the strength and hugeness of a mountain. But can you also believe in gentle power, like that which slowly unfurls a rose?

One kind of power can make a puppet dance. An entirely different power trusts His or Her creation to move independently, completely free to dance as she pleases.

Because of unhealed pain from your past, power may seem tinged with cruelty. Did a bully ever try to break you? Then it may take some doing before you can trust in a God whose power includes mercy.

Other expectations of power may relate to old fears. Ever see kids go through the biting stage? What a discovery, that you can take charge of a situation dentally! But soon the power of teeth becomes hard to control. Sometimes a person of any age will feel compelled to bite — or the equivalent. And then power seems terrifying.

But you can ask God to help heal any discomfort that you may feel about power, whether the problems be present or past, conscious or subconscious.

Call on God to ease your relationship with the full range of power, of love, of spiritual light, plus any other attributes that you hold dear. *Nothing you request could be too wonderful to be completely possible.*

So take care what you wish for…God to be. You will surely get it.

35. Trinity

God models for us how to have three mighty attributes: Power, love and light. Why all three? Just one or two aren't enough.

Power brings the ability to fulfill our desires. But *without love*, it's frightening. Sometimes powerful people close off their hearts. Success without love feels empty for everyone involved, even the one who supposedly succeeds.

What about power *without light*? Only for ego-based gratification will that work. Bullies, for instance, can usually do power pretty well. And a bully could even be in love. But when light is conspicuously absent, what good can come to the loved one or anyone else?

Religious zealots may be the scariest bullies, even if motivated by love. Power is there but no light, and being deluded about truth cannot substitute for authentic spiritual experience. Heaven protect us all from do-gooders like those who brought our world the tragedy of September 11.

Light means the experience of pure spirit, whether you understand it as freedom, feminine energy, the joy of God, the overarching levels of deep space or something even bigger. Deep within each human soul is the drive to receive more light.

We yearn to know more, to have more, to be more. How can we do this without harming others? Thank the infinity of light. When you combine *light with power,* now you're talking — especially if love can also be invited into the conversation.

Initially *love and light* may seem sufficient as a combination of attributes… but only for dreamers. Love-&-lighters with *no power* can't hold their own among people who specialize in only power; love-&-lighters are also vulnerable to anyone who lives with power plus *either* love or light (but not both).

Have you ever been pushed around by one of the highly confident souls with power and light…but *no love?* Besides being influential, they're so wonderfully connected to spiritual Source, they may even brag about it. Meanwhile, uh-oh! Unconnected from human feeling, they squash little things like other people's vulnerabilities. Inspired and highly competent, they're tempted to treat other folks like pawns on a chessboard. A game like that isn't fun. (Actually, unless the game starts with two equal players, it isn't even chess.)

Whichever game you engage in today, on a gameboard or off, see what happens when your side plays as Trinity: *Love plus light plus power.* Any missing attribute can be there for the asking, if only you'll ask God to help you develop it.

36. The Mountain

How could I meet with a God so distant?
You seemed like a mountain of not-knowing.
Heaping meditations onto each other, day by day
slowly a form emerged from a mist.
And I began to see you as an alpine splendor
solitary, shining with snow
against a sky that seemed
to symbolize an unattainable distance.

Traveling in more meditations, years within years,
longing grew great within me
until each day became a pilgrimage.
Not adventurous by nature,
I didn't dare imagine reaching your summit.
Instead, I hoped to climb just high enough
to know I really was on Your mountain.
Then, perhaps, I could touch the shining snow with my cheek.

Decades into this pilgrimage, my travel plans changed.
Sometimes I yearned for You in the form of a mountain,
but sometimes I'd seek you in other landscapes, too.
Wherever I stood that day, I'd search for You.

I have stood lost in an echoing cavern,
crying as I called out Your name.
I have called it in gratitude,
swimming far into a still lake, fragrant with pines.
This fool even put aside her heavy heart
and blew You soap bubbles
across an unending desert.

Gradually, occasionally, I've come to hear
a companion's voice on this journey,
a voice different from either my solitude or the presence of friends,
Your own silent presence within me.
I've started to recognize
how it can stretch like a desert vastness
or sparkle like the waterfall at the edge of a lake.

One day, in meditation, I myself grew like a mountain,
my human form huge and free in blue space.
Inside my cheeks, I felt your presence
heavy, so heavy, yet small.
That most familiar presence of love
fell as tears. The temperature was snow.

37. What Enlightenment Isn't

Here are 10 things that can be mistaken for spiritual enlightenment, but aren't.

1. Wearing the latest yoga *clothes.* Or any kind of clothes (including none at all). Enlightenment doesn't show on the outside. It shows on the inside.
2. Having the correct *opinions* to explain reality. That kind of "Enlightenment" was tried in Europe during the 18th century. Had it succeeded, historians wouldn't consider that "Age of Enlightenment" a mere fad, on a par with Baroque music, a cute preparation for the period known as "Romanticism."
3. Following a *teacher.* Or not following a teacher. No worldly diploma admits a soul into the club of Earth School Graduates.
4. Converting others to what's right. Enlightened people mind their own business, having nothing to prove. Helping people, when invited, is different from missionary zeal.
5. Seeming *relaxed and mellow.* Enlightened, some folks do become more serene, while others seem more dynamic; all are more loving. But how will this show? You can't fathom a person's level of consciousness from mere behavior.
6. Having everyone *like* you. Jesus didn't.
7. Having *charisma.* Hitler did.
8. Being *thin*. Golly, at no other time in history would it be necessary to mention this! Sure, Buddha may have been chubbier than St. Francis of Assisi, but both guys were There.
9. Being *flashy*. Psychic-level abilities, like astral travel or describing angels down to the number of feathers on their wings, are optional side dishes. For enlightenment, the main course is clear and present communion with God.
10. *Detachment.* Never feeling pain, fear, sorrow or other unpleasant emotions might seem like the greatest possible motivation to become enlightened. Although an attitude like this could be caused by excessive bliss, more likely it signifies denial, involvement in a cult, a serious psychological problem or just a convincing act. What detachment *doesn't* necessarily mean is higher consciousness. Enlightenment means feeling whatever human beings can feel in life…along with something bigger.

38. What Enlightenment Is

There must be as many definitions of spiritual enlightenment as there are names for God. At least this makes for a dazzling number of definitions....

Even if it seems intimidating to add a definition of your own, do it. Only those with a specific goal can recognize when they finally attain it. As noted by Matthew Kelly in his brilliant book, *The Rhythm of Life*, "Most people can tell you exactly what they don't want, but very few have the same clarity about what they do want."

Admittedly, not everyone likes to list goals. So I'll help by supplying *my* 10 favorite signposts to enlightenment. Editing someone else's ideas can be easier than writing a first draft. Whether you edit my list or make up your own, decide for yourself. Decide something! I believe enlightenment means:

1. Experiencing yourself as a package of consciousness — spiritual energy — that happens to include a human form.
2. Knowing that this version of yourself, the part about pure consciousness, is the real core of your identity.
3. Understanding the Divine play on earth primarily as energy.
4. Observing that same Divine play in the people you meet, without feeling the need to fix anyone.
5. Seeing through myths about life, especially when they're presented to you in the guise of "reality."
6. Functioning smoothly at all human levels: Relationships, body, mind, intellect and emotions. Do you spontaneously live with a natural balance which you can restore...simply by remembering to rebalance?
7. Trusting the natural flow of your speech and silence, your actions, your human likes and dislikes.
8. Having made your peace with the aspect of life force energy known as sex. Until then, it doesn't matter how much consciousness you otherwise have. Other people can still control you.
9. Witnessing the glorious, loving presence of God — available whenever you seek it.
10. Knowing that after you have "arrived" at enlightenment, your journey in consciousness continues.

A student once asked his teacher. "Does enlightenment sneak up on you gradually? Or does a special moment come when everything clicks into place?"

His wise teacher laughed, then said, "It's a gradual click."

39. Stretching Non-Judgment Too Far

"Why do you practice yoga?" asked the woman who sat ahead of me in the van. Three yoga teachers and I were being driven to the airport. I'd finished a loosely structured spiritual retreat, taking only the occasional yoga class, whereas my companions had just completed a demanding course to advance their credentials. They were professionals at yoga; I, a mere practitioner. Still, I'd been at it for 35 years, so I knew pretty well what motivated me.

"For enlightenment, of course," I said. "Why else would someone do yoga?"

All three ladies whirled around in their seats to stare at me. At their shock, I was equally shocked. It was like the scene in the movie "E.T." where the boy meets up with the young extra-terrestrial and both shriek at each other in horror.

Not exactly shrieking, we just stared at each other with lifted eyebrows. To break the awkward silence, I asked, "How about you?"

The most outspoken one said, "In yoga, I stretch as far as I can. But in life, I certainly don't judge myself. It would be wrong to place demands on what yoga does for me. If it helps me feel better, that's good enough."

How far the pendulum has swung! Yoga and meditation became wildly popular in the West during the sixties, through gurus like Maharishi Mahesh Yogi. Back then, students aimed unabashedly for The Big Goal, enlightenment.

Forty years later, there's a new generation of spiritual seekers, 22 million yoga practitioners alone. Many teachers avoid any mention of enlightenment. Aiming to reach the widest possible market, some tell newbies, "Yoga can give you a better butt. Plus it may bring you a little relaxation."

Sure, it's wise to avoid scaring students away with excessive woo-woo. But omitting discussion of any significant spiritual goal altogether? That's taking things too far...or not far enough.

Whatever you do for your spiritual practice, be it yoga or whistling in the dark, set a worthy goal. As any good yoga teacher will tell you, you're the one responsible for stretching yourself.

40. Shopping List

Yesterday I recounted my awkward discussion with Connie, a yoga teacher leery of setting goals in her spiritual life. Our conversation was followed by an awkward pause. To fill the gap, she offered to describe something really inspiring — a miracle, in fact. Here's the story.

Connie lived with her boyfriend. Together they struggled to make ends meet. So it had been a very big deal when a friend volunteered to teach her grocery shopping. Despite having spent plenty of time at the mall, Connie never had developed consumer skills with food. She'd shop at upscale markets, buying whatever appealed to her. Days later, she'd despair. How could she have spent so much on groceries yet have nothing to eat?

Hearing Connie lament, her friend, Joan, proposed a bet. "Let me take you shopping for a week's groceries. If you spend more than $50, I'll buy you a 50-cent can of Coca Cola. But if you spend less than $50, you'll treat me."

Joan helped Connie write down her first shopping list. They even clipped a few coupons from the newspaper. At the supermarket, they loaded up Connie's shopping cart. And although they didn't do math as they traveled the aisles, at checkout the groceries totaled exactly $49.50.

To Connie, this was a miracle. And the next week while shopping on her own, she found a special sale on hot dogs — just five cents a pack for the top-rated brand. Connie called Joan. "How many packages do you want?"

"I'll take 20."

Connie was thrilled. Here was $100 worth of free food for Joan's freezer. At checkout, the clerk joked, "How can I tell you like hot dogs?"

"Never eat them," Connie said. "I'm a vegetarian." She was so delighted at this chance to reward her friend that Connie considered this as a second miracle.

Her hearty glee when recounting this story was worlds away from the primly patronizing way in which she had informed me that spiritual goals were unnecessary.

How I longed to say, "Honey, connect the dots. Miracles happen whenever you set goals in life, any context — shopping or yoga." Instead I chose silence. When Connie is ready to connect those dots for herself, that could be another miracle, one she'll co-create with God.

But Connie taught *me* something, too. Miracles happen in one context, but sometimes a second miracle results when we apply that special memory to a different context. Think of something miraculous that has happened to you. If the context was material, apply it to spiritual life, or vice versa. Multiple miracles! Hot dog!

41. Broccoli in the Meat Keeper

Baloney really *does* have a place in your spiritual life. It belongs — to make an analogy between your aura and a refrigerator — in the meat keeper.

Everyone can become a really good aura reader. When you do, one of the first things you'll notice is that an aura has specialized compartments, a.k.a. *chakras*. They're like the built-in storage shelves of a refrigerator. Open the door and you'll find a fruit keeper, vegetable bin, meat keeper, and so forth.

How likely are you to confuse the tall, cool shelf for milk cartons with the freezer? Unfortunately, people sometimes do that inwardly. To an aura reader, it shows.

In auras, separate chakras are set aside for emotions, intellect, spirituality and other necessary compartments of human life. Even though people can (and do) deceive themselves, auras always tell the truth, one chakra at a time.

What if, for instance, a woman believes that she's brilliant at figuring out everybody's feelings? If that's true, the energy at her heart chakra will be huge and vibrant. Special emotional gifts, such as empathy, will show as well. Yet sometimes the folks who brag most about their perceptiveness have closed-off heart chakras. *Ideas* about feelings are being processed, not the genuine article.

This can change, of course. Any imbalance in a chakra can be healed… once the aura owner asks for help. Even more common than head-in-heart patterns are varieties of spiritual confusion. Religious zealots usually have fear or hatred in the third eye chakra, rather than showing signs of being God's special favorite (as imagined). Perhaps emotionalism is mistaken for spirituality — equivalent to keeping lettuce in the freezer. Why settle for that?

You can ask God to help align your aura so that you have genuine spiritual experience at your third eye, free-flowing emotions at your heart chakra, and so forth. In response, your inner life will be rearranged. For a while, you may feel as messy as a refrigerator being scrubbed out. But the result will be an enlightened aura, worth far more than a tidy or sanctimonious set of beliefs.

42. Divine Order

Some days your connection to God feels strong as steel. Other days it's more like broken spaghetti. But any day, in any mood, you can connect to God's presence as Divine Order.

The concept is simple. God's huge intelligence keeps this world in perfect balance, down to every detail. Intelligence operates at every level, from enough stars to fill any telescope lens to one perfectly sculpted eyelash on a microscope slide.

Divine Order can be contagious. Like a song that runs through your head, the rhythms of Divine Order can flow through you. Only instead of some irritating advertising jingle that got stuck in your memory, Divine Order will actually *help* you.

When brainwaves entrain to this mystical beat, your creativity will be stimulated to flow in synch. And God's soundless melodies will move you into your clearest possible recognition of Perfection Everywhere Now.

Therefore, Divine Order can help you to do anything better, whether driving through traffic, choosing a spouse or paying your bills.

And it gets better. Once you connect to that celestial flow, you can afford to "Let go and let God." Sure, you'll still need to think, to choose, to do your human best. Only, that human best…will be better.

If Divine Order is a spiritual law, why do we ever lose sight of it? *Entropy* is another law of this planet. Leave a perfectly good automobile on your front lawn for 50 years and it will turn into a pile of unidentifiable junk. The human version of entropy causes us to forget our connection to God. Instead we get caught up in frantic pursuit of a goal. Soon we begin controlling, rather than co-creating.

Or we waste time by perpetually playing Trivial Pursuit, staying busy without evaluating the what or the why.

Or (temporarily) we lose our belief in happy endings.

Whatever the cause, connection to your spiritual source can always be restored.

Simply affirm out loud, "I am Divine Order."

You may not see an obvious physical "Snap to," like the pattern that iron filings make when you unsheathe a magnet. Inwardly, though, you'll feel better. And as you muster the will and patience to watch, you'll catch God's intelligence making a clear path for you that is very real indeed.

43. Breathe in the Presence of God

When your finances are abundant, it's fun to check your bank balance. But how much more delightful it is to check your God balance! Instead of dollars, this money shows up as God presence within you.

How much is in your vault, the life savings account of your consciousness? Could be far more than you think. Why not find out right now?

Begin by taking a deep breath. Exhale fully. How do you feel?

That's a start, anyway. Now, pay closer attention to what it means to take a humongously, super-ambitiously, really deep breath.

Sit comfortably. Start breathing way down deep into your belly. Once that fills up, shift attention to your back and fill it up, rolling air up your spine all the way to your shoulders.

Try this deep breathing method when lying down, belly up, and you'll discover how much your back can inflate.

What about bringing air up in front, puffing you up from your belly to your chest? This will happen automatically, since your front connects to your back. You already know that you can puff up your chest. So favor your back. Just because you can't see it is no reason to ignore it.

Now that you've practiced full breathing, take some long…slow…deep… breaths. Listen for the presence of God and you'll find that the volume has been turned way up. Close your eyes and the light within may shine brighter.

Under the circumstances, your self-talk may gain extra power, too. Did you ever choose an affirmation and *breathe* it into being? Wow!

Affirmations are wisely constructed personal statements that you design to make your life better. The words could be as simple as "I feel that God loves me." Adding breath puts oomph into your affirmation.

How often will you bless yourself today with this rich gift? That's nobody else's business but yours. Only you can decide how often you'll consciously breathe in the presence of God.

44. Interesting People Sometimes Here

One afternoon, I walked down a street in Tokyo and idly read a sign in the window of a bar. The words made me stop in my tracks. The sign read, "Interesting People Sometimes Here."

Never before had I seen such understatement in advertising. If only I were a bar patron, I might have become this one's biggest customer.

Understatement charms people. It can also be a great way to make people laugh. Dry recognition of the obvious can defuse tension, too, like when you describe a sense of overwhelming dread by saying, "Well, yes, maybe I'm just a tiny bit worried."

Provided there's an underlying quality of sympathy, rather than judgment, you may be able to help other people by spreading around more understatement — as in asking a terrified friend, "So you're just a bit worried, are you?"

Yes, two cheers for understatement! Except beware a common form of understatement that isn't nearly so pleasant: When you do it to yourself.

Excessive modesty is understandable. Our most extraordinary talents come so easily, we think, "Shucks, that's nothing" or "Everybody can do that." One friend of mine memorizes people's phone numbers the first time he hears them. Another friend has such a keen sense of smell, she can use it to track deer in a forest. Gifts like these are wonderful, and dismissing their worth most unfair.

What makes modesty particularly unfair? Every thoughtful person goes through moments of self-doubt. We worry if we're good enough. Or we berate ourselves, and on closer examination the not-so-logical self-critique follows: "I'm bad because I don't possess every extraordinary gift in the world."

Couldn't this be just a tad too demanding?

At such moments — or to prevent future ones — give yourself the benefit of self-recognition. Your most *effortless* gifts may be the most glorious. Expressing gratitude can become a way to let God in on the glory. Consider, too, the greatest saying from Texas, a place not famous for understatement:

"It ain't bragging if it's so."

45. You Have Given Me a Face

You have given me
a Face within my face
through which I can taste other people's tears
Beyond that, when I choose
I can blink through indifference
and see my neighbor's soul.

You have given me
a Voice within my voice
and through it I can speak words that are real.
Beyond that, when I choose,
I'll improvise spontaneously
new words that wake up joy.

I don't quite know how it happens
or when it will happen again.
But I love when the old masks slip away,
and I softly breathe You in.
It can't just be coincidence
how we speak in unison.

You have given me
a Heart within my heart.
Beyond mere generosity or courage,
somehow, I'm being taught
to feel with wonder and surprise
how, deep within each person, beats
Your soft, Almighty Heart.

46. What If You DON'T Call on God?

Think of the need to call upon God as a continuum. Atheism is at one end of the God-Need Continuum. This counter-balances the other end of the Continuum, where a person calls on God constantly, which may not be as noble as it seems.

Ever hear the joke about Marvin and his ongoing conversation with God? "Every day, Lord, I pray to you. From the minute I get up until my last thought at night, there I am, pleading for mercy. In everything I do, I take care to do it exactly the way you would like it, following every one of your commandments. Frankly, I do a better job of praying to you than anyone else I know.

"I'm constantly calling on you, God, but what does it get me? Nothing! Why, Lord, why?"

Down comes a voice from on high: "Because, Marvin, you're a kvetch!"

Loving God is different from whining. Atheism may be far distant from your beliefs, but it's not a bad place to be, especially temporarily. It provides the opportunity to take full responsibility for your life.

Would the universe crumble if you tried this for a week?

At least you could do this experiment: Co-create from a *different* place along the God-Need Continuum, just for today. As you tackle life's problems, do your best, then call upon God as a resource — either more or less often than usual.

For some of us, it's important to realize that a deep connection to God need not mean constantly begging for help. Instead, you could treat God more like a toenail. Sure you bring it along everywhere; how often must you stop to admire it?

Acting like an outright atheist can be an amazingly challenging exercise. The harder you try to push God out of your heart, out of the people around you, out of animals, out of the enormous sky or even something as tiny as a teardrop...well, just see what happens. Push away.

Whether you consciously call upon God or not, both of you will do just fine. Of all the jokes God creates, one of the funniest may be the God-Need Continuum. We may wiggle around from one position to another. Yet the fact remains, we're stuck to it somewhere. A miraculous predicament!

47. How to Call on God

How intimidating is it for you to go to the movies? Once in the theater, do you worry about being worthy enough to see the show?

Compared to seeing a movie, calling on God is both easier and cheaper. Furthermore, you're guaranteed that "The God Show" (unlike entertainment produced by mere mortals) will rate way more than four stars.

Just like a multi-plex movie theater, God has many simultaneous screenings. You're free to choose any one. Automatically you'll attract the qualities of God being broadcast in that particular theater.

For example, would you prefer for God to show forth as the Holy Spirit, omnipresent, pervading all? Then ask for it. Close your eyes, take a deep breath, and think as a sentence inside your head, "God, please help me to experience You as the Holy Spirit." For short, you can simply telegraph, "Holy Spirit."

Would you prefer a more specific (but still abstract) name for God, like "Divine Power" or "Divine Love"? Again, just think the name. Easy does it.

Automatically, a few simple words will connect you to God in precisely the form you request. And here comes the really amazing part: The rest of your reality will morph to match. As you continue to watch that day's movie, you'll catch on to the plot. Keep watching on a regular basis and you can even join the fan club for that particular God show.

Heisenberg's Uncertainty Principle tells us that an experimenter's consciousness can affect the experiment. Measurable reality can change — yes, our precious so-called "real life" is mutable — and just because of one person's thinking. For me, it's a stretch to accept that even a few elementary particles could be altered by a person's intention, yet physicists have proven it's true.

I find it even more amazing how someone as perfect as God is willing to appear differently based on my whim.

But that's true, too. Just try the experiment. Not only will God show forth different qualities, depending upon your choice. A whole day's worth of reality will change around you, and simply because you prefer a God of Power today, compared to Compassion God yesterday.

48. You Choose

One of the more fascinating human freedoms is your ability to call on God in any form you desire. All celestial beings are holograms containing the Divine presence. So you can request the experience of God in any form and co-create with That choice.

When was the last time you experimented with this freedom? Just for today, call on God in a new way: As a Divine Being, guardian angel or personal guide. Or call on God in the form of an ancestor you revere or a type of animal to which you feel a special bond.

Is that *all* God is? No. But any expression of love, joy, peace or truth can enliven your spiritual life. You could even call on God as a favorite color or flower. It's your choice.

Experimenting can help you to release the common fear that if you called upon the *wrong* form of God, the *correct* one would strike you dead. Behavior like this might be expected from a bullying father or jealous spouse, but from the tender Creator of dewdrops?

Certainly, your choice will have consequences. An earth-centered aspect of God, like an animal guide, will help to switch on your connection to nature. Commune with your guardian angel for messages of deep compassion for your human self. A bigger, more transpersonal tenderness comes if you'll call on an Ascended Master like St. Teresa or Isis.

How vivid will your experience be? That depends on the clarity of your body-mind-spirit. If you do a spiritual exercise on a daily basis, over time the benefits will be cumulative. If you regularly get enough sleep and physical exercise, that will bring clearer consciousness, too. More clarity in your consciousness brings more exquisite experiences of God.

Yet calling on That needn't wait until you're perfect. Whatever your state of consciousness you can connect, and the process of connection can move you forward spiritually.

Granted, in material life our choices are limited (at least in the short run) by money, social status and the opinions of others. But in spiritual life? That's strictly between you and God, the Fulfiller of Desires. So ask for something great. That's not greedy, it's smart.

49. Turn off That Noise

When the goal is to switch on your God light, does it make sense to turn on a neon sign too? If you were operating a casino, you might install a light show to attract walk-ins, but flash in your meditation room won't impress anyone.

Bright artificial light makes it harder to see a candle-fine flame. And although this example of visual overwhelm seems obvious, the auditory equivalent may not, at least initially. Many tapes made for meditation include background music. It's supposed to help a person connect to God. If silence were a terrible threat, instead of being the point of the exercise, this would make sense.

When your goal is entertainment or hypnosis or putting God at ease — absolutely, switch on the Muzak. But God is plenty relaxed already, and you deserve better than some ride in an elevator. Your destination, after all, is the God within.

This place demands silence just as our human planet requires air fit to breathe. Unless you set up your worship environment to foster inner silence, you won't go far…except, perhaps, in mood. Watching a travelogue about Mt. Fuji could make you feel good, too, but wouldn't you find it more impressive to visit in person?

Then why do so many people play contemplative music?

- Sometimes it's a habit. If you experiment spiritually *without* that music, you just might go deeper.
- Perhaps music eases a fear of going within. Spiritual newbies can have a kind of *psychic barrier,* or spiritual virginity, felt as fear of letting go. If you fall into the unknown, will you ever come out? Let me reassure you that you will.
- Initially, it may bolster confidence to invite a friend or teacher to physically sit in the room with you, someone who has already been where you're going. Once you're through the psychic barrier, that initial trepidation will end.

Whether you're already an experienced spiritual seeker or not, now is an excellent time to explore silently going within. After you return, play music. It will sound better. So will everything.

What if you feel you simply have to play something during your prayers? Sing this sentence inside — just once will do it: "Wherever I go, protect me God."

The light, love and power of God will never fail.

50. Ask the Healing Question

Unfathomable are the reasons for physical pain. Sometimes they include a hidden lesson, an unquestioned and out-grown choice, even a secret payoff. If you can find what the reason is, healing will come so much faster.

- One unselfish woman thought she deserved to suffer for humanity's sins.
- One conscientious man wanted to rest from a job he hated. Illness was the only way he could let himself leave work without losing face.
- One dutiful woman believed she must follow in the pattern of others she'd known who had suffered.
- And a lonely man craved the more caring attention that pain seemed to bring.

Illusions all! There could be another way to satisfy the deep need behind any of these patterns. So the first step in healing chronic pain is this: Ask, ask, ask.

But don't be a relentless interrogator, like a movie cop slapping around a sullen prisoner. Ask compassionately, prepared to receive any answer with unconditional self-compassion. Not all pain can be healed by this method, but at least you'll know that you gave it a chance.

Pain might be written into your Life Contract in such a way that you can't erase it. You could have signed up for lessons about surrender and coping. Or maybe this current pain was set in motion during a previous life. Life isn't fair… unless you consider *reincarnation*, which provides adequate time for the consequences of a person's actions to come back and be understood. This possibility softens the harshness of pain. Since you can have as many lifetimes as you wish, you can afford to spend one learning pain's unique lessons. Well, if you did set this up previously, why not ask to re-visit the planning meeting?

Ask, ask, ask. And if you don't have the faith that you'll ever get well, invite a friend who *does* have that faith keep you company while you look within.

You have the right to know, "Why do I have this pain? What must I learn so the pain will be gone? Once I start doing my part of the healing inwardly, which outer resources will help me best?"

Ask to be given the answer in your dreams. Ask to be inspired with knowledge when you awake in the morning. Or sit and write a dialogue with the pain. Once you've warmed up the conversation, pop the big question. WHY?

Pain's seeming unfairness can be the most brutal part. Let a spiritual answer assuage that. It's comforting, even if you're told only that the pain has no lesson for you at this time and is just something that you must go through.

51. Phooey on Hell

Rev. Donna Dearmore, a Unity minister, recounts this story from the early days of her career. She was on her way to perform a wedding ceremony when a man accosted her on the steps of the church. He said, "You can't marry that couple. Don't you know the groom has been divorced?"

Dearmore continued to walk up the stairs. The man grabbed her arm. "If you marry them, you'll go straight to Hell."

She paused, choosing her words carefully. "You, sir, have no right to send me to Hell. Only I can do that."

Now, the man in this story could be seen as taking a courageous action, based on his fear of Hell. Belief in The Hot Place generates more fears than a scoop of detergent brings up suds. What if you make any choice in life that displeases God? An innocent mistake could, supposedly, send you forever to the realm of fire and brimstone.

Well, phooey on that! Why choose to believe in a jealous, petty God who would allow his precious creation — you! — to be punished forever?

Every belief brings consequences, and the fear of Hell can be used to justify any mischief. A coercive attempt to stop someone else's marriage is actually mild when compared to the way that some religious zealots have rationalized terrorism and war.

No matter how thoroughly you've been indoctrinated with the fear of Hell, you can overcome it.

Why carry within you the image of a harsh, punishing God? You can imagine another image of God that is similar but loving. Let them work things out so the punishing one walks away permanently. Then welcome the loving one into your life.

Rev. Dearmore is right. Only you can send yourself to Hell. Or to Heaven. And you make the choice on a daily basis, not only after you die. So, for you, which will it be today?

52. Heaven's Road, Paved with Intentions

One misconception in our collective consciousness goes like this: "The road to Hell is paved with good intentions."

True, intentions alone are no substitute for right action. But to malign good intentions because they don't always (apparently) work makes as much sense as saying, "Healthy food could make you fat." Sure, if you eat enough of it. Does that mean a person would be better off eating junk food or ceasing to eat altogether?

Really, the dangerous kind of "good" intention proceeds from belief in personal superiority, e.g., "I'll hurt you, but only because it's for your own good."

What an inspiration it would be if collective consciousness were to acknowledge *the positive power of intention*. But don't wait for others to figure it out. Make your choice now.

People who have been raised to fear God often worry about some kind of sneaky spiritual trap, guaranteed to send the miscreant straight to Hell. Such a belief mocks both you and God.

Of course, you can trust your heart when it tells you than an intention is good. Although intention can't substitute for right action, at least it's the basis. If your choice turns out to be a mistake, you'll learn your lesson and show better judgment next time. On The Learning Planet, who could do better than that?

Positive intention only makes life better, not worse. It's especially indispensable before you start any spiritual exercise. Pause for a second, take a deep breath and actively set an intention. A simple sentence will do it, such as:

- "God, help me to experience You more clearly."
- "Give me guidance."
- "Prepare me to be Your perfect instrument."

For the rest of today, you're invited to explore the positive power of intention. At the start of a new activity, even something as simple as sending an email, ask inwardly, "Why am I doing this, and what do I aim to achieve?"

Especially if you're about to do something big, think through the consequences. A fuzzy or negative answer won't do. Choose intentions that are worthy of you. Then confidently take action. Quick as thought, you'll pave the way to Heaven — for yourself, for others.

53. Push Buttons

Ever feel cut off from God? Maybe you just haven't been treating yourself enough like a machine. Yes, you can view yourself as a glorious machine for making contact with God. Every chakra in your aura contains a kind of push button for starting up a Divine walkie-talkie.

Consider that push button at your third eye (between and above your eyebrows). This button can help you make a *spiritual* connection. Close your eyes. Take some deep breaths. Now, with your imagination, push the button in your forehead. Easy does it. Once does it. You've turned on the communication channel for Spirit, so talk away. Ask a question and an answer will follow.

What, *that's* your answer? So, maybe it's not what you expected. Since when was God here to be what you expected? Your answer could be nonverbal, sculpted in silence. Maybe you'll hear it, feel it or see it. Whatever you get, it wouldn't hurt to say "Thanks" before you think the equivalent of "Over and out."

Perhaps you would prefer to connect *emotionally*? Again, show proper respect for the process by first closing your eyes. Slow down with a few long breaths. Now you're ready to push the button located at heart level.

Do this with consciousness to automatically open up the communication channel. Talk to your Love. Ask Him or Her to join you within your deep heart. Or you do the traveling. Curl up and rest inside the loving heart of your God. Your walkie-talkie works in both directions.

Got the idea? Each of the chakras within your aura (not just the third eye and heart chakras) can work like a walkie-talkie. The *communication* button at your throat is especially good when you're feeling lonely. All of us, even the most popular, have moments of isolation. Push on that button, then cry out to God as loudly as you like.

Most days, you'll feel how delighted God is to be with you. Always was. Always will be. Some days, alas, no button seems to work properly. Trying your favorite one brings no satisfaction, and others seem equally useless. That doesn't mean God is broken, nor that you've been abandoned, just that your part of the machine is shut down for a little maintenance work.

Maybe some health project needs attending to, or it's a good day to do something new to re-install hope, like petting a puppy. This may seem small consolation. But push buttons are tiny things too. And any day now, your body-mind system will run smoothly again. Then once again you'll be like a toddler in an elevator, so eager to push the buttons.

54. Just Show Up

In deepest darkness, in loneliest night
I will show up and bring my God.

Blasted by cold wind, in the rain,
I will turn stubborn. As smart as a bat
I will hang upside down in the dark if need be.
Somehow I can endure…and bring along God.

When the easy times come, and I work in a flow
when success brims within me, pouring unstintingly,
and joy overfills my cup,
in that messy, delightful stream of abundance,
I will show up and thank God.

Mustering all my available grace
I keep striving, keep aiming to do my best.
On the days when my shiny best seems inadequate
I will give up only to this extent:
I'll still bring in my humblest light, ordinary consciousness.

To One so great, my cheers and groans
may seem inconsequential, yet
perhaps they are part of my charm — or His joke.
I expect to inquire about that
when I show up to laugh along with God.

55. God-Colored

Just for today, as a spiritual exercise, dare to call upon God as one particular color, like blue, pink or yellow. Then, every time you happen to notice that color, see it as a kiss from Heaven, a sign that God is with you.

Make your choice. Take a moment to acknowledge the blessing.

To enhance it, ask a question about the God-qualities encoded in that color. It will be easy to let this new shade of love into your soul. The color will seep through as effortlessly as if you were bathing in sunlight.

To clarify, no, I'm not suggesting that you start to worship balloons. Or even that you carry out this colorful research into God for more than one day. Today's experiment is designed simply to help you get out of a rut.

Believing in God as only one form, how boring is that? You probably know at least one person who insists that the Lord will maintain one particular appearance throughout eternity, like a bearded old man who sits on a throne in the sky. Well, throughout your short lifetime, your appearance has changed, hasn't it? The baby you, the pre-schooler, the teenager, and so forth — at each phase, you looked different. That appearance corresponded to a special charm, unique kinds of knowledge, subtly different ways to use your perception.

If *little old you* could manage that much variety, why not your Maker? It could actually be considered insulting to limit God by expecting Him or Her to maintain one rigid, set appearance forever. It's bad enough when today's aging movie stars try to look like twenty-somethings a few decades too late.

Still, you may be especially fond of a particular personal image of God. Then combine That with your chosen color du jour. Have Jesus hold a squirt gun full of blue paint and imagine that he has sprayed your sky. Let Lord Krishna play orange music with his flute. Combine any of your senses with your imagination and you'll find new ways to dance with God.

56. Unmask Spiritual Superiority

"My God is better than your God." Now that's a scary thought — especially if somebody else expresses it to *you*. Actually, God can be understood at every possible level of consciousness. So every religion, each house of worship, helps people at a particular vibration.

Religion could be compared to an orange. In one view, it's is a round ball of juice sold at your supermarket. But that orange can also be seen through a microscope or be arranged by a painter as part of a still life. You could peel and taste an orange section by section. Having different ways to explore one and the same orange, why shouldn't that be considered a bonus? With religion, each expression is valid...unless it claims superiority.

But you knew that. Here's where things get interesting. Aura reading can help you sort through the conflicting claims, helping you to tell fact from fantasy. Consistently you'll find that the biggest zealots have a hugely undeveloped third eye. Witness this story, proudly told in a radio interview by Tim LaHaye, co-author of the popular *Left Behind* novels. At a religious conclave, he spotted the Dalai Lama:

"I just stuck out my hand and shook hands and said, 'Has anyone ever explained to you who Jesus Christ *really* is?'" Then His Holiness LaHaye graciously offered to give an hour of his time to convert the world-renowned Buddhist leader.

Well, find photos if you can of both these men circa 2001, when this conversation took place. Read their third eyes and have a good laugh. Which man shows a vibrant, clear connection to God? Here's a hint. Guess which fellow found it necessary to describe the other's spiritual status as "very pious and *probably* very sincere."

Today and every day, you choose your best way to co-create with God. Never believe anyone who asserts that only one way is valid and — such a coincidence — instructions belong exclusively to him.

If this kind of "very sincere" new friend insists on boasting about his spiritual superiority, know it to be a masquerade that has nothing to do with God.

Costumes can be fascinating. But when you read people deeper, masks fall away. Beware those who insist that you must hide behind one.

57. A Perfectly Good Answer

Did you ever ask God for guidance and, in return, get a big fat nothing?

Does no answer necessarily mean "No"? Only if you believe your fears.... Nor does silence mean that you are spiritually hopeless, incapable of ever receiving clear guidance. "No" is tougher to accept than a loud xylophone chime of a "Yes." But a gentle silence gives you permission to figure things out for yourself.

Perhaps silence *could* be a kind way to say "No." What you would like to do is wonderful, but maybe the timing is off. Or what you wished for may not be in your best interest; a finer solution is on the way. But maybe, lacking outer encouragement, you're simply being given the space to think your own "Yes." That would count as a sign, too. It's like *the wise way to flip a coin.*

The following technique is way too much fun not to try. All you'll need is a coin with two sides. Heads will mean "Yes," tails "No." Now ask a simple, personal question with a yes-or-no answer.

After you ask, flip that coin. See what you get. Then *notice how that makes you feel inside.*

There's the guidance that counts! When you groan inwardly, that answers your question as clearly as some lightning bolt from on high.

Another excellent way to seek guidance is Shakti Gawain's technique of *holding a situation in the Light.* Say you're hoping for a certain outcome to materialize. Play the scene out in your imagination. If the story flows with plenty of sprightly energy around it, you've received a "Yes." Proceed as if it will work. But what if, inwardly, your desire tumbles down with a thud? Then you've been given something different: A chance to think.

Frustration can stretch us, provided we're willing. Along with flexibility, benefits can include humor, curiosity, determination and graciousness.

Almighty God is willing to compromise. Otherwise you'd never have been given free will. Life as co-creation — sometimes it's awkward, yet always it's preferable. What a spiritual nightmare it would be if you had to live utterly alone.

58. Organizing Religion

"Been to church lately? When's the last time you went to confession?" Zealots can ask you questions like these or you can guilt-trip yourself on your own. What if, say, during the entire month of Ramadan, there was one 15-minute interlude when your observance of the holy fast was not perfect?

Here's my perspective, having co-created healing sessions for clients who've called on Ascended Masters related to every major religion (and many of the lesser known ones, as well). Divine Beings don't give a hoot about your reputation at your local house of worship. Religion is a *human* thing, helping people to evolve and create community among the like minded.

What makes going to church especially delightful is having a personal relationship with one of the founders: Not a social acquaintance, not perfection at worship, but having your consciousness make direct contact with an Inner Teacher.

Only *you* can personalize the faith of your fathers and mothers with a genuine relationship. What if spiritual seeking only exaggerates the points of difference between your beliefs and those of others in your congregation? It's nobody else's business. Religion speaks to people at every level of consciousness, uplifting everyone. If certain words bring you down, rather than up, just don't say them.

When singing a hymn, leave out any words you don't believe. Other worshippers, if they notice at all, may assume you don't know the tune. Or that you're crying. Or maybe *they're* crying. (Hey, sit next to me at any religious service. Lend *me* tissues....)

Seriously, some of the most spiritually evolved people you'll meet are refugees from a religion that turned them off. What if you actively hate what was shoved down your throat in Sunday school? What if you have been scarred by the behavior of leaders or fellow worshippers in your old church? Well, re-organize that religion!

Unlike physical scars, psychic hurts can vanish without a trace. Whether or not you still believe in the founder of your former religion, do yourself this favor. Meditate, thinking the name of your choice of Divine Being. Ask for help with healing any unresolved incident or relationship. Quick as a flash, miracles happen, with old pain that was stuck in your aura lifted out permanently.

Within — or without — the boundaries of organized religion, the story of your spiritual life is perfect. Why? Because you say so. No religious authority from your past can stop your co-creating a perfect life with God right now.

59. Alone By Choice

What if you don't wish to call on any Divine Being, angel or ancestor to help with your spiritual life? Will it matter?

Unquestionably, staying true to yourself is the fastest way to evolve. Yet spiritual do-it-yourself can be tedious. Why struggle for years to solve problems that could be lifted by one quick prayer?

Another drawback to mere self-help is this: Imbalances can be hard to detect at their own level. For instance, a woman who's over-intellectual may not feel her feelings, merely label them. And her spiritual life may amount to ideology rather than experience. Despite all her best efforts, she could be the last one to spot limitations that all who know her find obvious. How helpful to collaborate with someone who has a bigger perspective!

As for helping others, we'll do that better, too, with an assist from beings at the highest possible vibration.

Let's say that you find psychic-level debris in another person's aura. Later in this book, you'll learn some ways of removing this. These ways are efficient precisely because they're done by Divine Beings at a higher frequency than the psychic level. How long would it take to change a flat tire if you couldn't use a jack to raise your car?

But the most compelling reason to ask for help may be to overcome your own resistance…to receiving help. Have life experiences caused you to feel disillusioned about God, even downright contemptuous? Back when your heart and faith broke, this reaction was completely understandable. But now you can choose to move past it.

Experiences of disillusionment lodge in a person's aura. On that level, real structures persist, recording every bit of the longstanding pain, fear or anger. These things are physical, in their metaphysical way. After they have been healed, the brilliant gifts of your soul will shine all the brighter.

Of course you can tough out any pain. That even builds character. But hold on. Just how much character does a person really need?

My advice is to go ahead and send out a call. Ask for an angel, a sprinkling of fairy dust, any expression of Divine love from beings whose wisdom and spiritual clarity are greater than your own.

60. Spin Cycle

Sin means falling short, with the implication of failing God. Sure, it's possible that you have goofed a few times in your life, falling short of the standards you set for yourself.

Once you start to tumble, the lack of balance can spiral, spinning you around until you gather a wild and frightening momentum. But God can help you say, "Stop!"

It's like what happens if your washing machine is rocking back and forth with an imbalanced spin cycle. Can that be stopped? Sure. Not your favorite washing experience, but you open the lid, redistribute the laundry and start over.

In life, as in laundry, the need for a re-set need not be considered a personal failure. Self-talk helps make the difference. Please, call problems a cycle of *spin*, not *sin*. Whatever has happened, you can act responsibly now and, as needed, make restitution to yourself or others. Actions may have been mistaken but you can take change old patterns, so long as you never give up on yourself.

To forgive yourself, how about using your sense of proportion? One unbalanced load does not mean a washing machine has become irreparably defective. Similarly, regardless of what has happened before, you still are a good person. Each day you start fresh, with no mistakes. And whenever a day seems like a bad one, you can stop the washer, halt the clock, rewind the time machine — do whatever it takes to start over, right then.

Once I went to hear the Dalai Lama give a talk. Some 5,000 people were gathered. I came to hear someone I respect immensely, but many in the audience came with an attitude of much greater reverence, verging on worship. He was onto this. I'll never forget the gist of his opening, even if I must paraphrase the words:

"Some of you here have a high opinion of me. But I must tell you, I'm human, too. I have my problems and my neuroses, just like everyone else."

Yes, he definitely used the word "neuroses." I was shocked, then remembered that *everyone* here is at Earth School. Each person goes through spin cycles. Inner helplessness keeps them rolling on but we can change that by calling on any Divine Being for help. We can reach out to people too, as needed. Then the trick is simply to accept help, which all human beings must do sometimes.

Right where you are, time has interstices, finer holes than any mesh sieve. Exit through one of these into spiritual time. Take a deep breath and, otherwise, steady yourself as best you can. Remember that no more than your best was *ever* required of you.

61. The Perils of Whatever

When you ask for spiritual help, it's no time to be vague.

Beings from the other side aren't necessarily all-wise. All you know about them for sure is that they're not stuck in our three dimensions. My dead step-mother, for instance, may have lost her gambling problem when she moved out of her body, but that hardly puts her in a league with The Delphic Oracle.

What kind of guidance do you wish to attract? You have the right to ask for beings whose spiritual evolution, wisdom and ability to love are at least as good as your own.

So don't just be a good sport, letting life twirl you around like a pinwheel. Saying "Whatever" may make a person seem socially agreeable, but spiritually it's a big waste of time.

Once a spiritual healer did a session where she aligned with the vibrations of an Ascended Master. Her client was most impressed with how she looked after-wards. "You're glowing," he said. "How strange! After I channel, I feel so bad that all I can do is sleep for three days." What made the difference? She asked to con-nect with a Divine Being. He settled for whoever showed up.

It's the same when you ask for a healing. Why imagine that God automatically knows what you want? *You* are the one in the mud body. Illusions are built into earth experience, with fear and pain thick as the air, which will make your suffer-ing seem very real. To beings off-planet, it's not quite so vivid.

Ever watch a reluctant passenger ride a roller coaster? When she comes staggering off, *you* may observe some temporary anxiety but *she* is the one who wants to throw up right now. Her discomfort is visceral, not theoretical.

From a celestial perspective, each of us is an adorable, eternally blessed light being…no matter how rotten we feel. Should 20 burdens be weighing on you, Charlie, that makes you the expert witness.

So give listening ears a clue. Decide which burden feels heaviest. Ask for that one to be removed first, if possible. Divine Beings may decide to solve your prob-lems in a different order than you would, but at least they'll have your wish list.

Spiritual helpers of your choice can serve as extraordinarily helpful friends. Asking doesn't make you ungrateful, nor will it disqualify you from getting help. So ask. What would you prefer?

62. Oh My (Greek) God

Studying religions of other ages, one hears about worship methods that can seem strangely familiar. Take the gods of ancient Greece. Back then, if you chose to be helped by Hestia, goddess of the hearth, you'd consecrate a place for her in your home. This location might correspond to the part of the house where, today, you'd put the family TV. Granted, in those bygone days, you'd probably spend fewer hours just watching The Goddess Station and more time cooking up offerings.

However archeologists from the future interpret *today's* rituals (Heaven knows what they'll make of our TV-watching habits) we're free to interpret *yesterday's* rituals. Will we take the "holier than thou" approach, interpreting sacred practices of the Celts, Romans, Egyptians and others as worship performed by ignorant pagans? Or were the ancients, like us, given effective ways to reach out to God?

Sure, Greeks made statues of their gods and performed ceremonies to enlist their help. Will we ever know the extent to which these worshippers relinquished their personal power? Could they have co-created with beings who, through deeper perception, were seen, heard and touched? Did thoughtful people search their hearts throughout the day and ask themselves, "What would Heracles do?"

One way to tell is to revisit ancient cultures courtesy of a past-life regression. Having led many clients through past lifetimes, as well revisiting a fair sampling of my own, I've found that, for some ancients with pure hearts, religious rituals worked beautifully. Gods appeared in their light bodies. They talked. And they definitely responded to human cries for help. So divine intervention didn't occur just to the heroes of Homer's *Iliad*. It happened constantly to everyday people…and still does.

What if you called on a being like Athena, Artemis or Apollo? Does that mean you'd be worshipping an idol? Some of my clients have requested the help of these magnificent beings. In each case, I asked God to protect the room energetically, said the god's or goddess' name aloud one time, immediately felt that Being's presence enter the room. I summarized my client's intention. Then the three of us co-created spiritual and emotional healing to fulfill that intention.

At the end of each session, I said "Thank you." Hardly what I'd call worship! Frankly, I'd have to grovel more to get a table at some snooty restaurants I could mention.

Trust me, if I can do such things, you can, too. Divine Beings include the Greek gods, Egyptian gods, any so-called "mythological" beings whom you'd feel comfortable inviting into your home. Ask and they'll come, no strings attached. In the process of co-creation, neither you nor they are puppets.

63. Silence Collector

Some collect stamps, others jewelry or lamps.
But let my collection be silence.

Traveling the world, its new cities and old
I crave what is best: Hidden peace.

On my own, staying home, would I ever have known
the world's cities are, secretly, quiet?
The creative near-boil of a Manhattan condo,
(where even a late-night sleep can simmer);
watching high-altitude clouds in Denver
while a thousand-headed hammerhead
gathered its wondrous, thunderous force;
on a dry day in London, listening, amazed,
when so-very-proper gentlemen volunteers
in my subway car
wordlessly leapt up to carry my suitcase —
All these silences pull me straight up by the ears,
quenching curiosity yet deepening
a most ancient longing.

You're a city, too, God
fierce and mild,
silence filled.
Wherever we visit, I'm listening.

64. Happiness, Not Hype-in-Us

Life is a dance with veils. Call it *maya*, call it myth, call it one strange way to rock 'n roll...whatever. If your goal is to co-create with God, you have some veils to lift.

The tricky thing about myths is their kooky version of truth in labeling. Nobody tells you that a myth is a myth. Instead you are told it's a truth. To complicate matters, there's usually enough truth to the myth to make it seem real, so any falling short of the hype appears to be *your* fault.

For instance, have you ever been told that it matters to be good looking, successful, popular or happy? All this is true, sort of. But:

- Good-looking by whose standard?
- Which version of success?
- Just how much popularity do you really require, and with whom?
- As for happiness, can you define your own? Or will you settle for hype-in-us — a world of false expectations?

Politics, sociology, and other disciplines can give you tools to understand how money and power motivate certain groups to promulgate illusions. Question your reality and it will become a lot more interesting. How you spend money, for instance, can become a way that you reward people who live with integrity. With every bill that you spend, you vote.

Even if society were illusion-free, you'd still need to find your own version of truth. Every goal that you seek has a highly individual spiritual component. When you find the real thing, you'll know it.

As you seek truth behind the veils, don't concern yourself with how others might answer — or how they'd judge you for asking.

What is real happiness? Who defines popularity or success? You can recognize things like this well enough. Take a peek beneath the surface. God has tucked all these good things and more neatly into your day.

65. Your Soul Mate

One of the strangest scavenger hunts on the planet begins here: Romantic searching for *The One*. This maya-inspired ideal inevitably causes a person to overlook partners who would bring genuine happiness. The Soul Mate Myth sets up expectations for a lover to whom attraction is instantly obvious, forever larger than life.

Try this reality check:

- How many of the couples you know consider themselves soul mates?
- How many knew it instantly with an oomphy, dramatic love at first sight?
- Now, how many of those couples have actually *stayed* married?

That number of soul mates is, most likely, extremely small. And if you know more about the life of a couple who have this rare blessing, you might be shocked. The love relationship works and (most likely) so much else doesn't. Each karmic gift has been bought at a price, in this life or lives past.

Here's what happens far more frequently than finding "The One." You'll meet a stranger's eyes and feel an instant frisson of recognition. Does that necessarily mean you are soul mates? Hardly. Hello! You've just met before — in a past life, maybe in hundreds of them.

Perhaps your Life Contract this time around has set you up to have an important relationship with this person. When meeting, you'll feel attraction all right, but as soul mates? His destined role in your life may not be peaches and cream. It may be more like horseradish…or ipecac.

And perhaps your contract together will cause you to follow this sequence: Infatuated, deceived and disgusted. Perhaps the real beauty part of this relationship involves your finding the strength to walk away.

Fortunately, a person's love life depends on free will as much as destiny. If you're single, there are hundreds of singles with whom you could make a love match. Give one of these workable relationships a chance and the experience of love will probably *dawn*, rather than hitting you like a stun gun. Unlike most idealized encounters with so-called "soul mates," this kind of love is less likely to be a fantasy.

Real love need not be overpowering. Nor is it reserved for a certain kind of soul mate. Today, in even an inconsequential relationship, you may find a quiet kind of love you never noticed before. Take time to smell these wild roses.

66. Your Life Work

For many of us, the greatest fear in life is never finding "The work I was meant to do." Supposedly each person has One Predestined Work. According to the hype, it's your main reason for living. Only for some reason, you're messing up the plan by being too obtuse to figure it out.

Myth alert!

Destiny does exist. But its role in simplifying life has been...oversimplified. In what kind of world does God hand every 21-year-old a clear announcement of vocation, with the precious life choice gift-wrapped down to a perfect bow?

Not here on The Learning Planet! Career selection usually involves free will, seldom mere destiny. For most of us, the process will matter as much as the choice. And *many* kinds of work may thrill your soul.

Sure, sometimes a person's path is clear cut. That's a special blessing for earth life, not to be confused with standard operating procedure. Mozart began his career early. His musical talent was obvious. Did he waste even a single day wondering what he'd be when he grew up?

On the other hand, Mozart wasn't given a lot of days. He died at 33, remember?

You, on the other hand, probably have a longer Life Contract, along with the privilege of considerably more ambiguity. So what if choosing your life work hasn't been easy? All you've missed has been one rare gift: Having the choosing process be simple.

Lacking one noisy, irrevocable, indisputably center stage event — this would make for a lousy bullfight, but for a human lifetime it's not so bad. Spiritually, and even materially, you can't fully evaluate your life while you're stuck in it. Meanwhile, if you're impatient to flip to the answer at the back of the book:

Yes, probably, in your way you'll be at least as successful as Mozart.

Whether you contemplate your career, your life as a whole or one single day like today...the perfection may be hidden but it's huge...as large as life.

67. Heredity

Heredity happens to be a fact. Why is it also a myth? The distinction hinges on exclusivity. To believe exclusively in science robs life of half its truth — and the more interesting half, at that.

You'll hear, for instance, that diseases run in families. So do inner patterns. Negative ones cause disease. Medical intuitives help patients heal by identifying these underlying imbalances. Inner change can cure the related illness.

For example, what if diabetes runs in your family? If family history is all you believe in, there's scant recourse except getting checkups until the disease is diagnosed. But if you believe in holistic medicine, you'll supplement medical checkups, exercise and sensible eating by exploring your inner patterns.

The underlying problem with diabetes is often living without joy. Learning this, you'll grab each opportunity for joy as if it were the brass ring on a merry-go-round. Could that proactive inner search keep you off insulin? Better believe it!

Fatalism about disease isn't the only problem with the myth of "Heredity as personal destiny." This mechanistic idea diminishes life in countless ways. As a face reader, for instance, I find that many people assume that heredity shapes the face. So limiting!

Heredity serves merely as a mechanism, never a cause. Your *soul* shapes your face. According to a sacred, spiritual alphabet, facial characteristics (like ear angles) symbolize inner patterns with work, power and so forth. Over time, choices will alter your face, based on this same sacred alphabet.

Certain attitudes run in families, but your free will matters more. Depending on how you live, you'll develop the face you deserve. How simplistic to believe that faces are shaped only by genes, with their tedious habit of being either dominant or recessive. Your soul can seek out the genes of a distant relative, or mutate, or even attract a so-called "accident" — whatever will shape your face to out-picture your evolving soul.

This ongoing process explains why compatible couples eventually look alike, why children in well-blended families grow to resemble each other. Or consider large families with a "black sheep." This rebel gains a reputation for not acting like the others. Well, she probably doesn't look like them, either. Spot that rebel instantly in the family's group photo!

As you co-create with God, you can explore every nook and cranny of this amazing world. Deeper perception will show you details about how God lives and breathes in human form. On earth the soul is expressed, not invalidated, through the laws of science.

68. Question Fame

Pop artist Andy Warhol famously proclaimed that in our media age everyone would achieve celebrity…for 15 minutes.

Trick sentence. My point in writing it wasn't Andy's quote so much as to call your attention to the impact of a certain word. When you read *"famously* proclaimed," didn't that make his statement seem extra credible? These days, having an utterance be famous appears to matter more than whether it's true.

A can of nuts from my supermarket says, on the lid, "Famously Fresh." A dry cleaner or restaurant in *your* neighborhood may put the tantalizing words on its window and wow! Fame is supposed to make you sit up and take notice.

Supposedly fame constitutes the highest praise — at least until you ponder what the word actually means: Just that somebody has won a popularity contest.

For today's pop culture, nothing matters more. But you can choose just how popular that culture will be with *you*, including whether or not to join in the current fame frenzy.

In reality, nothing matters less. Celebrity is tantamount to neither wisdom, virtue nor talent. Long ago, people would quip, "If you're so smart, why ain't you rich?" Now the expectation has shifted. Smart people should be famous, shouldn't they? And deciding whether to notice a stranger often comes down to the question, "How come I've never heard of him?"

If he lived today, Warhol might be proud. America's commercial culture is packaged airtight as a can of Campbell's soup. But with deeper perception, you wield the can opener — not to mention the ability to cook your own soup from scratch.

Question fame. Notice how often you're expected to equate it with value. Instead, you can choose to value genuine originality, human striving, heroes sung or unsung.

Here's an exercise for today. When humanity parades by, turn on your own candid camera. Ordinary people? Little people? Why need there be any such thing as somebody insignificant?

Moreover, when it comes to *your* life, have extraordinary conversations, co-create magnificent work and big fun. In God's world, only a fool would settle for just 15 minutes of glory.

69. Home Alone

Most of us have a complex relationship with our own solitude. Loneliness hurts. To feel lonely occasionally is human, yet many of us find this painful, then increase the pain by berating ourselves. *Should* it be a problem, feeling lonely? Of course it should, if it is.

Some folks circumvent this kind of difficulty by treating solitude as a horror to be avoided at all costs. Better to be with anyone, no matter how dreadful. Supposedly, having a relationship avoids the problem of staying home alone.

Whatever your comfort level with solitude, your choice — more than anything else — determines how much you'll enjoy it. When solitude comes unavoidably, it's more apt to seem like a problem. Yet, if you crave "alone time" each day, it can seem like a luxury, as in the case of a minister I once taught to meditate. Seeking a polite way to excuse himself from his wife and eight children, he tried hiding out in a broom closet. Soon little voices assaulted him, excitedly asking, "Daddy, Daddy, what are you doing?"

When you know the spiritual truth about solitude, it may release you from the grip of that silly myth, loneliness.

You have never been alone. God has been with you all along…and still is, whether you know it or not, whether you breathe out or breathe in.

God sticks to you more persistently than peanut butter clinging to the roof of your mouth. So, of course, you can find God on demand, whenever you like. Whether you go inside to meditate (with or without a broom closet) or, instead, you seek spiritual truth *outside* yourself, eventually you can find God. Everywhere you'll find God and more God.

How vivid will the experience be? That depends on how awake you are inside. Plus, how willing are you to entertain *this* notion: Your omnipresent Creator need not be confined to a solid, physical form like your own.

The myth of loneliness is tied to expecting God to arrive in a physical body. But even if that happened, you'd still be walking in yours and, therefore, you might still seem separate from God.

Hey, you seem to be separate from other people, too. More illusion!

To make a success of this human life, you may as well play along with the Myth of Separation to some degree. Sure, here on earth, your individually shaped, dense, slowed-down physical form is real — even if that's not all you are. But when this illusion weighs on you, close your eyes. The sense of being body-bound can drop away instantly. In your consciousness, you'll move freely. So travel as far as you need to until you can enjoy being home alone…with God.

70. Personal Responsibility

Supposedly, one of the perks of being spiritually "saved" is to have all one's sins forgiven, cancelled forever. But you'll be far better off if saved…from the Myth of God as Replacement for Personal Responsibility.

A close relationship with God is one thing. It would be something else entirely to escape the consequences of your actions. So long as you live on earth, nobody can save you from having *karma*. It's no more optional than breathing.

Karma means that every thought, word and action produces consequences which, inevitably, will return to you. Return they will, regardless of your belief system. So a wise person takes responsibility. (And, to the greatest extent possible, that wise person co-creates with God.)

Being "saved" according to the born-again mystique does confer one inarguable benefit: Knowing that God loves you. No action of yours, no mistake can cut you off from amazing grace. Wonderful!

Yet forging a super-secure relationship with God requires neither high drama nor the theology of fundamentalist religion.

If you've ever been a parent or an artist, you've tasted the fierce love of a creator for her creation. As a lover, teacher, healer, athlete, scientist, parent, pet owner, even as a cook — for every role in life where you have felt real passion, there you have sampled a version of God's love for *you*.

How open will you be to receive this today?

Imagine if God's love were an ocean and you wished to scoop out some water for your personal use. If you reached in with a thimble, you'll fill that up with no problem. But do you think it would be too, too much to reach in with a huge bucket instead?

No container of yours could possibly be too big for the ocean to fill.

In real life, for God's love to fill you, you also get to choose an enormous container. It's your heart. How receptive are you? Until you're totally satisfied with the amount of God-love you feel, you can always ask to open up more.

So keep pestering God. Let that love grow within you until there is room for nothing else in your world. Strengthened by that, you can go out and create magnificent karma.

No need to rush this sacred process. It's the greatest love story on earth, in a version that has been saved…for you alone.

71. Perfection

Of course we seek it. But where can perfection be found?

Perfection in life appears spontaneously for minutes, sometimes for hours. But beware The Myth of Permanent Perfection.

Imperfection is neither your personal flaw nor a problem to overcome. It's the nature of life on earth. If you're expecting all wisdom, all joy, all the time...I hate to break bad news to you but you've come to the wrong place. Perfection doesn't exist here, at least not on the surface of things.

Allow me to introduce you to Planet Earth: Part school, part amusement park. Here, our only constant is change. *Ever* changing — how perfect is that?

Whenever you achieve success in your terms, enjoy it but take a deep breath. Any second, your personal roller coaster will take another plunge downward.

Screaming is okay. So is laughter. You signed up for a wild ride, in a place where illusions seem stable but not much else.

If you want perfection that lasts, bring your attention to God's realm. Whatever method takes you there, you'll find all joy, all good, all serenity, all wisdom, all loving kindness, all day and night and beyond. This ample perfection is God's permanent signature.

What's the attainable equivalent when you seek God in daily life? Gratitude...one day. Another day, you'll find perfection only through acts of selfless service. Yet another day, you'll feel invited to set a new goal and follow it, resulting in a delectable new kind of balance and peace. The very next day, your balance could come crashing down. Then your only hope for perfection might be to follow as few rules as possible.

Who decides? You do, and preferably early in your day. Choose what today's adventure is to be.

Please, listen for your inner "I wanna." It matters as much as seemingly loftier personal guidance. Make your choice, then flow with it for the next 24 hours. Something perfect will happen. But predicting it isn't your job. Enjoying it is.

72. Spring

Spring could start today, if only
you'd open the window to let the sounds in.
Unpredictable robins will start
a chorus that scatters small noises until
you admit that you can't figure all of them out. Suddenly
you'll collapse back again
inside your small room.
And you might be the same, except that within
you've been definitely, yet deftly, indeedly
touched by Spring.

Take a break for variety.
Why not, Silly? Stroll out there.
Sun has shifted. It's brighter with all the old air re-arranged
like grungy bathwater dumped out and replaced.
This tub of our sky
is now brimful of squeaky clean air.

Likewise your old ways, those familiar sorrows, that heavy lifting,
can be gone if you're willing.
In their place, a new version, pure Spring
is showing off her begin-again ways.
Feel the daffodils' gaiety. The insistent
wake-up call of a crocus
may startle you out of all reason,
old reason anyway.

And then, should you feel
like a hole has been knocked in your head
fear not. It's called Spring
and it's good for you.

73. Help Always Comes

Sometimes troubles strike suddenly. More often we slide into them, one worry at a time. Either way, the effect is the same. A day comes that feels like night, then another, until one dreadful question lurks right at the edge of consciousness: "Will I ever escape this?"

So it is vital to know that help always comes. Even if you feel so defeated that inwardly you doubt you could even deserve to feel better, you do and you will.

Blaming yourself isn't fair. Nor will it help you. Reach toward the Light in whatever form you can find it.

For example, take some concrete action to solve your problem, even if you must start with something imperfect. Prayer will help, but it will help faster if you'll also do your human part.

For another example, talk to friends and family who have a positive attitude. In times of trouble, community can be an enormous resource.

Life insurance doesn't come only through policies and cash payments. Now is the time to benefit from the support systems you've built during the good times. If you always make sure to have a life outside of work and your main love relationship, you'll have many resources.

Gathering this kind of "insurance" is a perfectly healthy motive for joining a church or club, getting together with friends to exchange Reiki or other healing arts. Apart from happiness in the moment, friendship will help keep you whole when your life falls to pieces.

So resolve that, after you've overcome this challenge, you'll build up your support system. Keep an eye out for new friends and follow up with invitations to get together. That will be especially appropriate because you'll have grown. Yes, a difficult episode in your life will force you to reach extra-deep inside, resulting in a fuller expression of your soul. You'll have more to give everyone.

In tough times, it takes spiritual wisdom to keep your heart open to the soft goodness built into life. If you need to, remember the spiritual law of cause and effect. You've been a lighthouse to others. That karma must inevitably return to you, either through people you have helped or through somebody different.

Go put a candle of hope in your window so that your help can find you.

74. Waking into Silence

- Do you wake up instantly, eagerly, like a pop-up ad on the Internet?
- Maybe you prefer to wake up languorously, giving a sensuous stretch.
- Or perhaps you wake up slowly, fighting all the way? (One clue would be that you've worn out your alarm clock's "Snooze" button.)

However you wake up, don't miss out on the day's most potent time to co-create. Indulge in the first silence when you awake. It's the human equivalent of dew on the grass — sweet and redolent of delicious subtlety.

Before you even open your eyes, reach out to God. Feel the love. Feel the support.

If today you were on your honeymoon, wouldn't you start off your day by hugging your spouse? Well, God is the love who is there with you, always was with you and always will be.

Say what you like, do what you must, sharing the first words of your day. Or just speak as God does sometimes, painting brushstrokes of silence.

75. After the Love Potion

What, nobody has offered you a love potion lately? Surely you've heard the tales, whether in Shakespeare, fairy tales or other romantic stories. Someone administers the love potion. You fall into a charmed sleep. Upon waking, you fall in love with the first person you see.

Mischief abounds in these stories, but you could circumvent problems by brewing and administering your own love potion. The following recipe is foolproof.

Before going to bed tonight, choose in advance the first thing that you'll see tomorrow. Place it close to your bed — that picture of a loved one, that blooming flower, that painting to inspire you or some written words chosen to start your day right.

Now all you need is the potion itself. Tonight, before drinking your last glass of water, hold it in your hands, call in a Divine Being and request help for brewing your magic potion. Explain just what it is supposed to do. Will it, for instance, deepen your ability to love?

Ask freely. There's no reason why your particular brew can't bring love *and* wisdom *and* joy *and* discernment *and* a more vibrant connection to God.

Be sure to include The Accident Clause. If, on first waking, you should forget about the potion and look at something unplanned, it won't count. Your day only beings *officially* from the instant your eyes light on It.

Go drink your potion in total confidence. (Even a sip will suffice.) Sleep well. Tomorrow you'll awaken into a magical day.

76. Welcome Back, Body

When you go through a spiritual growth spurt, what happens to the usual way you relate to your physical body? The physical connection may become tenuous. Unless you take action, you could turn flighty, like a helium balloon whose tether has quietly snapped.

Paying attention to your physical body (a.k.a. *grounding*) shows in your root chakra. That's the part of your aura located right above where your legs come together.

Aside from enhancing psychological balance, your root chakra's strength is directly proportional to your worldly success, including your ability to earn money.

Grounding brings health benefits, too. You'll find it easier to stop smoking. Weight control may come easier. Altogether, you'll have more fun. No matter how big you grow in consciousness, keep pace with your mind-body connection. Many techniques can help you achieve this, and some are so simple, it's ridiculous. Here are two of my favorites:

- Have you ever walked on *money*? It's easy when you tape a copper coin, like a shiny penny, inside each shoe. Explore how your foot fits inside it and you'll find the perfect spot. For instance, if you have high arches, tape the penny beneath. And if you wear orthotics, that's easiest of all because you can secure a coin to the underside that you'll insert into your shoe.
- Another quick grounding method originates with world-class healer Donna Eden. In *Energy Medicine*, she recommends rubbing the soles of your feet with the back of a stainless steel spoon. Instant results!

Should these methods not entice you, find others. What matters is that you learn to live with a strong, grounded body connection.

The root chakra is the level of quick judgments, stereotypes, practical solutions — not necessarily the highest wisdom, yet it passes for common sense. Developing strength there doesn't negate your precious spiritual awareness, your heart and the rest. If they're more developed than your physical connection, use them to help you ground. As long as you're having a life on earth, you may as well make a strong statement here.

77. Delicious Dunking

So, you've resolved to become more grounded. Here's my very favorite technique of all, guaranteed to bring you back from the ozone.

Take yourself to the kitchen or bathroom. Find a towel, plus two containers big enough to dunk your feet into, be they bathtub and sink, two buckets or a couple of your biggest soup pots.

Fill one container with ice cold water. Load the other with water so hot that it's as hot as you can touch without burning yourself. Once you take off shoes and socks, you're ready.

- Dunk your bare feet in the hot water. Soon your brain will process a clear message: "Whoa! This is hot."
- Immediately step into the other water bucket; keep your feet there until they feel unmistakably cold.
- Alternate several times. Though the resulting body sensations may be unpleasant, you'll notice them, which is the point. Dry off your feet, walk around and check out how you feel. Aren't you deliciously grounded?

Novelist James Joyce once wrote about a character, James Duffy, who "lived at a little distance from his body." Luckily, you can do better. Let this technique help you to score a touchdown.

78. Love at First Sight

"The first time you see your face each day, what do you notice?"

Try asking this if you're looking for a conversation starter. Some responses may surprise you. One man who told me, "In the morning, my eyes take so long to focus, I'll go through my whole routine in front of the mirror, shaving and all, without taking one single good look at myself."

Many of us do just the opposite. We start the day by glaring at a perceived flaw. It's as if our entire self-worth depended on miraculous improvement. Rather than frowning at their faces, some people glare at the scale instead. News here is likely bad, too. Even lost weight seldom satisfies a dieter. Instead it's seen in the gloomy context of an incessant journey toward some unattainable goal.

Well, what if there were another way?

There are at least 50 great things to see about your face. Who can stop you from choosing one of them?

Try this. Gaze deeply into your eyes and applaud the beauty of your soul. Or choose some part of your face that is — admit it — gorgeous. Stare at it. Praise it. Know that *this* can be what others are drawn to when they see you today.

A face reader would even know what that face data *means* in terms of a soul-level talent. (Did you know that nearly everything about your physical face links to something admirable, if only you have the knowledge to interpret it accurately?)

Why be harsh when you have every right to be appreciative? As a professional face reader, I find that most clients routinely fret over flaws that other people barely notice. Not only do self-disparagers force themselves to take the bitter with the sweet, the proportions are off. They're overlooking pounds of sweet to emphasize a few ounces of bitter.

How you see yourself for the first time this morning matters a lot. This image will imprint on your subconscious mind at its most impressionable, setting the pattern for your self-image all day.

Beyond that, your mirror gazing style is contagious. No, folks won't necessarily obsess over your pet flaw. But subconsciously they'll catch your vibe.

Why be diminished in their sight? Start each day by seeing something magnificent about your face. It's certainly there.

79. Pack It Right

Without thinking much about it, many people pack up their new day with yesterday's troubles. It's an automatic transfer, day in and day out. But you can do things differently.

Before you leave home today, you can pack up a *special card of inspiration*. It's so easy to adapt this technique from Cognitive Behavior Therapy. All you do is write down a statement about something you'd like to be able to do well — even if, in the past, you've told yourself that you can't.

- I am punctual.
- I manage my time really wisely.
- I live within my means and save more money than I spend.

Choose your words carefully because they'll be going deep into your subconscious mind. Then, carry your card with you. Look at it early during your day, plus whenever else you could use a boost.

Change cards sometimes. You'll figure out what you need to write on them. Plus you can ask God to inspire you.

Keeping your day's cards current takes so little time. On a day when nothing you have written so far seems especially interesting, write something new. For this deck of cards, you can do no wrong. You're the ace!

80. Express Yourself How?

Kids don't have to plan for it. Before noon a three-year-old has tried more creative things than some grownups do in a week.

How about you? Do you do the same things most days, starting right from the first step you make out of bed? Living the same old, same old — how boring is that?

So here's my challenge to you. Do something creative early in your day, within the first hour if possible, while your subconscious mind is most impressionable. Soon everyday chatter is going to blab in your brain. You deserve better. Design something brand new and soul-worthy.

Creativity doesn't mean that you necessarily must play the accordion or tap dance. Creativity can be expressive action, problem solving, doing something as ordinary as brushing your teeth but adding an element of novelty.

So many things can become creative, even something as deceptively simple as switching hands when you hold a toothbrush, combing your hair from the opposite direction as usual, finding a better way to pack up your lunch.

Packing outside the container, thinking outside the box and moving outside the rut, you may be amazed what a new day can bring in return for some extra creativity. God has given you the freedom to pursue endless opportunities, but only *you* can bring that freedom into your life.

81. Let Today Be a Holiday

Let today be a holiday, a holy day of wonders.
Once you wake up and begin,
your heart will sing
just because, just because.

Celebration's in the air. Companionship's delightful.
Even if you must work today
it feels like play
just because, just because.

Gifts and parties wherever you go, it's great to be invited.
Busy or still, time flows as it will,
and you flow with it
just because, just because.

May the whole world, all animals, Your people, stars and treetops
share one delight (in secret or not)
at all life's sumptuous changes:
Daylight and starlight,
breezes and sneezes,
rough or tender,
green or winter,
one rollicking game of a world right here
because why? Just because.

It tastes like candy in your mouth the whole day long
Your wonder-mint, the day's delight
just because, just because.

82. Down to Earth

God, I suspect, recognizes our auric energy first, with the physical form as an afterthought. Many of us have the same experience. Nevertheless, it's advantageous to treat the physical level as though it were real.

Some spiritual seekers do the equivalent of walking on tiptoe, never fully *being* here. By contrast, earthy people accept and notice the obvious. The truth is, no matter how spiritually gifted you may be, you won't have much worldly success until you're grounded. This planet isn't called "space," you know.

Of course, we've all met folks who take earthiness to an extreme, being either excessively literal, rigidly habit bound or crushingly materialistic. Earthiness isn't to blame here, just too much of a good thing. And that's one problem you probably don't have to worry about. I say that because you've chosen this book. Like me, you may be more apt to suffer from too little earthiness than too much. So know that you can *choose* your degree of earthiness.

I love the old saying, "In your lifetime, you will have to eat a peck of dirt." It's true. If you don't ground yourself voluntarily, life will do it for you. As a graceful alternative, try this relatively enjoyable way to "eat dirt."

- Take a moment to close your eyes. Feel the fleshiness of your body, its weight, heft, solidity; then notice how you connect to the earth beneath your feet.
- Eyes still closed, shift to your usual way of being in the body. Do you favor your head over the rest? Could emotions be taking most of your attention? Or does energy seem like the main thing?

Whatever your habitual body awareness, some adventure is good for the soul. So explore your body now as if *physical solidity* mattered most. Your body has an outline, just like a drawing in a coloring book. Fill it in, using awareness. What color do you feel in each place? Go from head to toe, then front to back.

But what if some part of your body feels bad — whether hollow, invisible, half-dead or twisted by pain? Color it in that way, not trying to pretty it up. For self-healing, nothing beats self-acceptance. Be with your body just as it is.

Do this exercise even once and you'll be initiated into more earthiness. For even more grounding, at random intervals today, wherever you are, *emphasize* the earth aspect. Let yourself be fascinated by things like the heaviness of furniture, the physical characteristics of people, the very embodied presence of a pet. And may the element of earth bring you its special excellence, rock-solid peace.

83. Ready, Aim and Enjoy Fire

Of all the elements within your body, only one seems dangerous. Fire within you or outside of you can burn beyond control. Dare you trust it?

Inner fire has its loveable side, however. Its concentrated excitement shows in the light *behind* the light in your eyes.

Fire is, actually, indispensable. Fire in the belly contributes to having a strong-running digestion. And how about appetite for life? To know what you want and pursue it actively — surely that's fire at its best.

Burning bright, your fire element will protect you with pride when you've been belittled, bring courage when you have been frightened, and bestow a piercing kind of clarity, concentrated as lightning, whenever you need it most.

Sometimes justified anger will burn within you, turning up the amount of energy for you and everyone around. Scary? Maybe. But you may as well aim with your will, steady yourself for victory and let fire be fire. Fearing that passion would be to dismantle your power.

Of course, fire is dangerous. More dangerous still is not to use it. Sex, for example, is a form of fire. Another is ambition. Seeking a shortcut to safety, you could shut down all your fires, one by one. You could…except that you're way too smart to settle for that cold imitation of life.

If one of your fires threatens to burn out of control, bring some of it to the altar of God. Celestial light burns at higher frequencies than human flames, transforming them. So try this Fire Ceremony. For equipment you'll need only a candle, a book of matches and a smidge of time.

- Begin by striking a match. Notice the rough sound, the edgy smell — perfect to symbolize how challenging it can be to direct human fire. Next, apply your short-lived flame to the waiting candle that stands for God's presence. A human flame always can unite with that steady, pure light (provided that you take the initiative to ignite it).
- Once that softest of fires glows up, your match will have served its purpose. Let the candle bless you with its light. Consecrate that light to a worthy goal. How? All it takes is one quick thought. Add a Q&A with God, if you like. Then make a wish and blow out your candle. Ceremony complete!

Now comes the good part. God's creative flame will come to illuminate you…mind, body, heart and soul.

84. Water Babies

Have you ever touched the skin of a newborn? Babies hold so much water in their skin, they feel as plump as a wet sponge. Life on earth will dry them out considerably.

By your advanced age, you may not feel especially connected to the element of water. Vulnerability is one of its qualities, like the fatigue accompanying sweat, the embarrassment of dripping underarms, the surrender that comes with tears. Which adult is crazy enough to welcome that?

A smart one! Water strengthens you too, bringing flow, freshness, flexibility and change. Emotions and ideas, at their best, are reminders of the way that water moves. When your heart pumps blood through your arteries, the rhythmic flow keeps you strong. Even the tiniest cut brings a bright red reminder that your body depends on mysterious waters beneath the surface.

Take a moment now to experience the water element within you. Because it's half hidden, you may be surprised at how much happens if only you'll do this: Sit, close your eyes, and set the intention to learn more about your body's water element.

Let its presence catch you full in the face. Beneath your eyelids, for starters! Notice the delicate pools at each tear duct. Your nostrils and ears contain moist caves. As for your mouth, it's a slow-moving waterfall. Subtle sensations like these may remind you how tiny quantities of water, usually taken for granted, are essential for every flashy experience of sight, sound, smell or speech.

But why stop noticing there? Continue by exploring the moist covering of your skin, especially concentrated at hands and feet. Drink a cool glass of water (or just pretend to) and feel the familiar relief of quenched thirst.

The in-and-outs of water within your body do more than bring balance. Personal splashes and drips can remind you how deeply you are connected…to animals, plants and people, plus the body of earth Herself.

What a symbol of God's presence! Water is the element we can touch but never hold. Besides playing theme and variations within your body, water moves weather for the whole world. And the size of water is amazingly varied too, whether written large in oceans or tiny in puddles.

So give thanks for the ever-changing flow of water in your life. Could an awareness of God's fluid presence be the true fountain of youth?

85. Metal Detector

Who would be crazy enough to call metal one of your body's essential elements? An orthodontist? A jewelry salesman? No, the truth is even stranger than that — an acupuncturist.

To someone skilled in Chinese traditions of healing, metal shows in your skin tone and your various pulses. Even the way you smell can reveal the balance of metal along with your other elements.

Physically, metal is said to rule your navel plus your large intestine. In terms of character, metal brings the gift of endurance. Its corresponding stress reaction is grim tenacity.

Acupuncturists can even find evidence of metal in how you walk. (According to them, a person's dominant elements are literally taken in stride.) A direct walk, full of determination, conveys that you have as much metal as if you wore a knight's suit of armor.

Metaphysically, metal has meaning, too. To me, it means taking earth life seriously. Do you have a healthy respect for the reality of so-called "reality"? If your answer is "Way too much," metal could be weighing you down. If "No," you might benefit from increasing the metal element in your body-mind-spirit.

But being *incarnated* need not feel like being *incarcerated*. Having chosen this life sentence, we might as well "Render unto Caesar what belongs to Caesar." Money is metal and that's just the start. Valuable watches have metal, and we put marriage vows into metal rings. Authority figures, like police officers, wear metal badges. Sports trophies are metal and so, too, a soldier's symbols of valor in war.

Even civilians may have to fight against grim qualities of metal. Some of us carry physical reminders of this element as embedded bullets or surgically implanted hardware. For laughs, there's the quick version: Did you ever accidentally bite down on a bit of aluminum, like the wrapper around a stick of chewing gum? Instant metal! Ouch!

A good balance of metal, however, makes a person more effective in life. Today, take out your spiritual metal detector and go prospecting. Some of the folks you encounter will seem floaty, revealing their absence of metal. Others may appear grim and joyless, real-life tin men. Pay attention to metal, welcome its best qualities, and you this will help you to take in whatever you need.

To a large degree, elements in your body depend on your consciousness — not only how much metal enters your system but the metal's quality. Ask God to transform the metal in your aura. Let it attain its highest vibration. God is the alchemist who can turn dullest lead into glorious gold.

86. Knock on Wood

Wood inspires. Polished wood beneath your feet is more luxurious by far than some mere red carpet. More elegant still, consider exquisite wooden furniture. For sensuality, touch a sculpture or bowl made of beautifully crafted wood. For luck, of course, a smart person knows to knock on wood, not lemons or tapioca.

According to an old saying, money doesn't grow on trees. But fruit does, and I know which one I'd rather eat. Nuts are even more spectacular, tasting like essence of tree strength, only crunchy.

But the best thing about wood may be this: Symbolically, it's part of your body. Traditional Chinese medicine tells us that wood is one of the five main elements. We need wood for proper functioning of eyes, liver and gallbladder.

Green is the color associated with wood. As its quintessence is anything better than the tender shade of chartreuse that you see on the first leaves and grass every spring?

In your personal system of metaphysics — that's the system you're fully credentialed to use, regardless of whether you're licensed to practice acupuncture or Chinese herbal medicine — what does wood mean to you? Where would you find it within your body?

As with all of the elements, you can actively use your consciousness to balance the wood within. Too much emphasis on wood? Then keep off your grass-colored clothes. Choose the brown of earth, the red of fire, the blue of water, the gleam of metal; go figure out which you need most. And make your choice more than sartorial. *Wherever you put your consciousness grows stronger in your life.*

But maybe you'll choose to add *more* wood to your life, not less. Through self-discovery, you might find that a tad more wood is just what you need. This most creative element gives a person spine. Rippling with wood energy, your strong bones rise up like fence posts. New growth appears regularly at your fingernails.

Enjoy wood wherever you find it today, whether as trees or creativity. May the latter grow strong within you, making your friendship with God evergreen. This is a great day to be alive, with you and God co-creating wonders. Knock on wood!

87. The Element of Wonder

Of all the elements in your body, surely the most mysterious is akasha. Your doctor won't tell you how much you've got, since modern medicine virtually ignores it. Of course, today's skilled, hardworking physicians are a mere blip in the history of medicine. For at least 5,000 years, sages have recognized akasha.

It's in your aura right now. *Akasha* means the element of deep space. Its quickening quality relates to mystical experience. When you can carry akasha in your consciousness, to that degree will akasha shine out from your aura. And what a stunning find that is!

- Don't confuse space with mere air. To tell them apart, go outside. Watch a breeze move through the natural world, setting the leaves on trees all atwitter (and maybe some birds, too). That wonderful element is *air*, not space.
- To reach for *space*, look up, especially at night, when the black sky opens into an unbounded canopy. What you see will clue you into space, and so will the wonder. Gazing at a star-filled sky, did you ever wish for a heart big enough to hold it all? Ah! That kind of wonder makes life's illusions fall away, increasing the amount of akasha in an aura.

To observe akasha in auras, let a rose teach you. Time-lapse photography can show what happens as a rose blossoms. Or simply place a budding rose in a vase and watch it, day by day. When opening up, that flower gleams with akasha.

Be sure to watch akasha at airports when passengers walk through an arrival gate. Everyone's aura is temporarily plumped up. Some people love carrying all that akasha from a flight. They're the ones whose faces glow; they walk with an extra majesty. Akasha makes others uncomfortable. Watch these passengers shake it out of their auras — like a wet dog after a bath, spraying the unwelcome water in all directions.

Frequent flyers build up more than free mileage. They awaken akasha. Pilots carry loads of it aurically, and astronauts most of all. Read their auras from photos if you can, to preview your future.

Why your future? Sooner or later, you will reach world-class levels of enlightenment. Aurically, you'll combine akasha with a radiantly balanced set of chakras. Ever hear the term "cosmic consciousness"? Akasha puts the "cosmic" component into your consciousness. But not to worry. You can blast off into the realms of akasha without physically leaving the ground. Do it today by opening up to wonder.

88. Surprise Is in the Air

Of all the elements in your system, air may be the most surprising, even literally. When you feel surprised, doesn't your breath change first? You might jump in surprise, burst into tears, clench your teeth or even expand your consciousness to include a larger-than-normal chunk of infinite space.

But the most common reaction is simply to gasp.

"Ah!" says your breath, recognizing a wowser. Or, sometimes, life's small, sad surprises evoke a quiet sigh. Amazingly, regular old air within you has the versatility to either sigh or gasp, sound ragged or steady, pour out through one nostril or the other or both.

If you wanted, you could spend your life charting the nuances of breath. Likewise, you're free to disregard it entirely…. But you won't, not when you realize that your relationship to air symbolizes your relationship to God.

Whenever you wish, you can breathe deeply to re-connect more strongly with your spiritual Source.

Considering the mightiness of that resource, isn't it silly how often we forget to use it?

For instance, when trying extra hard to do something well, do you ever hold your breath? That symbolizes forcing your human ego to go it alone. (As if that would make anything better!)

Any time the stakes are high, or you're learning something new; whenever you feel frightened, self-doubting or lonely, breathing bigger can only help.

Nor does breathing only connect you to God. Have you ever considered how widely the air is recycled? Within three days, any breath of yours has traveled around the globe and been shared by every human being alive, one nose at a time.

Call it "air" or something bigger. Ignore it if you dare. But every instant of life, you are processing That presence. How will you draw it in today?

89. Listen for the Glisten

Whenever you like, you can choose to be breath-aware. And what a great gift this is for co-creating with God.

When in your day will you most likely forget to breathe? It's probably those times when you could use God's presence most. Well, a more generous breathing pattern can be yours. Try this easy four-part breathing technique.

For starters, know that you can play your breath like an accordion: In, hold, out, hold. While you do this, affirmations are especially powerful. They're like a hymn of praise that you sing into an echoing silence. Try this combo:

1. Breathe in: "I open to the presence of God."
2. Hold the breath in: "I accept the presence of God."
3. Breathe out: "I co-create with God."
4. Hold the breath out: "I surrender the fruits of my actions to God."

You know, for many of us, doing a simple breathing exercise can become an initiation. We get it through our wonderfully thick heads that they have holes in them. Grace can flow in there! And we realize that a breathing *technique* can make the "hole" process extra efficient.

Why be only a passive recipient of the presence of God when a technique is available? Use one to actively summon more grace, so you don't have to passively wait until more grace happens to descend.

So often we take God's presence for granted, like seeing dewdrops first thing in the morning. If you're actively watching and listening, you'll find the glistening.

90. Treasure Chest

Thanks, God, for giving me Your treasure chest.
When I reach there, which jewels will fill my hand?
Passion-filled rubies or peace within pearls,
aquamarine oceans in miniature,
emeralds that help me breathe a strong green air,
the joy of diamonds (my survivor stones),
or sapphires, whose bright depths of indigo
propel me past known space?

Your treasures do not only bring
exalted moods, breakthrough experiences.
When I feel most in need, dirt-stained, alone
when doubts and old resentments seem to be
the real truth of my life, I reach inside
and know that every gem I grasp, I keep.

Even when weakened by despair, I'll find
some precious jewel shining within that chest.
Soon after, my full soul comes back to life.

Wisely, You thought to line my treasure chest
with the best hue of all, simple and plain,
the earth-brown cloth of hope.

91. Joyful Bones

Search your mind for an image of bones and, chances are, it won't be pleasant. There's the spookiness of skeletons, the fear of osteoporosis, a wince at even one quick mental image of a broken bone.

When's the last time you heard someone say, "Something *wonderful* is going to happen. I feel it in my bones." Or how about a simple compliment? "Golly, my bones sure feel great today."

Yet bones are the great stabilizing power within your body. With every step, each gesture, you move at least one bone. So instead of thinking of bones as dreary, you could enjoy moving them around and thank them for supporting you. Consider them a symbol of God's everlasting love, under your skin, tucked in deep.

Wild Thing, take those bones out for a run in the grass. Show off their versatility with sports. Perhaps you'd prefer to ascend stairs with them, then descend, displaying your dignity like a god striding down from Olympus the easy way.

After any bone-moving adventure, you deserve a reward. Go rest your bones in a chair. Amazingly, their upholstery (i.e., your skin and muscles) can actually fold. Note: This isn't just sitting. You have aligned your kingly frame into stately repose. God's artistry shows in the marvelous contouring of your wrists. And could each fascinating foot really contain no fewer than 33 bones?

Probably you've heard that bones are white. Supposedly they're silent, too. Boring! I prefer to think that mine are made of gold. When tickled by my positive regard, they laugh. Whatever you choose to think about *your* bones is nobody's business but yours.

Spiritually those human bones help you to participate in one of the ultimate educational games, where your huge energy presence appears to be contained in a physical form. Without bones, how lame would that illusion be? You'd be little more than a blob.

Dogs (who may be the most joyous animals alive next to enlightened humans) know the value of a good bone. Hey, they're onto something. And today happens to be a particularly great day to delight in bones, especially yours. Did you know? This book comes with a free software program, *The Bone Program of Joy.* Yes, you can think of it as a bone-us.

Here's how to install this new program in your consciousness. Use one powerful thought to give thanks for the power of God in your bones. Instant download! Day by day, you will accumulate strength by running this program. But some benefit has started already. Although nobody else may see it yet, as of now, your bones are officially glorious.

92. Creative as Your Knee

May all your joints become sources of pleasure, starting today. Beyond movement, joints express creativity, you know. It's creativity where it counts most, being an artist at life.

Hold a pen. Turn your head. Either action could be done innumerable ways: Ingeniously, timidly, gracefully and expressively. That's true even if joints are painful. On a day when your creative options seem limited, why not see what fun you can wring…or stretch…or tease…from one simple joint?

You might also bend that joint toward a useful symbol. Each part of the body has symbolic meaning. Mind-body experts invite us to explore this, for both prevention and healing. It isn't enough to pay an expert to fix things. Healers say that they succeed best if a patient is willing to find the inner pattern underlying a physical problem, then change it.

Even if you're perfectly healthy, learning about the body's symbolism can enrich your life. Otherwise, consider where your issues have landed in your tissues, or a cosmic point lies in your joint. Where means what?

- Toes: Resilience about how people treat you.
- Ankles: Willingness to accept feedback about your actions.
- Right knee: Getting along with male authority figures; humility.
- Left knee: Getting along with female authority figures; self-respect.
- Hips: Trust in your belief system (and being willing to exchange it for a new one, after the old one's outgrown).
- Lower back: Feeling secure that your work in the world will provide all the money you need.
- Middle back: Overcoming self-doubt and guilt.
- Upper back: Finding and accepting emotional support.
- Shoulders: Choosing *when* you're responsible for *whom*; releasing the rest.
- Elbows: Maintaining appropriate self-confidence; releasing false pride.
- Wrists: Flexibility when you're asked to change direction mid-action.
- Fingers: Confident handling of life's details, including knowing when to let go.
- Neck: Willingness to look at people openheartedly, rather than with judgment.

Every so-called "bad knee" or other offending joint offers a bittersweet invitation to evolve. God waits inside every experience, so a bum joint can link you to something better. In sickness or in health, your soul will stay married to your body. To honor both, plus their Creator, explore your body's symbols.

93. Full-Body Prayer

Traditional positions for prayer demand that you flex your joints. Ponder that, as you explore the symbolism built into your body.

To sit in the Eastern-style lotus position, you need humility of the sort that moves your knees outward. Reaching toward God, you're stretching your human self just as wide as you can. Hand *mudras*, or postures related to yoga, vary enormously. Although these ancient positions for prayer are innumerable and highly specific, traditional meanings for fingers alone are quite simple.

And they're fascinating to contemplate. In palmistry, as well as yoga, fingers are associated with planets, so I'll add that information as well:

- Thumb (Earth): Strengthening your ego, your human identity.
- Index finger (Jupiter): Increasing knowledge; yearning and restlessness; the courage to move past previous limitations.
- Middle finger (Saturn): Developing patience; allowing perspective beyond human emotions, the dispassionate wisdom known as equanimity.
- Ring finger (Sun): Feeling fully alive; extra energy used wisely.
- Pinky (Mercury): Communication with people, animals, Divine Beings; finding God in everything; open-hearted listening to others.

Western-style prayer posture is younger and simpler. You start by bringing palms together. That tilt of wrists symbolizes surrender in action.

Next you place hands together. This aligns all the joints related to action, from starting a project (which corresponds to the knuckle nearest your palm), through re-energizing yourself mid-action (symbolized by the next knuckle), to fashioning all of a project's final details (extra oomph at the last finger joint) .

Fingertips are especially fascinating. They symbolize the junction of subjective-objective life, where you release your actions into the world. That's also where you open to the intent behind *other* people's actions. By placing fingertips together, you're allowing yourself to re-pattern all this.

As for kneeling in prayer, it means surrender...but totally different from lotus-style surrender. With legs together, you reach toward God by taking action as an individual. And, as you know if you've ever knelt for any length of time, you're putting extra pressure on the knees, your two pads of humility.

However you move your joints today, make it a living prayer — flexible and original, this day's unique offering.

94. Circulate

Put your feet up and relax. I mean, really up. Armchairs are especially good for this, but you might also use your bed.

Depending on the furniture available, you can find a way to invert yourself. Prop yourself upside down, using your arms or a pillow for balance. Position your head way below your feet, balancing the rest of yourself carefully to avoid putting pressure on your head, neck or shoulders.

And there you have it: All the benefits of a headstand with no danger of dents. Whoosh! Now your blood can really circulate.

Inverted postures have been used for thousands of years. They're a simple but powerful way to rejuvenate all your organs. Your brain, in particular, will benefit. Praying upside down can be especially enjoyable.

There are just two times NOT to do inverted postures. Women, avoid them during your menses. And everyone, flip over *before* a meal rather than after; digesting food is hard enough without doing it upside down.

After your armchair-asana, remember to come out gradually. Suddenly standing up could make you faint...definitely not our goal. That would be rejuvenating you in mind, body and spirit. Build up your time to 10 or 15 minutes a day and soon you'll be hooked on your chair, as it were.

Circulation needs challenge in more ways than one. Physically, you can approach this through chair-assisted headstands or yoga or aerobic exercise. But you can also regenerate yourself with new social, psychological or spiritual ways to put yourself in circulation. The more, the merrier!

Today, will you voluntarily turn your life upside down (or sideways) in one direction at least? That might involve reaching out to a new friend, pursuing an unaccustomed activity, even something as simple as taking a new space in the parking lot. To live juicy, circulate.

95. Such a Delicious Life!

Heavenly, when food sings in your mouth, then goes on to nourish your body for days or years to come! Spiritual insight is no substitute for proper digestion. But, if you're fortunate, they can supplement each other.

How good do you feel right now? Digestion is one way to tell. Even if your career and family life are going splendidly and you're looking marvelous, even when your belief system has you sitting on top of the world, poor digestion can sound a wake-up call. Hello! It's not just your belly. Some aspect of your life could be hurting.

Very specific messages are symbolized by the human body. Digestive problems tell a story that starts, "I'm having trouble dealing with my life because...."

Stress can cause this. Perhaps you've denied your own happiness, sacrificing for others beyond what is really necessary. Sometimes digestive troubles disturb a reality that seems to work perfectly. Except your body-mind-spirit has news for that thin slice of you called "everyday self." *You deserve something better.*

For instance, Glenda was perfectly satisfied with her life. She was committed to a "Movement" that answered all of her questions. Unbeknownst to Glenda, this movement was really a cult. Fortunately, her soul recognized this.

To the young woman's horror, her digestion suddenly stopped working properly. For weeks, all she could keep down was sweet potatoes. It seemed like a cruel, inexplicable fate.

But the search for medical help moved Glenda back home and, eventually, caused her to ask some new questions, which led her to exit the cult.

Whatever their degree of drama, digestive problems should get our attention. "Quit bellyaching" is bad advice. If that belly hurts, take care of it on the health level and also investigate the metaphysical meaning.

Ironically, the same person who ignores physical signals may also be trying hard to develop intuitively. Every day, the same prayer:

"When will I know things unmistakably, in my gut?"

Every day, the same gripping nausea. Hmmm.

Of course, a day free of pain is a blessing. But a day with it can be blessed, too. Wrapped in any pain is a spiritual invitation. Will you dare to open the gift?

96. Love that Poop

Life lessons appear in the most curious places, including one that, in polite society, is always covered up.

Elimination, like other bodily functions, is rife with spiritual symbolism. Holding onto the old is one kind of problem. Running through too much of the new, too fast, is another. Bananas may balance the physical flow in either direction but won't bring long-term relief to the spirit. What will?

Consider that you've been invited on a *reverse treasure hunt*. Which patterns are due for release? Ask inside. Find them. Then get rid of them.

And speaking of treasure, let's give credit where credit is due…but often lacking. You're apt to enjoy dinner every night, but when's the last time you gave thanks for what you did with it? That would include the next morning's creative act of elimination. You could have a worse motto than, "Love that poop."

Symbolically, there's not much difference between releasing old matter into the toilet, cleaning out your closet or changing something about your work life that has been a nuisance. Perhaps a once-vital friendship has become a burden. You know what you'd like to release. Could now be the perfect time to let it go?

Of course, it's wise to evaluate before you release someone or something from your life. But once you decide to say "Yes" to a "No," go boldly forth. Let old-fashioned poop be your inspiration. Make it a ceremony or, at least, give the act your undivided attention. Only then can you fully enjoy the release.

Although TV commercials don't broadcast the fact, you may have noticed that life isn't only about being a consumer. After taking in, we digest, release and then must either recycle or let go. Otherwise how can we possibly have room for what's coming next?

Nature abhors a vacuum. Your replacement (and upgrade) may be totally ready to come into your life. But you still can't receive any new goodies until you create space where they would fit.

Yet how often do people celebrate releases or even pay attention? Could there even be a feeling, deep down, that the process involves something dirty? Each release is precious — and not because you're going to enshrine the discard in memory.

Nobody's required to start a Poop Museum. But you can value letting go. The old saying has it perfectly right: "Let go and let God."

97. Stop Flying OVER the Radar

Why strengthen body awareness? It can improve sex and keep a person healthier all around. Even food tastes better if you are fully present in consciousness while eating. In addition, body awareness can help a person to dress better, to stand out in a crowd, to dance better (maybe even to develop a sense of rhythm).

Spiritually, it's enormously important to be thoroughly grounded. Most of the clients who come to me for third-eye openings already have huge third eyes. Why can't they tell? It's because they lack grounding at the root chakra. So we co-create opening up the root chakra instead. With a stronger connection to physical reality, surprise! Spiritual experience automatically becomes clearer.

Another benefit of body awareness is that it keeps you from flying *over* the radar. Probably you're familiar with the expression "Flying *under* the radar." That's a military strategy for flying undetected into an enemy's territory, something done on purpose. Flying *over* the radar is neither voluntary nor conscious. Results can be heartbreaking. And the problem is common among spiritual seekers.

Why? Someone flies over the radar by living mostly from the heart chakra up. The person hasn't developed comparable strength lower down on the aura. *But success in life is directly proportional to the size of your root chakra.*

Most people on earth today are liveliest at the chakras related to physical survival, sex, and power. Frankly, they're pretty oblivious to chakras from the heart up. So, what happens if *you* are mostly conscious where others aren't? Everyone's thoughts, actions and values are shaped by spiritual consciousness. To the extent that you're coming from higher chakras than other people, you'll be flying over their radar.

How many times has this happened to you? You're in a group where everyone's trying to solve a problem. You offer a suggestion that, to you at least, seems pretty inspired. But nobody seems to notice. It's as though you said absolutely nothing.

Being ignored is tough enough. Making it worse, you know that your offering came from the very best part of you, full of truth, beauty and all the rest. It's enough to make a person feel invisible, crazy, or both.

But there's a remedy and it's actually pretty simple. Learn to inhabit the human side of life, starting with your body. Put more attention on physical awareness (strengthening Chakra #1). Then do something creative each day (great for Chakra #2). Live with power, not just love and light (enlivening Chakra #3). None of this will weaken the chakras that are already strong. And you'll be amazed how much better people respond when you meet them at the level — or at least closer to — where they send out their radar.

98. Breathe Like an Artist

Inspiration comes in. Exhilaration goes out. You can have these whenever you choose. Breathing in either direction connects you to God. And God couldn't be less stingy.

So many activities can teach a person about sacred breath: Singing or playing music, swimming, doing any sport well, acting, public speaking. The ancient science of yoga offers breathing techniques galore. But you don't need to be ancient, or expert, to custom-design your own breathing technique. Here are principles that you can safely combine however you like. Just take care never to strain your body by doing any pattern that feels uncomfortable.

So go, be a breathing artist. Before you lie a fresh palette and canvas. Use each of the following principles like a differently colored tube of paint:

1. You can breathe with *just one nostril at a time,* directing the flow of air. To do this, push down on the side of the *opposite* nostril with a finger or two. Breath re-routes automatically.
2. Breathing *in* through your *right* nostril activates yang energy, potent as sunlight.
3. Breathing *out* through your *right* nostril releases impatience to move into your future.
4. Breathing *in* through your *left* nostril awakens your yin energy, steady as moonlight.
5. Breathing *out* through your *left* nostril releases fear from your past.
6. Using your *mouth,* rather than your nose, shifts the vibration of breathing, emphasizing what is human rather than transcendent.
7. Each *in-breath* symbolizes opening up to a new blessing from God.
8. *Holding* the in-breath is a way to integrate that blessing.
9. Each *out-breath* is a way to express your latest discoveries, your chosen form of service.
10. *Holding* the out-breath, you surrender the fruits of your actions.
11. Combine *thought* with a breath to energize it. You could add an affirmation, a name for God, a hymn. Choose words for whatever you'd like to have become more abundant in your life.

Breathing artist, that's all you need to know. Of course, you can paint a gorgeous exercise just for today. Your breath is God's breath, in human form. The potential is dazzling. Go throw some dazzle back at God.

99. *Physically Fit*

What is fitness?
Fitness is *delight*
in what your body can do with its special kind of intelligence.
Fitness is *surprise*
as you discover new ways to move, new sports to try, new strengths.
Fitness is *patience*, loving each performance plateau.
(Once surpassed, it will stand only as a monument to persistence.)
Fitness is *health*,
since you get best results
when you respect your body, never mistreat it.
Fitness is *sensuality*,
because self-aware energy opens up enjoyment of *all* physical joy.

Even though fitness may involve setting long-term goals,
you must seek it day by day:
Fitness is *listening*, when you learn to let your body speak to you.
Fitness is *touching* the warrior strength within.
Fitness is the *taste* of physical confidence, different each day.
Fitness is the *smell* of your own perspiration,
the stretch of your muscles,
that delicious soreness after an especially challenging workout.
Fitness is *looking*…better, more alive within yourself.

May your fitness become contagious, a reminder to all you meet
that a body need not be something to criticize,
or a mere status object for showing off good looks,
or a possible location of illness, something to worry about.
Ask any child who is learning to walk:
Fitness is a way to thank the Universe
for the incomparable gift of being alive.

100. Unique

There are two kinds of people in the world....

Sure, and only about a million ways to complete that sentence!

No wonder it can be so tough to figure out who you are. Well, maybe your job isn't to figure it out at all but simply to explore it. Start by assuming uniqueness. Nobody else is like you. Sure, human bodies share many common characteristics, but inwardly each person is a one-of-a-kind.

Outwardly, this is true also. Face reading will show you uniqueness, even with identical twins. Strange though it seems, with each passing decade, they will diverge more and more, physically. And if you observe their behavior, you'll find that each twin's facial changes correspond to distinctive personal growth.

However you choose to explore uniqueness, you'll discover it whenever you look deeply enough. Sure it's natural to expect everyone else to be "just like me." But soap bubbles are as natural as that expectation, and about as realistic.

Do you still need extra incentive to explore uniqueness? Then know that your search will help you to appreciate the distinctive way each person represents God in human form. Is it to be the *power* of God, the *love* of God, the *truth* of God, or the *playfulness* of God? Which physical attributes go with that person's specialty? How was her mind constructed to explore that aspect of life?

Don't leave yourself out of this inquiry, either. How might *you* represent an aspect of God? Which words or images come to mind?

Yes, uniqueness is puzzling and complex, even when observed from a distance. Managing to express your uniqueness fully? That's still harder. Nobody else can offer you precise mentoring.

So loving your own uniqueness can be difficult. Will it be easier to start by loving the uniqueness in others? Or would you prefer to begin with self-love? Many of us cycle back and forth between the two, allowing others a bit more uniqueness, then accepting our own quirks more graciously, and so on.

Start whichever way you like. Just be willing to see God in that person — not as some abstract transcendent perfection, but in a way that's both humbler and harder — uniqueness turned *human.*

101. The Blind Spot

When you learn to drive, one of the most surprising discoveries is how every car has a blind spot. No matter how adeptly you use the mirrors, they'll never reveal what's directly in back of your car. To see that, you must make the extra effort to broaden your perspective. No doubt your teacher for Driver's Ed. trained you to turn your head and check before changing lanes.

Well, spiritual life has a comparable blind spot. Only we're not usually taught about it, perhaps because even the most evolved spiritual seekers aren't tutored to pass one big test. Instead you were *born* with license to move through life in your human vehicle. But if you'll train yourself to compensate for the big spiritual blind spot, you'll avoid unneeded crashes.

Never expect anyone else to be "just like me."

It's natural to feel more comfortable with others when we can establish commonality. That stranger really comes from the same home town, went to your school, or shares your religion? Superficial proof of "just like me" can be so reassuring.

But the spiritual blind spot involves something deeper than social similarities. It's human to expect others to share what is structured deep within you. For example, you might have this: A huge heart chakra but a chronically closed-off throat chakra; being an empath about intellectual matters *only*; sensory wiring as clairaudient more than using other senses; having a highly reactive nervous system, including exceptional awareness of your physical surroundings.

Living this way is natural for you, no more peculiar than expecting your car to have bumpers. Yet the people you care about most could have *none* of these inner attributes.

The spiritual blind spot is easy to correct. You need only remember to make the effort to overcome it. This can become as automatic as turning around every time you attempt to pass another car.

Whenever you talk to someone, turn around inwardly. Take a look. Find out who that other person is, really.

Deeper perception will help. So will your *intention* to explore each person's God-given uniqueness. And that term "God-given" isn't used lightly. Is your goal to co-create with God, rather than from your own ego? Then, whenever you deal with other people, let them be who they are. Familiarize yourself with what God created long before you drove onto the highway.

102. Each Amazing Story

Each person's spirit tells a story. You can read it in that person's aura.

Here's one way to do this. First, think the name of a Divine Being like Buddha, Jesus or Saraswati. This instant connection, however abstract, will wake up your consciousness. Automatically you'll be lifted from the realm of everyday thinking to a more receptive state of awareness.

For your second thought, set an intention, such as, "I wish to learn what it is like to *be* this person."

Next, direct your consciousness to the person's aura and the databank called the "Third eye chakra." (It's located at the center of the forehead.) Either aim your eyes there or place one of your hands a few inches off the person's forehead, with your palm facing the chakra. Ask inside, "What is a gift of her soul, spiritually?"

Whatever you perceive next will be the answer to your question. How useful is that! You know that illusions about spirit are thicker than grease on French fries. Here's your chance to learn the truth directly. It comes straight from your research subject's aura. And the clearer your own experience of consciousness, the more accurately you'll interpret whatever is going on with that individual.

Just remember, immediately after you plug into an aura and question, *everything* counts...whatever you see, touch, feel or notice in some other way.

So, what can you find, sharing someone's third eye? Sometimes there's confusion, sleepiness or dogmatic rigidity but, even along with that, you can find inspiration.

Sure, occasionally you'll find a wicked person, somebody who prefers hurting to helping. Since wickedness doesn't necessarily show on the surface of everyday life, that's useful to learn (if slightly depressing). Protect yourself in future by avoiding this person whenever possible. If you must interact, don't engage your energy; simply go through the motions.

What about someone whose third eye reveals zero interest in spiritual life? Maybe he's successful materially, pretty balanced psychologically and reasonably healthy, too. Let him enjoy his blissful indifference while it lasts. Most of us only start seeking when life has knocked us around a bit. The *timing* of each person's spiritual life is part of the uniqueness.

Finally, look just one bit further. Can you read the fine print on each aura's care label? "Made of joy. Meant for joy." That's a lifetime guarantee.

103. Photo Synthesis

You can read anyone's aura from a photo. That means a regular picture, not one of those special Kirlian photographs sold at psychic fairs. Granted, your regular way to look at pictures gives you certain kinds of information. Aura reading will supply something different. Do both, one after another, and wouldn't that count as the ultimate photo synthesis?

To prepare yourself for photo readings of a person's energy field, get comfortable with reading auras in person. Use any technique you like, including the following one. Conveniently, the aura you choose to read first could be your own.

Whether you're reading yourself or another person, you'll find the communication chakra in the same place, at the neck. Practice approaching it either through sight or touch. Stand in front of a mirror and look at your throat. Or put one of your hands in front of your neck, the palm facing your body.

Now that you've experimented with that a bit and found which position you favor, you're ready to begin.

1. Close your eyes, settle down with a few deep breaths, and think the name of a Divine Being.
2. Set an intention by thinking a sentence like, "Help me to gain wisdom."
3. Open your eyes. Breathe deeply and aim your hand or eyes at that throat chakra. Then ask inside, "What is going on with this person's communication?"
4. Accept whatever you get.

After a month of reading auras in 3-D, just 10 minutes a day, you'll be ready to use the same technique with a photo. Select one that shows only one person, rather than a group of two or more. Your photo should be taken from a straightforward camera angle, so the front of your subject's face and body show clearly.

Hold the photo up to eye level. Then use the same technique you did before, connecting with hand or eyes to *that* person's throat.

Doubt is the only obstacle. What removes it? Remember this. The purpose of deeper perception is to co-create with God. Since your goal never was showing off, let ego worries fade into the background. Each insight you gain is a blessing that can help others.

Can't you think of anyone you could help with your God-given talents? Then why waste time on self-doubt? Get going.

104. Too Many Tests

Sometimes a skeptic about deeper perception will put herself through a punishing test. Only rather than thinking she's being mean to herself, she'll confuse this with a noble rigorousness.

The "Too Many Test" syndrome goes like this. The woman will read her aura once, researching her throat chakra. But horrors! What if she's just making that answer up? To prove she's right, she'll do the same research again. If she doesn't come up with precisely the same answer both times, now she has a real basis for confusion.

- Which answer was correct?
- How can she explain the differences between them?

Really, there's one simple answer: Waste of time.

Yes, at last, a definitive answer! It is *a total waste of time* to set up any spiritual practice as a test. That goes for aura reading, prayer, healing, meditation, you name it. Even breathing could get bollixed up if you didn't trust that you would get enough air.

Just do the technique and give thanks for whatever results come your way. If you'd like more practice at aura reading, do the technique on someone else.

What else will help you to gain confidence? Never belittle your gifts by speaking about yourself negatively. Don't whine, "All I got was xyz." Say with pride, "I got xyz."

When you first learned to walk, undoubtedly someone cheered your first steps. How do I know this? Because I'm assuming you learned how to walk before the age of 10. Human beings usually have the common sense to cheer each other on when it comes to walking (if not always in spiritual matters). So there you were, taking those first brave little steps and an adoring grownup said something like:

"You're walking! First steps, wow! Wonderful! Hooray!" Huge praise and kisses followed for the rest of the day. With reinforcement like this, of course you were motivated to keep on walking until you got really good at it.

What if, instead, the grownup had said, "Pathetic! You fell down, you know. And even with the few pitiful steps you managed to take, your form was terrible." Tested unfairly, you *still* might be crawling.

So please, if you've been testing yourself (or, even worse, God) about any aspect of your spiritual development, cut it out. Proceed as if life — yourself included — could be trusted.

105. Soul Safari

Why merely talk to a person when you can take a soul safari? Soul is the distinctively human essence of a person. And it's there for the finding. Just don't expect soul to show on the surface. To explore soul, use deeper perception:

1. Be willing to give a few minutes of undivided attention.
2. Take a deep breath.
3. Think the name of a Divine Being so you can Get Big in your consciousness.
4. Set the intention to connect from your soul to a particular person's soul.
5. Ask inside for *language*, words that will help you capture the experience. (Otherwise your discoveries may be too abstract to remember. Requesting language for a soul safari is like bringing a camera along when you make your trip-of-a-lifetime to Africa.)
6. Take a few more deep breaths.
7. Whatever you experience next will count. It's information about that person's soul. So accept it. And be sure to write down any words, describe any images.

Seven simple steps! Information will come on the level of your consciousness, so don't expect a roaring lion. Instead, you'll experience a quiet, familiar kind of knowing. That very familiarity can be tricky. Because consciousness flows so effortlessly, soul-to-soul, nothing about your first few journeys may seem terribly exciting. With practice, though, you'll get it. You'll stop expecting a sweaty, bumpy ride, hyped up for tourists.

Once you settle down enough to appreciate a quieter journey, the "animals" may surprise you. Maybe you'll discover that a person you considered rather uptight has a soul that runs free as a wildebeest. Someone else's soul might move like a timid animal that even the most skilled safari guide couldn't coax into the open.

Soul can hide out for years, a secret kept from a person's own mind as well as from you. So don't consider it a failure if you turn up little of note. Your perception could still be very accurate indeed.

In one more unpredictable twist of safari, sometimes soul is the *only* aspect of a person that will let you in. Behavior and energy will shut you out, yet soul remains active, glaring straight at you (as happens with some rap music). Each person's soul is fascinating, distinctive and utterly unpredictable. Go on safari a few times today. Sure, you're qualified to be your own tour guide. And don't be surprised if God shows up too, flashing bright sunlight into the jungle.

106. Consider It

A spiritual seeker traveled far to meet a wise man. Not surprisingly, he found one. When asked the secret of life, the wise man said, "At the end of your days, all that will matter is two things: What you learned and how you treated people."

Being considerate is no mere frill. It extends deep below surface manners. To become truly considerate, you must feel out the other person's point of view, then proceed gently.

When two people interact, both get to play "trick or treat" — not just on Halloween but every day. Which will you choose, to be clever and tricky or to treat the other person with kindness?

Spiritual gains aside, considerateness is an excellent business investment. If you get your immediate aim but damage the other person's fine level of feeling, your victory will be temporary.

Instead, nurture the finest level of feeling in every relationship. This isn't being obsequious. Only genuine kindness has the power to transform the human heart.

What brings that wonderful transformation to a screeching halt? Irony. Postmodern society hooks us on being sarcastic — cute, yes, but also poisonous. At best you'll make friends with irony junkies, sharing their needles.

Genuine considerateness is worth the inconvenience of giving up superiority. Don't be considerate just for the sake of scoring better on your Life Review. You'll benefit long before that.

Each kind word or deed creates openings within yourself. And each one of these can become a new way to touch the heart of God.

107. Laughing Meditation

To get high on laughter you can't beat this technique, adapted from a method I learned at Yogaville. Although you can do it alone, the more the merrier. Laughing Meditation also happens to be a terrific party game. No bystanders are allowed, so give your more serious guests the option of hanging out in the kitchen while you and your noisy buddies take over the living room.

Your group will need pillows, blankets, whatever each person needs to lie comfortably on his back; 20 undisturbed minutes; a timer. As host, you'll be time-keeper. Ask all participants to turn off their cell phones. Ready, everyone?

Everyone lies down, not touching anyone else. You, the host, call on a Divine Being. Ask for spiritual protection during this meditation, so only energies of the highest vibration may enter the place where everyone is.

Together everyone does a minute of chanting. Some groups like to sing "Om," a mantra of peace. Others like to chant "Peace" or "Love." Or you could sing a round like "Donna Nobis Pacem."

Now comes the good part, laughter for 15 minutes straight. Only one rule: *Everyone must laugh out loud, more-or-less uninterruptedly, for the full time.*

At first, that means faking it. Your first ha-ha's will sound ridiculous but, eventually, a real laugh will issue forth from the lips of some susceptible silly. Uh-oh, here goes the whole group. Soon everyone will be surfing an ocean of laughter.

Unlike TV laugh tracks, real-live group laughter can sound bizarre. Some wonderful loudmouth will yuk it up with a booming belly laugh. Someone else, intentionally or not, will snort. The sounds may become increasingly outrageous until waves of laughter will roll through the group.

Whenever the wave dies down, do what you can to laugh in some really *strange* way that normally you would never do. Strive for exaggerated sounds; the more embarrassing it feels to make them, the better the release. So smash your laughter boundaries with an evil villain's laugh, a chuckle that's exaggeratedly con-descending, or giggle like a teenage girl.

Animal sounds can be a hit, too. Try to chortle like your Inner Baboon. It's hard to drop your dignity to such degree, but *somebody* in the group has got to make the sacrifice. Your wackiness will soon become contagious.

After the 15 minutes are up, close with one minute of the same kind of chant-ing you did before. Now you can go forth with a renewed, re-charged aura to do some magnificent co-creating with God.

108. The Laughing Pool

Throw your cares into the laughing pool
and watch them sink.
These sacred waters make a new sound
because laughter there neither starts nor ends
but merely is.
Find the flow.
It's how you feel right after
any good laughter is done.

Throw your cares into the laughing pool
and be still.
Even the ripples look beautiful
because they picture joy in motion,
never tragedy.
Sorrow? No sweat.
Nothing can out-deep
the place where all is well and wet.

Throw your cares into the laughing pool
and watch them sing.
Touch and smell the joy. For behold
the tranquil presence of God all around!
This one pool is made
made and unmade
of God's fleshless flesh, Type-All blood
and His great backwards-reaching tears.

109. Divine Imagination

Enjoy one of the blessings of heaven without the inconvenience of dying. Did you know? On the other side, whatever a person thinks will manifest instantly. Validation of this comes from people who journey out of body, like Robert Monroe, as well as mediums, like James van Praagh. In heaven, you'll build your dream house through effortless imagination and make it so real you can live there.

On earth, too, you can use imagination to create your heart's desire. Only here it won't happen instantly but through persistence. Compared to the afterlife, results on earth manifest slowly. Here, life is set up to have physical things seem more solid than thoughts, so you'll need faith to persist in using your manifesting power. At least nothing solid can stop you forever!

If you haven't yet found your way into creative imagination, here's the most important thing to know: It need not be visual. Use any of your senses to create, the more the merrier.

Whatever you imagine for spiritual purposes, absolutely everything in your story — each place, action or object — will serve as a *symbol*. The lover, boss, parent or child that you imagine may not choose to respond in real life as you have wished. But eventually, you'll still receive the essence of your request. No need to force things, either. In manifesting your desire, God will simply substitute another person to play same that role in your life.

Ultimately, anything that happens between you and others is symbolic. Life roles can have more staying power than any particular players cast in your Divine comedy. For instance, you probably know someone who has married several times, with each new relationship just like the old one. Meet "the wife." And millionaires who lose a fortune often make one again. That's "the business."

More persistent than these symbols are your underlying patterns of knowledge, growth and expectation. Creative imagination is great because you can use it to change these deep patterns.

The technique is simple: Start with a purpose, flow characters into a story, let it climax and, at the end, release the whole story to God, knowing that everything has been a symbol. To seal the deal, give thanks. Here's one set of words:

Take what I've imagined, God. It is a set of symbols that I release to you completely. I look forward to what this sets in motion for my life. Thank You, God, for the wonders we co-create together, with respect and love for everyone concerned.

Of course you can co-create through imagination! What would you most like to manifest? Start your wish list today.

110. Candy Adventure

Considering that anything can become a symbol for your creative imagination, you may as well throw in some candy.

For this exercise, I'll use Tootsie Rolls. But feel free to substitute any toffee, taffy, chocolate, licorice — you name it. Any sweet will become calorie free, consequence free and, of course, free of charge.

For your intention, choose to resolve a relationship where there's a problem. This could be business or pleasure, love life or in-laws, you name it. Your intention will be? Your cast will be? The star, of course, must be you.

This episode of creative imagination takes place *inside* a Tootsie Roll. Enter the long tunnel and crawl inside. Smell that chocolate. Does it make your body buzz with excitement? This adventure is going to be delicious.

Set the scene: Table, chairs, flowers. Would you like a violet flame to transmute negative energy? How about a window where scenes of inspiration can flash by as needed?

Setting the stage hasn't been terribly hard work. Still, you deserve a reward. How about some wall? It is, after all, made of Tootsie Roll and conveniently self-sealing, so any bit of wall you pull off will be replaced instantly. Yum, this meeting is going to go great!

Now bring in the people. Of course, you'll take care not to coerce them. Allow them be who they are, act as they act. Can you help it if you outsmart them every time?

At each important point in your meeting, take another delicious bite off something. (What are those flowers in that vase made of, anyway, jelly beans?) If the meeting goes especially well, perhaps you'll let another person in on the secret so you can toast each other with a fresh slice of peppermint table....

Before ending the meeting, enter the heart of each person and bring a Divine blessing.

Then, after everyone else leaves the room, ask inside, "What was the best part about this meeting?" Feel it. Put it into the very walls, then pull off a bite, and slurp it right up. Personally, I find it fascinating (not to mention convenient) that love, light, even power, can co-exist with candy.

Finally, come back to awareness of your physical body. Before opening your eyes, say aloud, "Take what I've imagined, God. It is a set of symbols that I release to you completely. I look forward to what this sets in motion for my life. Thank You, God, for the wonders we co-create together, with respect and love for everyone concerned."

III. Cute Gadgets

Some of the best ideas for creative imagination come from technology. Alas, every-day gadgets don't carry romantic associations (like the Taj Mahal) or holy vibrations (like Lourdes). But think about it. All gadgets exist for a purpose, and some have an obvious spiritual equivalent.

Lourdes holds holy vibrations because miracles have happened there and countless pilgrims have come, intensifying the beauty. But even more people have been helped in a dentist's chair, despite having a love/hate relationship with that modern-day wonder, a dentist's drill.

Is there something you'd like to release from your subconscious mind? Then imagine an office that's gentle as well as dental, with soft chairs, luscious music, celestial mobiles dangling from the ceiling, cartoons on the wallpaper, etc.

To imagine your Cosmic Dentist, choose a Divine Being. Then bring on the Novocain, a squirt of grace straight into your gums. Instead of numbness, however, you may feel a kind of serenity. Give yourself whatever you need so that this procedure will not hurt in the least.

Miracles can happen in your chair of creative imagination, not simply drilling out old tooth decay. Ask your Divine Dentist to help you remove any pain or fear, even addiction. After it's drilled out, watch your dentist plug up the hole. No need to worry about mercury-leakage from these fillings! Yours can be made of favorite flowers, precious stones, even fairy tears.

You get the idea. When you want something on the *inner*, think of some gizmo you've seen on the *outer*. Then adapt it.

Even if you're so un-mechanical that you can't put together a broken clothes-pin, God will give you the manual for any gizmo in a creative visualization. And you'll be able to master it, quick as a blink.

Children play games like this all the time. With an adult's experience, you can play even better. Besides, kids aren't the only ones who deserve fun and miracles.

112. Superhero to the Rescue

Society places such importance, these days, on being famous. If you could have huge fame, without all the negative side effects (like no more privacy), wouldn't one of the best parts be all the people you could know?

Marilyn Monroe, for instance, got to sing Happy Birthday to the president. She married a great baseball player, later a great playwright. Imagine the fun if you were famous enough to telephone any celebrity you admired and have that person respond by gushing at *you*.

Now, let's take this concept one step further. God values you as much as if you were the world's most famous superstar. Besides that, on the *inner*, you have access to every hero. So, ta da! *Using creative imagination, you can call on the hero of your choice, receive a warm welcome and get any help you need.*

Whose work do you really admire? Which politician, athlete, scientist, saint or artist has inspired you most? In meditation, summon that hero to bring you a blessing.

For example, say that you've always loved paintings by the great French artist, Jean-Baptiste-Camille Corot. One of his specialties was to include the "Corot spot," a small bit of bright red strategically placed within a picture that would otherwise lack much color variety.

Only think once of Corot and zap! You can become a red-spotter…in your own way. What would you like your red spot to represent? How about the concentrated love of God, centrally placed in every scene?

Easy. Done.

Fast forward after this hypothetical meditation. For instance, you're at a wonderful (but tense) family gathering. Grandpa is turning 80, and much as you love him, you know this dinner will last for hours, with bickering and boredom served up at every course. Well, bring on the red spots! And if nobody happens to be wearing red, rely completely on your imagination to place those spots decoratively around the table.

Imagination isn't only for times when your eyes are closed. And a superhero can rescue you in countless ways, mighty upliftment coming as inconspicuously as Corot brushing in a small dot of red.

113. Paint Chips

When re-painting your home a different color, it's wise to begin by gathering paint chips. And before investing in a new set of drapes, surely you'd ask for a sample swatch of fabric. Some professional designers go so far as to keep a scrap book, stuffed with samples, cut-out magazine photos and the like.

In a similar way, you can collect concepts for future sessions of creative imagination. Why not? Who else is going to be the decorator of your own interior?

But what if you're too busy to make a physical scrap book? Not everyone has the patience to fuss over another craft project. Luckily, all the samples you need can be glued to your memory. Just make a mental post-it as each visual goodie in your life parades by.

Quick as thought and twice as sloppy, pick up your paint chip. You'll own it forever (in memory, anyway).

Try scooping up some delightful samples today. What charms you? Delights you? Intrigues you?

Collect your favorite places or fashions or cars, even hairstyles or houses. Every kind of beauty is transferable.

While traveling in London you might glimpse a staid old mansion, satisfying, eminent, Victorian, with its façade of weather-worn bricks. Suddenly you catch the shock of its door, painted the most astonishing robin's egg blue. Well, don't be a fool. Scoop it up!

Fast forward in your day to meditation time. Imagine a place in your home where you've just discovered a secret passageway into another world. Beautify it with your paint chip of purest robin's egg blue.

God's infinitely creative world is here to be your resource. Use it to decorate your sacred chamber. Then enter.

114. Enter that Sacred Chamber

Why enter a sacred chamber? So you can have a sacred experience, of course!

Get going, kid. Close your eyes. As you draw the place, you'll enter into it. Like the hero of the great children's book, *Harold and the Purple Crayon*, you're the artist whose creations become real.

So pull up a couple of chairs, one for you, another for the Divine Being of your choice. Or call in your guardian angel. Do you miss a mother or father who has crossed over to the Other Side? Invite anyone you would like to come, then sit with joyful expectancy.

Whoever arrives, play along with it. If there's a distinct absence of flash, take that as a compliment. God provides just what you need so, clearly, God has confidence in you.

The more often you visit your sacred chamber, the more real it will become. So dare to picture the Holy of Holies that you carry deep in your heart.

115. Beats Gardol

One of my favorite TV commercials from childhood was for toothpaste. Supposedly, brushing with Colgate would coat your teeth with a mysterious substance, Gardol. The resulting protective shield would shine out for all the world to see. Gardol would keep your teeth forever safe from decay. Besides that, the commercial implied, you'd be alluring, glamorous, even amazingly popular.

Many of us would like special protection, and not just for our teeth. So take this precaution: Put on the psychic equivalent of Gardol, something that takes no more time from your day than brushing your teeth.

To begin, imagine a small building, your portable sanctuary. This could be in the form of an igloo, a greenhouse, a teepee, a huge crystal or any other simple structure that you find appealing. Design the walls out of something transparent and add a door that can open and close. You'll need it.

Walk through that door, close it, and set up an Agreement with God about the nature of this sanctuary. For instance: Light shines back and forth through the walls, as does warmth. Sound travels. So can feelings and healings. What doesn't reach you? Other people's negative energy.

Once you're clear about your sanctuary, put it on: Count to three, then let the sanctuary merge with your body. Sure walls like these can wrap around you. Why not? Let them gently merge with your skin, leaving a fine mesh over your nose, mouth and ears. Breathe through it. See through it. Talk through it.

So comfortable is this seamless covering, soon you'll forget you have it on. Yet the protection will work anyhow. Other people's negativity won't stick to you.

Being protected by this portable sanctuary, other people's light and love will reach you, just as yours will reach them. But the energetic effects of malice and other negativity will be screened out, as much as any shielding could do. And this once-a-day protection can help you stay clear.

In the evening, before your final prayers, imagine yourself back at the original site of your protective builiding. Count to three and let the building unfold from your skin, popping back to its full size, resuming its original shape.

Imagine walking out. Let a healing rain fall on you and the building, both.

Tomorrow, your building will be just where you left it. Like anything you create through imagination, repeated use will make it more real. So count to three today and, quicker than brushing your teeth, enjoy some cosmic Gardol.

116. Loveys for Grownups

Kids have the right idea with their loveys, if not great finesse in execution. And you're just as entitled to keep around a special teddy bear, a favorite chair, a magical perfume. (Unlike a two-year-old, you won't have to drag yours through the mud to show you care.)

To see how fresh and potent a lovey can be, start by choosing one to represent a Divine Being or angel.

This isn't worshipping idols. Your lovey will work more like a cell phone. You pick it up, use the speed dial, start talking. Even folks who seem inseparable from their phones aren't worshipping them, are they? (Actually, wouldn't that be great! What if everyone who has ever annoyed you with bad manners on a mobile phone were using it to speak directly with God?)

Meanwhile, back to you…and your new lovey. Choose it. Name it. Now it can begin to help you.

- The old way: You come home, sit in your armchair in front of mindless TV, ease your aching back, eat junk food and zone out.
- The new way: You come home, greet your lovey, commune for a while, then enjoy glorious food, superb entertainment, delightful relaxation.

Nobody else on earth needs to watch while you hug that teddy bear. Nobody else needs to know that it speaks for a Divine Being. Let it console you for all the hurts of the day. Or share your excitement and triumphs. Or bring you healing energy. Simply ask.

Sure, at first you may feel foolish. In time, you won't just be pretending. The connection between that sacred being and your lovey will become real. No, Moses or Merlin can't be confined to some silly old stuffed animal. It's just one extra special location — no sillier than having a person say that he "belongs" to a particular synagogue or mosque — or that only one official prayer may ever be used on the cosmic cell phone.

So play with the lovey of your choice, even if it feels like pretending at first. When you're done, take a moment to notice that other feeling deeper down. Unmistakable! Peace!

117. Youthing

Un-age me today, God.
Help me start new,
willing to feel
my way through unknown...
everything.

I'll stop my worrying.
You make the sandwiches.
Tuck in Your trademarked
small bits of wonder.
I'll think of you after each
astonishing crunch.

Even the sweet
comforts of home
will taste better with salt and stirring.
And I love the surprises:
How any moment
celestial delivery boys, wearing disguises,
may come to bring my pizza.

118. Ask for an Amulet

No, you won't find it on Ebay. Nobody else has seen it, let alone owned it, nor will anyone else even have the chance to own it. Only you can possess this Divinely-designed amulet.

Why request it? Imagine how it might change your life if you could own a sacred relic. I mean something really big, like the Ark of the Covenant if you're Jewish or the Holy Grail if you're Christian.

Well, this amulet is your equivalent. Not only will it be hugely powerful and holy, but it will be designed just for you. And despite bringing a *timeless* blessing, this amulet will be *timely*, bringing into your spiritual life right now exactly what you need most.

What will that be? Faith or realism, kindness or power, ambition or patience?

Start thinking about it but don't decide yet. Today's job is to contemplate these three choices:

- Are you ready to *ask* for an amulet?
- Do you agree to *accept* its blessing?
- *Which* Divine Being will you ask to bring it to you?

Although you could do a quickie version, grabbing this brass ring out of the ethers, for best results give the process three days. For today, it's enough to explore those three essential choices. Though simple, they're deep, especially the first two.

So ask those first two questions many times today, not to test yourself but so that your answer can deepen.

As for the final question, any Divine Being would be delighted to help you bring forth your amulet, but try several different celestial presences on for size.

Making your amulet is glorious. So is the process itself, excellent practice for other kinds of co-creating with God.

119. Ask in Your Way

Yesterday you were given the tantalizing assignment of preparing to receive a sacred amulet. It's defined as a gift or adornment from spirit that can be used like a spiritual engagement ring, rich in symbolism and magnificent in design. Funnily enough, when this particular object gets lost you'll feel good, not bad, but we'll explain that part tomorrow. Of more immediate concern....

How can you, of all people, imagine an amulet? What if — Horrors! — you're "not visual"? Then practice the spiritual sutra, "What, me worry?"

Both your amulet and its purpose will come to you based on unique gifts of your soul. Some people effortlessly receive an image, but images are productive only if they come without effort. Alternatively, you may use an idea or a wish, an emotion or physical sensation, even the start of a song.

However your senses operate naturally, there's no requirement for a detailed vision, like some architect's drawing. After all, you're not requisitioning a particular brand of roller blades. Amulets bring *spiritual* presence.

Here's how to discover the physical shape of your amulet. Close your eyes. Take some deep breaths. From your heart space, ask to become aware of the amulet shape you need most. Then take more deep breaths, without trying to figure out a thing. You'll hear, feel or see an answer.

That's asking, and receiving, in *your* way. Why should "Have it your way" only apply when you visit Burger King?

Take a few practice tries today, just for fun. Construct one possible amulet shape. Then play with another. By the end of the day, choose one.

What you learn about yourself in the process of refining that shape could be even more important than the amulet itself, powerful though that will be. The lesson is priceless: *How* you notice the things around you. Exactly those senses will serve you best for co-creating, whatever the exercise in deeper perception.

120. *Your Amulet's Mysterious Blessing*

During the last two days you've been building up to request a mysterious object, invisible except to your deeper perception. Co-creating with a Divine Being, your amulet will appear in symbolic form, bringing you a great blessing.

In a moment, you'll finally receive your amulet. But first, let's preempt some common worries. What if the amulet still feels vague or you worry that it can't work because you're making it up? Know that, in the celestial realm, subtle is good. Often inner experience seems different from regular life, more like watching a movie or a cartoon. Well, that's still plenty real for producing results in your life.

Besides, unless you're satisfied with what you receive inwardly, who says you must be a passive recipient? Demand more. For example, let's say that at first all you get is "A candle." Feel around, get the heft of that candle. What is it made of? Ask inside, "Why a candle? How will it help me?" Relax and breathe. Spontaneously, you'll receive an answer.

However much you understand, the full blessing encoded in your amulet will move steadily into your spirit until you own all that it has to offer. How long will this take? Maybe the "medicine" in your time-release amulet could take a day, a month, a year. Who cares?

Who will even *know*, for that matter? Once your amulet has done its work, it will vanish automatically out of its etheric dimension. Such is the nature of an amulet.

So now you know how an amulet works in general as well as what yours will do in particular. Time to receive it already!

Do this with a ceremony, making it as elaborate as you wish. At a minimum, give the process your undivided attention. If you like, create an altar with flowers and sweet incense. Light a candle to symbolize the light of God. Do anything else that you consider appropriate for such a sacred occasion.

Then think the name of a Divine Being. Ask for your amulet — however you've imagined it. Ask for the blessing you desire. Then tell the Divine Being where to put it. Yes, you get to choose this part of your body. After all, you're the one who knows that body best, including the associations and symbolic meanings that different parts of your body have for you.

Feel or imagine the amulet being placed within you. Give thanks. Then trust that the rest will follow with no further work on your part. The knowledge encoded in your amulet will merge with you completely, surely as today's sunrise is guaranteed to melt into the rest of this glorious day.

121. Thank That First Teacher

The third spiritual teacher is the one who gets credit. But usually it takes at least two earlier teachers before a person really starts learning.

First you'll be annoyed as well as helped. A teacher will disappoint you in some way. Your second teacher may seem inadequate, too. Finally you'll dare to trust one more time. Then comes the teacher who can supply what you need.

Plenty of teachers are not for you. At least they don't seem to be. Yet even experiences you've rejected may become valuable in retrospect. You'll realize that Teacher #1 and Teacher #2 did show you something worthwhile.

One teacher may simply have helped you to overcome TV manners. In America, at least, it's not uncommon for classroom newbies to behave as if at home in their living room, snacking and chatting to each other as they critique the teacher's material, delivery, hairstyle, and so forth. A teacher who says "Stop that" may not be granted a second viewing, but the student will know to treat future teachers more respectfully. Here are some other clunker experiences where first spiritual teachers could have brought you something surprisingly valuable:

- Maybe a past teacher helped you to overcome resistance to learning.
- Another teacher could have taught you to boldly ask your real questions, regardless of what others in the group might think of you.
- Did a self-proclaimed expert appear qualified when he really wasn't? That teacher may have reminded you to choose future teachers more wisely.
- Saying "No" to information from one teacher could sensitize you to recognize, in future, the caliber of information that you would greet with a whole-hearted "Yes."

A worthwhile spiritual teacher is one of a kind. Did you once expect yours to be as close as the nearest McDonalds, available 24/7? Eventually a student learns that a spiritual teacher is at least as valuable as a good hairdresser, worth tracking down. After the equivalent of a really bad haircut, you learn to appreciate quality.

Regardless of what your experiences have been so far, know that God has sent every teacher your way with a purpose. And God noticed how you opened up your heart again and again; you persisted until you found Teacher #3.

So give thanks for all the "imperfect" ones on your path. They led you to now.

And especially don't count it as a failure if, sometimes, *you* get to be another person's first teacher.

122. Magic Mirror

In the old fairy tale, Snow White's wicked stepmother had a big mirror. Evidently she never heard the expression "Get a life." So the dame spent a heck of a lot of time in front of her mirror. As you may know, she was particularly obsessed with this question: "Mirror, mirror on the wall, who is fairest of them all?"

Fairy tales about this narcissistic power freak could discourage a normal person from keeping a mirror handy. But please! Mirrors need not be vanity things to have magical powers.

See what happens if you keep a mirror where you work, e.g., on your desk. The trick is to place it where you'll glimpse the thing (and yourself) unexpectedly. When your face pops into view, let it serve as a random reminder to ask your reflection the really important question: "How am I feeling right now?"

After all, you know every nuance of your face. You recognize the glow that comes from enjoying yourself, the glower that shows when you're not. Certain muscles are held differently, depending upon how you feel in the moment. You are, in fact, the world's expert at decoding the deep meaning of those eyes, those cheeks, those lips, those jaws.

Let's say that you have a good friend at work and, suddenly, you spot that friend looking dreary. Wouldn't you offer to help? Often we wear one face in public, sink into an entirely different visage in private. And that's just the face which your magic mirror can show you.

Why magic? Your free will is such that, combined with self-honesty when you first see that image, you can change what needs changing.

If sorrow shows, for instance, that's not just something to cover up. It is something to heal.

Whatever the problem, ask for assistance from that Helping One within, the one with the irrepressible sense of humor and the strong will. Invite the Wisdom Bringer or the Compassionate Witness. You know exactly which aspect of God can help most.

The very act of calling on That can show you something worth seeing. In your mirror, just as well as anywhere else, seek the omnipresent Fairest One of All.

123. Heal without Inner Ouches

You have at least one gift for healing. It may be emotional, spiritual, musical or athletic. Sometimes a person's healing gift is even mechanical, like one man of my acquaintance who fixes computers with a spontaneous laying on of hands.

It can be just as satisfying to heal people.

Having a gift, however, doesn't guarantee that you know how to use it safely. It's smart to find a qualified teacher, even if you wind up needing only one lesson.

By analogy, what if you taught yourself to read long before first grade? Maybe your mother would hide the morning newspaper from your precocious, innocent eyes.

Maybe you'd read so well, you wouldn't even move your mouth, as many early readers do. But what if, in your self-taught innocence, you pinched your arm every time you came to a question mark?

Quirky habits aren't unusual for self-taught healers. A good teacher can help you to avoid inadvertently hurting yourself as part of the process. So even though the gift itself comes for free, you'd be wise to invest in some training. You won't only improve how much you help others; energetically you'll be protecting yourself.

Wherever you are in your evolution as a healer, what can you learn today about your gift and how to use it with even more finesse?

124. Holiday in Your Heart

How do you shift into the spirit of *holiday*? Society helps out during a legal holiday, bringing the momentum of collective consciousness. But how can you take a holiday, make a holiday, just because you decide to do so?

No need to change the whole world's calendars. It may take only a slight change of emphasis. Although specialties of a particular celebration are unique, changes like these are typical for the spirit of holiday:

- Big work pressures recede and everyday *worries slip away*. No matter how heavily the years weigh upon you or how deep the ruts of your usual life, suddenly you feel like a kid again — at home in the company of loved ones, adventurous, free and ready to play.
- *Time changes* during a holiday. Rushing isn't needed. (Neither is ambition, since worldly success no longer matters.) Holidays occur in *present* time; the past becomes relevant only to the extent that it can contribute fond memories, favorite traditions.
- Money pressures don't matter. In the holiday spirit, you can scale down any entertainment to fit your budget. Suddenly you feel *effortless gratitude* for all you possess.
- *Happiness* becomes your main job. It's easier than usual to live from the heart. Effortlessly, you'll cut people slack. (Ever notice? At home, some folks might seem pesky and annoying; on vacation, they're transformed into quaint characters.)
- *Laughter comes easier* and more often while you're on holiday. Now's the time for games, silliness, corny jokes. Why not?

Actually, "Why not?" is a good motto for holidays, as in "Why not enjoy?" and "Why not today?"

125. Suspense

Just for today, *suspend judgment.* This works better than trying to practice non-judgment. You simply allow people to be who they are and do what they do.

What about that maniac on the road whose driving is a disgrace? How to get over society's latest villain whose image is played and replayed on TV? Who will take care of the payback?

God will.

To some degree, God always has, through spiritual laws of payback. For a taste of it, think for a second what it must be like to be in the mind-body-spirit system of the person who has behaved so badly. A certain kind of consciousness is expressed in every action. The worst punishment of all may be having to live with oneself.

Meanwhile, all *you* need do is live with yourself. Protect yourself as needed but otherwise let others go free, knowing that God is in charge. Just for today, don't merely know this. Believe it.

How can you tell for sure that you haven't engaged in judging people? Your neck will feel good. Move it and it will bend comfortably in different directions, flexible and free.

For the sake of no more pains-in-the-neck, suspend judgment. It's one freebie you can always give yourself.

126. Anonymously

Part of the test would be the lack of label.
Never would I be told of any test,
nor would wise words of comfort come to me.
How could they? No one else in my world knew
how sore I felt, how inwardly alone.
I coped and hoped and then I blamed myself.
Nothing I did could make it go away.

The sorrow, fear and solitude seemed like
a prison sentence. Later I would know
that, like incarceration, I served time
until a karmic debt could be repaid.

Eventually the situation cleared.
And, day by day, my life came back to me.
Hope grew — and then surprise — how that dead time
had been gestation for another life
within (what seems) the same identity.

I'm starting over, more adventurously
because this inextinguishable self
has learned a thing or three about God's anonymity.

127. Unexpectedly Powerful

God has given you enormous healing powers. Everyone has been given at least one awesome gift for healing. It's very individual, a way that you can help people, animals or the environment.

Just what is your gift, exactly? This question may be fraught with heartache. Nonetheless, you can find the answer. Prayer will accelerate the process. Or you can let events guide you. Another way is to take initiative and experiment with different healing techniques. Will it be healing with words? Spiritual transformation along with a Divine Being? How about psychological healing? Or will you co-create best as a physical healer?

There you are, gamely experimenting with one technique after another. When results come surprisingly easily, *that's* a clue. When joy flows along with the healing process, pay attention. As blessings accumulate, finally, you'll get it through your smart head: Aha!

As your talent becomes evident, you'd be wise to study with an experienced teacher in your field. Untutored — merely inspired — you'll still bring blessings. But a teacher can help you to learn faster. And who will be protected most by your gaining more skill? You, the healer.

As you refine your gift, a good teacher will help you to discover how much power you've had all along. Yes, that can be way more than you expected. It's like this gardening story.

Once I purchased landscaping pebbles from a quarry to cover the edges of my garden. Knowing that I'd need lots of the pretty little rocks, I literally ordered a ton.

Finally delivery day came. As the driver backed toward my driveway, I couldn't see over the edges of his dump truck any more than I could tell you what God ate for breakfast. How huge was this truckload going to be? Would I have trouble containing it all on my property? Trying to reassure myself, I thought, "You're only receiving what you've ordered. Relax. You can handle this."

Down went the business end of the blue truck. Pebbles started to rattle onto the blacktop, depositing what looked like a decorative little puddle. "Now that he's tested my driveway, here comes the rest of the load," I thought warily.

But that was it. The driver laughed at my surprise. "It's bigger than you think," he said. "Once you spread it around, you'll see just how much you have."

So much for worrying that my mighty ton would spill over the driveway and engulf my neighbors' yards. Our healing gifts are like that, bigger than we think yet manageable enough to fit into the neighborhood.

128. Puzzle Boxes

You were born with the ability to speak every language on earth. Each baby vocal-izes like a miniature Tower of Babel. Even if you couldn't do it easily now, years ago you tried out strange consonants, amazing vowels, even clicks of the tongue. Even-tually you specialized in learning to speak one or more languages.

Similarly, when growing up you have experimented with four completely dif-ferent puzzle boxes, each containing a different reality about life on earth. By age five, you could appreciate them all. Soon after, you chose to specialize in one or more of them. But I'll bet that, in theory at least, you can relate to each of the following:

- Babies play with the puzzle box of *spirit* until acclimated to flesh-and-blood bodies, a process that can take months or years. And even after that puzzle box is closed and locked, each child of God remembers the special combina-tion to open it back up again.
- A toddler's puzzle box is *energy*. Often you'll catch two-year-olds looking at auras or listening to them. And much as they love being tickled, toddlers will laugh even more if you play by poking them off-body.
- The next puzzle box is *myth*. Preschoolers demand daily stories about heroes. They play hero games, wear hero clothes. All the world's a stage, at least for someone fascinated with this puzzle box.
- Eventually, each child is programmed into adult reality. In our post-modern culture, this box is labeled "*Science*." It starts when we're told things like, "Cover your mouth when you sneeze or you'll spread germs." We're raised to act as if the laws of biology, physics and chemistry were life's defining truth.

After kids have become familiar with all four puzzle boxes, individual choice be-gins. Scientific belief may be society's shared language, but relatively few adults live solely inside that box. Instead, privately, each of us custom-designs a *box of belief.* Any of the four puzzle boxes may be included.

Don't expect this distinctive combo of myth, science, spirit and energy to show in obvious ways. It's invisible. It is also essential — as deeply personal as a person's hands or feet. When you co-create with God, helping yourself or others, respect each person's collection of puzzle boxes.

Showing this kind of respect helps you to evolve as a co-creator.

129. Four Worlds of Healing

Human bodies seem similar enough. Therefore, methods to heal them would seem constant, too. Yet four radically different kinds of medicine work on this planet, each one a world apart.

- *Scientific medicine* works best if you believe in the power of doctors, germs and drugs.
- *Myth-based medicine* brings best results for those who love stories, whether as movies or books, songs or teaching tales. Different characters show how to break up stuck patterns; heroism's the inspiration. One way or another, a healing tale works like a treasure hunt, with the climax being an Aha! experience. Abracadabra, your treasure is found. You remember how health can return.
- *Energy-based medicine* depends on your receptivity to deeper perception. This world of "alternative medicine" includes everything from sniffing bottled-up *aromatherapy* to chatting with the flower fairies in charge of a *zinnia*. To the degree that you identify more with your subtle bodies than your physical form, you'll heal best through energy.
- For a no-frills approach, you can't beat the healing power that comes directly from God. Personal prayer, devotional reading, coaching from a teacher, even a saint's intercession, this is *spiritual medicine.* If attuned to it, this is how you'll heal fastest.

When spiritual medicine connects the patient's consciousness to its Source, miracles follow. Yet this form of medicine really is no more miraculous than any of the others. All four ways are wonders, with most people responding primarily to one, secondarily (or not at all) to the others.

Therefore, when you need healing, the smartest thing you can do is to figure out which world(s) of medicine you believe in most strongly. Your personal truth matters here, not the theoretical superiority of one level over another. Each of these worlds within our world is valid. So don't base your decision on the advice of anyone else, however well meaning.

Four worlds of healing — one unique choice. Trust yourself to decide what is right for you.

130. Healing Outside the Box

These days, it's fashionable to admire people who "think outside of the box." It's deemed a highly desirable way to solve problems.

But sometimes you can do better and *live* outside the box. Consider all the changes you, for one, have survived so far. Even if you don't believe in reincarnation, surely you've noticed that you've had several lifetimes…all within this one.

Probably it will take more than your supply of fingers and toes to count up all your changes of housing, cities, lovers, friends, careers, ways of dressing, even religion. Living in this era of speeded-up karma, you lack the dependable (if frustrating) familiarity of village life as it has survived through the ages, where you were given your place and, more or less happily ever after, lived there.

Now humanity is being pulled full speed ahead to a state of enlightenment. Whatever unfulfilled desire or personal boundary holds you back, guaranteed it's going to become an active part of your life, sooner or later.

Nowhere is this accelerated evolution more poignant than with our boxes of belief. It's possible to change all the aforementioned externals, from housing to religion, without once moving outside that favorite old puzzle box. What calls it into question is crisis, especially the need for physical healing.

In the extremity where even an atheist may cry out "Help me, God," comes an unmistakable summons to break out of your reality box. You'll be driven from one "failed" approach to another, until you land where God has intended you to be all along.

I think of a dear friend, Emma, who battled breast cancer. First she worked with her primary belief, spiritual medicine. Then she turned to her second favorite, energy medicine. Finally Emma tried an approach that didn't especially appeal to her, healing stories. She believed in them, hard as she could. Still, nothing helped. Tumors spread all over her body until she looked like a goner. Finally Emma allowed herself to go through chemotherapy, the despised alternative. Only then was her health restored.

What's the moral of this story? God is bigger than anyone's box.

So never push your beliefs about medicine onto another person, any more than you'd coerce that person to follow your spiritual path. Illness can become a blessed opportunity to awaken, yet nothing on earth is more frightening.

When you encounter someone whose box is being smashed, don't give answers. Instead, bring what is really needed, compassion.

131. The False Lure of Synchronicity

Coincidence has its uses. Sometimes the book you most need to read will tumble off a bookstore shelf, pointedly landing right at your feet.

Synchronicity is a wonder. It helps you feel cared for by spirit and brings adventure to everyday life. Each day, you wait to see what God will deliver to your doorstep.

This effortless grace works best, however, when supplemented by common sense. Synchronicity comes with a catch: Distinguishing the true pull from the false lure.

"Everything happens for a cosmic reason," some people say. With all respect, I disagree. In a world of unfathomable complexity, plenty of things happen for reasons that are, for practical purposes, trivial.

If you go out walking and step in some dog doo, does that mean you must take it home, put it in a picture frame and hang it up in your living room?

Even meaningful coincidences can arise just to grab your attention. The event that wakes you up may not be an end in itself, so much as encouragement to keep searching.

One of my clients, Beverly, was in the market for a retirement home. Driving in the country, she saw a man at work. As they chatted, he told Beverly about some unadvertised land available for development. It turned out to be the perfect site for building her house of dreams.

Being a believer in synchronicity, Beverly was delighted with how she had chanced upon this property. She found it enticing that the helpful stranger was a builder. Before hiring him, fortunately, she took some practical precautions, one of which was having me read his aura. Turned out, several major integrity problems were evident. Maybe it was no accident that this man was puttering around in his front yard that afternoon, unemployed.

Beverly's synchronicity was a mixed bag of blessings. Yes, the man led her to a meant-to-be piece of land. But no, he had no further role in her life, not if she was smart.

Synchronicity tests us in many ways. Sometimes newbies to spirituality assume that teachers are so interchangeable, a perfectly good one will be located as close as the nearest elementary school. Finding someone at your vibration is a more meaningful coincidence than propinquity.

Sure convenience is appealing. But, in a world where the tests can outnumber the freebies, question synchronicity. Never make it a substitute for common sense.

132. Prayer Clunkers

"I'll pray for you."

Is that a treat or a threat? Depending on who makes the offer, a wise response might be, "No thanks."

The goals of your prayer volunteer may be very different from your desires for your future…or God's. Alas, conversations with God about other people can turn as nasty as any other form of gossip.

Does anyone, individual or group, have the right to pray that you convert to someone else's religion? How about "inspiring" you to bring forth grandchildren, to materialize a particular job, to move closer to home, to vote for another person's favorite politician?

Prayers like these connect people subconsciously, binding them by psychic ties or worse. If you could see how complicated these patterns become, you would be appalled by the tangle. Energetically pulled and tugged by a web of astral-level debris… Ouch! And the chaos feels even worse than it looks.

Coercive prayers are sticky, earth-bound projections of personal pride. Yet other prayers may be the real deal, shimmering gold, sacred and powerful. It's like having two car dealerships in your neighborhood, one selling superb luxury vehicles, the other offering broken-down wrecks.

When you pray for others, how can you avoid sending a clunker? Connect first to your own Source. Get your personal prayers out of your system. Then begin your prayer requests for others, and send out light, love and power wherever you choose.

This un-coercive offering will reach only those who want and need your particular vibration of blessing. Even a second's worth can bring huge results. Plus, an ample amount of light will be left over to protect *you*.

Whether or not others pray for you, you'll drive down the highway of life in a God-given, tuned-up car. And the residue of your selfless prayers will give you the equivalent of an extra bumper.

133. Prayer with Power

Do you have big ambitions for prayer? Why not? Your prayers can help anyone, anywhere, whether living or (physically) dead.

Prayer is your best way to help even those who don't request help, provided that your efforts remain un-coercive (i.e., you don't try to pray friends into an outcome of your own choosing).

For prayer, all you need is time, intention and God. Use the rules other people have taught you or feel free to break them, or else make up your own method entirely. As someone who co-creates with God, instinctively you'll make choices that bring power to your prayers. And you'll participate fully as the person you are, not as someone whose attention is divided, half begging God for favors while the other half worries, "Do I have enough faith? Do I deserve to call myself a Muslim/Buddhist/Christian/Jew?" (Show me any religion and I'll show you a unique flavor of guilt.)

Whatever your religion, what makes a prayer powerful? It's the degree to which you are aware of God. The clearer that awareness, the more oomph to your prayer — and you're responsible for that part. God shines like the sun, bright as can be. Yet a cloudy sky could make the sun's presence seem iffy. Unawares, you may be carrying clouds along with your desire to pray, so take a moment to puff them away. Relax your body, using whatever method you find most effective. Downplay doubts or fears by setting an intention. What do you wish to accomplish?

Then call on God. Once connected, you'll know what to do. For how many years have you been perfectly capable of using a telephone? Then you're used to talking with someone who isn't physically present. Have your conversation. Include any friend or situation you like, letting it be released into Divine care.

When you're done, I would recommend that you don't do the equivalent of slamming down the phone. Wait a moment in the silence, just in case God has an immediate answer to what you've asked.

Then give thanks, not only because it's common courtesy; not because God's feelings would be hurt otherwise, but to remind your subconscious mind that — despite any lingering doubts — you really *did* just succeed in talking with God.

Finally, after any prayer, please treat your body considerately. You've really gone somewhere in consciousness, and human bodies need transition time. Making sure that you get this isn't God's job but yours. So pay attention to your body. Include a stretch, perhaps. Then open your eyes.

Now you're ready to go forth. After prayer with power comes *life* with power.

134. Variations on the Theme of Prayer

Just as there are thousands of names for God so, too, are there countless variations on the theme of prayer.

Variety might seem to come mostly from the innumerable matters you can pray *about*. But sometimes you might feel stuck, sending out the same old routine prayers in the usual way. In that case, remember that you're free to vary *any* of the components of prayer. Think about how you might change each of these standard components:

1. Awareness: You become aware of the desire to pray.
2. Preparation: You prepare yourself and find an appropriate setting.
3. Communication: You call on God and send out your prayer.
4. Release: You let the prayer go, trusting in the best possible outcome.
5. Recognition: You're alert to receive the first bit of blessing, inner peace.
6. Appreciation: You give thanks that your communication has been received.
7. Transition: After some transition time, you shift back to regular awareness.

It's especially easy to experiment during Step #3. For communication you could:

- Sing God's name, dropping it into deep silence.
- Muster up the memory of a favorite scent. Then imagine God deep inside that fragrance, like the center of a flower.
- Dance, either physically or mentally. In the ancient practice of hatha yoga, each posture has meaning, both for purifying the nervous system and as a symbolic offering. Any way that you position your body can become a sacred position, bringing special qualities to prayer.
- Choose a favorite color of light. Then give it a symbolic meaning to enhance your God-connection. Each hue can correspond to a special attribute, and don't be shy about creating your own. Just for today, bright turquoise could mean God's ability to break all rules, yet never bring lasting harm. Today's pale green could symbolize Divine persistence in making things new. Be a prayer artist!
- Cook up an association between God and a favorite food. Make the flavor so real you can taste it. What a delicious appetizer before you ask for God's help!

You wouldn't consider belittling God's ability to create. Why let mere habit diminish yours?

135. Love, Find Me

Love always finds a way, it's said.
I wish Love would find me,
come when I least expect it
and light my way.

When mess and clutter overtake
both office space and home
and there's no time to fix it,
what happens to my calm?

Vacation seems impossible
with so much work to do.
Can't I find one small piece of peace
pervading through?

My mobile phone, e-mail and fax,
depended on but loathed,
could I reclaim the life they were
originally bought to help me with
finding some kind of — What's that word? —
I can't even remember it now…Oh yeah, balance.

The ultimate convenience and
post-modern luxury
may be the order only I
can choose to see.
Though miracles are welcome here
and love's my destiny,
Heaven helps those who help themselves
That would be me today.

136. Pullouts

Ask for a *pullout* today. Pulling out of your aura something that doesn't belong there — it's one of the easiest ways to improve your life.

Improve which aspect? Sometimes the answer is obvious: Improve my emotional life; heal that persistent pain in my shoulder; overcome difficulties that I face at work.

Other times, there seems so much to fix, it's overwhelming. Still other times, everything seems to be going pretty well. Good or bad, if the choice is difficult, you can simply ask for overall improvement.

Now, whom will you request to do the work? Call on God, of course, but I recommend that you also enlist the help of a Divine Being, someone in a body made of the highest vibration of light. Here I'll use the example of Archangel Raphael, whose specialty is to bring healing.

Sit comfortably and close your eyes. Think His name. Then, either imagine Him or watch with your inner sight. As He stands before you, ask Him to pull out the problem, so it can leave you completely and forever.

Be in the silence and observe the wonderful healing that follows. Perhaps you'll help by blowing out air through your mouth or singing tones or naming names. Perhaps you'll simply contribute amazement, noticing how Archangel Raphael pulls certain symbolic objects out of your aura.

Play. Make it up, if you must. In this ceremony of healing imagination, you'll be inspired to work with ideas that best fulfill your intention.

Pulling out is only Part One of this process. After it's done, always follow up with Part Two, putting energy back in.

Nature abhors a vacuum. Unless you put back something different from what was removed, the old stuff will return. I'll bet you have at least one friend whose sad love life illustrates this point. She'll dump a horrible lover but never put back self-knowledge or self-esteem. Consequently, within a short time, she'll find a "new" lover who's just as bad as the old one.

End your pullout, therefore, by asking Archangel Raphael for a *put-back*. May he fill you up with new white light, with clearer self-love, with audible ocean waves of peace. Ask for whatever feels right. When you're filled up, give thanks.

How could you not be grateful? One complete spiritual healing...changing the rest of your life for the better...something that easy and fast...Wow!

137. Signs and Wonders

Your everyday mind is a distinctive blend of ideas, feeling and spirit. All your life, you've heard this within, as thoughts or pictures or both. Yet some of us expect that God's voice, heard within, ought to sound completely different. Being taken over by an utterly alien voice, this is supposed to be reassuring? Sure, it could be a sacred experience to speak in tongues but what about thinking as a blend of *yourself plus God?* This would be co-creation!

Out goes your question. In comes your answer. It's a bigger truth than you might have found strictly on your own.

Co-creation isn't flashy like some kind of spiritual ventriloquism. Occasionally you might ask for some flash, a special sign. Well, go ahead and ask. *Never be afraid to make an ask of yourself!* You could do worse than seem like God's super-demanding child. Long before you came along, this Father of yours has had ample experience with brats.

Besides, who is this Big Guy? He's someone who loves His children even when we ignore Him. God waits for us to be interested, however long that takes. He respects our free will enough to let each of us make the first move.

So it won't wreck things if you ask for a wonder. But when it comes — which it will, in *God's* way — will you recognize it? Answers to prayers can seem quirky, surprising, annoying and otherwise anything but actual answers.

I love what happened to Sylvia, a friend of mine who was pregnant. Since she had a history of miscarriages, upon learning that she was pregnant, old fears were stirred up. First thing one morning, she sat up in bed and prayed for reassurance. Could God please give her a sign about whether she'd carry this baby to term?

When Sylvia got up to make the bed, a special stone fell off her night table, a Shiva lingam. It landed on a pair of her husband's trousers; he'd left them on the bed. Actually, this ultimate fertility symbol landed right on the fly of his trousers.

Sylvia told me, "The funniest thing just happened." After describing the stone's tumble she concluded, "Now I've had my laugh for the day. I only wish that my sign would come." Well, you may be thinking, "Would the message have been any clearer if handwriting appeared on the wall?" What was Sylvia waiting for, reassurances in Aramaic broadcast directly from her pillow? Her healthy pregnancy ended with a magnificent baby, and maybe a lesson as well.

Remember this story — not necessarily the well-aimed Shiva lingam but the way signs happen *as part of life*. Don't let yours be obvious to everyone except you. With trust, you can recognize that your life is filled with signs and wonders.

138. Landscapes for Your Soul

Landscapes are an especially potent place to activate creative imagination. Each of us has at least one scene in nature that speaks powerfully to the soul. Imagine yourself there and you can co-create wonders.

Soon as you start thinking about that place, full-body memory will rush in to support you. Invite a Divine Being to keep you company, if you like. Definitely add a desire, a story line, and voila! It's easy to make your wishes come true when you dream them at such a great wishing place.

For instance, are you an ocean lover? Then close your eyes and imagine a sunny beach. Dunk your feet in the water. Watch babies with their toys, playing in the sand. Hear them splash and shriek with joy.

All the guests at your beach can have as much fun as those children. Here everyone, no matter how troubled, remembers how to play.

Now it's your turn. Stand up. Walk into the waves. Ride them, letting the water bring you up, then back down again, graceful and rhythmical.

Did you come to this beach with any troubles, such as worries about a person or job? Well, let the worries wash away as you body surf. Any troubles that stay stuck within you can, at a minimum, rock in the surf with the rest of you, soothed by the healing ocean.

So go with it, flow with it, this Divine Rhythm where everything changes yet stays perpetually good. And give yourself credit, too, surfer. Feel how beautifully you flow with each wave, as though you had always known how.

In the far distance, bigger waves sound out their Om, God's eternal song. Hear those waves crash, again and again, breaking nothing. Then send out your prayer to merge with this sound.

Your wish is granted. Feel it?

When you're satisfied, come back to shore. Sunbathe or snack, knowing that all of your hard work has been done. Finally, stretch, open your eyes, and give thanks.

Like any successful vacation, this session of creative imagination will rejuvenate you. When you return to everyday life, feel the pep in your step, the ease in your knees.

139. Healing Pine Forest

Enter a Healing Pine Forest with creative imagination. This sacred place is sure to invigorate you. It's as if, despite all complications, deep down you were as simple as one perfectly shaped pine cone.

To start, imagine yourself so grateful to be here, standing among the feathery evergreens. Shuffle bare feet through soft fallen needles. Go naked, if you like. Nobody will mind.

Breathe deeply enough to fill yourself up with pine fragrance. Now the healing process can start. Ask God to cleanse you *energetically* with white light, swirling from top to toe. Choose a method to cleanse the various systems of your physical body:

- Would you like a scrub of gentle pine needles?
- How about a pine-scented rain?
- Or would you prefer for your skin to slurp up a luscious, pine-scented mud?
- Maybe you'd prefer to do the scrubbing yourself. Then here's your exquisite, transparent bar of pine soap.

Close your eyes and, instantly, materialize your cleansing method of choice. Now start scrubbing, friend. If you're aware of any *health problem*, start there. As the radiant healing energy enters, you may feel a shift, soft as a friendly wind through the trees.

Ask to cleanse your *digestion*. Your organs, your cells, even the taste in your mouth are being purified. Open up channels to produce *soma*, super-refined natural chemicals that enhance deeper perception.

Next, cleanse your *elimination*, internal organs plus that mysterious inner-outer organ called skin. Your body needs a strong capacity to say no. Remove all obstacles to removal…gracefully, easily.

Your *reproductive* system deserves help, right? Let healing light dissolve any stored up pain or frustration. Fatigue is removed, while every obstacle to your healthy desire releases. Open up your capacity for pleasure.

Circulatory system? Sure, let it flow. Bring new health to your heart, your veins, your capillaries. May your very blood be re-charged. Nothing like the freshness of pine! Feel it buzz through you, bringing a joyful exuberance.

Invigorate next your fine *endocrine* system. Throughout your glands and hormones, let the great cleanse begin. Sparkling chemicals will bring you a new start on life.

Lymph drainage comes next. Your body's mysterious extra system for cleansing, let it be strengthened now, gland by gland and cell by cell.

Bones, joints and muscles will follow. Feel your skeletal system gain new health starting right now. Remove all that doesn't belong and let this be done in the most gentle and tender way, soft as the side of a perfect pine needle.

We've saved the best for last. *Respiration* is such fun to cleanse when your tool is the evergreen vibration of pine. Down to your deepest lung fibers, be healed.

And ta da! Now comes the *fill up*. What fun when you're deep in this forest! Ask God to bring you a radiant green energy, the quintessence of evergreen.

Imagine new vitality being poured into you until it's crammed into every available space. Much has been removed. Now even more is being added. And you don't need to figure out where. Just get stuffed.

Before leaving this sacred pine forest, did you know? You can speed time up. Let the bright sunshine of daytime morph into a serene twilight. Feel the moon rise, full and glorious. If you wish, the serenity of a perfect evening can cling to your feet. Look up at the stars. You may feel a big new kind of joy thrill your soul.

Now is a perfect time to stretch your body, give thanks, and open your eyes.

140. Clear Mountain Breeze

Sometimes it's fun to open to something new. Sometimes it's more than fun. Opening up to something genuinely new could save your life psychically.

Hey, find any excuse to come with me now on today's inward adventure. Sit comfortably, close your eyes, and bring your intention along as you climb our imaginary mountain. How big a mountain? Right-size it.

Choose the weather, too. You're invulnerable here, so march through a hurricane or blizzard, if you wish it to symbolize your life now. But you also have the option of ease. You could set out on a sunny day, when the only visible snow is glimmering on a neighboring mountain top.

What a glorious journey! Hear the firm stride of your shoes, a percussion that strikes against the big mountain silence. What is the temperature like around you? Notice how the air smells sweeter once you have moved above the tree line?

Questions will make your experience stronger, so here are some more: Do your legs feel amazingly strong? Are you holding a marvelous walking stick? Notice any friendly animals along your way?

Going still higher, let yourself recognize a familiar exhilaration. You remember this wonder. It's the quality of a sacred journey.

As you approach the peak, know that inspiration awaits you at the top of the mountain. In anticipation, the very air changes. It's rarefied, with such purity that it energizes you, almost the way food would, but faster. This magical air so potent, it's enough to make you feel you could fly.

Finally you stand on that mountain top. Do you find a Divine Being here, ready to share the amazing view?

Within your own body, mind and heart, you have such a feeling of power. *You can do anything.* Know it. Believe it.

Connected to your full inner strength, ask for a vision or words about your new beginning. Should your experience of this be clear, celebrate. But if your experience isn't so clear, don't give up. Demand that God give you a sign within 24 hours.

And now find a souvenir of this journey to put in your pocket — a pebble, some snow that won't melt, you name it. (You know what that souvenir symbolizes for you, right? If not, ask inside.)

That's just one of the things to consider as you descend from your mountain. Walking, maybe singing inside, celebrate what you've accomplished. The next part of the life before you… it really is open, brimming with new possibilities to co-create with God. Stretch and, when your body is ready, open your eyes.

141. Abundance, Complete with Desert

In this spiritual exercise, you will create greater abundance of anything you'd like to increase in your life. Everything will be here but beverages, so I recommend that you drink a tall glass of water before setting out. Yes, my friend, you're about to visit the desert.

Sit comfortably, where you'll have no distractions. Close your eyes and imagine that you've been walking on a spiritual pilgrimage. Turn your head and find that you have brought along a whole posse of Divine Beings and angels. Remind them of the purpose of your journey, a specific intention with meaning for you, including any desires for wealth and success.

Right after you've listed it all, you arrive. This desert is vast, stretching far as the eye can see. On every side, feel the peace. Let the land pull you down into earth energy, cleansing you with each step.

Whatever discouraging experiences you've been carrying, any fears and frustrations, release them now through your feet. Maybe you can even hear them leave. Let the silly old weights clatter downward forever. This place is too sunny and beautiful for you to be walking with burdens.

And look up. Although the earth near you is flat, in the distance stand high cliffs, natural towers of sacred stone. Such magnificence! Doesn't it feel like God's country? Here is a place where your wishes can come true.

It's not just the vastness, the silence, not even the calmness built into the air. This place is so connected to earth that, of course, all pretense must fall away.

False ideas about what you "should" want or have — expectations that come from others instead of you — how could burdens like that stand a chance? Here it's enough to be only, authentically, you. Feel one desire of your soul come through, clear as never before.

Run it like a movie and watch that desire play out. Then let the show finish with a sign of success, something tangible, something you can wear or tuck into your pocket. Take it. Give thanks that this, or something even better, has been set in motion for your life now.

Just for fun, why not leave this desert by riding in style? Here comes a magnificent horse or a camel, a llama, a unicorn.... Take your pick. Then get on and ride. Feel the fun of it.

Ride with your posse into the sunset. Then, when you're ready, take a few breaths. Stretch and open your eyes. You've just swapped one place of miracles for another.

142. Space Ranger

Come play in deep space. It will satisfy an ancient longing. Or maybe you'd prefer a different benefit, like landing more firmly on earth afterwards.

How could a space voyage ground you? It's like the old trick for practicing a tough piece of music. Usually you'll practice at a manageable speed. But sometimes a smart musician will go through that music impossibly fast, missing notes like crazy, and who cares? The contrast helps a musician to play at normal speed later with far more assurance.

Whatever your purpose for taking today's trip as Space Ranger, protect yourself by asking a Divine Being to co-pilot. Mission accepted!

Now position yourself physically. Sit with your feet on the floor. Then clasp your hands, interlacing fingers. Separate the palms and place them atop your head. (If your elbows stick out, that's a sign you're doing this right.) Raise your hand position up several inches — part yogi, part ballet dancer. Here comes the payoff: Close your eyes and, inwardly, look up through the top of your head. Your hand position will guide your attention effortlessly upwards.

Breathe deeply and set your intention. Do you, for instance, seek inspiration concerning a particular problem? How about entrée into bigger consciousness? Remember, there's always grounding. Ask for whatever you wish.

Now hands down, start imagining. You're in the waiting room of a space station. Huge windows look onto the most wonderful airships as they take off and land.

Additional planes await takeoff. Choose one you like, then walk over to the runway and board it. Seat yourself comfortably in the cockpit. You, after all, are the pilot — well trained by Spirit and, therefore, supremely confident. Your co-pilot, that venturesome Divine Being, sits next to you. Bring in a whole crew of angels, if you like.

Clearance comes: Smooth takeoff, fast flight. Feeling the smooth ride, check back with your intention because it may already have undergone a shift.

Ready, now, to jump into hyperspace? Switch it on with one quick thought. Continue to design (and instantly manifest) your space mission just as you'd like it to be, down to the finest and most fabulous detail.

Before returning, you might wish to select a souvenir. Fasten it onto your aura for keeps.

Land your ship safely, Space Ranger. Welcome back to terra firma. Open your eyes and feel solid ground beneath your feet. Give thanks for one more successful spiritual mission.

143. Welcome, Power

You didn't come into this life to practice being a victim, did you? Yet, as you wake up your full potential, victimhood may still lurk within, half-hidden but real.

Could you have some victimhood left to release? One way to find out is to finish the following sentences:

- People take advantage of me because….
- Although I'm smart about most things, problems still come up when I deal with….
- It's hard to believe in myself when….
- When discouraged, I feel like "The story of my life" is….
- Even though I've grown enormously over the last few years, I still shrink down into a puddle of misery and insecurity when….

No question, patterns of victimhood aren't worthy of you. Here's a graceful way to dislodge them. You can do this *power wash* either as a visualization or literally, in a bathtub or shower stall.

Peel off outward clothes. This will make you totally present to the truth of your human self. Then soap up and scrub away. As you do so, speak out statements like these:

"Subconscious mind, pay attention. I completely release any patterns of victimization within me."

Rinse off, and this time speak variations of this affirmation: "I welcome my full power into…."

Will it be your heart? How about your voice? Could there be some part of your body that would just love an infusion of power?

You name it, you've got it.

Don't be afraid to err on the side of generosity. Could any amount of power be excessive? No way!

If you're feeling really bold, boost the flow of power with Divine co-creation and sing it out:

I welcome God's power into my heart, into my heart, into my heart.

144. Riding on God's Grace

On a sad day, I sank into my wishing place
I lowered eyelashes and asked for God's grace.
The problem? My friend, all the troubles we'd had.
And I wished from my heart we could be friends instead.

Nothing happened. I thought, "This is so just like me.
I am hopelessly trusting. Kid, grow up some day!
Stop this wishing and recognize, like an adult,
bad things happen that can't be fixed. It's not my fault."

Having settled things sensibly should be enough
for a sensible person, but I'm also tough.
I am stubborn and trusting, hopeless though it be.
So I wouldn't move 'til God's love come back for me.

I recalled a whole list of good things I *did* have.
I remembered a time I fell deeply in love.
Then tears came. That romance, just like my friendship now
had broken irreparably, hurting me so.

I rode waves of emotion, crashed, felt as if shame
and helplessness ought to be my middle name,
when a new thought came, quietly, I don't know how
that more of God's power could join with me now.

This new power could keep me from victimhood, plus
I could dare to be kind, I could still dare to trust.
My heart changed. I began to breathe in stronger air
and gave thanks for this new proof that God is right here.

145. Divine Economy

Once you ask God for help, your healing will come. Whether the problem be physical, emotional, social or financial, a heartfelt prayer sets in motion a compassionate response. So trust that help is on the way.

Demonstrations of Divine support won't be one-size-fits-all, necessarily. Were your problems? When you remember that you're on The Learning Planet, the variety of healings makes more sense than ever.

Why isn't it fair to demand a big, obvious miracle? On some level, you may expect drama on a grand scale, like the parting of the Red Sea. Special effects would definitely make for a more thrilling movie. Still, what would you learn?

Out of kindness, most Divine cures come subtly. That's why, when you ask for help, you'll receive the smallest, most intimate version possible.

So take it as a compliment when miracles don't clobber you over the head. How much lovelier when a soft invitation is sufficient to open your eyes!

Divine economy is at work. You'll receive exactly the size of help you require, in the way that best helps you evolve. God isn't stingy, just wise.

Maybe your answer to a prayer will be the thought to consult a doctor or other professional. No failure! You're still being invited to co-create your healing, balancing subjective and objective, practicing discernment. To act responsibly in material ways will not limit your spiritual evolution — exactly the opposite.

Today you can travel through life like an Eagle Scout. Learn to coax a tiny flame into a warming campfire.

146. Accept Your Healing

It isn't enough to pay someone to heal you. Whether you consult a physician, an acupuncturist, a partner in prayer or some other specialist, his effectiveness depends on you. Are you ready to accept your healing?

Acceptance need not require the skills of a spiritual contortionist. Invite your body-mind-spirit system to bend around the principle of gratitude. In other words, expect your good.

To speed the process along, it can help to let God know that you'll welcome whatever self-knowledge is needed. Once I sat in session with a client who had loads of problems. At a certain point, I started to give her a homework assignment. Jokingly, I asked, "That's okay, isn't it? Or would you rather have me do all the work?"

She snapped back, "I want as little to do with this as possible."

Whew, that was a tough session! Sure I was committed to doing my best to facilitate healing. But for several seconds after she spoke, I stopped wanting to help her at all. Even after I willed back my willingness, facilitating any healing at all was a slow slog.

Beneath the surface of a health problem can be a toxic pattern of thinking, like a stuck emotion or some other undigested experience from the past. Who else is supposed to digest your experience? Without a patient's receptivity, nobody else can find the full pattern, let alone move it out.

Sometimes a patient accepts help during an official healing session but, afterwards, she still resorts to body blame-talk, like "My bad back." If that's you, cut it out. (By which I don't mean trying to surgically remove your nether portions.) If you're going to send words to some struggling part of your physique, please be friendly. What, are you going to accept your healing but loathe your body?

And speaking of acceptance, consider fighting disease *gently*. When you pray for a healing, ask that it come as fast as you can handle…with balance. Haven't you known people who demanded immediate, drastic and total removal of all that stood in their way? Results may not be pretty. Somewhere between zero miles per hour and racecar speeds, you can find a way to drive through life's highway of healing without crash and burn.

May common sense inspire you along with openness to God's healing power. Think of all those years of medical school you *don't* have to attend. Within you dwells a brilliant healer who knows the greatest medical secret of all — how to call in the grace of God, then get out of the way.

147. Three-Way Stretch

This fun technique won't bring you total fitness. But it can circulate your life force energy, tone your muscles and make you feel extra-alive in your body. All this in less than five minutes? Not bad.

Actually, there's more. With this technique, you need no special equipment. Like a great marriage, you can follow though in sickness or in health. Finally, the Three-Way Stretch is even creative.

Okay, now that you're psyched, start where you are. Exaggerate the position of your body until you are stretching every muscle group from head to toe.

Twist and turn, sidle and scrunch, until you've made your position really interesting. Throughout your body, you have opposing pairs of muscles. One pushes while the other pulls. Squeeze part of your body from one direction. Squeeze a second part. When a whole bunch of body parts are well squished, squeeze harder and hold the position to a count of three. Then release.

Count that as Round One of Three.

Now take a very different second position. Perhaps you'll move some muscles in the opposite direction. Squeeze, count to three and release.

Then take a third position. Once again, squeeze count to three and release.

There! You've done the essence of yoga. (Also, essence of cat.)

Beyond the benefits and advantages of this technique, here's one more reason to love it. Symbolically, Three-Way Stretch is co-creation in motion. You start where you are, with your human self, then reach as hard as you can in God's direction, then let go. Will one stretch do the trick? Sometimes, yes. But often there are many directions for stretching, so don't limit yourself to just one.

148. Hugs

Have you had your hugs today?

Psychologist Virginia Satir has written, "We need 4 hugs a day for survival. We need 8 hugs a day for maintenance. We need 12 hugs a day for growth."

Of course, your actual mileage may vary. Some of us happen to need more.

How can you get enough hugs? It helps if, every day, you're with at least one hug-ready person. Avoid explaining that you're hugging for strictly medical reasons, which would be only slightly less alarming than if you said, "I'm hugging for your own good. It's tough but I'm *that* dedicated to keeping you sane."

My advice is just to ease into the hug-a-lot habit. Greet each friend with a smile and a hug. You're being generous, really.

What if you still lack enough hugs for your minimum daily requirement? Maybe it's time to make friends with some trees. Otherwise, be really bold and hug yourself. Adding a few endearments or affirmations won't hurt, either.

"I love myself, no matter what."

Narcissism, no. You're not giving anything to self that you're unwilling to share with others. Self-hugs are revitalizing and, once replenished, you'll have more to give your loved ones.

After all, your very best friend may be a non-hugger. Accept that this is not someone to wrap your arms around. Plenty of other ways will be available to show affection.

Figuring out how many hugs *you* require and making sure to get them — now, that's your responsibility.

If you go to a fine restaurant, soup will be on the menu, and many choices may be offered, including a daily special. In that same spirit, demonstrate versatility as you gather each day's delectable collection of hugs.

149. Heart Hug

Experiment with a Heart Hug. It's probably the opposite of how you hug now.

This hugging style for the new millennium is informed by the metaphysical difference between the body's left and right. Your *right* side relates to yang energy, what you're like in public: Doing, doing, doing. By contrast, your *left* side expresses yin energy: What you're like with those who know you well, just being you.

Appropriately, a handshake connects two people's energy on the right side. Handshakes ought to be yang, considering that they establish a public bond, perfect for the workplace or when meeting someone new.

Perhaps out of habit, most of us hug in the same direction we use to shake hands, right to right. But if you'll embrace from the other direction, you'll touch heart to heart, connecting from your yin side, maybe also your inside. It feels very different.

Long as we're considering direction of hugs, let hugs in general teach you about the other person's willingness to connect with you. What will you notice today? Here's a start:

- *Shoulder*-only hugs are dutiful.
- When *heads* don't relax into a hug, there's a spiritual with-hold.
- Turning away at the *throat* signals lack of communication.
- Willingness to hug at *heart* level symbolizes receptivity to emotional connection.
- What about the brave soul who'll *meet you fully,* body to body, from the solar plexus all the way down to the legs? There's a moment of complete connection, a brief surrender to oneness.

I count hugs as one of the all-time greatest human discoveries, ranking right up there with shoes. (Ever think how brave that first footwearer must have been — or how silly that primitive fashion statement must have looked?)

Hugs make you huge, big enough for two. My friend Catharine Rambeau and I call them "Huges." Whatever you call them, explore their immense spiritual potential. Build your capacity and you just might wind up holding a space big enough for God.

150. Daytime Story

Being an adult, you can choose your own bedtime stories — daytime stories, too. Subconsciously you always tell yourself some story or other. Usually it stays in the background, but not with today's exercise. Do stories like these sound familiar?

- "Things may start well for me but they never end well."
- "Certain people just don't like me. Never have, never will."
- "When I'm finally enlightened, things will be better."

Note especially that tricky last one. Stories that sound ennobling may be the worst. One way to test a story's value involves your body. After you think an idea, how do you feel physically? Try on the three statements above. Do they make you feel better in any way? Oops, better try on their improved versions, below. You don't want to walk around with a power chakra shaped like a donut!

- "However things start for me, they always end well."
- "Certain people just don't like me. But for every one who doesn't, there are 500 who do. And these are the people I consider important in my life."
- "I'm wide awake spiritually, and growing more enlightened every day."

Sad old stories can be perfectly true. They have just one drawback, making you feel dead inside. Here are paired story topics, mutually exclusive. Either version can be true, depending on your choice. Notice the radically different consequences for your mind-body-spirit:

- "Fate rules my life, not free will" versus "Free will rules my life, not fate."
- "Heredity is the most important factor in my health" versus "The most important factors in my health are within my control."
- "My doctor is responsible for keeping me healthy" versus "I am responsible for keeping myself healthy."

You get the idea. Tell yourself some new stories today. What empowering tales they can be!

Subjectively you'll be much stronger. Now you'll only need do the objective part and make choices wisely. Maybe some of your choices will be new, possible because you've started to tell yourself more empowering stories. As you apply your will, you'll find the strength (and sheer spunk) to be healthier than before.

151. Sleep Comfortably

Ever been so tired that you couldn't sleep? One solution is to *just feel comfortable*. Lie in your bed like a king in your horizontal throne. Feel the luxury of it.

Even if you don't drop off to sleep right away, you can enjoy the comfort of resting your body, snuggling under the covers, breathing to any rhythm you choose.

Insomnia can be a horrible problem. Sleep experts offer helpful advice but they may not be able to tell you about the spiritual benefits of your situation. When you can't sleep, don't worry. Use the time to co-create with God.

Dark of night happens to be a superb time for spiritual exercise. What if you go through your usual ones yet you're still lying there awake? Try a new prayer. Or simply lie in companionable silence next to your Beloved. If you're sleeping with a human partner, too, here's one situation where three in a bed could be good.

Still awake at midnight or 3:00 a.m.? Know that some devotees of God purposely wake themselves up at these hours to meditate. Let the deep stillness puddle around you. Splash in it, then ask God to take away any problem you name. Afterwards, fill up with blessings.

Should mere "blessings" seem intangible, night is the perfect time for imagining blankets of light that flow over and into you, the first one violet, the second indigo, and so forth, all through the rainbow and back again. That ought to be enough comfy covers until sleep tucks you in!

Alternatively, use night wakefulness to commune with departed ancestors or any loved one you wish to summon from the Other Side. Call on a Divine Being to chaperone, holding a protective light. Then think of the person you wish to contact. Let the words and images come. May the wisdom flow.

But what if you ask and nothing happens? Don't call it a failure any more than you need call it insomnia. Invent a conversation. The person you're seeking may be inspiring you from the Other Side. However vivid your experience, give it a proper ending. Say three times to the person you've spoken with: "Leave here now. Go in peace."

What if you awaken early in the morning? Don't call that insomnia, either. Right before dawn is an especially potent time for spiritual exercise. It's said that ancient Vedic seers would do breathing techniques at 3:00 a.m., and this would satisfy their need for food of any kind the rest of the day. You might find it more interesting to materialize worldly dreams. Lying in bed, imagine them one at a time: Each new relationship, every career boost, all the delightful vacations.

Maybe you didn't talk to God enough during the day. Next time you're offered a night-time date, consider it an honor.

152. The Changing Nature of Sleep

Some sleep problems may be an opportunity to re-evaluate your spiritual life and give yourself more credit. Even if you feel like you're slogging through molasses, there may be more to the recipe.

Ever hear about American history's stickiest disaster? As described in *Einstein's Refrigerator* by Steve Silverman, in 1919 a large vat of molasses exploded in Boston, forming a gooey kind of tidal wave. Slow as molasses? Hardly! It rolled down the street faster than horses could run.

Back to now, here you are, faithfully co-creating each day and wondering "Where is my flashy experience?" Yet enlightenment is creeping up on you, more subtle than a river of sloshing molasses but perfectly valid nonetheless. One symptom that you're evolving spiritually is the changing nature of dreams and sleep.

Becoming more conscious of consciousness, a person develops inner wakefulness. If a *dream* ends in a way you don't like, you may be able to change it. But learning to move in and out of dreams can startle you awake.

Sleep used to cover your consciousness with a thick veil. Gradually, that veil grows thinner. Like someone familiar with a dark bedroom who has been given a night light, you may find yourself waking up.

Rather than berating yourself for having developed yet one more ailment — insomnia — congratulate yourself instead. Learning to witness sleep gives you more hours to be awake inwardly. You'll enjoy more fully how your body relaxes yet, in awareness, you won't sleep. Even your mind can sleep while your inner self remains alert. As your mind-body system learns this neat trick, sometimes you'll startle yourself wide awake.

Any life passage can disrupt sleep. Remember puberty? How about pregnancy or parenting an infant? And when your baby leaves home, sleep may be the second thing to be dumped out of your empty nest.

Biological life events can disrupt sleep as badly as *biographical* changes. Going through menopause, your life will be shaken up like a rug, with loads of old dust tossed out, so of course the resulting sleep patterns may not be pretty. Equally disruptive are death and divorce (yes, they're two separate things, although this can be hard to tell if you're forced to go through the latter).

Whatever causes sleeplessness, seek medical help as appropriate, but also consider that you've been given extra time to commune with God. And when all that communing actually wakes you up inside, this is a *good* thing. Can you function fine during the day? Then believe that you've slept long enough. And, yes, it does count as sleep if you rest your body in bed while the rest of you stays awake.

153. Healing Heart Café

Bring to the Healing Heart Café
each person from your past you've loved and lost.
Call one forth now from memory
and see how she comes willingly.
This meeting will set you both free.

Begin with your first lover or perhaps
a parent who appeared inadequate.
Imagine his recounting how, through everything,
he cared about you. Tell
the truths you crave to hear, each sweet detail.

Next comes the part where you may feel
ridiculous. So what? Big deal!
Proceed regardless. Make your guest
speak words that will explain and heal.
Assume one factor was his love
and not its lack.

Need your invented truth be reasonable
or the apology stingy and short?
In this Café, you are The Perfect One,
admired by all and popular
beyond your wildest dreams.
In fact this place is made precisely
of outrageous things.

Bring in love from past lifetimes, if you wish.
Bring in a circus, mermaids, gods or elves.
Nothing's too strange — or kind to your deep self
so long as you are healed before you leave.

154. Truth in Labeling

What if this world had truth-in-labeling? Would you recognize the joint?

Instead, earth is a place where things are seldom what they're labeled. Take *healers*, for example. Some doctors are genuine healers while many merely possess credentials. Plus, as you'll discover with spiritual discernment, *everyone* can do healing one way or another, if desired (a statistic that includes you).

Similarly, society bestows certain labels for *teachers*. Some accredited ones do honor to their profession, working like dogs and glowing like saints. Yet many of the best teachers on earth work unofficially. (And, once again, *you* may make cameo appearances as a teacher, official credentials notwithstanding.)

Religious leaders, however huge their congregations, have the job for one reason only. They're teaching what they most need to learn. Humanity's brightest lights of consciousness are seldom the ones in a pulpit. Meanwhile, shining acts of wisdom may come from just such unaccredited leaders as…you.

No matter where you live, people are easily read according to certain "supposed-to's." How convenient that everyone's labeled, some with high status, others with low. How convenient yet how misleading! Wouldn't it be refreshing if each of us were labeled properly — stamped with the equivalent of prices and ingredients, updated daily.

Today at your office, a co-worker's insignia might read "50% off." Unless you were looking for a sale on intelligence, this would not necessarily be a good sign.

But labels like these might at least cause you to keep your wits about you, rather than taking people at surface value. Fortunately, you can always read behavior. And, when you're ready to go even deeper, you can find precisely those up-to-the-minute truth labels I just joked about. They're not pure fantasy. They're real. They're in auras.

The human energy field can be read at will, just like a price tag. As a child, you learned regular literacy, choosing when to switch it on or off. You can do the same now, only better. If you'd rather read faces or body language or something else, do it! Make your own signs and labels.

Deeper perception is activated by choice. So don't fear that once you get started, you'll have to read everyone deeper, everywhere, in every situation. This morning, if you read your cereal box at breakfast, that was because you wanted to. Literacy is a resource, not a compulsion. Well, the same goes for deeper perception.

Which sacred labels will you choose to read today?

155. Objectively Speaking

To be successful in life, it's necessary to be objective. What actually happens, in contrast to how you feel about it?

Events are objective; interpretations, subjective. Putting together both sides of life is called *objective-subjective balance*, and it's one difficult trick. Usually folks favor one side over the other. This even shows physically. Here's how a little face reading can tell you who tends to do which.

Hoist up a mirror to help you learn about the structure of your right ear. Discount the lobe and pay attention to the relative proportions of the rest. Your *inner circle* neighbors the ear hole, recessed like a shallow wading pool. Probably you also have a fleshy border separating your inner circle from the *outer circle*, which lies above and beside the inner circle.

Once you've found these two ear circles, compare their relative sizes. With a bigger *outer* circle, your default position in life is to be objective. A larger *inner* circle suggests that your subjective side is stronger. *Equal* proportions indicate that objective-subjective balance will come more easily to you than to others.

Everyone can choose to be balanced, but understanding a person's proclivities helps to awaken compassion…and maybe add a new kind of objectivity as well. Also, once you've learned to read ear circles on yourself, you can go forth and read ear circles on the rest of humanity over the age of 18. (That's the minimum age to receive a face reading; it takes that long for the physical face to strongly reflect the soul.)

Face reading aside, what's the *practical* significance of being objective? What an objective thing to ask! Being objective, you'll be results-oriented, interested in rules, keeping track of what happens when and how. If, on the other hand, you care more about how you *react* to objective matters, you're being subjective.

Just for fun, try this experiment. Today, whatever your usual predisposition, emphasize noticing the *objective* side of life. Stick to your schedule. Believe only what's literally said. Enjoy the show! (And if this is how you live anyway, have fun being self-conscious about it.)

Closer examination would reveal that objectivity is an illusion, other people's "facts" usually being different from yours. But for today don't go there. Keep your reality simple.

By now you may be thinking. "Help! I couldn't stand doing this even for five minutes."

And doesn't that tell you something? Give yourself those five long minutes to learn how the other half lives.

156. Subjectively Speaking

Believe in yourself. Believe in others. Whether or not you find this easy to do depends partly on how you balance objective-subjective reality. Being objective, you'll tend to believe in people who can boast prior success. Being subjective, you're free to hope for the best in everyone. This can help you aim for a better life than circumstances might seem to warrant.

Subjective experience begins whenever you *interpret* objective reality. Sometimes you can learn the most interesting things about people only when you refuse to give up on them.

Yet emphasis on subjective life may cause torment as well as triumph. Will you take things that happen too personally? Could your emotional life become too intense? Perpetual interpretation can keep someone focused exclusively on psychology, religion or spirituality, i.e., to people with other interests, a bore.

Over-emphasizing subjective experience can diminish your life until you add balance. Short of being read by a skilled *empath* (someone who can directly experience what it is like to be you) how can you expect other people to understand what matters to you? At best, you'll communicate only with kindred spirits, and maybe not terribly clearly even with them.

Let's say you have a friend whose level of involvement in subjective matters matches your own, plus your belief system and education are, more or less, identical. Even that friend won't have a clue about your unique subjective experience unless you communicate. For fulfilling relationships, a naturally subjective person may need to work harder than someone oriented more towards objective life.

Still, if you're deeply subjective, it's unthinkable to be any other way. You despise mere facts. To you, facts are like black-and-white photos. Interpretation adds the color. Without subjectivity, human life wouldn't seem fully human.

Go ahead, then. Today, *indulge your subjective side.* Then, if your complicated inner life causes pain, take a good solid exhale and resolve to be more objective for a while. Evaluate what has happened. Decide what, objectively, you can do about it.

Perhaps you've found my description of subjective life either puzzling or irrelevant. Aha! You're objectively oriented. So your assignment for today will be a little different from what you read above.

When the people you deal with today show their strange, subjective colors, strive to be extra understanding. Subjectivity isn't contagious, like measles. It won't turn you into a whiner. And you may develop a touch more patience with your own inner life.

157. Speaking of Balance

Whether your way of relating to life is naturally subjective or objective, you'll have more success if you strive for balance. That can come easily if only you'll remember to use a certain computer program.

For context, your natural inclination about objectivity could be compared to computer *hardware*. Whether you are way subjective, objective beyond belief, or an intricate combination of the two, you've been wired that way since birth. Think of it as part of the (exquisite) way God created you as exactly who and what you've come here to be.

Objective-subjective balance, however, is a matter of maintenance. To continue our analogy, it works like computer *software*. You can easily install the balancing program right now, or upgrade your earlier version. Just speak out this affirmation:

The objective and subjective aspects of my life
are in perfect balance right now.

Drop this affirmation into the silence. Listen for the thud. Inwardly you may feel a shift; outwardly, you'll hear the words fade away. Meanwhile, your inner computer will adjust instantly.

This can change your life.

Repeat this balancing affirmation when needed and many commonplace problems will disappear. For example, my client Anne recounted a problem with her neighbor, Christina, who had dropped in to visit. After the first hour, Anne became uncomfortable, wishing that her guest would leave. After five hours, Anne said, "I prayed really hard. And finally, God helped me out and Christina left."

"Why didn't you just *ask* her to leave?" I asked.

This had never occurred to Anne. She's highly subjective. Mostly, this works fine. Anne is a talented artist, a generous friend. She just needed to learn how to toughen up with more objective-subjective balance.

This guesting incident became a turning point for Anne. She reprogrammed her inner computer and, thereby, discovered a happier way to deal with friends, strangers and strange friends, too.

An ounce of *objective* action can be worth a pound of subjective cure. Of course, for some of us, what's needed is the opposite — a refreshing ounce of *subjective* action. Either way, if you'll affirm your objective-subjective balance, you'll receive precisely what's most needed.

158. Green Light Ahead

You have a place of sacred guidance where wisdom is yours for the asking. One old image of inner listening portrays an angel hovering over one shoulder, whispering into your ear. Unfortunately, a devil is also pictured, equally vocal, in residence over the other shoulder. No wonder many of us don't feel inclined to ask for guidance. Yet you have a reliable voice within, tranquil and subtle, still and small.

What if you worry that misinformation lurks at one of your shoulders? Well, which sage ever advised paying rapt attention to your shoulders, for heaven's sake? Shrug off that fear. For most people, guidance speaks at your heart. For most others, guidance speaks at your solar plexus (i.e., your gut).

Which is it for you? Here's one way to find out. Frame a question to which you'd like an answer, such as, "What will help me to feel peace today?"

The answer will come to your mind most clearly if you also prepare your *body* to be receptive. Sit as comfortably as you can, uncrossing arms and legs. Take a few deep breaths and close your eyes. Speak your question within, as if you owned an extra pair of lips located right inside your body, at heart level.

After you ask, relax by taking another deep breath or two. Be open to whatever comes next.

If nothing appears by way of guidance, ask again. Only this time, let the extra pair of lips be located at your upper abdominal area, inside your rib cage.

After experimenting a few times, it will become clear to you whether you prefer listening for guidance at your solar plexus, your heart or somewhere else. From then on, you'll be effective at asking for wisdom whenever you wish.

Unsure whether an important action is a good idea or not? Ask inside. When an answer comes, it's your go-ahead from within.

If you're stopped at a traffic signal, it's a relief when the light turns green. With some practice, your inner guidance can become as clear as any traffic signal.

159. A Moving Experience

Children under 10 sleep better than grownups. They sleep all over the bed. Ever tiptoe into a sleeping kid's bedroom and laugh? Feet, arms and head have moved where you'd least expect them. But, really, why shouldn't we all sleep that way?

Asleep or awake, kids move creatively. For them, it's spontaneous. For you, it may not be. Nonetheless, you can do a grownup's *daytime* equivalent of a kid's night workout. Just take every possible chance to move in an unexpected fashion.

Go for it! Stretch. Twist. Dance in slow-mo. Explore. Not only will you keep your body more flexible, but you'll have way more fun.

Have you noticed? Creative movement is like laughter. With each passing decade, we grownups tend to do less of it. Yoicks! Are we practicing to fit quietly into our coffins or what?

On the other hand, some of us buy dedicated workout machines just for stretching. My health club, for instance, sports four of them. Maybe you've seen one of these rack-like contraptions; they come complete with diagrams of different ways to stretch. I find a certain humor in seeing folks all dressed up for their workouts, stiffly reading instructions posted on the official contraption, then studiously forcing themselves to go through the motions. They're so earnest about being flexible.

Many of those same positions could be done against a tree. Or in secret, isometrically, while standing in line at the checkout counter. Any minute, you could have enormous fun behind closed doors, rolling around on the carpet.

On behalf of your long-suffering body, I challenge you. Do 100 different movements today.

Which? How?

Who cares? Just make them up. Don't force your body, of course, but do have fun with it.

Admittedly, with some of your adult responsibilities, physical creativity could seem inappropriate. Will your boss applaud if, during today's meeting with an important client, you explore 17 thrilling new ways to stretch your shoulders? Somehow I have a hunch that you won't be given promotions for this kind of thing.

So do it secretly if you must, and *promote yourself*...into a state of greater vitality. Physical flexibility can go spiritual, you know. Stretch yourself into readiness for more spiritual grace.

160. Popularity

Give thanks today for your reputation, such as it is.

If it's bad, you have a terrific opportunity to exercise objective-subjective balance. Who doesn't like you? And whose problem would that be? Objectively and honestly, what would it take for you to be respected more? (As you know, you're allowed to find that price too high.)

But perhaps your current reputation is splendid. Then know that you are receiving the karma set in motion by two important choices:

- First, you've demonstrated a pattern of living with *integrity*, a habit which can only improve your life over time.
- Second, you've appealed to the *right audience*. In life, certain people will never appreciate you. Others will. It's a matter of wavelength. A fashionista who wears only chic black clothing can't be expected to swoon over your well-worn blue jeans, however comfortably they fit.

But do you still worry about what "they" might think of you? If you've given people a chance to know you and they've declined, that doesn't mean *you're* not worth knowing. Despite your previous high opinion of them, *they* could be the ones not worth knowing.

As for people who sniff around you like dogs, then bark off in some other direction, what's their problem? Maybe they'll come back. But why let someone who acts like a dog leave *you* wearing a leash?

No matter how fabulous their reputations, strangers are mere fantasies in your life, unreal until you get to know them. By their behavior towards you, they reveal who they are. No matter how popular a man may be, if he treats you badly then he has modified his reputation with you, right? Right!

As for a friend who has always been difficult, stop expecting her to change. You're in the relationship for something, so either get it or give it, and then spend as much time as possible elsewhere. If you're wise, the only popularity that counts is your standing among the people you respect.

Sure, you're in the business of co-creating your reality. So it's frustrating when every conversation isn't lovely. But sometimes the highest perfection for a relationship happens only after you drop it.

Having a gut instinct to flee the room — what's that supposed to be, chicken liver? Your inner "No" can be part of a magnificent spiritual invitation for everyone concerned. God isn't afraid to leave people alone. How about you?

161. Spiritual Success

To clarify career choices, it can help to distinguish your *human* work from your *spiritual* work. Your spiritual career need not be how you earn your living.

Spiritually-oriented people often gravitate to jobs where low pay is common, like becoming a holistic healer or spiritual counselor; an actor, musician or writer. Why do it full time? Wait until part-time goes really well. Then quit your day job.

Unfortunately, some advisors are staunch supporters of drama. Supposedly, it's a test of your faith to gamble on your livelihood, forcing your spiritual work to become your main source of financial support. What, you'll write a better novel if you're starving? As if! Some wealthy role models claim that you won't attract (or deserve) fulfillment until you're willing to risk all. Easy for them to say *now*!

Drama certainly has its appeal. And it's true that the Donald Trumps of the business world thrive on winning and losing when stakes are high. But are you that type? Here's one way to tell. *If you are, you won't have to push yourself to gamble. You'll have to push yourself to stop.*

Otherwise, you're in the majority. Being a risk taker is fairly rare. It's a form of neuro-physiological wiring, built right into the soul. Risk takers rate high on the "Sensation Seeking Scale" developed by psychologist Marvin Zuckerman. Unless bungee jumping or gambling turns you on, probably you lack the thrill gene. For you, common sense will serve better than gambling on your success.

Many full-time spiritual workers have made a brave choice that keeps life harder than necessary. Even the business world doesn't necessarily reward the best and the brightest. With spiritual enterprises, monetary success can be even more capricious. So full-timers risk financial problems. Then desperation can put hooks in their work, consciously or not, as they struggle to bring in business.

Alas, some spiritual full-timers don't deserve special status any more than some full-time (but not especially talented) psychologists or teachers or workers in other professions. Sometimes a person craves the ego-boost of saying, "I do [fill-in-the-blank] full-time." Does that make her better than someone who also has a day job?

One of the smartest people I've ever known was asked, "Have you ever considered becoming a college professor?" First he laughed. Then he said, "I'd rather be free to use my brains as I see fit. Besides, I've already given myself tenure."

You, too, have something really valuable to offer the world spiritually. And you've had tenure from birth, though that hasn't stopped you from continuing to develop your gifts. What outward sign of success do *you* need to feel confident?

162. Elections

It doesn't happen only at the polls.
You vote with every choice in daily life:
Your use of time, how late you go to bed,
your work, and the extent you do your best,
your friends, and how close you allow them in.

Elections can remind you of the need
to activate your independent mind.
It's not enough to gossip, guess who'll win
or read official polls as if they're true.
The multitudes — their attitudes — don't count.

Nor are elections time to criticize
the candidates as not perfect enough.
They're what they are, their faults not your excuse.
Hold it as spiritual practice if you must:
Find the most good you can and vote for that.

163. Invisible Coins

Love may make the world go round, but money keeps us from getting dizzy. It's one of the great stabilizing forces of the planet.

Financial survival keeps us going to work and, through that, involves us in society. Have you ever known kids so rich they'll never need to earn a dime? The ones I've met have left me wondering if this isn't one of the hardest ways for a person to grow up.

Needing to produce a paycheck motivates a person to live unselfishly. We're forced to produce tangible results, something good enough to pay for. If ambitious, we'll push ourselves extra hard, giving our best at every level — spirit, soul, emotions, intellect, mind, body and environment.

When you can manifest a dream, bringing results all the way from spirit through to the environment, bingo! Money jingling in your pocket symbolizes success in an unmistakable fashion. You have, for now, won the game.

Yet the game depends partly on luck. Rough karma can come as financial hardship, producing an unmistakable jolt that grabs a soul's full attention. Beset by money problems, a thoughtful person won't only seek immediate cash but will re-evaluate long-term career, personal values, everything that matters, including (like it or not) the people who were supposed to be friends.

It's disheartening when money trouble causes some friends to expose their shallowness. Some friends! But you'll see their pride followed by a fall if you watch them long enough; anyone who believes that affluence equals virtue has a big lesson coming. Maybe that ex-friend's trouble won't come financially, but life has other ways to make a person scream.

And when pain comes, every bit of kindness from others counts for so much. I like to think of it as God's invisible coins. They break the usual rules about money, or even math itself. When you give one you get one. Receive one and you'll want to pay it back. Or you'll pay it forward. Or you'll do both.

No matter how you spend that money, it will bring you interest over time. How it lifts the spirit to see God's money multiply!

About material wealth, it's said, "You can't take it with you." But nobody can prevent you from leaving this lifetime with wealth that can be spent all over the universe, your supply of God's invisible coins.

164. Your First Marriage

Even if you've avoided the wedding altar so far, you're still influenced by memories of a marriage. They were imprinted on your subconscious long before you were born. At the moment of your conception, in consciousness, there was a marriage between your birth parents and you — regardless of their state of wedlock and, even, if you were later adopted.

Since this affects who you are today, you may as well learn about this first marriage and, perhaps, do something about it. First look at photos of your father and mother, if available. If not, no problem; bring attention within and ask to see an image of each parent around the time of conception. You might see a face, encounter an aura or have some other experience. This will be the most complete knowledge of which you're capable, so even if it's subtle, trust it.

- Notice what your father was like, his strengths, his fears. That way of being human is encoded within you, so send yourself just the right kind of compassionate love. While you're at it, how about sending him some love, too?
- Now do the same with your mother. What was she was like then. Send love to her presence deep within you. And can you send her some extra love, too?

Thanks to free will, you're so much more than the influence of either parent. But subconsciously you've carried their marriage pattern all these years. No matter how good, it represents limitation for you now. So ask God to help you release the complete subconscious influence — everything but their unconditional love.

- Use a third snapshot to finish this ceremony of healing. See your parents as a couple, either through a photo or inwardly or both. When conceiving you, how did both parents relate to each other? Energetically, this has influenced you deeply. So imagine how they felt, right down to their hopes and fears. Witness it, bringing God's blessing to everyone involved. Then ask God to remove this imprinting from your body-mind-spirit. Now you'll get to be yourself, just yourself, from this time forward.

Yes, you can set yourself free to find your own joys, your own strengths. Re-parent yourself if you like. Choose spiritual parents who inspire you or ask God to do the job directly. Let these role models influence you, all the way through to your subconscious mind. With a perfect marriage deep within, you'll expect more from this life. And you'll claim it with more confidence and joy.

165. Your Sex Life

Guaranteed, throughout most of human history, you wouldn't be asked this question: "How's your sex life?"

Don't let pop culture shape how you'd answer that question today. Dissatisfaction is common, due to the expectation that "Good" equals "Hot-hot-hot." Yet of all the stages of love, this is only the first. Usually, limerence (i.e., infatuation based on lust) peaks after just six months. Going through a succession of Stage One relationships is an interesting way to sample *life*, but not necessarily a profound way to sample *love*.

But what if you're expected to settle for love without sex? Reading your mate's aura can help you uncover covert activity. Pornography is the Internet's most profitable industry. Infidelity, in one form or another, will show in a person's aura.

Aura reading can also help you answer the practical question, "Am I better off with or without this lover?" To research this, explore your aura, chakra by chakra. Then imagine the two of you together, just as you were the last time you made love. This will shift your aura into what you were like energetically. Read yourself again. You'll learn specific ways that you become a different person while in the relationship. Maybe your sexuality becomes dull but your heart and communication expand, or vice versa.

To make your research more complete, imagine yourself in the future, *half a year* after having split up with your lover. Read yourself again. Then, for a second time, imagine yourself half a year in the future, only this scenario has you two still being together. What happens to your aura now?

For even more daring research, imagine yourself *five years* into the future, once with you still in the relationship, once where you aren't. Supplement each scenario by reading yourself in the way that you trust most.

Don't forget the most important, inspiring question of all. Use deeper perception to investigate *your special excellence as a lover.* Connect with a Divine Being, bring awareness to your own aura (especially at the belly chakra) and research away.

Deeper perception will help you to challenge the myth that love depends on having a certain idealized kind of sex life. You deserve to understand love in your own way.

And as you deeply evaluate your love relationships, you'll make better choices. Whatever strengths you discover within yourself can help you to find fulfillment where it isn't…yet. And if your sex life is great, deeper perception will help you appreciate that more, too.

166. Renegotiate That Contract

Before this incarnation, you signed a Life Contract. It outlined your life up to the age of 21 (or for some people, 28). Until that age, all your major events were scripted, both the good, the bad and the ugly. All major players were scripted, too, from parents to teachers to playmates.

After you turned 21, what changed? Increasingly, free will has shaped your life. Although certain terms of the contract continue to affect you (like your number of life breaths), most of what happens after 21 depends on your choices. Increasingly, you live with the consequences of your actions — which is why, for so many spiritual seekers, life gets better with each passing decade.

Benjamin is an example of someone whose contract was front-loaded with harsh lessons. By the time he reached 30, while doing a spiritual exercise, he learned something surprising. This lifetime had been planned as a short one; frankly, it was mostly a dumping ground for bad karma. There would be just enough time to squeeze it in before his next incarnation, where he'd do more significant things.

Only Benjamin did far better than expected. He did so well, in fact, that during his spiritual exercise he was invited to extend his contract for this life, changing it so that he could include more of that cool "next-lifetime" stuff.

Few of us consciously renegotiate our contracts to that degree while still on earth. Yet many of the small clauses are negotiable. To do this, call on God and say out loud which part you wish to release, then what you'd prefer in its place. For example:

"God, I seem to have set up a Life Contract where, in my love life, I'd always be the giver, without getting much back. If it's okay with You, I request to change that part of my Contract. Starting right now, I prefer to become a magnet for generous people as my friends, and I'm ready to claim a fulfilling love relationship where I can give and receive in perfect balance."

What do you have to lose by asking?

Whether or not you renegotiate your contract, know that having an earth life of any kind is a great privilege. Each human being, without exception, can gain distinctive kinds of learning not available elsewhere. This spiritual learning occurs even if, in human terms, the life seems like a failure.

With someone like you, who works so hard to make your life the best it can be, there's no limit to what you can achieve spiritually. Make something great of this Life Contract and you'll be poised for graduation to something better. Not just in some other life but here on earth…now.

167. Your Job

Really, you have just one job. It doesn't matter who actually hired you and for what, or even if you're officially employed. Sure, monetary salary comes in handy. But regardless of how big or small the paycheck, your job is to stay connected to the Home Office.

At work, you'll show up clearer some days than on others, just like the sky. Your responsibility is to make the attempt, regardless of inner weather.

However you earn your living, remember that God is your real employer. So be sure to check in for spiritual guidance just as you would ask an immediate supervisor. Some of us prefer to work independently; others feel more comfortable checking in often. Do whatever is your preference.

In this job of yours, there may be some problems but no insurmountable obstacles. Ultimately you can't lose. There is always a way to authentically be yourself and do your best.

Whether you work with many others, with just one other person, or alone, it's still a job where you can show up fully every day, doing your best. Granted, this can take great courage, but it's a kind of courage that grows with practice.

Sometimes, you may find yourself doing one of those screaming prayers, where you must have God's help or you'll never get through the day. Soon afterwards things flow wonderfully, easier than easy.

Earning a living in this tough world, who knew it could teach a person so much about tenderness?

168. The Complete 360

Being in a relationship is like running track. Each long-term relationship (including the one you have with God) runs you through the full circle of emotions at least once.

Some tracks take you mostly through positive emotions, with negative ones as small blips, whereas other circles of relationship are built just the opposite. Complicating your sense of the full 360, each relationship doesn't begin at the same starting line. This makes it hard to predict which stretch of track will come next.

It's easy (but spiritually lazy) to peg folks as all good or bad, and the 360 concept can bring a fuller perspective. With a good friend you could start moving through stretches of love and they will predominate for the whole track. With emotions like anger or jealousy, when you go around that part of the circle you will make allowances far beyond those you give other people. Since you started with love, you'll always give your friend the benefit of the doubt. Interesting!

Judging people as "bad" seems inevitable when you start at the messy part of a track or if it's simply a larger proportion of the full circle. Petty annoyances may tempt you to judge every bit of the relationship as bad, since that's how the relationship began, but why oversimplify? Even with someone you despise, if you pay close attention, you may find illuminating short moments of respect or delight. Also interesting!

And even a gorgeous friendship can include speckles of colors that clash. Well, well, well.

By inviting you to remember the full 360, I'm advocating neither masochism nor lack of common sense. When self-preservation requires that you ditch a toxic relationship, do it. The 360 approach is just for relationships that you have committed to already, ones that you're ambivalent about, and how you think about past relationships that ended badly.

Denial could make the negative part of a track seem more tolerable. An alternative coping method is to dump every friend once you run past the first turn. Or wherever the track of relationship ends, you may evaluate it unfairly, based on where you said goodbye. Yet if you're willing to keep a broader perspective about the full 360, a valuable kind of spiritual maturity can develop.

Is each stretch of track pleasing? Not necessarily. But it can be incredibly interesting. And, like any good long-distance runner, you'll find great satisfaction if somehow you can stay the course. Let every bit of the track make you strong and you'll learn this life's lessons right down to your bones.

169. Unlikely Pen Pal

When it comes to pen pals, of course I'm going to recommend something a little different. Most of us are familiar with the kind of "pal" assigned by a school teacher to educate you about the big, wide world. But the kind of Pen Pal I'm suggesting today could actually change your part of it.

Who is this new Pen Pal? It could be that old pain in your back. Or that disappointing job. Maybe your unlikely Pen Pal will be moodiness, an addiction, or some recurring pattern that hurts your relationships.

You see, this new "Pal" is a part of you, a portion that doesn't usually get friendly treatment. It's so much more convenient to DRESS UP a difficulty, DESPISE it or DENY it. Now everyone wants reality to be 3-D, but this is ridiculous! How can you get to DELIGHTFUL, DE-LOVELY and DELICIOUS if part of you is, frankly, half-dead?

It's common to treat chronic problems like outsiders, not pals. You might complain to a friend about "My bad knee" but never speak directly to its face (as it were). How can you open up dialogue with a dysfunctional, distant or despised part of your own self?

Bring out pen and paper, belly up to your word processor or get out a tape recorder, whichever method helps you to communicate with flow; certainly some recording device will be needed for the Pen Pal Technique to work properly. You could think of it this way: "The problem is real, so I am willing to make the process of solving it just as real."

Invite a Divine Being to witness your conversation. Announce out loud that you call upon [whatever is the name of your Pen Pal]. Set an intention for healing. Now you're ready to start.

Warm up with small-talk questions, like "How long have you been part of my life?" and "What would you like me to call you?"

After every question, record an answer. Even if it feels like you're making it up, keep the words flowing. Soon you'll relax enough to trust the process. Then your consciousness will make the shift into expressing what might be called a disowned voice within yourself.

Once the words flow nicely, ask and answer the big questions, like "Why are you here?" and "What will satisfy you?"

Maybe this kind of dialogue doesn't seem lofty. It's not a conversation with God exactly. But making yourself whole by this method will help you to co-create a life than honors the best in your Pen Pal…and the rest of you.

170. First Time Blessing

What if today were your very first day here on earth?

See your body as if it were new. Yes, you have been born in a big way, fully grown, with the size and age exactly perfect for an earth experience. Nice job!

Feel the delight of movement, the peace of repose. Habits of worry or criticism have become irrelevant. Let this be a day of gratitude for your body.

Loveable? Admit it. In its unique way your body is absolutely gorgeous. Would you please check out those eyes?

Even the underwear you put on can become a novelty. In no previous lifetime have you owned garments precisely like these. Don you now this apparel of gaiety. It's enough to make a person sing "Fa la la."

Fastening your clothes with zippers or Velcro, owning adornments like a quartz watch, carrying a calculator in your pocket, how amazing all of this is! In centuries gone past, even royalty couldn't afford treasures like yours.

Your home holds even more mysteries and delights that pamper your body.

And when was the last time you gave thanks for little things like aspirin and modern dentistry?

Everything about your life — people, pets, places — what if you were discovering them today for the first time? Might you feel a love-at-first-sight-ish wonder at all their best qualities?

In everything you do today, let go stale familiarity. What will you receive in return?

That's just part of the mystery. Please accept this day's First Time Blessing.

171. Inside Out

In years gone by, I've dared to make mistakes.
And, risking failure, sometimes I've won big.

Sometimes, with friends, I've dared to play the fool —
been jealous, angry, shown some fearfulness.
And yet I would not change the honesty.

With work, vacations, even choosing clothes
I've shown no flair for glamour. Nonetheless,
I know when I've shown courage, even if
to others it seems I just muddled through.

Despite apparent mediocrity,
with the occasional flash of something more,
inside me, life has been reversed. I'm like
a coat that has two sides. Where's the brown cloth
when, inside out, I shine like a full moon?

Appearance and reality might merge
if I'd consider this outrageous thought:
What if, along with everyone on earth,
through good times, bad times, all our inside-outs,
we have been one plain thing consistently:
Simply magnificent. Dare we see that?

172. Your Spiritual Mission

When you came to earth, you packed an extra suitcase, you know. Besides being prepared for your human life, you brought what you'd need for your *spiritual mission.*

This mission, or job as a world server, shapes how you walk through life. It shows in your aura from birth, continuing until your very last breath. To a skilled face reader, it shows physically (not necessarily as plain as the nose on your face but deftly hidden in pattern and nuance). When you can read the soul through a walk, a voice or a scent, you'll find it encoded there, too.

Whatever it takes to recognize your spiritual mission, do it. This gift of yours is far too magnificent to ignore.

All you need do is show up in a room and your aura will get busy, moving energy for everyone else in that room according to your specialty.

Yes, it's your destiny to serve the world, regardless of whether or not you give yourself credit.

What valuable thing could you do, simply by showing up as yourself? Perhaps you're a molecular empath, a peacemaker, a destroyer of stupidity, a transformer, a memory holder.

Becoming conscious of your spiritual mission is a delight, for you'll learn about something you've always done successfully (and without effort). To the extent that you can spot the ripple effect, it feels good in an altruistic, soulful and very familiar way.

By analogy, you know how you relax all over when you put on a favorite pair of shoes, the kind that supports your tender tootsies just so. Even more comfortable than that is your spiritual mission.

When you get wise to it, you'll add consciousness to inherent talent. This means you'll perform your spiritual mission better than ever. So ask inside. In God's perfect way, the answer will reach you. And eventually you'll be able to turn around and see its trace in every footprint you have left on this earth.

173. World Server

What a sandwich you're making in the cosmic do-it-yourself delicatessen! Slices of bread on the outside symbolize your *human life*. For the tasty filling, you add a *spiritual mission* to help the world.

Putting this combo together isn't necessarily easy. Some of us assemble the bread first — the human part — but then have trouble choosing the filling. A great longing arises within us for the missing ingredient. We wonder, "Is that all there is?" Everyday life tastes like dry bread until we figure out how to consciously serve the world.

Other sandwich makers begin with the filling — helping others spiritually. Consciously or not, we're perpetually snacking on service. That's because we are natural teachers, healers, empaths, transformers of one kind or another. Being givers brings a good taste to life but doesn't necessarily fill us up.

Besides, life gets sticky with nothing to buffer direct contact with sandwich filling. So we come to feel human kinds of lack. We wonder, "When will life give back to me?" and "Will I ever be successful?"

If questions like these resonate for you, maybe it's time to claim your human life. Find ways to put yourself first. Seek to express your soul, not only your spirit. This will give you the equivalent of daily bread.

Is it selfish to put your human self first? Some of us do have a clause like this in our Agreement with the Universe. But a one-sided Agreement like that can be renegotiated.

Beyond that, your aura may carry an outdated religious vow, even a family curse reaching backwards through generations. Portions of your own soul may have (temporarily) become detached from the rest of you, causing reluctance to enjoy the human part of your life.

All sandwich-making problems can be overcome. Ask God to show you any missing ingredients. If that doesn't produce results, ask God to bring you a human healer. God responds to every heartfelt request. So never be shy about seeking answers.

"How can I balance my spiritual mission and my human life?" Whatever the answer, it is going to be delicious. You are, after all, destined to create a one-of-a-kind sandwich, and it's a hero.

174. Elusive Genius

Everyone has genius. But genius for what? That's the nagging question. Nobody but God is a genius at everything. If only each of us could have real genius for something. What a tantalizing thought! But how could that be true when so few people ever seem to rise above mediocrity?

Alas, we're looking for genius in all the wrong places. The biggest collective myth in America today has us seeking genius in show business. Or we'll assume that genius equates with easy success in the world. Well, consider that genius means "only" this: It prepares you to do something spiritually that nobody else has ever done before, or to do a different version of something that others have tried.

For this very reason, you can't expect genius to win you instant public acclaim. First you must develop your genius, use it, believe in it — even if you don't yet understand it fully. How else can you find the courage to do something that nobody expects?

Here are some ways that you can become a talent scout for your own genius:

- Remember that genius can be spiritual, rather than worldly. Imagine that you're standing before the pearly gates, having your Life Review. Which qualities would be praised? Living that, enlivening that in others, could constitute your genius.
- Which activities, inner and outer, are absolutely your favorites? List them, then figure out what they have in common.
- Use deeper perception. Read your aura, your face or your heart. Set the intention to discover the gifts of your soul.
- Go about your usual business. When the day is done, review your success and give yourself credit for what you've done well.
- Or let the arts help. Poetry is all about finding the special excellence in people, places or situations. So write a poem about yourself. Or exchange poems with a close friend, where each writes about the other. Drawing, photography, music — any art form that the two of you can swap — may be just what you need to set off an Aha! about your own genius.

Even when you've figured out where your genius lies, that won't guarantee fame. You'll have to settle for what genius does: Make life better for someone, somehow. Just as Hollywood contains only so many multi-million-dollar mansions, only so many people can be rich and famous. But all of us can own real estate in God's neighborhood.

175. Five More Clues

Still not convinced that you've found your genius? Don't worry. Originality can be elusive. Try this extra handful of clues.

1. *Effortlessness:* You're always good at your genius topic. Skill comes without struggle. Training may still be necessary but your soul won't sweat. Mozart still had to practice his scales and, like him, you'll benefit from learning solid technique. But with genius, your intelligence matches the requisite knowledge so perfectly, it's like turning the key in a lock.
2. *Timelessness:* When you work at your genius activity, time flows so smoothly, it's like sampling eternity. Afterward, you feel energized. While in the throes of especially strong inspiration, you may even forget to sleep or eat.
3. *Passion:* No question, your genius ignites strong passion, convenient or otherwise. Other people may comment on your vivaciousness, charm or energy (when doing one of your specialties, anyway). With a cosmic "Whoosh" you've been given strength for what you came here to do.
4. *Pain:* Ultimately, your genius brings joy, to yourself and to others. Daring to express that gift may bring up huge pain. Yet genius will motivate you as nothing else can to overcome any obstacles. Looking back, you may even be grateful. Struggles you couldn't avoid will cut beautiful facets into that gem.
5. *Frustration:* Genius makes a person constantly cheerful only in Fantasyland. Here on The Learning Planet, genius often shows as frustration. Do you feel anger or jealousy when others do a particular kind of work…and do it badly…to great applause? Do you keep feeling, "I could do that so much better?" Well, prove it. Frustration can cause you to seem opinionated, critical or pushy. But humor the confidence underneath it. Eventually you'll find effective ways to turn your talent loose on the world.

Never give up on your genius. As you develop even a faint sense of it, give thanks. Instead of demanding more, more, more, use what you've got. Do something related to it every day; surely you can find five minutes.

What if, despite your best efforts, you still can't find your genius? Ask God to show it to you within three days. God will — either through dreams, thoughts, or comments by others. Admittedly, finding your genius may seem impossible, a hopeless mystery. But refuse to give up. Eventually, you'll *consciously* use your genius to bless the world. And that's when you'll find astounding possibilities, mysteries, hope.

176. Jump over It

Have you been to the Hollow lately? For many of us, that landscape is all too familiar. Nothing specific about the place is memorable except for the déjà vu of frustration. Here is where your sweetest dreams fail. You're in the gap between inner hopes and external results.

Right after putting on a clean shirt, you drip food on it. After your long-awaited phone call comes, you lose the connection. On the very day that the scale shows you've lost five pounds, you find yourself snacking at midnight. Have mercy!

And yet you'll go forth tomorrow, trusting life (foolishly or not) and probably you'll tumble into that hideous Hollow all over again.

Dealing with frustration becomes even harder when there's something that you really, really want, like a particular promotion at work. Doing your best is no guarantee that you won't fall into the Hollow. So how can you find the strength to go on? Let this be your motto: Genius at work.

Yes, seriously. Genius includes qualities like these:

- Genius helps you to persevere, or to turn around and then persevere again.
- Genius won't let you accept an outdated "No" for your answer today.
- Genius tells you to jump and to hope, even when the human part of you knows full well that soon you may come crashing down.
- Genius keeps supplying you with strength, with dreams, with learning, with new determination to express your special excellence.

Let life continue to test your genius. If only you'll keep dreaming subjectively, striving objectively, eventually genius will jump you clear across that Hollow.

And what if it turns out later, the journey of your life wasn't about reaching any particular destination? What if the whole point was to develop your jumping muscles? Because you consciously aim to co-create with God, know that (at the very least) God will be there with you, either in the Hollow or way past it.

177. The Fun of Fear

Being scared of things may not sound like great entertainment. Yet fear is one of the specialties of life on earth. It keeps us stuck in a highly entertaining — even educational — illusion. Here's how a recruiter might pitch it to you, persuading you to incarnate:

"Check out The Earth Ride, a spectacular opportunity for spiritual evolution. The whole planet is designed with polarities, some hidden, some not. Your challenge will be to steer your way though them.

"Right from the start, you'll have a uniquely designed vehicle that changes while you travel. Nothing around you will seem secure, with everything around you changing constantly. Yet you'll find something to hold onto, and this will keep you from falling off.

"And did I tell you about the suspense? Although you'll always be an energy presence connected to God, you and everyone involved will forget about that part. It will seem that you travel alone.

"Timing, also, will seem weirdly off. Your vehicle will move really, really slowly. Consequences of every actions will be slow, too. As for the place where you ride, that's so dense, even thinking can be hard sometimes. All this makes you learn as never before."

Now your enthusiastic recruiter reaches for the clincher: "The Earth Ride is such a compelling illusion, it's guaranteed that you'll believe in the physical forms and their labels. To make this happen, earth life uses two amazingly powerful forces, fear and pain. Together, they make this a ride to remember."

Sound like fun? So often people look at fear as an unfortunate surprise, yet it's absolutely necessary for The Earth Ride to work.

In an interview, actress Reese Witherspoon explained why she was desperate to be in a scary movie. She said, "I just love to be scared. For me that's the only time I can really forget I'm watching a movie."

By similar logic, what can you do when you wish to *remember* the truth of a situation? Question fear. As you awaken spiritually, you'll find that our earthly amusement park is set in a playground of Divine love. Secure despite all earth's illusions, you'll recognize who you are, the bold spiritual being who volunteered for one wildly adventurous thrill ride.

178. Half the Battle

If you're smart, you can recognize your friends. You also can recognize your enemies. There's no need to pretty it up. Some people have only their best interests at heart (and not much of a heart at that).

Regardless of friends or foes, what matters most is taking responsibility for your own life. Fortunately, that's in your power every day and every tomorrow.

Co-creating with God is no substitute for making human decisions — the best you can, one small choice at a time. Wise actions will accumulate, shaping your quality of life 20 years ahead.

A less lofty, but thoroughly necessary, way to safeguard your future is to be willing to recognize your enemies. Sometimes the people who strive hardest for goodness blind themselves to its opposite. So consider yourself warned.

Selfishness, cruelty, greed, and so forth are real, if not properly labeled. Noticing that a rotten fish smells won't lose you virtue points. So when you get a clue, don't blame yourself for being "judgmental." No belief system worth believing in says that your gut-level instincts are wrong.

Admittedly, seeing evil everywhere can signal the need for psychological help. And undue fascination with evil is worse than a waste of time. But sometimes you'll encounter enemies clustered as thick as ants around honey.

Back during your outspoken childhood, if someone produced a bad smell, you noticed. You probably said so, too. Keep the clarity, if not the naïve free speech.

Recognize your enemies. It will win you half of life's battles because, at least half the time, once you understand what's happening, you can simply refuse to engage.

179. Vampires

Even experts make mistakes. We'll recognize enemies at work but not in our families, do a great job of screening platonic pals but consistently fall in love with losers, show smarts with money but gullibility with politics.

Any goof is possible. So the interesting question becomes, "How do you deal with it?"

After you've demonstrated a bit of human vulnerability, do you typically feel guilty or do you sugarcoat the truth?

Objectively, a situation could have been defined so that too much was expected of you. Maybe *you* set the unreasonable expectations. Or perhaps you allowed someone else to set them.

Either way, co-creating with God does not demand that you soldier on, suffering fools (or worse) in a valiant attempt to act loving toward everyone. Ouch! A one-way relationship leaks energy worse than a broken bucket drips water.

Struggling to be "a good person"? There's another time waster. Usually you can say "No" to an enemy and "Yes" to a better path that puts you with an entirely different set of people. Sometimes you may have to wait a while for that new path to open up, but open it will.

A dutiful daughter once praised her invalid mother, then told me (with a straight face), "Along with her being very sweet, I *have* noticed that she is a psychic vampire."

Sweet or not, mother or not, a toxic person does not deserve your wide-open love. For someone like this, it's doing plenty if you simply go through the motions. Holding back is smart, actually. You never can give enough anyway. Why try?

Millions of people on this earth right now could make better use of your love and attention. Instead of depleting you, they'll take just a bit of what you have to offer and make good on the investment. Probably, they'll glow right up.

Not-so-great friends can be worth helping, too, even if they don't give off much of a shine. But enemies? They're another matter entirely.

Remember who's who. The next time you're wrestling over how much more to give somebody who exhausts you, check to see if your neck — and your brain — are still working properly.

Let psychic vampires find other victims. You have too many friends to help, friends who are worthy of the name. Don't make a mistake about that.

180. This Glorious Contract

Before birth, it looked easy:
Both sorrows and great joys.
I knew sometimes I'd stumble,
my ears hurt from the noise
of wicked people cheating,
proclaiming victories.
Yet through my soul
God's strength would come
with unrelenting ease.

For years, my human self
has moved through mysteries
of Earth School at its worst and best,
all previous knowledge
of my Contract
thoroughly erased.

Discouraged or confused
or fumbling, feeling lost
there's one part of the Contract
where my unknowing stops.
I can remember, as if back
in full eternity
to move within and breathe;
then I will seek and spin and turn
until the truth finds me.

Sure as free will while I live here
my home is never lost.
Direction, help me find you.
True compass, point me north.

181. Seeing Beyond Eyes

Where does your soul show? Quick, your first thought!

Most people answer, "My soul shows through my eyes" — a correct answer, in its way, but limiting.

Your soul shows in your *life*. And wonderful though your eyes are, how big a percentage of your life is contained within those two little dots?

Granted, soul doesn't show very clearly in most people's lives, not yet. But it could.

What is your *soul*, anyway? It's an individual chunk of God-stuff, more spectacularly distinctive than your mere thumb-print or retina. This is your human identity, complete with very specific likes and dislikes, talents and terrors, all very suitable for this world of polarity.

Don't confuse soul with *spirit*. This is the same individual chunk of God-stuff that heads for Home.

Those moments of exquisite bliss, yearning prayers, breathtaking sunsets...every peak experience that you have cherished has enlivened your spirit.

Though less well known than spirit, your soul is equally important in the overall balance of inner life, and this week you'll have a chance to strengthen your soul expression, day by day.

Today's assignment: During each of your major activities, take a quick moment to ask "Why am I doing this?" or "What's in this for me?"

When your answer comes as *delight* — a direct, full-body experience, not mere "goodness" as proclaimed by your head — in that moment, you are living with soul.

182. Getting to Know You

Don't be shy. Introduce your soul to the rest of you.

Given how complex you are, how will you recognize something as simple as your own soul? Aim for zing.

Zing, the feeling of aliveness, is a full-body enthusiasm. For instance, "soul music" isn't just agreeable to your ears. It sets your feet tapping.

How about "soul food"? Whether yours is fresh hot collard greens, peppery chili or your favorite flavor of ice cream, just the thought can make you salivate, waking up the truth about what tastes good to you.

Your soul is quintessentially human. And should you feel yourself drooling to recognize it (perhaps in a manner reminiscent of the previously-mentioned ice cream), try this:

Allocate 10 minutes today for soul searching. Then plant yourself in front of a full-length mirror. Talk for one minute about one of your planned activities for today. Freeze.

Notice your facial expression and body language. Replay your tone of voice. Then, if you're really bold, hold up the palm of one hand and sniff it.

Now announce something else you could do, whether it seems thrilling or boring. Give one 60-second description after another, always subjecting yourself afterwards to the same test.

Has it become obvious yet? Some activities are merely dutiful. Others actually thrill your soul.

Sometimes you can *adapt* necessary activities, based on what thrills your soul. Even an apparently boring task can contain a nubbin of joy. Waiting in line at the post office, for instance, what if you were to quietly hum your favorite song? Or pop a bit of cardamom into your mouth and chew on its ever-surprising flavor.

What other secret (and socially acceptable) ways could you sneak more soul into your day?

Any activity that thrills your soul will reverberate throughout your body and kindle the light in your eyes. It's like having God call you by name. Only, in this case, you're the one who calls forth your own presence.

183. One Advantage of Wickedness

Guess how many people today live with soul? My research on auras suggests that they are distinctly in the minority, only about 1 in 300. Many of those fortunate few are selfish, shallow, even wicked. Why? Spiritually-oriented people have more qualms about going after what they want.

You see, living with soul means expressing yourself humanly. Spiritual seekers typically prefer transcendence. Both directions, roots and wings, show in particular parts of your aura, spirituality at your third eye chakra and soul at your high heart chakra.

Not yet familiar with the latter? The *high heart chakra* is located at your upper chest, between the throat and heart chakras. This part of your aura reveals the degree to which you live with soul and also impacts your immune system.

Waking up your high heart chakra won't take much time really, only one hour a day of doing what thrills your soul. Do 10 minutes here, 20 there, and it adds up fast. Besides, those thrilling activities can be variations on what you must do anyway, like cooking dinner, exercising or doing a routine shopping trip.

For instance, instead of cooking a dutifully healthy (but tedious) dinner, figure out which cuisine would positively invigorate you. Your "soul food" might be Mexican, Chinese or Greek. Make at least one dish in that style to nourish your high heart.

Why might you, a spiritually-oriented person, not already be living with soul? Your expendable time and energy may go into helping humanity or being a world server or seeking clearer experience of God. Also, you may feel ambivalent about squandering your time on mere human happiness.

Will it help if I promise that this is good for you and your aura? Consider it medicine or, at least, a woo-woo kind of vitamin. A minimum daily requirement of human happiness is needed to wake up your high heart. Far from detracting from your work as a world server, this will help you succeed. Besides, who says that in order to co-create with God you must give up having fun?

Now, wicked folks do tend to have fun. Often they have very active high hearts... accompanied by dingy third eyes. Can this still be attractive? Sure. Picture someone who scowls yet the eyes shine so brightly, they fascinate you. Fortunately, your aura can become charming without coercive hooks.

Help your aura to give the equivalent of a huge and genuine smile. Beam out some contagious joy today.

184. Braincalm

If someone tried to squeeze you into a cage, wouldn't you complain? Well, that someone may be you.

When was the last time you actively considered ways to break out of that comfortable (or not-so-comfortable) routine you've set for yourself? The problem with most people's lifestyles is that we have built them too small, with space enough for survival but not room enough to stretch the soul.

To open up a more generous space, here's what you *don't* need: A thinner body, a different lover, a winning lottery ticket or drama of any kind. A vast, often unexplored, middle way extends between wild-hot fantasizing and tepid realism. Finding that middle way begins when you dare to speculate.

Go and braincalm — that's my advice. Brain*calm*, rather than brain*storm*, because the creative act of imagining can bring you peace. Simply make a list, on paper or by speaking ideas into a recording device. For an excellent reality show, get a friend to camcord you as you improvise. Besides providing entertainment, observing how you free associate could later turn out to be useful.

What belongs on the list of activities that might thrill your soul? Sure, consider a new career. But also ask about doing the same kind of work in a different setting. For instance, with one of my clients, the prospect of continuing to teach high school Latin made her aura droop, yet teaching for a college Classics Department energized her so much, it was like receiving a lightning bolt straight from Zeus.

Hobbies often thrill the soul more than official careers. Eventually they can earn big bucks. Ever hear of Ford automobiles or Apple computers? Some of the world's most successful companies began purely as fun. Besides, a career that never earns you a nickel in profits could still turn your aura into pure gold.

Ultimately, all you'll need from your braincalming list is another, smaller, list of what actively thrills your soul. From this, you'll choose one hour of activities each day. Yes, one hour a day is all you need for a lifestyle that turns your aura positively glorious.

185. A Pet, Not a Pest

So, you've decided to adapt your daily routine in ways that thrill your soul. I hope this doesn't seem like one more chore, or even a diversion from the loftier-seeming goal of co-creating with God.

Your human self cries out to be honored. Does doing this require that you cram even more into your super-stuffed hours? Ridiculous! Probably all that's needed is a slight adjustment to what you're already doing.

For example, how might you tweak *exercise*? Let's say that every day you spend 30 minutes riding an exercise bike while you watch the evening news. Why choose that show? Probably, you're being dutiful. Responsible people must do such things and, by gum, that means you!

But maybe there's a different TV show that would make you laugh, which is what your soul really craves. Perhaps you could read an interesting book while you pedal. Or maybe your soul would applaud more if you spun your wheels outdoors and, literally, got somewhere.

How big an inconvenience need it be to indulge your soul? Not much! Once you figure out where the thrill is, you may have to reshuffle a few activities but that's no more than the amount of trouble you'd take for a new puppy. And think of the love you'll receive in return — *love of your own life*. This, in turn, gives you a stronger basis for co-creating with God.

How can you know for sure what would really thrill your soul? The surest method I know is the "Thrill Your Soul" technique.

- To start, do a preliminary reading of your aura, chakra by chakra.
- Then make a list of choices, the more specific the better, not simply "Art" but "Painting with water colors," "Painting with acrylics," "Drawing with pastels."
- Research each choice by saying it out loud three times, e.g., "Drawing with pastels, drawing with pastels, drawing with pastels." In this context, your aura will morph into what it is like when you're making that choice.
- Then read your chakras again; especially be sure to read your high heart chakra.

Can you tell if your aura likes a particular choice? Hey, can you tell if a dog's wagging its tail?

If you owned a dog, you'd show it some affection. And you'd walk it daily. Why not indulge your own soul at least that much?

186. Better than Santa

"He's making a list, checking it twice, gonna find out who's naughty or nice." Ever hear that Christmas song about Santa Claus? Well, you can do one better. You can make a list about your soul's desires. Checking it once or twice, afterwards, will tell you which parts of you are alive, which are numb.

Why make a list like this about yourself? Meaning well, we can define goodness so strictly that we omit the joy part. For many of us, the price of responsibility is ignoring our deeper desires. Sound familiar? Then be reckless. List *anything* that might make you happy. Your catalog of joys will be longer, and probably way more interesting, than a simple Santa-worthy shopping list.

It's best to make your list excessively...unrepentantly...exuberantly large. Afterwards, you can always narrow it down (a process that won't work in reverse).

On previous days, I've given you some different techniques for exploring the consequences of life choices. Here is one final method that's super-deluxe. To "check your list twice," *fantasize* about each possibility.

You know, there's a direct relationship between the juiciness of an idea and its corresponding daydream. Sometimes you can't tell how great an idea is until several minutes into its corresponding daydream. Certain ideas will bounce around your brain like pure pleasure, while even at the fantasy level, some concepts morph into chores with all the charm of cardboard,

It takes a big combination of soul-thrill activities, pieced together like a crazy quilt, to satisfy your human nature. This complex garment may not have the simple appeal of conventional Santa Claus, costumed in red-and-white, easy to spot as he glides down your chimney punctually in the wee hours of December 25th. Still, you may be better off seeing a coat of many colors, fascinating every day of the year.

187. Praise Dance

Some of us have always worshipped God through dance, even if we haven't been doing it lately. What, you just did a few steps before breakfast? If not, you can start now. Just think, *praise dance* could make this day glorious.

Name it anything. You could call it interpretive dance, trance dance, improvisation, monkeyshines. When you find yourself somewhere incredibly beautiful, even a *place* can set you dancing. But most people find the easiest way to begin is with soul music — whatever that would be for you — whether a pop song, drumming or a sacred chant.

A familiar longing will move through you. Perhaps a particular feeling of joy will make its rhythms known. As you move, that feeling will intensify.

Allow yourself to speak through your body, simply and directly. What could be better than movement for expressing things like:

- I open my heart to You.
- Fill me with Your light, then with always more light.
- Make me strong. See how I offer all that strength back to You, praise upon praise?
- Words way too corny to say out loud will work *just fine* when you dance them.

Maybe you'll dance with friends. Your eyes can be open or closed. Will you need to acknowledge other dancers? Do so only to the degree this feels comfortable.

Group dance proves the truth to the saying "The more the merrier." Fellow dancers can help you to turn up the energy. Yet dancing alone is good, too. So long as God is there, what else matters?

Around the world, people are praise dancing right now, regardless of what they call it. Don't sit this one out. Human applause may not reward you. But for hours or days afterwards, you will feel better. Every movement, even the slightest turn of your head, counts for something: Glorious praise.

188. Swirls of Light

What if you were walking through a desert? Imagine that a dust storm came up and threatened to choke you. Wouldn't you pay attention?

Desert dust is an exotic thing to imagine, but the psychic equivalent is common. For starters, you feel lonely and isolated. A problem worries you, then becomes a truly big deal. Soon the emotion of that problem gets under your skin, stinging and itching. Like grains of sand, the pain can blind you to all in your life that is good.

How fortunate, then, that you always have the power to bring in your own kind of whirlwind. God will be there, standing at the center and wrapping you inside a swirl of light.

Try this out as a spiritual exercise. Stand straight and tall, preferably outdoors. Open your arms wide. Spread out your fingers and push your palms upward, ready to embrace what is good.

Make your own prayer, silent or aloud. You'll know just what to say.

Next, take a deep breath and imagine bright light several feet above your head. Pull it in, spiraling around you all the way to your feet. (Which color is the light? Which direction should the spiral take? Again, you'll instinctively know.)

If you want to be fancy, you could hold a crystal in your hand, circling it to attract an extra-enormous amount of light. Or you could use your voice to make spontaneous sounds, pure tones that help move the energy.

However you co-create your swirls of light, do it three times. You'll draw in light of protection, of peace, of strength.

Afterwards, continue your conversation with God until you feel complete. You'll know how to end this ceremony — whether by feeling the vitality of your body, making an affirmation or simply saying "Thanks."

Had you just escaped from a desert windstorm, you'd walk with a grateful step. Having just received a swirl of sacred light, your step may carry gratitude, too.

That's advanced co-creation for you! It wasn't a reaction to external drama. You took initiative yourself. Well done! And for this occasion, you even created your own weather.

189. Dance

It isn't just a dance.
Your life depends on it.
Your pace, your grace, your stance
express your truth. So speak up!

Set yourself free today
to stretch or spin or bow,
letting your unimpeachable soul
have its say, no matter how.

Dance, especially if it seems scary.
Refusing will bring you worse pain.
So what if it's not the safe thing to do?
Dance anyway. Dance yourself sane.

In each form where you've been embodied,
deer or monkey; hedge, willow or pine,
your soul learned how to reach
then bow down.
So remember it, shake it up, follow or lead with it.

However brief, that transcend-dance
makes your body forever a shrine.

190. The Lotus of Your Heart

In the lotus of your heart, God lives eternally. For thousands of years, spiritual seekers from the East have contemplated this image. As a modern person, however, you may seldom see water lilies unfurl at the surface of a tranquil pond. Like me, you may relate better to an analogy about seeking God through an artichoke. After all, seeing isn't always believing, but eating almost always means digesting.

So, if you've ever eaten an artichoke, bring one to mind as a spiritual symbol. An edible flower, as much as it is a vegetable, artichokes demand to be eaten in a unique manner. You must pull off one petal after another, turning each one upside down, then scraping off each bite.

Is that a great analogy or what? To seek God, peel away. All your customary myths and meanings will be put aside, perhaps even turned upside down. Even taking a bite of food stops being normal. You must go for the truth as you find it, one piece at a time, exploring in the way that the experience demands.

Nor does the artichoke's symbolism stop here. Outer petals taste downright bitter compared to the deeper ones. Well, hasn't that been your experience on the spiritual path? Your first explorations may not have seemed especially sweet. With regular practice, though, you develop a taste for the mystery food.

And as you draw closer to the artichoke's *central* mystery, the petals grow so refined that they turn nearly transparent. You could liken this to the rewards of deeper perception, where each person tells a unique story, one you couldn't have anticipated. The elusive presence of God, rather than your personal imprint, has become your teacher now, drawing you forward one person or experience at a time.

As enjoyment grows, so does your longing. Delving into the mystical beauty of creation, petal upon petal, the growing sweetness delights you. Yet your craving intensifies. Despite all the wonders along the way, you want that core delicacy, the artichoke's heart.

What must you do now? Pull out each petal. Scrape away every single thistle. No longer will you dawdle over each leaf, the way you examined your first, coarse petals. Priorities shift with experience. Your excitement grows as you rip away edible and inedible parts alike.

Empty out every shred of what you've known so far. Only then can you reach the prize.

Forever dwelling in the lotus of your heart, at the center of this world, grows the concentrated presence of God. Go taste it.

191. Soma

To fully develop deeper perception, your body will have to produce something that you may not have heard of yet, *soma*.

It's a cluster of chemicals, like vitamins, only way more subtle. Soma refines the human digestive system. Modern science may not have focused on it yet, but 10,000 years ago, Indian sages were onto it. They recorded knowledge of soma through the oral wisdom tradition known as *Sama Veda*.

Here's the practical part. In English. When your mind-body-spirit system is ready for a more refined experience of consciousness, you produce soma automatically. One clue is a sweet taste in your mouth.

Another clue is having food taste really, really delicious. You're the best one to know which foods would make soma for you. Although I'm in no position to investigate this scientifically, I do have a hunch that natural foods will work better than those whose lip-smacking qualities depend upon additives like MSG. And I have identified one food that's especially great for soma production. Can you guess?

Not chocolate, Silly. It's the sacred lotus globe. Probably you'll find it in your supermarket under a different name, artichoke.

Well, artichokes must not have been available to the Vedic seers, because they never explained that eating them can give you a preview of soma. Today's food scientists (the same ones who don't yet investigate soma) are at least wise to artichokes. It's an established fact that this particular vegetable contains an enzyme that sweetens whatever you eat afterward. So in the spirit of East-meets-West soma research, try this experiment. When the season is right, start your dinner with a first course of freshly cooked artichokes.

When your body produces *soma* naturally, even a glass of water will taste extraordinarily good. And one of these days, you'll produce soma regularly. Then your increasingly refined digestive system will further refine your consciousness. Effortlessly, perception grows deeper, so you'll excel at your choice of art, music, dance, any techniques for deeper perception.

Soma wakes up your senses to the reality within surface reality. As if that alone weren't all the fun a person could desire, consider this:

Physiologically, soma can help you to experience God more gloriously. Beyond the white light of basic God awareness, you can enter a golden vibration where you commune with Divine Beings directly, clearly, effectively.

Let's toast your glorious future with a fine glass of water and, perhaps, an artichoke leaf. Cheers!

192. A Cosmic Concert

Certain kinds of music can revive body memory of a past life. Did you once dance with your tribe around campfires? Maybe you sang for royalty or were initiated into sacred temple dance. In countless previous embodiments, you have danced or sung or played instruments. Deep down, you never forget.

Knowledge of these past incarnations can flow when you recall the performer you've been. So let music connect you with strengths from your past.

Whenever you hear a song, guess the time and place where that music originated. Then pretend that you're living there. Imagine your costume, perhaps, or the place where the dancing was done. Dance, if you can. Really let yourself go.

What is there about those Strauss waltzes, those mountain chants from Peru or the dervish rhythms from Persia? The sound of a drum can remind you of times long ago in Africa, Australia or South America. Does something special happen when you hear sacred music from the East or evangelical songs from decades ago? Well, that's some of your soul music.

Listening, you may remember a familiar urge. Of course you performed, one way or another. If certain gestures come back to you, trust the process.

Music and dance are memorable for good reason. They bring on ecstasy. Moreover, both soul and spirit are involved, which is rare. Not only does the body move and groove, expressing a very human enjoyment as soul, but simultaneously the spirit expands and transcends. Wow! This is the equivalent of standing in front of a slot machine when it comes up all cherries.

How is this wealth of transcendence stored within you? Carried from one lifetime to the next, encoded in consciousness, these are among your deepest memories. In your body right now, memories of ecstasy go all the way through to your cells. Thus, the practical point. Any time you make contact with strengths from a past life, you can awaken them to use *now*.

And this is no superficial connection. Your body comes along with your mind, heart and spirit.

So enliven some of this ecstasy. List many kinds of music you like. Add sounds you enjoyed as a child. Make it your business to play a bit of each.

Before you turn on that sound system, call on a Divine Being. Set the intention to re-awaken positive cellular memory from any past lives that correspond to the music. Also ask to heal any negative memories stored with the music. Then listen with your full being, wide open to all experience. Whatever miracles that follow, subtle or strong, will be part of God's concert.

193. Face up to Human Truth

If you're like most people, your training in seeing faces stopped by the time you were five. By then you'd been indoctrinated into a set of illusions. *Skin color* supposedly explained race. You learned to rate *attractiveness*, then do a quick scan of *facial expression.* Put all three items together and you could peg a "good" person versus a "bad" one. Mission accomplished.

Yet race doesn't necessarily show in skin color, not with the accelerating pace of inter-marriage. Equally out-dated is the expectation that certain features spell ethnicity. An arched nose could be Italian, Jewish, Black, Navajo or Vietnamese. When you look with the intent to find an *individual*, stereotypes dissolve. Then you can pose a far more interesting question: What does an arched nose *mean*? In thousands of face readings, I've confirmed that an outward curve at the nose corresponds to a talent for creative work.

As for attractiveness, its all-consuming importance in today's vanity culture is one more illusion. Learning to read faces for character, you'll discover a fascinating paradox. To the extent that features have average proportions, they win beauty points. But to the extent that the features are quirky, they correspond to strong soul-level talent in areas like work, relationships and power.

Fortunately, most of us are mixtures. Among dozens of characteristics, each of which has meaning, some are average and others unusual. Thus, we combine beauty and individualism. When you read a face deeply enough, everyone's a winner.

Most people believe they can read the soul through the eyes. With training, they definitely can. Usually, though, folks just fasten onto one mood. A magnificent, complex soul equated with one transitory emotion? Puhleeze! That's like confusing the clothes on your back with the body beneath.

Another facial myth relates to detective work. Ever hear that you can spot liars by reading expression? Unless you use deeper perception (like reading how faces change over time or aura reading), the odds are only 50-50. Even trained FBI investigators are fooled half the time.

Sure, faces can tell you the truth...just not in 30 seconds. Whether or not you learn a detailed system of face reading, you can find deep truth in a face. Like any other aspect of co-creating with God, first get quiet. Ask to connect with a Divine Being. Set a worthy intention. Be fully present, right where you are, and on that basis ask your questions.

Let sacred knowledge flow to you, tender as the inside of your cheek, and you will honor every human face as perfect.

194. Not Just for Saints

Haloes aren't only for saints, although you might get that impression from sacred art. If you're alive, your halo is perfectly fine…and you can read it in depth and detail.

Auras — that, of course, is the more common name for the celestial light surrounding a physical body. Auras can be read by anyone willing to take a small amount of trouble in exchange for a large amount of wisdom. To read auras properly, must you see them clearly, blazing with color? A few people do, most don't. I don't, for instance. Yet that hasn't stopped me from helping people and myself with the gifts that God gave me.

So if you don't see auras in flaming color, relax. It isn't necessary. Everyone has talent for aura reading. Hardwired into your soul, as basic as your handedness and sexual orientation, certain gifts for deeper perception have been yours since birth. Seeing colors gets all the hype. But, as explained in *Aura Reading Through All Your Senses,* you may have 11 additional gifts, and these are only the most common ones.

Be confident that you do have a full set. These gifts enrich your life at every level, from the most ordinary tasks to your most elegant co-creating with God. So, what the heck are these alleged gifts? Do you feel like the last one to know? Here's one way to investigate:

Wherever you go today, consider each person you meet (in person, on TV or radio) as if it were important for you decide right then whether or not to become friends. How much could you learn about each person? What helps you decide?

- For you, does friendship begin with emotional radar?
- Maybe it's more a matter of how you physically feel, responding to that person's presence.
- A handshake could give the information you trust most.
- Or could you be listening for qualities of voice?

Unless you choose friends purely based on how they look, don't think the only gift that counts is clairvoyance. You don't need clairvoyance to be a really good aura reader, not any more than you must live like a saint in order to have a halo…and have a home in the heart of God.

195. Drama? Optional

My, how folks love drama! In a world of polarity, contrast brings out life's vividness. First you roast yourself in a sauna. Then you hurl yourself into an icy plunge pool…curiously refreshing.

Yet much of life's drama is optional. To learn a life lesson, must a person always go through a big test? Often we can substitute thoughtful living:

When there's a problem, invite God to help you co-create a solution. Even when you're feeling surly, you still can ask for Divine help. The help you receive, without struggle, may be amazing.

Natural cycles within life, if only observed, can move us forward harmoniously. One delicate moment is all an experienced bird needs to take up a shifting wind, hover within it and find a new direction. That kind of gentle dimension may open wider for you today. And maybe this story will help:

A college friend of mine, Maggie, attended a huge concert given by the 60's folk singer Donovan, when he was at the height of his fame. Maggie noticed that he kept one stick of incense burning near him. Strumming his guitar, Donovan thrilled the crowd, and Maggie was grooving along with everyone else.

Suddenly, in the midst of a song, the incense tipped over, scattering ashes. Donovan stopped immediately, startling the audience. "Must pay attention," he mumbled, to Maggie's astonishment. Then the singer got up, rebalanced the incense and resumed his singing. Rather than breaking the spell of his performance, he'd intensified it. What a lesson in flow!

We can always choose to flow along with God. That's why, so often, painful drama is optional. When seeking a solution to problems, stay alert. Often you can catch answers early, not by nipping a problem in the bud so much as by smelling a flower's perfume. Could much of the drama in your life be a bad habit?

After you pray for help, don't overlook the gentle response.

196. Thunder

"Why do you dislike dogs so?"

That was a question I hadn't thought about in years. With my friends Victoria and Ed Fatula, I had been discussing why all of us preferred cats to dogs. But I was no mere cat lover. I was a dog loather, and had been since childhood.

As I explained, it started with the first dog in my life. He belonged to Kathy, my friend from second grade who lived two floors down in my apartment building. Whenever I'd visit, her enormous German shepherd, Thunder, would jump on me, chasing me into the corner. I'd face the wall, cringing, while he'd bark like crazy, striking me with his forepaws.

Eventually, Kathy's mother would call him off. Although Thunder never bit me, the terror remained. And some rubbed off whenever I so much as saw another dog. "Poor Thunder," I said, concluding my story. "And poor Kathy, too. Her mother was crippled. I suspected her dad was an alcoholic. What a miserable family it was."

Ed asked, "Did it ever occur to you that Thunder *liked* you?"

I gasped. He continued, "Especially in a household like that, with so much pain, maybe he liked your energy."

What a way to re-evaluate a childhood memory! Love? Never once had I considered this as a possibility.

Obviously, a contributing factor is that, as a seven-year-old, I knew nothing about dogs and how they show affection. That is hardly the limit of my ignorance. Here on The Learning Planet, I'm still learning more every day about the simplest aspects of being here (not only how to co-create with God).

And now, thanks to Ed, I'm delighted to have found a new clue to help me understand dogs and, maybe, more than that, too.

We've all heard that, supposedly, perfect love casts out all fear. Well, this new version of the Thunder story reminded me of something important. Love that casts out fear need not be perfect — not yours and not the other person's, either.

As with Thunder's fondness for me, his rowdy (and misinterpreted) love may not have been perfect at all. Yet it still counts as a possibility worth considering.

To find blessings beneath the surface of life, we must be willing to question. Next time, I'll remember to ask and maybe you will, too. Sure the fear was real, but could love also have been there all along?

197. The Secret Art of Walking

Walking could give us a hint, though usually we don't get it. We think walking is about moving forward, right? But really it's the most perfect symbol of evolution, where obvious progress is only half of what happens.

How is walking done? First answer: You move one foot forward, then the other.

Well, what about the part in between? After each forward march, you must stop. Walking smoothly requires an alternation of act and react. The hidden *let go* part matters at least as much as the forward motion.

Unless you're prepared to rest, how can you stay in balance? Until you stop insisting on forward movement, you'll never really progress. In fact, you'll fall over.

To feel that hidden balancing, stand up and take a few thoughtful steps. The yang aspect has always been so obvious. Sure, you must move your best foot forward. But before you take your next step, the yang must turn into yin. Instead of striding, your *walking* foot will become a *balancing* foot.

Will you catch that moment of grace?

Whether you walk, run or dance, it's the same sort of two-step. All life on earth is written in binary code. Act, then rest.

Life is filled with variations on this theme. That good night's sleep sets you up for a day of activity. A love relationship has tides that flow in and out. Even though your career moves forward, sometimes it seems to be stalled.

Love where you are. Find your balance. Then circumstances can shift to help you move forward.

In spiritual life, certainly, each of us dances a two-step. No matter how exalted you feel, grounding will follow. "Rah Rah" times, where you feel wonderfully connected with God will alternate with "Blah Blah" times when you couldn't care less.

Sometimes we confuse this necessary phase with "losing faith." But just as surely as the sun's time will follows the moon's, your faith will return.

Spiritually, cycles in your life don't just repeat. They signify progress. Know that whether you leap or you pause, whether you balance gracefully or fall down for a while, you are dancing into God's arms.

198. When Wicked Men Appear to Win

When wicked men appear to win,
let them have their day.
They cannot win your soul
nor will they keep their victory.

Unfathomable is this world.
Events are being shaped
in ways you need not understand
to (some day) celebrate.

Although it stings to see the smiles
on people you despise,
when you pray for the good of all
your sorrows will downsize.

So fight injustice where you can
with quiet certainty.
Let fools enjoy brief triumph.
You'll have lasting clarity.

Eventually Pride trips and falls
into his well-earned place.
Trust that each story's going to end
with an enduring grace.

199. How Many Chairs?

Of all spiritual truths, *self-authority* may be the hardest to learn. It means valuing your own truth.

Authority figures are so much easier to depend on: Your parents, a favorite teacher, a guru, the rich or famous or beautiful.

Yet, once you're an adult, nobody on God's great earth knows better than you do about what is true. Even the most enlightened person isn't superior regarding truth-recognition abilities. In every relationship, every situation, at any moment when you desire to know what is true for yourself, you can.

How will you find out? The inner language depends on your individual set of senses for deeper perception. Maybe you'll find a resonance, a light, a sensation in your body that informs you when all is well. Plain old fresh air may be your cosmic symbolism. Who can tell? You.

And whatever is your favorite way to recognize truth today, it may be different tomorrow.

The one thing you can count on is this. Inner truth is not outwardly obvious. When teaching aura reading, I often demonstrate it this way. Lightly resting my hands on the back of a chair, I stand before the group. Softly I say, "Don't expect inner truth to be flashy. We go wrong when we expect it to be like this."

Then I pick up the poor chair and smash it onto the floor, hard as I can. The clattering sound does create a delightful, obvious kind of drama. In fact, I'm proud to say that over the course of my career I've broken a chair or two.

As for you, smart reader, how many chairs do you need to break? I bet you can get the idea that spiritual truth is *inner* without having to wreck a single piece of furniture. And even if you did, for a lifetime of self-authority, that would be money well spent.

200. Graduate from Cults

Being enslaved by a cult is like having bad breath. Often the sufferer is the last one to know. But once the problem has been overcome, everyone around can breathe a good-smelling sigh of relief. Here are questions to ask about any group, whether it's a chartered organization or just a loosely-gathered bunch of friends:

- Within this group, will you be respected as an equal? Question any "all-wise" superiors.
- Must you uphold any credo? In a healthy group, you can disagree with some or all of the group's beliefs yet remain a member in good standing. You don't need to sneak around just to belong.
- Does loyalty to this group demand intolerance of others? Are outsiders considered losers? It's a good sign when members and non-members alike are respected.
- Will you be accepted as you are? Or, to be considered worthy, must you change? Cults hook members with secret guilt that they're not as perfect as they should be.
- Are others in the group interested in you as an individual? Or are you accepted only to the degree that you blend in? You deserve to have your opinions matter.
- Do group members use special words, reflecting their "superior" understanding? In a healthy group, you're not constantly translating speech from outsiders, reinterpreting it to fit into your belief system.
- Is your group a "Movement" that aims to save the world? Will you be satisfied if most outsiders never feel the need to belong? Outside of cults, personal freedom is considered a good thing, not a problem to fix.

In the first rapture of joining a cult, a person feels super-confident, as if finally you have found The Answer. Graduating from cults, that giddy confidence disappears. In its place you gain something gritty, a more adult kind of freedom.

Undeniably, it takes courage to relinquish the support of a cult. Living on your own, you may not always feel so sure that you know all the answers. Your friends won't be a chorus of believers who echo your every word.

Graduated from a cult, you will speak in words that are yours, not jargon from some all-wise authority figure. Yes, you'll have to settle for ordinary human words. But God will hear them just fine. Actually, the worst thing about cult thinking is this: It won't allow a person, really, to be alone with God.

201. Deprogramming

"Not me," you say. "I'm a free spirit. Nobody controls my mind."

Sounds good. But even if you have never been in a cult, some classic deprogramming techniques could still improve your life. Try these.

Ask yourself what you believe about life, about truth, about people, about politics, about God. Is it exactly the same stuff you were told growing up? When you allow your beliefs to change gradually, it means no cult can contain you.

Have a friendly conversation with an outsider, someone who doesn't share your belief system. What, you don't know anyone like that? Maybe it's time to make a new friend.

Whom do you hold as the authority in your life? Do you often preface comments by quoting a source other than yourself? Whether it's the head of your religion or your astrologer, your spouse or your hairdresser, question that authority figure. Only one human being is qualified to know best about your life, and that's someone you never have to pay.

Of course you can be your own authority figure — maybe not omniscient but smart enough. Wherever you go, deep inside you have a truth signal. That gut feeling of right or wrong is a link between your human self and your Higher Power. When that delicate inner link works, who needs to clunk along with a chain gang?

202. Going Spiritual

No matter how deeply you believe in God, it's not enough just to "go spiritual." After asking for Divine help, you'll still need to solve each problem on its own level. Lucky you, the human part of The God Team!

Everything that happens in your life can bring a blessing. Do you believe that? Even so, the game is to figure out where, exactly, that blessing might be. Sometimes, you have to hunt long and hard. And what you dig up may look an awful lot like a turnip.

How will you use it? That's where the treasure hunt becomes interesting.

Co-creation requires that you don't skimp on the human share of problem solving. Let's take the example of a lost job. In theory, that can be seen as a spiritual invitation. You are meant to build greater prosperity. So you ask God to show you how to make this happen.

Still, the answer to your prayer may be blocked until you take the next step, any step. How would you *prefer* to earn your living? Which skills are marketable? Take the best step you can. This will start more inspiration flowing your way.

Once again, merciful God is delivering your good on the installment plan.

When you read auras, you'll find clear evidence that some people mistakenly avoid human responsibility by "going spiritual." Sometimes a man will have a huge third eye, corresponding to great spiritual awareness. Yet his puny root chakra reveals that he doesn't take earth life seriously.

Any chakra will bounce back to its rightful size after old stuff-in-the-way has been cleared. But until that kind of healing is done, the man we're describing will show a spiritual kind of fight-or-flight response. Confronted by problems in everyday life, he'll flee into a state of transcendence. Temporarily, he'll feel better. But who will be left to fix things for him here on earth?

Career success usually demands strength at your lower chakras: Practicality at your root chakra, creativity at your belly chakra, power at your solar plexus. Being a person of faith with a dazzling third eye — sorry but that won't substitute.

Fortunately, everyone can have all the chakras be strong, all the time.

To make that happen, ask for an aura that's clear enough to make you really effective in life. Then let the fun begin.

Co-creating solutions to problems, you are guaranteed to grow...so long as you don't routinely escape by "going spiritual." Bring along your entire human self. When you have solved a major problem, that's who will get to enjoy the results.

203. Full Responsibility

However skillfully you co-create with God, you're still living in a world of cause and effect. Karma is an ancient name for the reaction to every one of your actions. As you sow, so shall you reap, whether you help people or hurt them.

But here's the tricky part. Karma applies to your thoughts and intentions as well as the surface level of behavior. What if you act friendly to someone for an ulterior motive? On the surface there's no problem. But see how you like it when that karma boomerangs back and you feel used.

Sometimes we believe that if we're pure enough, or we only have enough faith, we can rise above all problems. Personally, I think that's asking a bit much of our own anti-gravity boots. Plus it isn't terribly fair to God.

It's one thing for God to allow us to team up as co-creators. That doesn't give us license to rip up God's whole planet and design one more to our liking. Talk about "Give him an inch and he'll take a mile!"

So long as the rain on this planet falls down and not up, consequences will come back to the person who set them off.

Anyway karma is too good to waste…as a teaching tool. If you make a mistake, karma teaches you: "Fix things as fast as you can. Apologize. Make amends." Afterwards, you may as well relax. Thanks to karma, life will inflict the perfect amount of pain needed to balance the equation.

You see the implications, right? Stop with the guilt, already. For each person you hurt, it's enough to apologize once. More apologies won't fend off consequences.

As for somebody else's mistake, that silly person will get karma back, too. So you're freed from needing to become the sole avenger.

Fair as can be, karma gives everybody incentive to keep on learning. Even people who've never heard the word "karma" eventually get the hang of it. Witness sayings like "Fool me once, shame on you. Fool me twice, shame on me." Victimhood, so popular in the media, loses its luster for someone who understands that people create their own karma. Why dawdle at some pity party when you could go forth and create something better?

Thanks to karma, you've already created today's truthfulness, kindness, gratitude and patience. Day after day, for how long now, have you done the best you could? And since you've begun actively co-creating with God, what an upgrade! Today, for instance, you're setting in motion the most extraordinary blessings. No need either to cower with fear or cringe with modesty. Huge goodies, well deserved, are aimed right backacha.

204. Love That Inner Child

Has anyone you know been working for years to heal her wounded Inner Child? The task is probably impossible — just because of how it has been defined.

Intention matters enormously. Once you define any part of yourself as "wounded," an undesirable kind of ownership is set in motion. It's like people who talk about "My arthritis" or "My bad back." If only they considered the consequences, they'd never use such toxic language. And nobody could pay them enough money to even *think* that way again.

Who cares if some highly toxic expressions are commonly used? You do, when you realize what immense impact words have on your subconscious mind. Don't fling them around carelessly any more than you would a sharp knife. That includes how you speak about the Child within.

Since you come of age, that Child has probably lived primarily in your subconscious. Glorious she is, too…full of innocence, creativity and other delightful qualities. Of course, you can nurture this Inner Child, which will bring out her full magnificence. Perhaps, perfect parents have done this already, sparing you the trouble. But how many of us had perfect parents? We signed up for a Learning Planet, remember?

Why didn't God help you get that Inner Child part right in the first place? God could have, being all powerful. Plus God created you as a healthy soul, not a walking wreck. So doesn't it seem a bit weird if God put you through formative years that were difficult?

I'll dare to call this one of life's sweetest mysteries. Along with very individual tasks built into each person's Life Contract, certain themes come up for everyone. Sooner or later, each of us must answer questions like "Who am I?" and "How can I learn to love myself?"

In order to answer these challenging questions, you may eventually meet all your subconscious selves. Hail to your Inner Child, Inner Adult, Inner Teacher, Inner Healer, and all the rest of the gang.

Meet them. Greet them. Wallow in some of them, if you must. Only, please, have perspective. Deep down, your majority vote is healthy, whole and well. That's why, deep down, it feels safe — both consciously and subconsciously — that you can co-create with God.

205. Which Where?

Which place could possibly matter more than here? So often we rush through what's happening, treating it like preparation for the next big thing. Some hypothetical destination seems more appealing, whether for business or pleasure.

Yet HERE is the only place from which a person can fully enjoy life. Theoretical where's can prove disappointing or even non-existent. Besides, if it's true that "God is everywhere," wouldn't that include His or Her being right here, available to keep you company?

When you find yourself rushing off to where — wherever that is — whoa! Come back.

How? You could take a deep breath. Or drink a glass of water. Even eyelashes can help, if they're in good working order. Blink them fast as you can for 10 seconds.

Okay, now that you're back, agree to really be here. It can help to shift from usual awareness to deeper perception. Explore anywhere deeper, provided it's here. Take your pick:

- How do you look? Hoist up a mirror to remind yourself and read your face deeper.
- Explore your emotions. Whatever you feel inside, what's inside that?
- Physically, what's going on with you? Could one simple change help you to relax (and maybe even feel pleasure again)?
- Do you feel bored? Then what obvious thing about your same-old, same-old routine could you change right now, thus improving everything. Come on, you can do it just for now, for here, for once upon this time.
- Focus on someone or something alive that is near you. People, plants, pets, even a photograph can remind you of somebody else's consciousness. It's so different from yours. Make the shift to investigate, then bring awareness back to yourself. Without occasional contrast, even your magnificent self could feel like a prison.

Being here is the basis of spiritual experience. Nor is your HERE as tedious as it might seem. In the very place where you have been all along, you could find yourself inside a hymn, and realize that you know how to sing the words.

206. Suicide

Sometimes the most courageous thing in the world is to just get through today. Manage that and tomorrow will be better, right from the moment you wake up. Every new day brings the possibility of serendipity, one surprise that can change everything. When hope feels like too big a reach, entertain at least the possibility of one bit of help.

What if someone you know has committed suicide? It can feel as though an essential rule of the planet has been broken, like having gravity turned upside down. Statistically, your likelihood of suicide goes up when someone you know has done it. Yet you're no mere statistic, not with your indomitable free will.

Maybe you've been told that suicide means a soul is damned for eternity. I'd question that. Well-trained mediums who contact spirits of the departed know what happens in a way that transcends the shoulds of abstract theory. Consistently these mediums find that death by suicide doesn't keep anyone stuck for eternity.

Still, suicide is hardly an elegant solution to solving problems. Eventually that soul will return to earth and face a similar challenge until it is finally overcome.

What would be the opposite of committing suicide? When challenged by a death wish, or by the suicide of someone you love, here's what you can do:

- Keep your body-mind-spirit in balance. If depression is a problem, don't blame yourself. Experiment with over-the-counter supplements, like St. John's Wort, Sam-E and 5 HTP. If one of these doesn't work, seek professional help. Medication may be needed for only a short time, so why put it off?
- Redouble your intensity of being alive, right where you are. Gratitude is one way to do it. Before going to sleep each night, give thanks for 10 things that went right (a practice that is way more interesting than counting sheep).
- Serving others can lift your outlook. Help at least one person daily.
- And try changing your routine by doing at least one thing differently, or better, every day.

Prayer remains a great first resort, last resort, and middle resort. Prayer will remind you of the one fact that suicide doesn't take into account. Despite appearances at their worst, you are never alone.

207. Life of the Party

Smash it all, trash it all, God.
Anything
that stands between me and Thee,
party it out.

Gentleness would be
my preference, of course
and I'm aiming to co-create
joy, which means what?

Be in my heart, in my lungs, in my tongue,
You as the singer, my life as the song
Me as Your puppy dog, woofing along
and Your queen
and Your king
and the foot of Your throne.

Put my life back together again
when You're done.
After every removal dance
comfort returns.

And then better than ever, more whole than before
let's go out again partying straight through my door.

208. Truth Speech

Which language works best for co-creating with God? Any words will do. Almighty intelligence can understand even the silliest babblings. When speaking to *yourself*, however, you'd be wise to choose words more carefully.

Many of us employ a stiff and formal speech when addressing our loving Creator, limiting ourselves to set phrases that we've been told are correct. Meanwhile, self-talk blabs away unexamined, whether a force for good or ill.

Yet self-talk matters enormously. Your most brilliant efforts at co-creating with God can be sabotaged by how you mutter to yourself when, supposedly, no one important is listening.

Just as every action produces a karmic reaction, sooner or later, each thought and word will come back to you. Self-talk is remembered *subconsciously*. And your subconscious mind is as literal as a young child, accepting as equally valid both self-criticism and praise, light-hearted jokes and sarcasm.

Accumulating into patterns of belief (technically known as "thought forms") self-talk makes your life either better or worse — and, alas, usually worse. While cooking a fine dinner, it's not unusual to produce a pile of kitchen scraps. Imagine if you served them on the same platter as the rest of your meal! That's the equivalent of subconscious self-talk. It has no separate trash can for carrot ends, plastic packaging or discarded giblets.

What you say about yourself today becomes tomorrow's thought forms, an assortment that may not be ideal for seasoning your daily bread. Deep down, do you expect success or failure? Subconsciously, what is your opinion of your intelligence, your talents, your attractiveness? Do you even like yourself?

"Of course, I like myself" you may think, indignantly. Rationally, sure. Yet some of your negative thought forms may be surprisingly hurtful, even hateful.

You can help truth to prevail. Learn the language of affirmations. Then use power words to educate your subconscious mind about who you really are.

The rules of this language are simple, starting with *Rule #1: Each affirmation must contain the word I.* Bashfulness, indirect tact, fear of bragging — none of this is applies to affirmations. Thus, "I like myself" is the kind of language to choose, far superior to abstractions like, "It is each person's right to have high self-esteem."

Which "I-statement" can you invent now for worthier self-talk? Speak it aloud many times today. Simple? Yes, but these words will help to shape the rest of your life. So let each phrase be lavish with praise, the highest truth about yourself. Sooner or later, other people may say those same words back to you.

209. Simply Positive

When we start writing affirmations, it can feel like being invited into a candy store where everything's free. No wonder we can cram way too much into one mouthful, the equivalent of chocolate fudge, licorice, and butterscotch plus a coconut cream. Here's a typical newbie's affirmation:

"Starting right now, whenever I am in a situation where I might feel tempted to look upon myself negatively, I remember that ultimately I am likeable and, therefore, I am deserving of good things happening in my life."

For a lawyer, this might be constitute simple speech, but for the rest of humanity, whoa! Too many words, too fast. Yesterday we discussed *Rule #1* of affirmations: *Each affirmation must contain the word I.* Now let's add *Rule #2*: *Keep it simple, Smartie* (KISS).

For KISS to work best, say your affirmation out loud. Pretend you are talking to your best friend, not some devious Supreme Court Justice of the Known Universe. Repeat the words, simplifying each time, until you arrive at something simple.

What if your statement remains complicated? Turn each delectable chunk into a separate bite. For instance, from the previous 35-word laugh-aff, consider the phrase "Whenever I am in a situation where I might feel tempted to look upon myself negatively." Feel it out, being especially alert to any pain that comes up. Question deeper and you might uncover a sweet little affirmation, cute as a red jelly bean:

"Whenever I meet people, I expect them to like me."

Once you've identified a simple "I" statement, run it by *Rule #3* for affirmations: *Be positive.* Subconscious thinking is literal. So you can't effectively break a bad habit by commanding yourself to "not do." Really, can you picture "Stop smoking"? If the urge comes to smoke, are you going to slap your face (from where, inside your own head?) and scream "No"? What then?

As a former smoker, I know that quitting is hard, yet there are better things to tell yourself than simply "Stop smoking." For instance, you might substitute some extra-deep breaths. As an affirmation, this might become: "Instead of smoking, I satisfy myself by taking deep breaths of fresh, clean air."

Rules like "KISS" and "Be positive" can improve *all* your communication, not just how you talk inside your own head. Need to resolve a conflict with someone else? How about asking God to help you co-create the words you need?

Use power words to express your desires — not for all time but for now. Communicate clearly and directly. Thus, you're more likely to resolve any problem in a way that is simply positive.

210. Beautifully Self-Centered

Every affirmation you design must concern your side of things, even if this seems to contradict the rule about keeping affirmations simple. What if your biggest problem is a horrible boss at work? Your simplest solution might appear to be the affirmation, "That fool I work for drops dead." Sigh. You know that the karmic consequences of such a statement would be nasty — not to mention the possibility that your boss might wish to permanently pink slip *you*.

Well, you still might be tempted to sneak around this problem with a stealth threat like, "That fool I work for turns into a nicer person." Tempting though it might be to involve other people in your grand plan to rule the universe, deep down you know better than to try. Every wish doesn't deserve to become an affirmation, any more than it would constitute a valid prayer.

Yet many people mistake the feel-good quality of a sentiment for the right to inflict it on others. "God, help my neighbor to worship my preferred version of You." Please! What if your neighbor wants exactly the same thing to happen to you? Don't do unto others what you wouldn't wish them to do unto you.

Trying to change other people never works, whether through actions or thoughts, affirmations or prayers. Even God can't change anyone...without permission. So what *does* happen when someone repeatedly tries to fix somebody else? Poison is created on the level of auras, technically known as *psychic coercion*. It can stick to both the sender and the receiver. Every bit of coercion has its distinctive nuances, such as where it will stick onto the receiver's aura. Beyond that, certain patterns are likely:

- The coercion *sender* will become more arrogant. To what degree does she believe that she has succeeded in playing God? To that degree, her relationship with God will become a fantasy; she'll also find it hard to have deep, true perception of the unique individual she has coerced.
- The coercion *receiver* doesn't necessarily hear and obey. But he may develop confusion about what he really needs, wants, feels or believes.

One way to avoid coercion is to use *Rule #4* of affirmation language: *Mind Your Own Business*. Human choice is sacred. If you feel tempted to change someone else, ask why.

Whatever the problem, you need not solve it alone. Sometimes it's just a minute's work to ask God to come in and help.

211. Here and Always

"Everywhere" doesn't work well as a street address, not unless you're looking for God's house. God can afford to be everywhere and always. God doesn't have to pay rent.

When choosing language for affirmations, your language had best take into account your kind of space and time. Sure, the fragment of God within you contains all the omnipresent-and-eternal attributes. Nevertheless, you the co-creator are having a *human* life.

So, when designing an affirmation, use *Rule #5: Affirm in the present tense.* Eternity works fine for God. But the human version — tomorrow — never comes.

Thus, you'll only frustrate yourself by saying, "I will feel centered and balanced, no matter what."

Phrase a request that way and you could be waiting a very long time. Eventually, you might wind up identifying with Sisyphus, the fellow from Greek mythology who was eternally doomed to push a rock up a hill; just as he neared the summit, his rock would come crashing back down.

Why feel like you're pushing one heck of a rock when, with a simple shift of tense, you could toss away problems as if they were pebbles? Choose words with the power of the present, e.g., "I feel centered and balanced, no matter what."

God's infinity within you expresses as "Perfection everywhere now." So don't feel tense about placing your affirmation in the present.

212. Right-Sized

When you design affirmations, downsizing won't be an issue, will it? Downsizing can be a hideous business practice, especially when management insists that (despite the wailing from ex-employees) now the company is perfectly "right-sized."

Dreams for yourself never need be downsized, not with the huge imagination God has given you. Yet you might wonder about the appropriate size for a dream. Just how big can you make an affirmation and still have it succeed?

Spiritual life is like an all-you-can-eat buffet. Only you know when you're just full enough. Deciding to "Say when" is a skill that develops with practice.

Constructing affirmations will test this skill. Use self-awareness to right-size your goals. Will a particular affirmation be a good stretch or an unbelievable lie? At what point does an affirmation cross the line?

For example, what would be your right-sized way to complete this affirmation? "I bring my weight to ___ pounds."

If the number you wrote down is 50 pounds away, that may be too extreme for your own good. Can you really know how you'll feel, even five pounds lighter or heavier? Once there, you might need several months to get comfortable with your new weight.

One goal at a time makes more sense. Only after reaching your first goal can you tell when you're ready to set the second.

So don't put in charge some ruthless Inner Pusher who will risk hurting the rest of you. Each part of your mind-body-spirit system has its own voice and, sooner or later, that voice will demand to be honored.

Another risk with oversized affirmations is that they'll produce no results whatsoever because, subconsciously, they cause conflict. When you ask for the moon, one part of you believes, another part wishes you *could* believe, and one more extremely important part of you hates being lied to.

In short, coaxing yourself is commendable but lying to yourself won't work. So follow affirmation *Rule #6: Big enough, yet believable.*

It takes wisdom to right-size beneficially. But deep down, do you have any idea how much wisdom you have been given? Exactly enough.

213. No Way

Having mastered so many affirmation rules, you've earned the right to break one. So let's reconsider *Affirmation Rule #3: Be positive.*

When an affirmation works properly, it can bring up negativity. What if, for instance, you say this affirmation: "I deserve happiness, today and every day." And say that your first thought is a sarcastic, "No way."

Don't push this down. Use it. Squelching emotions like pain, fear or resentment won't make them disappear. But *release statements* can. They're a special kind of affirmation designed to demolish old subconscious blockage.

To create one, start with your honest negative reaction to any affirmation. Put that inner grumble into words. Then language it as a *release statement* by prefacing it with words like "I release the false idea that" or "I release the fear that."

Immediately follow any release statement with an *antidote affirmation* designed to contradict the negative thought. Sometimes you'll need a string of these antidotes, forming a sequence. Afterwards, start a new cycle by repeating your original affirmation. This healing self-talk can be immensely satisfying, like finding the perfect comeback to an insult. Here's a sample cycle:

- *Affirmation:* "I deserve happiness, today and every day."
- *First reaction:* "No way." Then, after asking yourself, "What's the problem?" you find this belief, "Sure, I'll find happiness — after everyone else gets it first."
- *Release statement:* "I release the false idea that other people always get good things ahead of me."
- *Antidote affirmations:* "The good things I desire are coming to me right now. God takes care of other people, but God always takes care of me, too. I claim what is mine by Divine right."

With affirmations (and, come to think of it, any other conversation in life) sometimes your best choice to say is "No." It can be a superb power word. Just ask any two-year old.

Surely you know some people who work incredibly hard to express only the highest standard of spiritual truth. They will only say "Yes," never anything negative. You have to admire their discipline. But how come they make you so uncomfortable? Maybe you recognize something they don't. Denial is no substitute for a well-placed "No."

214. Entranced by Possibility – Part 1

No hypnotherapy credentials are needed to put yourself in a trance. Haven't you ever spent hours before a TV, with little recollection afterwards about what happened? How about reading so intently that even a small interruption makes you jump? Repetitive exercise can entrance you; so can dancing, a leisurely bath or music. Mindless eating is a common, if unintentional, way to topple into a trance. For some, all it takes is slouching onto a favorite armchair.

Comfortable, yes? But is a trance really an altered state? You don't need a doctor to measure your brain waves, not when the signs are so obvious. You're on vacation from the usual forms of self-control. Physically, you settle down. Mentally, you relax, too. All this means you are extra suggestible, but who cares? Life seems simple and good.

Uh-oh! If you were driving a car, this trance state would be like taking your hands of the steering wheel. It's as though you assume that other people can be trusted to be in control of your life.

Now, some trances really are fine. You could be under the spell of a favorite entertainer. The relaxation of laughing along with a laugh track could make that silly TV show worthwhile. But why not give *yourself* a chance to become the hypnotist?

Yes, instead of being seduced by an advertiser, you can sell yourself any message you choose. The influence of your subconscious mind is enormous. As with affirmations, the goal is to reprogram yourself in a positive way.

When you supplement affirmations with self-hypnosis, wow! You'll add huge power to your efforts.

Today's assignment is to choose a topic. What in your life would you like to change first?

Please, have mercy. Choose one topic at a time. "I am in control of what I eat" is enough for one day. So would be "I spend within my means" or "I graduate from smoking."

Even if your goal is uncomplicated, like "I am an expert juggler," it wouldn't be fair to combine this with "I star in a one-man band" plus "I ride a unicycle."

Easy does it. Someone very capable is about to answer one of your prayers — you.

215. Entranced by Possibility – Part 2

To use self-hypnosis, the hardest part is to commit to one project at a time. Assuming you've done yesterday's assignment, you've accomplished that. So you're ready to move ahead…into your head. Begin by writing the hypnotist's script. Get Big so you can co-create this script with a Divine Being. Then:

- *Brainstorm* a bunch of ideas related to your topic. Include both ideas, ideals and nitty-gritty behaviors. For instance, you can set a scene for the pattern you'd like to change. What will you release, and why? Which new pattern will you insert?
- Draft your script. Find the *main points.* Turn them into a *sequence,* and write it up like a short story. "I do a, b and c. My goals are x, y, and z." Finally, include an instruction to imagine yourself at the final goal. Be sure to *congratulate yourself* in words as well as an image.
- So far so good. You've sketched out your masterpiece. Now pace it. Just like a physical workout, you'll need to start with *a warm-up,* end with *a cool-down.* Hypnosis often uses a counting cliché you've probably heard a zillion times. Well, it's used so often because it works!
- Slowly count up from 1 to 10, adding reassuring words along the way that you're becoming relaxed, very relaxed. To bring yourself out of the trance, announce that you're *coming back* and count down from 10 to 1; remind your cooperative subconscious mind that you're preparing to wake up.

Nearly there, script writer. Hypnosis is powerful, so do a little extra editing. Scrutinize your words for anything that might seem hurtful to your subconscious mind. Language will be extra important when you're suggestible. Fortunately, by now you're fluent in the language of affirmations. Use those same principles here. Your script should be personal, present-tense, positive, specific, non-coercive and simple.

Read your script in a soothing voice. For self-hypnosis, boring is actually good! Thus, when you record your cassette tape or CD, take full advantage of this rare chance to feature your Inner Snoozer.

Once you've finished your recording, use it. Get comfortable in a chair or bed. Listen to your tape a few times a day, starting today, until you arrive at your goal. Sure, you'll have to follow through with your actions, but this is way easier than making a resolution without the benefit of hypnosis. Your subconscious mind has huge power. Now it's activated to help you fulfill your conscious request.

216. Paint Yourself into a Corner

All those hymns of praise you've been collecting,
sacred moments, ways of ease and joy:
you'll know how to use them.

All those names of God you've been collecting,
sounds of ocean, truth depths in a voice,
the freshest smell in daisies, roses' songs,
the light of knowing — all this,
did you know?
You saved it for a reason.

This language no one else on earth can teach you.
It's spoken with the voice straight from your soul.
Half-knowing, probably, you have been learning
how to hear His presence, His footfall.

You have collected more than you acknowledge.
And any day now, everything you hear
will sing that sound, chiming in perfect sequence.
You'll find yourself, then, painted into a corner,
where, even if you wished, there's no retreat.
Beginning now, the paint of sacred lightshow
is clinging to your ears, your heart, your feet.

217. Golden Silence

Why is silence called "Golden"? Here's a clue from your childhood. When your parents had company, did you ever sneak out of bed to eavesdrop? Then you may have noticed the pace of typical conversation, where people were so eager to speak, they barely let each other finish a sentence.

Admittedly, friends can interrupt each other in delightful ways. When they swap around inside each other's sentences, it can seem like telepathy. Still, there is something even lovelier, conversational pauses. They are evidence of listening.

At least, they can be. Silence strongly reflects intention. We've all heard the pompous silences of self-important people. And have you ever been hurt by an angry silence, hurled like a weapon?

Which kind of silence will you choose? By intention, you could allow Divine silence into your speech.

This can relax others as well as yourself, mentally and even physically.

By inviting silence, you invite conscious awareness that God, too, participates in the conversation.

When you remember to pace your speech, you'll find it easier to hear what other people are trying to say. Beyond that, whenever you frame someone else's words with silence, you're paying one of the ultimate compliments.

So sprinkle some extra silence into this day. You'll improve your inner listening. In the echoes of speech and actions, you may hear more than ever before.

When you return to speaking, experiment with this affirmation sequence:

I release all fear of silence.
Silence helps me become more aware as I co-create with God.

218. Other Ideas

When you're anxious to persuade people that you are right, you may miss out on some of life's most powerful learning.

Even ideas you never would agree with can become fascinating samples of otherness. Granted, the person before you is human, like you, but he may think in ways you never would. As you let go your assumptions, guess what? You, the intrepid explorer, will be rewarded with the full impact of another person's ideas.

The logic will prove to be marvelously consistent...and expressed with perfect clarity...through this being's unique mind-body-spirit system.

It takes courage to step outside the box of your thinking, feeling, wanting and believing. When you open to another's individuality, the differences may dazzle you, as though sunlight were reflected on glass, on brass, on wood.

Thus, the profound uniqueness of human beings awaits you, with surprises galore, whenever you are willing to accept them. My initiation into this under-rated form of exploration came at the University of Miami in 1971. After I gave a lecture on meditation, a student approached me shyly. With the air of revealing a deep, dark secret, she said:

"I'm not sure you'll be able to teach me meditation. You see, I'm not like other people. I have thoughts. They're inside my head. They're secret, and nobody else knows what they are."

See, you may have more in common with people, and their secrets, than you might otherwise assume. Even if you never get to be an explorer like seafarer Christopher Columbus or astronaut Sally Ride, you can travel into God's mysterious realms of true otherness, expressed humanly. The following affirmation can bring courage as you explore:

Safe in my truth, I am open to everyone's ideas.

219. Phony Baloney

Only you know what it means to be authentic. Might your desire to impress some-one else cause you to occasionally act like somebody you're not? Without meaning to, you might sometimes bend your truth to fit in with a crowd.

Take a moment now to request a warning *signal* from within. This will keep you from slipping into inauthenticity. Spiritual signals can, and should, be subtle. An Inauthenticity Warning Signal works best as a slight twinge of physical or emotional discomfort.

Take a deep breath with eyes closed and experience what it is like to be you, nothing fancy, just a basic sense of being yourself. Think the name of a Divine Being. Then set this intention. "I choose to receive a simple, non-painful warning signal about inauthenticity."

Close your eyes and take a few deep breaths. Your attention will effortlessly go to that signal, which could be a faint sensation in your lips, a particular emotion in your gut or a slight twinge in your knee.

What if your first thought is a walloping pain in that knee? Say inside, "Too intense. Change this to a milder version." Then take three breaths. Pay attention again and you will probably feel a faint version. (Otherwise, ask again tomorrow, when you're clearer. Finding a signal should be easy.)

Feel like you're making up your signal? You could be. Or God could be. Either way, it counts as co-creation, so why quibble? What matters is to *use* your signal. From now on, whenever it goes off, relax back into being yourself.

Even when you're not a phony, people may accuse you of it. Being yourself was so automatic. What will be your defense against false accusations? You'll have it when you need it from now on. Such is the power of your Inauthenticity Warning Signal.

Someone who doubts your authenticity may be asking for something that doesn't exist outside his imagination. For instance, he may find fault with your hairstyle for being "too neat" or "too messy," confirming his need to criticize. Or he may be going through a stage where only pain is considered authentic, anything else being despised as inauthentic.

False judgments need not sting. Know you are authentic, all the way down to the creases in back of your knees. A critic may not see that deep, but you can. And if you often find yourself worrying that *other* people are phonies, these affirmations may help:

I know my truth. I respect my truth. I live my truth.

220. Nothing to Prove

"Why can I see my friend's problems so clearly? Solutions seem obvious to me, but when I suggest them, she never listens!"

Hearing this lament from one of my students, I sympathized...especially because there were things that I could have told *her*.

Sure, it's tempting to volunteer answers, as if each human challenge were like a math problem, with the correct answer at the back of the textbook. But this is The Learning Planet, where each of us receives individualized instruction.

So, really, it's perfect that people won't change behavior unless they decide to. The best we can do is invite them. Except for your child under the age of 18, how many times is it appropriate to give each piece of brilliant advice? Just once.

Sigh! If there's anything harder than solving your own problems, it's watching people you care about fumble around, not solving theirs. Typically, this is what happens:

- You notice that your friend has a problem.
- Feeling as astute as a Sherlock Holmes, you figure out a solution.
- Tactful as can be, you share that solution with her.
- It's as though you said nothing.
- Clenching your teeth, you try to avoid judging this idiot.
- Then you attempt to forgive yourself...for having judged her anyway.

This perfectly human "Me fix it" attitude can send a well-intentioned person spiraling from one layer of judgment into another. Here's one way out: The more deeply you feel God's presence, the easier you'll find it to let people be. With God as experience (and not merely theory), trust inevitably develops.

Trust like this permits you, as a responsible person, to avoid coercing others. Having sampled God's perfect timing, you have reason to believe that people you care about can find it, too.

Therefore, the best way to avoid judging others today is to spend some time yourself to be alone with God. Ask to receive the joyful kind of patience that makes free will a delight — your free will and everyone else's. Later in the day, if you have a relapse into judgment, you may wish to remind yourself:

I am a balanced, healing presence.
Because I co-create with God, I have nothing to prove.

221. Delicious Traffic Jam

When traffic slows you down, would you like to jump for joy? More likely, any jumping fantasies relate to un-kinking your body. Yet temporary car imprisonment can become a chance to stretch inwardly.

Here's the Aha! I had one time when stuck in a traffic jam on the Washington Beltway. Moving at five miles per hour, I was grumbling about my ruined schedule when suddenly I realized...driving like this was my Comfort Zone. As a way to get from points A to B, the speed was lousy. Yet, in my heart of hearts, I preferred it.

In the contemplation afforded by highway gridlock, my thoughts turned to risk-taking in general. All physical risks disturbed me, not only fast driving. When playing laser tag with my son, hadn't I achieved a record of sorts, scoring in the minus thousands? Many people avoid extreme sports like bungee jumping; I, however, am leery of any sport more extreme than bowling.

For me, I realized, emotional and spiritual risks were just the opposite. Never had I shied away from a tough conversation or a chance to grow psychologically, always I'd been eager to explore new ways of reaching out to God. In short, throughout my whole life I'd been a wimp on the outer but a huge risk taker on the inner.

Then came the best part of my Aha! Maybe, just maybe, some folks could be as timid about inner risks as I was about the outer ones. What, have more compassion for them, my polar opposites? Automatically, I thought of my mother. When young, she was a fabulous athlete. In adulthood, she baffled me by avoiding even the tiniest baby step in the direction of personal growth. I would think, "How could she be like this?" Now I had to laugh at myself.

The Aha! hit me like a ton of bricks... being lifted from the back of my head. Yes, new compassion was born right there on the highway. In its way, this breakthrough was as dramatic as those stories in a newspaper where stalled traffic forces a mother-in-labor to deliver her baby right in the car. Except this birthing was inner, not outer. Given what I'd just realized about my preference for inner versus outer, how perfect was that?

Maybe a traffic jam will never "drive" you to lack of distraction. But everyone suffers times of inconvenient waiting, like a sick day, getting laid off from work or being stood up for a date. Next time you find yourself in a jam, I hope that you find, in your own way, a delicious aftertaste. May it be sweet and free for the taking. Prepare to receive it with these words:

No circumstance can keep my good from me.
I move forward in life at the perfect speed to claim my good.

222. Terrorism

You can't shake it off, really, the presence of God. We forget this, playing the game of life on earth. Angels never forget their connection to God. But angels don't evolve spiritually as we do, either.

Being human is not the same thing as being abandoned by God. It just feels that way, sometimes. To get the most out of The Learning Planet, you incarnated into a whole sequence of illusions:

- Separation from God.
- Separation from other people.
- Separation from animals.
- Even parts of your own body-mind-spirit system may be forgotten or denied.
- Over time, feeling immensely proud of yourself, you'll put the pieces back together. Separation ends.
- Only, watch out. Without warning that puzzle will, most likely, be broken apart all over again. There you'll go, finding a whole new set of pieces. Specifics will vary but, by the time you solve that new puzzle, you'll find it was very much like the last one, with similar themes of separation and oneness.

Why agree to put together these elaborate puzzles? Think about it. Which has taught you more about God, always feeling your connection or re-inventing it? Although the bond is always there, most of us are forced to strengthen it.

Terrorism, the great collective fear of this new millennium, makes separation seem worse than ever. At any moment, regardless of where you are, suddenly, you could be dead! This has always been true, of course. Tell me about any lifetime on earth, any place or time of incarnation, where in the end you went scampering away with your full set of human body parts intact.

Terrorism threatens to ruin the game, taking away much of the fun. But actually the game itself isn't being ruined at all. Terrorism can even speed up evolution. In moments of terror, even an atheist will cry out for God. To the degree that you feel threatened, you'll reach within deeper than before to find a sacred connection you can trust. Whatever happens, remember that you can co-create with God. Even if you forget temporarily, you two are still gorgeously glued together. These affirmations can remind you:

I am always with God. God is always with me.
There is no place where I could be and God is not.

223. Foreign (Yet Familiar) Language

Study any foreign languages lately? Unless you're as bright as a baby, it's tough. At first, you don't understand a thing. Besides, you sound weird. A perfectly competent person can feel tongue tied and discouraged.

With persistence, your efforts pay off. Eventually you can pronounce the strange sounds; you can even boss other people around in a new way, or say whatever else you like. But the best part of learning that language may be what it does to *you*.

Learning to speak a new language helps a person to think differently. Neurological pathways open, helping to keep your brain flexible.

Well, what if you were to study God's language? Imagine how much bigger you would think if you could escape at will from the Tower of Babel that is human discourse. God is fluent in your language. You already know that. What a far more interesting project it could be for you to speak Hers.

Deeper perception can help you to access some of that language. Aura reading, for instance, brings nonverbal information that goes way beyond your usual categories. Empaths can use techniques designed to enhance their natural gifts. Even questioning how soul expresses in someone's physical face — that can get you there. Whatever your favorite method, deeper perception will open up experiences that transcend surface expectations and words.

However you prefer to explore who a person is, deeper down, do it! As a side effect, you'll be tutored in God's language.

God speaks so eloquently through non-physical energy. As you become familiar with this vibrational speech, you'll open your heart to something very special about it. Notice a form of punctuation that can bring you ecstasy in any language, God's silence. Every time you hear it, you will be transformed.

God's speech could be the most rewarding foreign language you ever study. Try the immersion method, just 10 minutes a day. Use any technique you like for deeper perception. Soon extraneous mind chatter will peel away. You'll start speaking That language....

I don't promise you'll know everything about it any time soon. Like me, you can keep learning more every day of your life. But a person could do worse than to be schooled by delight. These statements can lead you to your next teachable moment:

I open myself completely to God's language.
It is safe for me to fully use my gifts for deeper perception.

224. Silent Day

How does one take a day of silence? It's easy. Don't talk. Commune with inner silence instead.

Did you know how many flavors silence can have, depending on your state of consciousness?

Did you know how powerfully silence can shape you, change you, take your connection with God to a whole new level?

Let experience move you to new depths beyond words. Going about your usual chores, a day of silence will surprise you. If you make time for some extra contemplation or prayer, silence may awaken you even more.

How about handling family members? Tell them in advance about your day of silence. Then carry a sign; if anyone forgets, you can point to the word "SILENCE" rather than mouthing it.

As for errands and chores, often a friendly nod is all that's required.

Silent day, holy day, where all is calm and all is bright....

Sacred experience can be yours for the asking (silently). And, for the days when you're not in silence, consider affirming this:

I hear how God speaks to me, both in words and in silence.

225. Friendship Song

When first we started to be friends
the melody began:
so faint yet true, unlike all other
friendship songs yet sung.

Fast forward 20 years and I
have learned our song by heart.
The orchestration's fuller now,
our singing grown more sweet.

New friends have come. Each brings our ears
one more distinctive tune,
some growing huge in resonance,
the others good but plain.

Friend, do you think God can hear all
our funny human noise?
I know that it has trained my ears
to listen for His voice.

226. Comfort Zone

How comfortable must you stay today? Before you decide, make sure you know about all three of life's exploration zones.

The Comfort Zone is marked by security. You know what to expect, more or less, and feel a certain confidence in your ability to handle whatever comes your way. Physically, your body relaxes. Even if you must exert yourself, you know you won't have to cope with anything wildly unexpected. Having used this set of coping circuits before, you'll know how to pace yourself now.

Many an argument could be avoided if, before stating opinions, each speaker would move into the Comfort Zone. Despite any challenges of the moment, your body-mind-spirit is a sanctuary where you can relax. Three deep breaths might get you there, or the old-fashioned method of counting to ten. You know how resourceful you feel in your body when in your Comfort Zone, right?

The opposite state is the Panic Zone. Here, too much is demanded of you. If overwhelm had a fragrance, the whole place would stink. Survival is the best you can hope for. But you won't enjoy that very much, not until you can find your way back to the Comfort Zone.

Third and, often, best comes the Learning Zone. Here you encounter just enough challenge to mobilize your strengths. Although you're invited to experiment and evolve, any pressure is gentle. Unlike the Panic Zone, you can think clearly. Unlike the Comfort Zone, you won't risk becoming either complacent or bored.

What will bring you just the right degree of challenge, neither too much nor too little? Certain people can pop you into the Learning Zone, which is good reason to seek out their company. But you could find this Zone even if you lived in solitary confinement. Just set yourself a goal with some challenge to it — neither enough to cause panic nor the same old, same old.

Whatever you're planning today, be it a day of work, a vacation or party, it's good to stay mostly in your Comfort Zone. But leave the door open to travel beyond it. Visit the place that can keep you feeling youthful as long as you live, the Learning Zone.

227. Panic or Victory?

Don't expect Pan, the Greek god, to bring along his pipes. If you must enter the Panic Zone, no official fanfare will necessarily alert you. Even physically, there may be nothing unusual. Unlike terror, everyday anxiety doesn't include bulging eyes, frozen feet or a sweat bath. Panic is both well disguised and commonplace.

"Stress" is our society's more usual term for it. One frustration piles up after another. Time or money, maybe the opinion of someone important — something piles on the pressure until there you are, strapped onto a torture device.

This situation might be worthy of a dungeon if not so exquisitely postmodern. At least if you were hauled off to the old-fashioned, smelly machine with all the screws, an official captor might introduce himself, something like, "My name is Griswold, and I'll be your torturer today."

Today, most likely there will be no proper introduction. Instead you'll be innocently checking your e-mails or trying to buy groceries. One more thing will go wrong. And ouch! You'll tumble into the Panic Zone.

Being spiritually ambitious, you may be tricked into thinking that you're in a high-powered Learning Zone. You might tell yourself, "If only I push myself extra hard, I can score big points with my relationship/my career/my evolution/my God.

Nope. On earth's game board, a player cannot move directly from the Panic Zone to the Learning Zone. (You can't pass GO, either.) According to the rules, before entering the Learning Zone, first you must return to the Comfort Zone. How?

1. Move away from the Panic Zone. Can you physically exit somehow? Otherwise, just change your posture and breathing pattern.
2. Think the name of a Divine Being.
3. Let the dialog of sanity begin. Ask inside, "What am I most afraid of?" Personal attachments push us toward the invisible torture machine. What could you ask God to handle for you? What would be a reasonable goal that you could set for yourself?
4. Choose your next action step.
5. Move back into your Comfort Zone. Let the Divine Being help you.

Eventually, you'll be ready to return to the game, relatively calm, your next action step ready. At your own pace, then move into the Learning Zone.

You can afford to feel confident. Pan will not win. You will.

228. Spiritual Gymnastics

What good is peace during your prayers if, afterwards, it disappears? Unshakeable peace is a worthy goal. If annoying people enter your life, they can give peace a vigorous workout. Which of the following techniques have you already tried?

- As a spiritual practice, you could think, "I see God's love in you," or any other uplifting affirmation. (Just avoid phrasing it coercively, as in "I know God can help you to stop being such an obnoxious idiot.")
- For self-knowledge, you could adapt a technique taught at The Focusing Institute. Ask, "What's most annoying here? Is this person expressing my shadow — something I do too much or something I don't do enough?" Let the answer come through your body, not just your mind.
- Or you could try the contradiction technique from Re-Evaluation Counseling. Figure out what annoys you most, then find a wacky, contradictory version, the wilder the better. For example, when somebody's cell-phone chatter annoys you, you might move away and discharge the vexation by saying, "If I'd known you liked cell-phones so much, hey, I would have given you more of them. Just think what you could do with 14." When your contradiction makes you laugh, it has worked.

Any of these techniques can restore sanity. Yet the desirable skill isn't mere coping, it's balance. This brings us back to a version of that earlier question, "What good is peace during your prayers if, in regular life, it disappears?"

Gymnasts can offer some profound wisdom. They need balance at least as much as you or I do. Whether jumping off parallel bars or rings or finishing some other amazing stunt, how does a gymnast land? You've seen the position, but I'll bet you haven't tried it lately:

Place one leg in back of the other, for balance. Stick out your butt, the farther the better, emphasizing your defiant stability. Next, *assume* triumph: Hold your head high. Finally you're ready to open your heart. Thrust out your arms and your chest. Spread-eagle to such an extent that even your fingers reach out, electric with expectancy.

So, how does that work for you? Maybe it will become your ideal balance stance. Well, maybe not physically. But you may move yourself that way inwardly.

Or find a different symbolic stance that you prefer. Once you find your position of spiritual stability, certain people may still seem really obnoxious…but not necessarily… and, most important, not to you.

229. When Holiday Plans Fall Through

That day at the beach didn't turn out as expected, did it? The rain, the fight — whatever the problem, all your planning has come to naught.

But that was the planning, not you. You're no nothing, so ask God to give you Plan B.

Once I asked a relative how she liked to spend New Year's Eve. "I sit and feel sorry for myself," she said. At least her candor was wise.

A holiday is too good to waste. When circumstances take the oomph out of your plans, go forth to find your oomph elsewhere.

Call on God to help you make new plans. Then, remember the point of that holiday. Was it to start a new year? To celebrate freedom? To give thanks for your abundance? Today might be a religious holiday, one of God's birthdays. Or today could be the less widely known holiday celebrating the birth of you. (Having most people ignorant of such a great occasion is all the more reason for you to party really big!)

Next, reclaim your power. Nothing on earth can break your spirit unless you cooperate. Don't let anyone keep you from celebrating. If you've been disappointed, so what? After the good cry you'll have a new try…so long as you never give up.

Some people have a gift for play. They'll find brilliant entertainment ideas from the newspaper or they'll stay home and turn the place into a play station. I'll never forget the holiday spirit of Jordan, a friend who lived in poverty materially but definitely not spiritually. She invited me over to her home for a royal foot massage, ceremonially done before a cheerily burning fireplace.

Another friend, Angela, owns a mansion so grand, it could be intimidating. Just to bring perspective, she decorated a bathroom bordello-style, presided over by a sculpture of a famous courtesan; suspended above the toilet, Cora Pearl opens her legs wide to all visitors. Now there's a festival!

If you're also one of life's playful spirits, all you need do is remember that you have a talent for holiday making. Decide to use it. Within minutes, you'll figure out a plan for your special day.

But what if festivity doesn't come naturally? Some of us find it a hard slog, planning fun. Even if someone else usually serves as your recreation therapist, occasionally you may be stuck spending a holiday at home, solving some unwelcome problem or tending a sickbed. At least you can pin a dandelion to your lapel.

Do something, little or big, to celebrate the truth about this day. Between your best efforts and God's help, the spirit of holiday will keep faith with you.

230. Grumbles

Uh-oh! Here comes another one.

When an annoying situation comes your way, you may as well bring out the Spiritual Warrior within and embrace your opportunity. Consider substituting the word, "Hooray," As in, "Hooray! Here comes another one."

But this isn't some magnificent challenge. It's stupid.

Good for you. You've just defined the sneaky but smart way lessons are generally taught here on The Learning Planet.

Some lesson! Who says there's anything to be learned from this mess, other than that I'm inadequate or that God hates me?

Earth School is set up for us to identify with our lessons. We learn from real-life actions and consequences. To ace each course, believe that, eventually, you can solve every problem in your life. Because intention is powerful, you will.

If this is a "lesson," it's pitiful. I wouldn't pay to see this as a horror movie. Why can't my life have more glamour to it, more pizzazz, something?

What, you think someone would pay to see what other people go through each day? In real life few of us "meet cute" or have a big budget for special effects. Instead of glamour, we get stuck with slow and dull. Why? My theory: Learning pops in better that way.

Obviously you haven't been to enough movies. A good movie could make anything seem interesting. No way could I make a triumph out of this.

Obviously, you're not paid as much as a first-rate feature film director. Add in the salaries of all the stars, the makeup crew, the lighting experts and scene designers. Movies are made by lots of people, with loads of resources, whereas you are the lone star here. (Plus your angel committee. Plus God.)

Trust me, I've been through this kind of wonderful creative opportunity before. I hate it. Why can't I have something different?

Lessons repeat until you can find a way to learn them. Whether you solve a problem in one moment of co-creating with God or you plod through a month of self-taught human discoveries, here's the good part. What you recall in the long run won't be the problems at all. You'll remember — and be so proud of — your solutions.

231. Shadow Boxing

How well does your *shadow* move along with the rest of you? The physical one works so well you couldn't possibly improve upon it. But how about your more mysterious inner shadow? That may demand some attention.

This darker side of your personality is wonderfully selfish, raw and stubborn. May as well enjoy it! If you don't, or push it too far away, that subconscious shadow can become a monster. It will take over when you are overtired, intoxicated or otherwise not exercising the usual control over behavior. You said what at that party? Uh-oh! The memory of a shadow-dominated performance could make a person writhe with embarrassment.

Is there some area in life where you regularly sabotage yourself? Probably that, too, is caused by your shadow. It's the origin of most negative actions that defy explanation.

With a psychological approach, here is what you'll do. You'll analyze that shadow, get to know it, work hard to cope with it. Phew, such hard work!

For a spiritual approach, invite God to help you to find a way that honors your shadow self and heals its pain. As the difficult truths become conscious, ask God for light and more light — not to remove this much-needed part of yourself but to help you live with it in peace.

Say, for instance, that you keep meaning to clean up your house. You have motive, opportunity, even the perfect weapon (your cleaning supplies). Yet somehow the crime against grime is never done. If anything, things get messier. Either you blame someone else or you get mad at yourself.

Now it's unlikely that God will personally intervene. But you can visit God at your inner sanctuary. Bask in Divine Order. After you bask, ask. Request to gently heal every way that your shadow self is involved in the messiness problem. Maybe inspiration will come right then. If not, open your eyes and do some research. You might call on a Divine Being to keep you company. Set your intention to heal your relationship with your own shadow self. Then lovingly hear its story.

You could dialogue, writing Q&A's back and forth. You could ask your shadow self to write a whole essay, expressing his point of view. You could try something wildly creative, like making a puppet show between the Mournful Neat You and your Happy Inner Wrecker. Or draw a picture of their interaction. Perhaps you'd prefer to dance out their stories, expressing each one, in turn.

What, you'd feel way too ridiculous? Hey, you're alone, just you, your shadow and God. Ridiculous can be good. To be silly without feeling ashamed is high art and, maybe, just what it takes to tame that shadow.

232. Tailgating

Imagine the Wacko Driving Academy where people are taught to tailgate. Teacher explains:

"Sometimes other cars go too darned slow. You've got to teach them a lesson. So creep up behind every car in front of you. Sooner or later, those slowpokes will clear out of your way, and then you can drive like you own the road."

Shucks, even in the Academy, that doesn't make much sense. Nobody but God owns the road. As for the brilliant strategy of tailgating, it doesn't get drivers ahead by much. Sometimes they'll move up by one car length before stopping at the next traffic light. Crashing is a distinct possibility, too, which won't save anyone time unless the tailgater is eager to exit this incarnation.

Driving schools don't teach tailgating, of course. Besides, much of it happens unintentionally. One man coped with his tailgater by slowing down, only to have her bump into him. Both drivers got out of their cars, surveyed the damage, agreed there was none.

Suddenly the tailgater burst into tears. She said, "I didn't mean to hit you. Please forgive me. I didn't even mean to tailgate. When will I pay attention? Until I hit you I had no idea what I was doing."

Tailgating has an equivalent off the road, and often it happens just as unintentionally. We don't mean to creep up on other people's space and boss them around. Sure somebody said "No," but that wasn't serious. Maybe we didn't speak loudly enough. We might as well ask again.

Pushing can become a habit, inflicted on one hapless person after another. No harm is meant. We just know for a fact what we want, whereas other folks seem to be on the wimpy side, moving through life with way too little motivation.

Just as cars on the road need space around them, so do people. Pushing them, even "for their own good" is a kind of spiritual trespass. *The degree of pushiness inside you on any given day remains pretty constant, no matter where you might go.*

How to avoid tailgating in everyday life? A psychological solution might be to re-evaluate personal boundaries. But a spiritual approach can be more fun.

That spiritual space around someone else, akin to the distance between driving cars — check it out with your deeper perception. That's the other person's aura, a delectable treat to appreciate. Usually an aura is filled with intelligence, creativity and other qualities that can fill you with peace. So when you feel the urge to push, stop to notice what you are pushing against. Then awe can become your median strip on life's highway. Wouldn't that make any car trip more fun?

233. That Bling is Such Tired Shtick

"Don't use the word 'bling' outside of the house," urged my teenaged son. "Everyone will laugh at you."

Of course, I had to take his advice. A 14-year old knows better than his mere mother about what's in vogue. Actually, when it comes to slang, just about everyone knows better than me. Mostly I'm stuck in my first teenage acquisitions: "Cool" and "neat" and, pathetic though it may seem, "Okeedokee."

As my son explained ever so patiently, the term "bling" originated as a way to describe jewelry belonging to male rappers, adornments like solid gold chains to go with the gem-studded rings. Since their proud owners wore so many chains at once, the proper term was "bling bling."

Okeedokee.

Afterwards my friend Molly comforted me about my inexpert usage of "bling." Molly lives in New York and is the most sophisticated friend I've ever had. She advised me to share the news from Manhattan circa 2005.

"Bling is everywhere now, in conversation as well as fashion." In fact, Molly concluded, "By next year, people will probably be saying, 'That bling is such tired shtick.'"

So much for fad glories....

But the very idea could make a person fall in love with God for the first time.

Here's someone who has been around how long? Bringing forth one fad after another, and sustaining us between them, ever fresh, ever fun — this is some far out Dude-Being! In your spiritual exercise today, you just might want to make contact with That. Among all other attributes, God has got to be wearing the biggest, shiniest bling.

234. Big Day at Earth School

It was more salt than cinnamon.
The lessons came one after one
until, at last, the day was done.
Such puddle splashing, God,
and (now my feet are dry)
what fun!

235. Portable Faith

What's the biggest difference between real life and your favorite sitcom? Your problems aren't punctually resolved in half an hour. So, in real life, it can help to carry a chunk of faith in your pocket.

What, a *Faith Object*? Sure. This will be a portable reminder of all in your life that is good. Start with any piece of jewelry. Or use a stone small enough to carry in your pocket or purse. Your Faith Object will be kept within touching distance, constantly available as a reminder that God is at work, even if you don't yet know how.

Once you've chosen your object, charge it up. Hold it between your palms. Close your eyes and dip your awareness back Home, into the shining, buzzing presence of God.

Easy to say! When you need a Faith Object most, that presence may not tune in loud and clear. But intent is what counts, so consider this step successful whatever your subjective experience may be. (And, while you're at it, have faith that a season will come when the presence of God sounds as clear as a bell, chiming into your heart on demand.)

Back at your programming ceremony, here comes the fun part. Remember a triumphant moment from your past. Will it be a scene of joy or love, a time when you actively demolished obstacles or simply a lazy moment of pure contentment? Whatever you choose, ask for the best part of that energy to be put into the object you're holding between your hands.

Finally, call on the Divine Being of your choice to be placed in charge of your Faith Object. Ask out loud for help with your specific situation. (Just don't dictate *how* it will work out. That's God's job.)

Now you have it, a freshly minted Faith Object. Any time you feel discouraged, grab it. You won't be disappointed.

Finally, remember that every thought, every hope from your heart, every attempt to co-create — every bit of this is as real to God as your Faith Object is to you.

236. The Promise of Crystals

In your home, right now, do the batteries outnumber the crystals? If so, you might wish to change the ratio. Crystals are small appliances for your spiritual life. They can help to re-charge your *consciousness*, which runs your body-mind-spirit (a more amazing machine than any appliance).

How can a mere rock help your spirit?

Precious and semi-precious stones, alike, move energy into your aura. When used properly, each type of stone can help you in a particular way. Pick up one of the following and notice how it makes you feel:

- *Clear quartz, rose quartz* and *amethyst* help your aura to attract frequencies of intelligence, self-love and spiritual transformation (respectively).
- *Smoky quartz* provides grounding.
- Whether white or pink, gold or green, *calcites* help you to evolve at a higher frequency, even, than quartz crystals.
- *Fluorites* magnify qualities of your intellect.
- *Herkimer diamonds* bring joy.

This is just the start of a very long list. Every kind of stone found in a rock shop can help you with a highly practical specialty, so crystals can be the study of a lifetime. To make the vast subject manageable, pick up one crystal at a time and research it on your own (no guidebook needed beyond your own consciousness).

Here's a super-adaptable research technique. You'll need one precious or semi-precious stone, either mounted in a piece of jewelry or unset, like a crystal point. If neither is available, go outside and choose an ordinary pebble.

Next, prepare your "research facility." Close your eyes, take a few breaths and ask yourself, "What does it feel like, being myself right now?"

Call on a Divine Being to join with you. (Just think the name, remember, and you'll be connected). Then set an intention to gain more wisdom.

Now, look at your stone. Note the color, the structure, the beauty. Hold it up to your heart chakra. Close your eyes. Take a few breaths. Notice again what it is like to be you right now. Be especially receptive to subtle shifts in your consciousness.

Ask inside, "What is this good for?" Any natural object, a leaf, a flower or stone has an answer for you, if only you'll ask. Actually, Mr. or Ms. Co-Creator, this is not a bad question to ask of people, either.

237. Psychometry and Beyond

However knowledgeable you are so far as a crystal explorer, this three-part experiment can move you forward. For equipment, you'll need a *plastic* object, like a scotch tape dispenser; an often-used object made of *metal*, like house keys; and a precious or semi-precious *gemstone,* whether set as jewelry or a plain crystal.

Prepare yourself, the researcher. Close your eyes, take a few breaths and consciously notice what it is like to be *you* right now. Call on a Divine Being to join with you. Set an intention to gain more wisdom.

For Research, Part I, pick up your *plastic* object. Hold it. Close your eyes and ask inside, "What does this tell me?" Take a deep breath. Whatever you experience next is your answer.

Probably the answer is, "Not much." Plastic is amazingly neutral. Even an item you've used for years won't carry many of your vibrations.

Do Part II with your *metal* object. Repeat the sequence of self-awareness, Get Big and set an intention. Hold the object and ask, "What does this tell me?"

Psychometry is the art of reading an object's vibrations, and metal objects store personal information best. So keys to your home can reveal how you felt when living there; a wedding ring tells the story of your marriage, and so forth.

To learn these stories you will need faith, fearlessness, spontaneity and language. Say aloud whatever you get. And phooey on any fear of making a mistake! To build up confidence with psychometry, find a sympathetic friend who would like a short reading. Borrow a metal object belonging to him. Research, then say what you get. Ask for feedback. Chances are, you'll amaze yourself, you're so good.

Psychometry is a ridiculously easy way to learn about a person's present and past. But to move into your future, do Research Part III on your *crystal*. Prepare again, with self-awareness, name of Divine Being and intention. Hold the object and ask, "What does this tell me about my future?"

Wow! Feel your awareness move into a new frequency? It's like when you were a child, perfectly content with the size of your body. Yet everyone said you were going to keep growing.

Right they were. Except they may have omitted this rather important fact: After physical growth stops, the really interesting spiritual kind intensifies. Let crystals remind you. Spiritually, you are becoming far bigger than you may think.

238. Crystal Clear

Gemstones can be worn for their beauty, flaunted as symbols of social status or treasured as symbols of love. Yet most of the jewelry you'll see people wear (no matter how elegant) combines pristine beauty with all the allure of a garbage dump.

The reason involves the spiritual purpose of wearing any gemstone or crystal. Energetically, it's alive, constantly transforming your aura. Sparkles that show on the surface are relatively slow-moving reminders of the stone's energy work.

Diamond or pearl, garnet or amethyst, even a humble quartz crystal, it's a hardworking energy factory. Gems constantly bring extra frequencies into your aura. But few things on earth simply give, give, give without ever needing support. Interacting with its owner, jewelry takes on negative vibes.

These become stored in its aura. Unless cleaned, even the loveliest stone will collect owner by-products.

You, the owner, may be brimming with sweetness and light. But certain conversations are like having someone spill drinks on your carpet. Stains accumulate energetically until, like a well-worn rug, your gem could be in danger of uglying out. Luckily you never need to assess how grimy your special stone has become. Just develop the habit of cleaning it.

This is basic hygiene for gemstones. After you wear one, or carry it, and especially if you use it for healing — by the end of your day CLEAN IT UP.

How? Place your stone on a specially treated Positive Energy Plate (available at www.kupmed.com) or a crystal cluster. Or create a *purifying vessel*, any non-reactive container that you have filled with sea salt or kosher salt. (Salt that you designate for this purpose will work indefinitely.) Bury the item in dry salt for at least 15 minutes. Or give it a sleepover, if you like, and pluck it out in the morning.

Some items are best cleansed in a super-saturated salt solution. Stir a tablespoon of salt into a bowl of water. If it dissolves, add another spoonful. Repeat until the salt no longer dissolves.

Do be careful about what you cleanse by this method. Use it only on something that won't be damaged by salt water, e.g., avoid jewelry set in metal. If in doubt, ask at your jeweler's or your nearest rock shop. Many free-standing crystals love a salt bath, and you can soak your entire collection together. After 15 minutes or longer, just rinse each stone under clear water.

Cleaning gemstones is that easy.

Prayer and meditation clear *you* out each day. Keep your crystals clear, day by day, and they can bring you *their* best.

239. Your Favorite Program

I can guarantee, your favorite program isn't on television. At least, it won't be, once you learn the art of programming crystals and gemstones. This kind of programming is both easy to learn and *necessary*, if you are to get your full money's worth as a consumer.

What if you had a grand piano in your living room but never let anyone play it? An un-programmed, high-vibe stone would be as much a waste as that piano. Crystals always transform energy. But they won't do it powerfully until programmed. This program will continue indefinitely (unless you change it). And, unlike any grand piano I've seen, a programmed crystal can easily fit into a pocket or purse, becoming your nice little secret.

It's fun when a beautiful piece of jewelry, admired by strangers, has a private meaning for you. Hey, sometimes that secret alone could get you through the day! But a programmed stone will do much more than that. According to the intent you put into it, your precious or semi-precious stone will reach out energetically, pulling specialized frequencies into your aura and, thus, into your life.

You may be especially successful if, before choosing your program, you explore the special excellence of a stone. Hold it and ask inside, "What can you tell me?"

Say that a Herkimer diamond tells you that it brings joy. A bead of blue lace agate helps establish balance. And a chunk of gold calcite energizes you, especially your root chakra. Let's say your original goal is to program all three stones for self-esteem. With more information about each stone's special excellence, you might adapt your programs like this:

- The Herkie will be programmed to activate joy about being yourself.
- The blue lace agate will be asked to help self-esteem grow along with your personal balance.
- And the gold calcite will augment your self-esteem whenever you eat.

To install each chosen program, write it down, using the language of affirmations. Call on a Divine Being. Hold the stone in your hand and say out loud what its program is to be. That simple! Or you can read ahead for the next few pages and do an even fancier version.

240. Thought Form Alert

Unintentionally, you may have programmed your home to hold worry or sorrow. But you can replace this with something positive that you choose on purpose.

Repeated patterns of thought, whether positive or negative, take on a life of their own. Technically, these patterns are known as *thought forms*. Once created, they influence future outcomes.

Here's an example of the power of thought forms. Do you have to deal with an appliance that drives you crazy, whether your car, your computer or your washing machine? That gadget didn't just come with a warranty. It also has an intelligence, a *deva* — the fairy-like being who is in charge of it.

When criticized, this deva will accumulate negative thought forms, just as a person would. So avoid saying (or thinking), "This stupid machine is always breaking down." Repeatedly thinking your insult will make it come true.

Wouldn't you respond the same way? Let's say you have a job. One customer treats you like dirt. The other treats you like gold. Which one will receive better service? With the grumpy customer, static may always get in the way, despite your best intentions. Well, that "static" is something real, negative thought forms.

But you can remove them in just a few minutes, anywhere, any time. Use your mighty power of speech. Say the following words out loud. Fill in the blanks with all the objects and people you wish to include in the healing:

1. God, I call upon you to bring a new light of truth here. Bring light into all the negative thought forms in [this object].
2. Lift them out, let them be fulfilled in the light, then completely released.
3. Now bring in more light, God, and create a complete set of positive thought forms, equal and opposite to what has been removed. Thank you, God, and it is done.

Ever been in someone's home after a fight? The tension felt so thick, you could slice and dice it with a Cuisinart.

Well, you were feeling negative thought forms, intensified by emotions. Even when mild, negative thought forms automatically bring down a person's vibrations. One reason why vacations feel so refreshing is that we temporarily escape the usual negative thought forms at home!

Give yourself a vacation today. Make your home, car and workplace energetically new. Wrap them shiny bright in positive thought forms.

241. Begin a Sacred Ceremony

Each new start holds the potential for sacredness. Think of the purity of new snow, the promise in new clothes. Each fresh beginning in life merits a ceremony of initiation. Bringing a Divine blessing, you can co-create a new start for anything — a crystal, a year, a home you are moving into, whatever you choose.

- Step 1. The Program

Choose a program. Wishing for "All blessings" would be too vague. How about asking God to decide what you need? That would be too passive. Don't you think God might find it baffling to sort through the gazillion small *human* things you desire? Play with ideas until you can write down a specific wish list, complete with priorities. Create your own program.

- Step 2. Cleansing

Energetically cleanse the item to receive the program. Whether it's a crystal or a suit of clothes, make sure it's clean. Spiff up that house as much as you can… without driving yourself crazy. If the main recipient of the blessing is you, make a ceremony of your shower or bath. After assuring physical cleanliness, you'd be wise to remove negative thought forms, as described yesterday.

- Step 3. The Altar

You deserve to have your ceremony be done in a sacred manner. Decide where this will be, then set up your altar. You'll need a candle in a holder and, soon, a match. If you wish, you may add a white cloth, flowers, fruit, incense, any special touches that would appeal to your sense of beauty.

- Step 4. Invitations

Of course, ask for Almighty God's blessing for your ceremony. Besides that impersonal omnipresence, it's wise to invoke God in a personal form. You might choose an Ascended Master like Jesus or Ganesh; Kwan Yin, Lakshmi or Athena. If you'd prefer an angel, perhaps you might call on Archangel Michael, who removes what doesn't belong, or Archangel Uriel, who increases mystical experiences.

A picture or sculpture of your Divine Being on the altar may uplift you. Otherwise picture Him or Her in the candle flame as you light it. Then speak the sacred name and welcome That presence into the room. Tomorrow you will speak out your program and it will go straight from your lips to God's ears.

What a combination: You to facilitate and a Divine Being to do the lightwork!

242. Complete Your Sacred Ceremony

Yesterday we considered the practical steps to stage a sacred ceremony. You've chosen what you want, prepared for the upgrade, set up a space for sacredness. Then you invited a Divine Being to participate. What now?

• Step 5. Co-Create
Before God, say out loud the program you've prepared. Add anything else you feel called to say or do.

• Step 6. Let God Co-Create, Too
Your turn is over, so relax and let go. Take a moment, in silence, to let your blessing be received.

• Step 7. Let Go
Once you're done your best, allow yourself to finish. One spiritual law unknown to many people is that you won't receive the blessing of a prayer until you let it go.

It's like eating at a banquet. If you stay at the table beyond when you're full, continuing to eat for hours, will this improve your digestion? At a certain point, a person has got to get up from that table and use the energy from the food to do something besides more chewing.

Naturally, after calling on a Divine Being to help with your sacred ceremony, you won't have the physical sensation of feeling full. Probably you won't see anything flashy either, to outwardly prove your success. But if a messenger of God does descend to congratulate you, driving a flaming chariot and showering you with orchid petals, do remember to send me an e-mail!

Usually the end of a sacred ceremony is very quiet indeed. This may seem like an anticlimax. The party is over. What's next?

Here you have one of the hard (but sweet) lessons of authentic spirituality. Pause to feel the sense of peace within your own heart. Recognize the quiet feeling that all is well.

Whether you've done a sacred ceremony today, or merely your usual prayer to ask for God's blessing, a quiet moment of peace can be your sign of completion. It takes great spiritual discernment to honor this silent moment…and elegant manners to pause one more moment longer to add your thanks.

Go forth confidently, knowing that you can revisit this silence at will. And, yes, you have been blessed.

243. Candle Flame

Within each stranger's eyes
there burns a secret, sacred flame.
It's hidden, usually:
One quick, soft beam.

Pass through the stare or glare,
beyond even your curiosity.
A childlike look of love
is yours for free.

Ask God to keep you company.
Then nimbly jump, jump quick,
into this candle stick.
One second's all you have to make the leap.
With that full face before you, between blinks
it is the perfect time
if only you will dare to tumble down,
to fall, and keep on falling, deep within.

Through trust, you'll find that you
have earned a privileged and holy sight.
Uniquely glowing flame,
you burn so bright.

244. When God Advertises

God does not generally do infomercials. You're also unlikely to see a newspaper ad for God's door-buster sale or have your e-mail pop-up with Celestial Spam. Furthermore, there's an excellent chance that your favorite radio program will never be interrupted by a salesman with the voice of Guess Who?

Having nothing to prove or to sell, the Prime Mover of our universe doesn't need to advertise. Yet "The God Show" still is broadcast on a regular basis. Tuning in depends on you.

Once you intend to find the presence of God, you can. Though subtle, it's everywhere: The space in the picture, the silence in the sounds, the cleansing fragrance of a deep breath, the *magnificence* of the physical body who's observing all this (i.e., the creation of God's that you know best). These reminders of divinity are not less awe-inspiring for being hidden.

For today's project, make it your business to find God's advertisements. At random times throughout your day, shift your awareness. You'll find evidence of God's presence in human acts of kindness, generosity, peacemaking or creativity. From the pulsating joy of the morning to the velvet of sleep, reminders of God have been tucked into every moment.

Admittedly, this is not like watching The Shopping Channel. Each ad consists of sneak peaks; each product is one-of-a-kind.

Besides, you're watching a different kind of show. This is your soul's all-time great love story.

God waits patiently for you to buy or not, as you wish. Never will there be sales pressure. Nor will you be forced to respond to any one-time offer.

But when you are ready to shop in God's store, all doors and display cases will swing wide open. Don't worry about finding an advertised special. Here your heart's desire is always affordable.

245. Crystal Ball, Improved

Ever wish you could tell the future? Previewing decades to come isn't easy. It may require a gem quality crystal ball, not to mention years of training and just plain luck.

But discernment about one particular choice, affecting your short-term future, doesn't require such fancy equipment. Simply hold your question in the Light.

Is it wise to ask for that raise? Would today be auspicious for that conversation you've been putting off? Those driving directions you got off the Internet, will they prove reliable?

To hold your question in the Light, imagine the scene unfolding. Does the mental movie go forward or stop?

Sometimes you'll fantasize beautifully, or simply feel loads of energy around a particular path. What matters is the energy, not which images accompany it. You have received a "Go" signal.

Other times, it's the opposite. Energy is lacking, so you must do heavy lifting to move that particular sequence of thought. You may even feel like Sisyphus, struggling to roll your rock uphill despite a familiar feeling of…Oops!

If that happens, don't blame either yourself or your guidance. Give thanks because you've just received a message which is just as valuable as the "Go for it" variety.

A heavy rock that won't roll uphill is your inner crystal ball.

246. Pretend Games

Here's a bold assignment for today. Allow yourself to feel God's huge love for you, even if it seems like you're only pretending.

When you have done something especially well, take a few seconds to acknowledge delight (or relief). This would be an ideal time to ask God, "Do you love me?"

Now, you've heard those call-in talk shows where listeners ask a question and then say to the guest, "I'll take my answer off the air." By hanging up the phone, they demonstrate sincere curiosity; they're willing to shut up and listen. Besides, they will hear the answer via radio more clearly without the distraction of a telephone. Why try to listen in two places at once?

Whenever you ask a question of God, whatever the question, it's wise to turn off the "telephone" dominated by talking and turn on the "radio" dominated by silence. Feel God's presence, subtle but real. Be attuned to shifts in that silence, plus anything else you hear as God speaks back to you.

Even if you still worry that you're pretending, flow with the other aspects of your experience. Be more interested in that than your doubts.

You'll find there is no bad time for listening to God, especially after you ask that vital question, "Do you love me?"

With trust as a listener, you'll discover an unconditional love… *like the kind that you can choose to give yourself.*

Connecting to God need not be difficult. Whatever your level of spiritual development, you can do it.

What if you find it hard to believe that God would talk to the likes of you? Pretend you are worthy. Make it a habit, free will at its finest, and begin today.

247. Like Clockwork

Co-create something with God every day on the inner. This could be prayer, contemplation, or any other inner exercise.

Outer techniques (like jogging, reading, discussing ideas about metaphysics) won't get you there as directly as going straight to the inner. God's pure silence and ever-fresh light can recharge you like nothing else.

For a spiritual exercise to qualify as *inner*, you can't simultaneously multitask, work out or be social. Spiritual exercise is a full-self activity, requiring undivided attention. You must be able to relax enough physically so that you can receive ideas at depth.

Whatever technique you use today may bore you tomorrow, so be open to changing your spiritual practice periodically. You'll know when. As for the what, you'll be the best judge of that, too. So many practices are available from teachers, books, sites on the Internet. Choose one practice that appeals to you and make it your day's offering to God.

This is the kind of "giving" that gives back to you, too.

Worst case, how will you respond if results aren't what you might wish? Well, that teaches you something. Either adjust your expectations or don't do that particular practice tomorrow. Find something else.

Spiritual growth is cumulative. Regular practice will make you familiar with exquisite nuances of consciousness. Body, mind and spirit are connected, and every subjective dip into pure being trains your physical system to hold onto more consciousness.

"Sure, I'll try," one student said. "I have so many problems and so little time. Still I suppose it might help if I had more of an inner life, so I'll try to find a chance to do some spiritual exercise."

"Try" is a failure word. Really it means, "I'll try, just to show my intentions are good. I'll *try,* but I'll never really *do* it."

Meanwhile time is ticking away. The minutes and hours of human life move as steadily as clockwork, and no excuse of yours or mine can make time stop. Only eternity might do it, the eternity glimpsed during your precious minutes of spiritual exercise.

So don't just try to be regular in your spiritual practice. Do it.

248. Humming Along

What is a hum? It's your inner songbird, perched somewhere between the tip of your nose and your heart.

Okay, literally, humming just resonates in your sinuses. But could the magnificence of your sinuses be under-rated?

Consider that your sinuses are a built-in, spiritual echo chamber. If really bold, you could compare your humming ability to a church organ. Actually, your version is better because you can completely master the instrument in just one lesson.

Whether this low-key instrument is on-key or off-key, it serves a glorious purpose. By listening to yourself hum, you'll bring your attention to a subtle junction point, halfway between outer and inner. This state of equipoise is the goal of many a meditation and, frankly, it's a style of meditation that sounds more interesting than most.

The technique is wonderfully portable, too. Humming can accompany nearly any activity. Or you can hum to sweeten solitude.

Like listening to banjo music, how can a person hum and not feel better? Whatever your mood, humming can modulate it into a more cheerful frequency.

Hum for your physical health as well. Even a few hummed "La, la, la's" can improve circulation in your upper respiratory tract. This can help you to avoid sinus infections. And you may even be boosting your brain power.

So if anyone shushes you, feel free to say, "I'm engaged in a holistic do-it-myself medical procedure. It will increase my production of nitric oxide, which helps dilate capillary beds and ultimately will enhance my blood flow."

What could be better than that? Maybe this: Humming reminds us that sacred singing need not be a public performance. Like Gregorian chants of old, which brought celestial splendor to ancient monasteries, any hum that you bring forth now can be directed to a special audience of One.

Prayer need not be expressed only in words, you know. And a highly uplifting co-creation can start with the simplest of tunes. Why not hum one today?

249. Bowling with Light Balls

Do you think bowling is fun in an alley, where you're restricted to a narrow lane with those embarrassing gutters? Wait until you try this version. With Spiritual Bowling you can throw balls of light anywhere, at any angle, and it's guaranteed that you will hit your target every time.

Speaking of a target, Spiritual Bowling provides you with something far more interesting than pins: People. Help them wherever they are, and for free. Here's how.

- Ask a Divine Being to help you create a huge ball of white light, pure potential on a spiritual level. This globe of love, light and power will manifest instantly, quick as thought.
- Choose someone to hurl it toward.
- Aim. Throw. Never a gutter ball!

Just be sure to avoid coercion. You're not throwing mere spitballs; these blessing balls have power. So avoid labeling them with specifics like "Take away Lori's asthma" or "Help Dave find a new job." Such sentiments may seem admirable. But you're not in charge of anyone else's health or work life. Dave and Lori will just have to use their blessings without any coaching from you, thanks very much.

Sending a Spiritual Bowling Ball is like giving cash for a gift, each dollar made of spiritual energy. Your recipient will know how to spend it, no problem.

If this kind of free money were sent to *you*, you'd know what to do with it, wouldn't you? Hope so, because of course you can aim Spiritual Bowling Balls at yourself, not only other people.

When you're the target, go ahead and stuff a specific goal into each light ball. Only be sure to add this: "All this God, or something better."

This way you agree to receive more than you asked for, and allow it to come however it will, including something far better than what you've considered.

Now, you may know that a bowler can become very involved in her swing. For starters, she's sticking three fingers directly into holes molded deep into the bowling ball. Yet successful throwing means that she must let go completely.

Imagine what would happen to you if, during physical bowling, you wouldn't let those determined little fingers release the ball?

Spiritually, letting go is just as important. So relax each time you bowl with light balls. Let go. Then count your throw as a perfect strike.

250. L'Heure Bleu

One of the loveliest times of day often goes unnoticed. The French call it *L'Heure Bleu,* the blue hour. After sunset yet before dark, this is when a landscape loses its ordinary colors and shifts into shades of the most extraordinary blue.

The deftness of this sky-painting can give you new respect for life's Exterior Decorator. Compared with God's daily twilight, even the great Picasso's "Blue Period" amounts to little more than a childish scrawl.

L'Heure Bleu can become a sacred time for you. Once outdoors in that mysteriously still air, surrounded by transformative light, you can re-align with your Source.

For centuries, great writers have used weather imagery to express inner life. Shakespeare, for instance, often used this device to great dramatic effect. You can do it too, neither for drama nor an audience, but for your own spiritual upliftment.

Let indigo light from L'Heure Bleu expand your consciousness. Or choose any alternate weather you like. If you like, your next celestial wake-up call could be sprinkled among snowflakes. Or maybe you'd prefer for God to seep into you, ray by ray, in the form of summery sunshine.

Be a rain maker, a cloud buster, a bringer of rainbows. Inside, choose any weather you like as you co-create this day.

251. Divine Newspaper

Just for today, I'll forget about TV news, radio broadcasts, my favorite blog, even the daily newspaper. Instead I'll only tune into God's announcements of current events.

Yes, today I'm taking a news fast. But rather than deprivation, today's spiritual exercise can bring me huge fulfillment. Instead of filling my mind with society's sometimes bizarre ideas about what constitutes "news," I'll decide for myself which stories matter.

Besides informing people of current events, media news can entertain us, even bestow a sense of community. But can't I do this too, and do it my way?

For entertainment, at random times I can pause to appreciate the here and now…whatever shows up. Unlike entertainment created by others, however, mine can focus on what matters spiritually.

The trick is similar to what a good director or editor does: Frame things right.

If disorder (or worse) shows in a shot, I can zoom in closer or angle out wider. Persistently, I'll keep playing with perspective until I locate something fine. Challenges notwithstanding, I can always frame a scene big enough to include God.

As for creating a sense of community, my reporting can extend to people whether I personally know them or not. It's easy to reach out with a smile, a friendly word or a helpful deed. No need to stop for a commercial break or turn over a page, I only need stay where I am and the world's best breaking news will find me.

252. Loud Money

Yes, of course you'd like more of it, but at what cost?
Have you heard too much gold can't be spiritually good
or full coffers equate to a coffined, dead heart?
Don't believe it. You merit a prosperous life.
Wealth need never replace joy's true source in you, God.

So invent money myths you'd *prefer* to be true.
To you, money could be all this — with interest, too:
Symbols of gratitude, God in disguise,
A moveable passion, creative joy flames.
Perhaps money just eases your spiritual path.
Let your credit and debit cards document growth
to Enlighten Mint, where all real money is made.

The problem would be loving riches alone
as if they were real, outside-in, valuables.
How lonely the clank of such coins! Gold-edged guilt!
Such poverty could deaden ears. So instead
resolve that you'll carry just coins that can sing,
bills as trills of a spiritual song to be shared.
Let it jingle with joy, be contagiously loud
to all who are listening for God in this world.

253. Your Spiral Staircase

Although most people agree that the earth is round, your part of it has been built as a spiral staircase. Each spiral is custom designed around a few themes drawn from a person's Life Contract. Perhaps you're learning how to keep your power while in a love relationship, or how to eat in a balanced, healthy way. You could be learning financial responsibility. Or perhaps the biggest job is simply to keep your sanity.

Whatever your themes, remember that *you* have chosen them all. After incarnating, you forgot them (along with the fact that you made any Life Contract whatsoever). Instead, while slogging up your staircase, you may feel perplexed, ashamed or amused at your lessons. On The Other Side you were such a kidder!

On This Side, your spiral staircase is set up like a huge shopping mall, circling ever higher and higher. At each floor, windows display goods from all kinds of amusing little shops. But the serious business at each mall takes place at the multi-level anchor stores, built at every level so you can't avoid them. Lord & Taylor again? Sure. But in your Life Contract, perhaps it's called "The Love Store."

Thus, you'll take a few steps, have a few minor lessons (akin to shopping at a few cute boutiques) and darn! You're back at Lord & Taylor. Sometimes it may feel like a recurring nightmare.

Stuck with the same love problem again? Not really, because you're always learning at a more evolved level. Now, some well meaning friend may say, "Obviously the answer to your problem is blah, blah, blah." This advice will be offered with such calm assurance, it makes you feel terrible. What kind of dummy were you not to know this, when advice came so easily to your friend?

Well, your advice giver marches along a different spiral staircase, where Lord & Taylor could be the equivalent of a tiny dollar store. Maybe the tough anchor stores for him are more like After Hours Formalwear and Priscilla of Boston.

Every person on earth is invited to master certain lessons. Even when you seem to repeat the same old theme, you're mastering it at a higher level. Imagine if the floors at your colossal Lord & Taylor were only numbered. Then you could tell for sure that you've trekked all the way to up to the 17th floor. But would that *really* make it more fun? You're still back there shopping again, only now you're in the Underwear Department....

Yes, God is merciful. God is also the tough kind of teacher who will test you relentlessly until you master each lesson. How else can you graduate from a first-rate school? When you get to the top of your spiral staircase, there is such a roof garden! And have you heard rumors about the graduation ceremony, complete with angelic choirs? It's true. So keep climbing.

254. *Disappointments and Delays*

Why would a loving God make our world so thick with disappointments and delays? If nothing else, they strengthen resolve.

How much spiritual muscle would we build if, always and instantly, we got whatever we wanted? Instead, life seems like a gamble. Sometimes we win, sometimes we lose. It can be incredibly discouraging, how a random task can take hours or days, weeks, even decades. And during the most infuriating times, nobody else may have a clue how frustrated you feel.

So here's one therapeutic way to deal with delays. To remind yourself that you're neither alone nor a failure, make a Wishing Box. This can start as any container dedicated to the purpose. But rather than make do with a stained old Tupperware container, please, choose something elegant. Buy it new or decorate something you already own.

When young, my son's special treasure box began as a blue plastic cube that had once held Johnson's Baby Wipes. With some stickers and glitter, he made it into something superb…according to his standards at the time. Your own Wishing Box need not be museum quality. But it should bring a smile to your lips and hope to your heart.

Then, whenever you have a wish, write it down. Place the paper inside your Wishing Box. Once a day, hold that box in your hands. Send it good energy. If you do Reiki or another type of healing, use that high-vibe energy to activate your wishes. Or you can treat the box like a dandelion gone to seed: Make a wish and blow.

After each wish comes true, remove the paper. Give thanks. Let the paper go, since it has served its purpose.

Delays and disappointments may never have a purpose that is clear to you. But however real your frustration, remember this. To God, your wishes are realer. Every one of your prayers will be answered with the timing that's perfect for you. Delays on The Learning Planet are God's strategic planning.

255. My Heart's Desire

My heart's desire, what is it really? Do I know? Otherwise, do I dare to find out?

Because each of us is uniquely designed, your heart's desire may be quite counter-culture. For instance, what if you are put together as someone whose life's ambition is simply to praise God? Outer accomplishments may matter little, yet you have no label like "Monk" or "Nun. Therefore, you may confuse your heart's calling with laziness...and keep looking elsewhere.

What out there do I really want?

Society might call many a heart's desire laziness, or have no name for it whatsoever, which could feel even worse. But the desires that matter most are private, between you and God. When you're ready, the two of you can negotiate all the important details. Who cares if the scope of your life doesn't look like a standard job description?

Whatever your heart's desire, you can find it. And once you've found it, you can name it, then figure out how to make it come true.

If you are still searching, ask God to help. Sit in meditation each day, doing whatever technique brings you joy. At the end, before signing off, ask to know your deepest heart's desire. Then spend a moment in the joyous, God-awe-full silence, not minding anything.

Sometimes peripheral vision is our first opening into clairvoyance. Or eavesdropping is our first hint of clairaudience. A Divine whisper could come through any of your deeper senses. When that happens, don't go frantically chasing after it. Instead, settle into yourself by placing awareness at your heart or solar plexus. And then simply be with the truth of your being.

Once you begin to know or feel the presence of your heart's desire, you are well on your way to accomplishing it. Do at least *one* small something each day to bring that desire to fruition.

Disappointments, delays or other frustrations count for little, compared to the weight of not knowing your heart's desire. Absence of a worthy goal in life can produce illness, poverty, all sorts of trouble. Eventually, you can feel such pressure that even the *wish* to find your heart's desire seems unrealistic. Yet that desire is absolutely real, part of the Divine pattern for your soul.

So have the courage to seek out your heart's desire. And if you don't know it yet, send out a call until it is answered.

My heart's desire: God, reveal it to me.

256. Longing for God

Do you long to be extraordinarily enlightened, attuned to God's presence with absolute clarity? A great goal like that may seem unattainable.

At such times, it helps to remember that God is fully available whatever your present level of consciousness. If you carry fear, pain or anger, you'll glimpse only a smallish fragment of God's loving-kindness and mercy. But even that small glimpse can bring relief...and help you to evolve further.

So however you feel in the moment, keep at your spiritual practice regularly, doing the best you can. Spiritual evolution is more than figuring out a "correct" set of beliefs; it requires the engagement of your entire body-mind-spirit system. Whenever you feel stuck, it could be growing pains.

Just as we can always call on God (and each call will be answered) so too can we ask for our next human teacher. Some of the best spiritual teachers don't have official credentials. Your next one could be a cleaning lady, a clarinet teacher or a reference librarian. Being in that person's presence, you will learn something important. Ultimately, spiritual wisdom is caught, not taught.

Inner discernment will help you to recognize a true teacher. And some of the most remarkable spiritual teaching happens aura to aura, from one person to another. Use your deeper perception to find out what's going on.

To honor the call of longing, what matters most is that you unfailingly spend time alone with God every day. Do it early each morning. Or do it before you sleep. Or do it any time in between, so long as you take that time regularly.

Use that time to seek, adore, question, actively co-create or simply be...in the presence of God.

257. Peel That Stuff Away

A ripe banana makes it seem ridiculously easy. I'm referring to the goal of peeling away life's illusions, so you can make contact with God. Stripping away illusions should only be so easy as peeling a banana. As you may have noticed, there is no cosmic banana skin.

Enlightenment is a do-it-yourself job, with more style required than taking a few easy tugs. Part of the problem with finding the truth about life in any given moment is that myths, judgments and illusions don't stand out with bright yellow skin. Therefore, the process of *peeling away* is abstract.

Don't begin with an object, but with a choice. In one situation after another, ask to find the truth.

This intention to find truth will show you one kind of experience at a time. Although real, it may be only one layer.

You may also find, at each layer, a set of your own feelings, judgments, beliefs, pat answers. Acknowledge them but know they are not Truth with a capital T. So it's time to take a deep breath, go back to the situation and start asking all over again: What is the truth here?

What, for example, is the truth of a ripe banana? That bright yellow skin is just the start. Ask a finicky eater. Before you get to the real banana, there are so many stringy wisps of not-quite skin, not quite fruit.

Similar bits of non-truth cling to everything in life. How can you lift them off? Be gentle. Only an ingrate would hack away at a sweet, soft banana. Yet it's understandable when spiritual seekers, made fierce by longing, bring out the equivalent of a machete.

To find wholeness under the surface of life, you can avoid both drama and dogma. Hunt for truth today, one exploration at a time. Do it gently. This quest for truth is sacred, remember?

In the (soft) blinking of an eye, you may find that time slows down…moving you in the direction of eternity.

258. Which Terrible Word?

Which of these words do you find harder to use, "Yes" or "No"?

If you're a *Nay-sayer* to life, it can be exceedingly difficult to squeak out a "Yes." Your first reaction to any situation is "No."

What a valid, even prudent, response that can be! Protecting yourself, avoiding relationships that won't work, being practical enough to foresee problems that others miss…no, there's nothing wrong at all with being a nay-sayer. Only just for today, challenge yourself with a "What-the-heck, yes."

- "Yes, I can."
- "Yes, that new idea sounds great."
- "Yes, your way of doing things could work."
- "Yes, I will give that new person a chance."

Whether you seemingly lose or win, that yes-choice will open up breathing space for your soul.

But what if, instead you're a *Yea-sayer*? Wonderful though it is to drive through life with a constantly revved-up optimism, could it be time to check your brake pedal? How about your turn signal? Enough with the affirmative action, already. Try out some deny-ative:

- "No, I won't keep that broken [fill-in-the-blank…appliance? job? relationship?]. Sorry, but you've exceeded my limit for fixer-uppers."
- "No, I won't help this time. Let someone else do it."
- "No, I won't pretend that things are wonderful when they aren't."
- "You say that you're telling me this for my own good? No, I don't think so."

Splurge today on a brisk, bracing "No" or "Yes," whichever one would be harder to say. You're bound to find some context where that one "terrible" word will do you good.

259. When Vows Are Ows

A vow is an ultra-serious promise. We make them *voluntarily* for weddings or as part of religious life. When we make them, we mean them. But what happens after a vow is no longer appropriate?

Can we break a vow without breaking faith? I believe that we can. And you have the right to decide this for yourself, using your full self-authority.

In some cases, you may feel that ending a vow is not only okay but absolutely necessary.

A vow's purpose is to learn something, to accomplish something or to serve someone in a particular way. This doesn't always take an entire lifetime to achieve. Besides, you might be amazed to discover how often a person carries into *this* lifetime vows that were made in a former incarnation altogether.

For instance, in one past life or another, many of us have promised to embrace a life of chastity, selflessness and solitude. Ever wonder why you can't seem to get a date? Something is *out*-dated — that vow, so rescind it.

Another example: You may have promised to be loyal to one particular person, no matter what. Well, "what" can be pretty terrible. It's one thing to love your child in one lifetime, something else to defend that same soul in the guise of a confidence man when he shows up this time around.

Vows of poverty are also pretty common. Sure you meant it, back when you entered the monastery. But that could have been 500 years ago. Got poverty now? Money may keep eluding you until you change that vow.

Where do vows show up? One part lodges in the same place from where they can be released most easily, your aura. A second component is stored in your subconscious mind, plus one final dollop lingers in cellular memory.

You could approach healing from any of these three levels. I favor healing at the level of auras, because they respond so quickly to simple ceremonies of healing. If you suspect that you're carrying a leftover vow from the past, try this method. It will take you less than 10 minutes.

1. Call on a Divine Being to help you. Also call on Almighty God as your witness.
2. Create the surroundings for your ceremony. Light a candle or do whatever else you feel will transform the place where you stand into a sacred space.
3. State your purpose, e.g., "The purpose of this ceremony is to permanently terminate an old vow that I believe I've been carrying."

4.   Describe the vow. How accurate must you be? Not enough to satisfy a lawyer or a patent attorney. Look, you're talking with God, who can fill in any details where you need help. Aside from that, know that your general feeling about this vow is to be trusted.

5.   State that this vow no longer applies to you. Need you supply reasons? No. But you do need to speak up loud and clear. Say three times, "This vow is now ended."

6.   Ask for help in bringing in the new attributes of life that are being freed up, e.g., "I now open up my life so that I can have a fulfilling love relationship." Continue your conversation with God until it feels complete.

7.   Close your eyes and take a moment to notice how it feels like to be you. Perhaps you will notice a shift in body awareness or inner silence. In any case, give thanks for the help you've received. In the days to come, your life will be freer because of the vow you have ended.

You're allowed to evolve, you know. Almighty God, of infinite resources, is bigger than any outdated promise you made one time.

Set yourself free now to find (and fulfill) a new set of promises.

260. Not So Crazy After All

Ask yourself which matters more to you, staying comfortable or claiming your spiritual birthright? Developing deeper perception can bring up your biggest fears. You could spend the rest of your life with those limitations. Or you could resolve to keep evolving regardless.

Once I was interviewed by a TV reporter from Baltimore. She'd driven down to Virginia with a camera man in tow. For two hours, she interrogated me and some of my students. All the footage would be edited down to a couple of segments for network news. Soon it became clear that only one of her questions would *definitely* be on the show.

How did I know this? The reporter asked this question three times: Once with a wide shot from the camera guy, once with a close-up of her (doe-eyed yet steely), and once with the camera focused on me.

Leaning toward me with a practiced and condescending smile, the lovely broadcaster said, "Rose, I know you read auras and teach people how to do it. I know you think it's all true. But, just between you and me, don't people ever ask you this:

"'Are you crazy?'"

Three times, I got to give her the very same answer. "The fear of going crazy is exactly what keeps those people from reading auras."

Now, your deepest fear may be different. Years ago you may have given up the pretense of sanity. Maybe you're more worried about seeming un-loveable or not fitting in socially or getting fired because of your spiritual leanings or losing control of your life or going to Hell or being tricked by The Devil...little things like that.

Whatever you are scared of spiritually may revisit you in the context of co-creating with God. Using deeper perception can bring up all sorts of deep fears. But if you'll keep on exploring and learning, sooner or later you'll pass each fear by, maybe once and for all.

See spiritual fears for what they are, illusions. Then you can bless humanity most fully as a world sever. Humanly, you'll enjoy life more, too.

261. God's Quicksilver Presence

God's *quicksilver* presence is out everywhere
soft as a kiss from the most tender lover
until I look for speed. Then You're racing
faster than dancing dust. Or, if I start seeking
complexity, Your complexion
shifts yet again and I'm into the spider webs,
dancing with fractals, relentless intelligence everywhere.

But when I seek God's *mighty* presence, That's everywhere, too
with immense strength in Your vibrating airways.
So-called "objects" contain such a wildness of space.
In each thing (once I listen), well, there You are
humming That most delectable tune.
Moreover, everything You've sung here
seems real. Neat trick!

Pure gold, moving silver, or granite hard,
You are the teacher, you are the bard.
While I get to be in Your lesson, Your poem.
Sometimes, like now, laughing my head off,
sometimes snoring, sometimes crying,
sometimes whispering "Amen."

Yes, God, Your quicksilver-changing, eternal
presence is out everywhere.
And you know what?
It's sticking.

262. Special, Today Only

To a child, everything seems new. Either it really is or else new concepts, like language, enrich the experience. That tomato, that song, that exercise in counting, that favorite toy — each one is new, new, new, every time.

By contrast, we adults have a sad tendency to know it all. We've tasted plenty of tomatoes, sung our songs, counted ourselves to sleep. We've even had sleighs full of toys.

So even if we haven't already seen a particular item, thanks to our vast store of concepts, even most *new* things can seem *used*. Sometimes, the familiarity seems sweet. Other times, the voice of experience drones on within us, heavy with languor or disgust, "Been there. Done that."

Not today, friend. Today you can smash all vestiges of "Been there. Done that."

At random times, all day and night, hang this sign any one place at any one time. Of course, this sign will be easy to post. Technically being imaginary, it will be visible only to you and, maybe, cats. Let the sign read:

The God Company Announces
Today's Big Sale
Brand New Merchandise
Your Satisfaction Guaranteed

Place this sign freely on any person or situation. Suddenly, it's as though you were shopping in the most delightful new store. Check out each bargain. Deep within it is the presence of God — in a form resplendent with power, love, light. Or you may find sugar, spice, salt, sushi, sarsaparilla or some hitherto-unknown flavor.

How many times have you asked God to show you a sign? Today, give a sign back.

263. Baby Yourself

Never again will you have a baby's guileless grin. But today's assignment can still open up new vistas of your innocence. It's a two-part assignment, one thing *to not do* all day long, and something else *to do* instead.

The NOT DO is expectation. Usually we grownups start this up within five minutes of waking, as though judgment were required to prove you'd lifted your head from the pillow. So complicated! Lose all expectations that limit your home life, just for one day, okay?

Now proceed to baby yourself in the outside world. Usually you'll reach for the morning newspaper or switch on the news and oh boy! In comes a whole cast of characters — politicians, experts of all kinds — each of whom may or may not act according to your expectations.

Well, for just one day allow these people to function without your standards helping them to shape up. Just for one day, let your expectations (however wise and complex) become one gigantic NOT DO. Let these people be who they are going to be anyhow.

Such a vast amount of inner time you'll receive as a bonus! This can give you all the more time to enjoy one sweet, juicy new DO:

Pay attention to your fascinating, wonderful body. You've seen babies chewing their toes, right? You've witnessed their delight at walking, correct? Well, today is your turn to wallow in physical joy. No toe nibbling is required, nor anything physically difficult. You'll simply get to explore your body as though it were brand new.

- Let your physical range of movement astonish you.
- Allow every sense to delight you.
- Notice how food enters your mouth, moves through nuances of digestion, and makes that very satisfying exit.
- Explore how breathing is fun.
- Even blinking can become a game.

You get the idea. When was the last time you had kid-like fun with your body? Don't even bother to answer. Living without time-related questions will place you squarely in the present...along with an extra dollop of joy.

264. Daily Requirement of C

Did you take your vitamins today? You took them while singing, right? No? Okay, swallowing pills may not be the best time to trill like a bird.

So when did you get in your singing? Those musical notes are exactly like vitamins…for your soul. Unless you purposely sing a full scale each day, entire notes may be neglected. Goodbye, voice vitamins A, B or C. And without your voice's minimum daily requirement, you may develop a dead spot inside.

For fun, listen with a musical ear to the people talking around you. So many words, so few notes! Most people favor certain pitches, ignoring others completely. But singing can help anyone to break out of boring vocal patterns.

Besides, daily singing can heal your throat chakra. So many of us have auras with more-or-less broken communication circuits. Is yours clogged with pent-up joy, stuck grief or way too little uninhibited self-expression?

To heal your aura, sing every note in the scale. While you're at it, let fun override duty. About time! Otherwise it is likely that you will walk your dog more often than you take your own voice out to play. Go ahead, growl out your low notes. Squeak your highest. Express any emotion you choose. Working your voice can feel great, and that's just the start of the possible benefits.

Affirmations work better when you sing them. Spontaneous melodies can decorate your prayers. Or improvise love songs to God. Just for fun, if you know a child under five, watch how that smart kid reacts when you sing your words rather than plain old talking.

One of the best ways to cheer up your own Inner Child is to make up a dopey song. A man I know sings out the street names as he drives, breaking up the monotony of his commute to work. Or try singing an official, composed song but change it by substituting one daring lyric, sung over and over again: "I like myself."

And remember those hokey old musicals where folks just burst into song for no reason? Try it. You could reinvent an art form; at the least, you'll have live entertainment.

Professional singing is everywhere, on concerts, radios, CDs, the Internet. Even TV commercials, when sung, are performed to perfection. It's enough to discourage us honest amateurs from making our voices known. Of course, certain people in your life might cringe when you burst forth with song. So don't invite them to your private concert.

God certainly wouldn't dislike your voice. After all, She sang the world into creation. Invite God to be your audience and sing, sing, sing.

265. Silly But Smart

Laugh yourself silly. It's the smart thing to do.

You were born a silly. From infancy, the smallest things made you laugh with delight. Someone surprised you? Either you'd cry or you'd giggle. Teach yourself something? You'd be sure to laugh then.

After a distressing experience, children discharge most negativity with a quick bout of tears; soon after, wisely, they laugh. Of course laughter is the best medicine. It's also the best illness preventer.

So why is it that with each passing decade, people laugh less? Shame on that worse-than-silly grownup who taught you inflexible dignity. Instead of a bouncing baby boy or girl, have you turned into a lump of seriousness? As if dignity ever brought happiness!

To counter excessive sobriety, laugh. Sprinkling fun into most situations can be easy as adding salt to your food. Make bad puns. Try on a goofy face. Or bring up some memory of horrible failure that really wasn't — especially effective if this memory is several days old. When it comes to failures, the staler, the better.

Feeling stale yourself is another matter. If you *must* sit decorously, what law says you can't also read the funnies? Besides, when's the last time you read a joke book? Kids can handle something that heavy, so why not you? Aside from being a much better reader now, here's another humor advantage you have over children: A grownup's well honed skill at irony. Don't just sneer with it. You can use a seemingly serious book or magazine to bring on a full-body laugh-gasm.

Regardless of how dignified you'll look, somersaults can be an excellent way to bring on laughter (unless they'd also throw out your back). If you're very physically fit, roll down a hill. Either the uncontrollable flip-overs will start you laughing or you'll laugh when recovering from the post-roll nausea. No, you're no longer a kid. You're way funnier.

Truth is, life's serious problems will stand on their own with no help from you. Problems can take on the solidity of walls but laughter knocks them down. So demolish life's rigid sorrows however you can. Usually, acting silly is smart.

266. Spinach Sculpture

You *were* planning to eat your vegetables today, weren't you? Well, how about using them for a spiritual exercise?

However artistically talented you may be — and however strange an artistic medium is spinach salad or cooked broccoli — you can turn that tasty pile into something fascinating. Sometimes you won't know what to create until you start toying with those greens. Well, go ahead. Just sprinkle on plenty of the ultimate condiment, imagination. It's not every day you get to eat your prayers.

And while you're at great food projects, please do your Inner Child a favor. Check out how you typically hold that fork and knife. Boring! Would it be so horrible if one time, in the privacy of your own dinner table, you were to switch hands? Get a grip, a different grip. Actually, how weird would it be to dispense entirely with the formal cutlery and dig in with your fingers?

We grownups can turn into food snobs, so fascinated by gourmet this and nutritious that. If that happens, we lose half the fun of food, which consists in how we eat it.

Back in childhood, you could do the imagination part just fine. When you were made to learn manners, solemnity and scolding entered your digestion. Sigh! No more chewing with mouth open. No more racing food around your plate, then eating the winner.

Some days the best thing you can do for yourself at a meal is to cut each bite into a puppet. Let those forkfuls of personality act out their tale. Then provide the ultimate applause...by chewing.

What, you'd rather rearrange colors? You happen to have a degree from MIT in building edible robots? Any imaginative activity will pack more joy into each morsel.

Joy changes food's chemistry. When you digest food with joy, you produce more *soma*, the physiological basis for deeper perception. Even for the sake of serious enlightenment, if you're smart and ambitious, give yourself permission: Play with your food.

267. Divine Temper Tantrum

Acting like a spoiled brat can be good for you. Just do it right (and not in public). Set aside 20 minutes for a kind of temper tantrum that's good for the soul.

Start by gathering all your supplies: A room where you can be alone, a timer and one big, fat pillow suitable for stuffing into your mouth, as needed.

Sound like fun? Oh, it will be…once your Official Temper Tantrum is *over*. For now, call in a Divine Being to keep you company. To help you remember His or Her presence, you may wish to light a candle. Perhaps you'd also like to sing a favorite hymn or chant Om. Do whatever it takes to create a healing space for this anger-clearing ceremony.

Now it's time for your timer. Set it for 10 minutes. Then go have a tantrum. Scowl. Pound your fists. Shake your butt in the air. Kick your feet. Remembering how to tantrum turns out to be far easier than remembering how to ride a bicycle.

Please don't skimp on the screaming. If you'll only take the precaution of stuffing that pillow into your mouth, you can yell like crazy without either losing your voice or inciting your neighbors to call the police.

Swear words are excellent. Voice all forbidden thoughts. Lightning will *not* strike you dead. In fact, you won't get into any trouble at all.

So have a fabulous grump-dump, be it justified or petty, righteous or merely spiteful — whatever. You don't edit your poops before releasing them, do you?

Actually, 10 minutes turns out to be a pretty long time to purposely act out anger. Toward the end of Part One, you may have to fake it. But don't worry. Sincerity isn't required for this performance, just plenty of noise. Do whatever it takes (short of injuring yourself) to fill those first 10 minutes with fury.

Then comes Part Two, 10 more minutes. Reset your timer. Sit comfortably. Now close your eyes and listen to your heart. Ask your Divine Being to bring light to every part of you where there has been release or rearrangement.

When that's done, you might also wish to thank your Divine Being. And notice how you feel now. Peace may fill every place where rage used to be.

Yes, heaven helps those who help themselves…to a well designed temper tantrum.

268. Toys

Toys designed for children will free your soul at any age.

- When is the last time you bought a jar of bubbles and sent them flying?
- Do you keep a kazoo on hand for emergencies?
- If you can't make it down to the toy store, do what a child does. Play with a tissue, a rubber band or a box. Any one of them comes complete with a dozen games. What, you lost the manual? Time for a new one. You could be hired to write it.

Pure silliness is all the excuse a wise person needs to play with toys. Many of us grownups work too hard at playing, just like everything else.

Once you get into the goofiness groove, finding ways to play is easy. You remember how you did it long ago. In fact, as an adult you can actually be *better* at playing than when you were a kid.

Next time you find yourself taking yourself and your problems way too seriously, I'd recommend that you slide down a banister or dance down a flight of stairs. (Staircases make excellent toys.) Or try the Upside Down Walk:

Stand up. Bend over until you can hold each ankle with the corresponding hand. Straighten up your legs as far as possible. Now that you're in position, walk around waving your butt in the air. If very coordinated, you may also be able to sing a goofy song or intone your favorite affirmations. See how far you can get.

The illusions of this world don't stick to kids the way troubles do to adults. Yet the heavy things in your life have no more lasting permanence than some cloud pattern in the sky. How long will one of these resemble a puppy or a map of the world?

Like clouds, your troubles can billow away — at least the portion that weighs on you inwardly. Let kids' toys remind you. This life of yours may be designed for serious evolution, but it's taking place in a toy store.

269. Wonderland

What if, just for today, you could open up bigger to God than ever before? Why not? Let the seeker in you rejoice. You're not asking for the moon... or to *become* the moon. You're not even requesting major event rearrangement, like meeting the love of your life. When you make your day's wishlist, simply put in this request: Ask that today, living normally, you will be open to *wonder*.

No mere concept or mood, wonder can become your spontaneous experience. It's the element of Life within life. Wonder appears by surprising you. Shrug off the experience and you're unchanged. But if you say "Yes," a new wad of wonder will land right in your lap (at the level of body, mind or spirit).

Thus, seeking a hefty input of wonder is not asking too much, nor need the request be difficult to fulfill. You've gone jewelry shopping sometimes, haven't you? Can't gold be hard and soft at the same time, shiny even as it absorbs light? Sink your senses into gold and you will bounce back in wonder.

It's the same with any aspect of life, whether natural or humanly made. Pay enough attention and wonder can be your reward.

Really this consequence is no more shocking than discovering that a forest is made out of wood. *This is God's world.* So the closer you investigate anything physical, you'll find the presence of its most essential component...its creator... its material...God.

Of all the elements, *akasha*, the essence of deep space, may be your easiest jumping-off point for wonder, being located beyond earth as well as within it. Questing, you can find akasha whether you look, up, down or sideways. Focus on the akasha component to make a mountain out of a molehill or morph a molehill into a mountain.

One way to wake up wonder is through loving people or pets, appreciating them deeply enough to reveal each being's unique essence. Or awaken wonder through service, working to the point of fatigue and beyond. Even physics can show you wonders of akasha, since elementary particles within the atom are almost unimaginably small — and link to each other across vast space.

But should no super-fancy microscope be available, know that prayer can get you there, too. Set your sights on akasha, close your eyes, and your consciousness knows how to take you. Fall straight up.

270. Who Is This Child of Wonder?

Begin to know her as great love, surprised.
Hearing a call to greater joy if she would only dare,
she chose "Yes": Leave familiar God
and be a human child.

Arrived on earth, how vulnerable this baby will appear.
Yet her soft, tender body merely is a symbol of
courageous trust and sacrifice,
the seeming risk she takes.

How hard it is to leave God's joy, forget Divinity
and all the wisdom learned in lives gone past.
Each human tear will hold
a small eternity.

Still has she chosen to be here and now.
She's come to join with us and brings this pledge:
We are to see this world together though our human eyes.
Divine sight is awakening us into the great surprise.

271. Cast the Burden More Creatively

Casting the Burden is a wonderful technique where we give up our troubles to a Divine Being and then let go. It's as though you were carrying a physical burden, like a bag of rocks, and now you are able to toss it onto the shoulders of Lao Tzu, St. Teresa, or some other capable being.

Sometimes this technique flows like a blissful dream. You feel peace. Immediately after you co-create, even a few seconds of relative peace can be an ample reward. Peace is one shape of the footprints of God.

But sometimes you'll heave that burden with all your might yet nothing happens. Say you've awoken in the middle of the night, racking your brains over a problem. You mutter something like, "Take it, St. Teresa." Then you roll over, struggling to get back to sleep.

Nevertheless, the problem keeps coming back, coming back. Well, consider that as an invitation to be creative. Ingenuity in bed isn't only for red hot lovers, you know. Ingenuity can be demanded even when you don't feel sexy or perky or in the mood for anything fancier than a good loud snore. Whenever and wherever casting the burden doesn't seem to work, stage it differently, with imagination, until you succeed. For example:

- Imagine that you are performing on stage, doing a complicated soft shoe routine, dancing right over your problem. Then you stop, change places with your Guardian Angel, point to him and say, "Take it."
- Stage a baseball game, where you see your problem being thrown to you in the form of a baseball. But no worries here, because if you strike out, see who is on deck. Krishna looks mighty strong standing there holding his baseball bat (and his blue skin makes a lovely contrast to the team uniform).
- Or wrap your request for help inside a yellow rose. Offer it to Kwan Yin. If worries come back, place your next request inside a pink carnation. After that, if needed, tuck your "Take it, Kwan Yin" into an enormous daisy. So long as you're stuck, semi-awake, you may as well say it with flowers — lots of them.

Sure, we're at school here on earth. And lessons aren't always scheduled for times when we're in the mood. But nothing and nobody can force you to be play grimly. Even when you feel as small as David facing Goliath, that's a great time to cast the burden. Let God in colossus form wield your slingshot.

272. Colorful Resolutions

Next time you make a wish or resolution, let it be *really* colorful. To do this properly, you'll need a full week, though only a few minutes each day.

Start with a suitable wish, something you really care about. Please, choose something attainable based on your efforts. Becoming a world-famous rock star won't work, being dependent on karmic caprice, but instead you could choose "I become a superb guitarist." Also, a negative wish, like "I stop eating candy" must be tinkered with a bit until you find the positive version, like "Because I take such physical and emotional pleasure in being healthy, I spontaneously choose only foods that are good for me."

Sit comfortably with eyes closed and imagine a scenario where your wish comes true. To add power, bring in a Divine Being. Activate all your senses, including your sense of humor. And now, here comes the colorful part.

- As though you were an artist gone wild, pour an enormous bucket of violet paint over the entire scene. Let that color soak into you and everyone else involved. Keep the paint coming until you've absorbed the perfect amount. Give thanks and you're done for Day #1.
- Day #2, pour on indigo paint.
- Day #3, drench yourself with sky blue.
- Day #4, let bright green seep through you.
- Day #5 is a cascade of sunshine yellow.
- Day #6, choose a bath of bright orange.
- Day #7, douse yourself in your favorite shade of red.

Why give yourself one full day for each color? You'll allow your body-mind-spirit system to soak it in completely.

Each hue is encoded with a package of information about a certain vibration. Now, as you may have noticed, everyday life contains a mixture of colors. By letting yourself take in the full sequence, you're helping your wish to manifest in the full range of earth frequencies.

May your fulfillment be, likewise, sumptuously real.

273. Rainbow Tea

Sun tea is good for your aura. But you can improve upon the well known recipe. Make rainbow tea.

Start with a clear glass jar big enough to brew several cups. Add teabags of your choice. Or use no teabags at all, if you'd prefer something that tastes more like regular water (but isn't).

Place your jar by a sunny window or outdoors where light will strike it but casual strollers won't. Now comes the fun part. On a slip of paper, write the name of a Divine Being, either alone or as a sentence like "Ganesh, help me to brew this rainbow tea."

Next, write your blessing du jour, like "Relaxation" or "More Self-Love."

Amplify the blessing with color, anything along the rainbow spectrum from red to violet. Write the name of your chosen color on the slip of paper. Then slip your slip beneath the brewing jar.

An extra option is to place an object with your chosen color next to the jar. This could be a gemstone or crystal, provided that your brewing place is very secure. Otherwise, make do with a colorful glass, even a piece of plastic or clothing in the right shade.

Water easily picks up any vibrations you add to it. Your rainbow tea will be steeped in blessings galore. The colorful frequencies help because — unbeknownst to you — your aura could have a deficiency of green. Or you might be lacking in yellow, etc. (Can't you just see the TV commercials?) Give yourself a week, if you can, to rotate through the whole rainbow.

Yes, rainbow tea is definitely water soluble. Any frequencies that you don't need will run through you, just like excessive amounts of any water-soluble vitamins. But the colors that you need will soak right into you. Be a thirsty sponge, then, and let the full range of God's glorious blessings plump you up.

Cheers!

274. The Two Journeys of Illness

Whenever illness disrupts your life, your soul is summoned on a journey with two destinations to choose from. The first is *Victim Land.*

Symptoms are the signposts here. How did your illness begin, with which problem? When more medical problems show on the horizon, do they represent the road before you or merely a mirage?

In Victim Land, nobody is terribly interested in your ideas or opinions, your imagination, your ideals or what makes you special. You count only as a collection of data and, supposedly, what matters most about you are statistics like your temperature and weight, plus the results of medical tests.

Survival becomes the goal. Because pain makes time seem to expand, even a few hours in Victim Land can drag into an eternity of isolation and fear. Worst is the temptation to (figuratively) start to rent property here, like a dismal second home, an antiseptic-smelling cabin which you expect to revisit on a regular basis.

In hospitals, staff sometimes refer to patients by illness instead of by name. Mr. Smith and Ms. Jones become "The Cancer Case" and "The Heart Case." Sometimes the patient takes on that identity, too, for self or family or friends. To the extent this happens, Victim Land can become a person's *primary* residence.

But an alternative journey is possible. When illness kicks you out of your regular life, with just the right body English (sometimes known as co-creation), you can land somewhere entirely different: *The Kingdom of Spiritual Truth.*

Here your belief system rules. Rediscover how you are more than your physical body. Commit to learning wherever you may be, even here. Could your awareness become extra sensitive in some way, once your life shifts away from the usual patterns?

In Victim World, you'd say, "I'm sick." But in the Kingdom of Spiritual Truth, it's more accurate — if a bit long-winded — to say something like, "I (a much-loved portion of God, always connected to God, embodied first and foremost in pure consciousness) am going through a temporary sickness experience."

Illness disrupts normal life. Yet it can also bring a new start. Inconvenient though it is to release your expectations, this may be exactly what's needed for your next step of spiritual evolution. Perfectly paced, you'll move back and forth between The Kingdom of Spiritual Truth, or Victim World, and your usual life. Gradually, in a fascinating way, you'll return to normal.

Normal — that's when things that used to be taken for granted now seem to sparkle like treasure. Whichever journey you took in your illness, everyday life will shine more brightly because you have traveled.

275. Inner Ghost Removal — Part 1

Sometimes a name will come up from your past and you'll be reminded of something you'd rather forget. Well, you have the power to banish that inner ghost.

First revisit the story behind this specter of regret. Every inner haunting has a story. You've told it to yourself so many times, reliving the pain or guilt, shame or fear. Revisiting that story one final time, by choice, won't hurt you.

So summon up your courage. Call on a Divine Being to keep you company. Step One of ghost removal is to remember the facts of the case.

Keep your mind open as if seeing the story unfold in the present. Be as objective as possible. Dare to believe that whatever happened wasn't merely bad karma returning or someone else's problem. Seeing your story anew can help you to change it.

Step Two allows you to go subjective. Each ghost brings up unfinished business. Strong emotions are attached. Feel them now. Denied negative feelings can actually feed a ghost; the haunting will continue until your unresolved feelings are laid to rest. You are doing this now.

When you're in touch with emotions related to your inner ghost, ask your Divine Being to bring forth a perspective you've never had before. Why is this ghost standing before you? It's not just to make your heart heavy but to bring you one final lesson. Which is what? Ask inside.

No cheery moral will be delivered, necessarily. But *something* will come to mind that can satisfy you. If not, prompt the information to come by asking questions like these:

- What do you wish you had known back then?
- What could you learn from this memory?
- Whatever it takes for you to feel right about that person or situation, give that to yourself. New emotions can be bought for surprising little, you know. Self-compassion, for instance, is on sale this week.

Dedicate this day to receiving all the *knowledge* you need to heal this inner ghost completely. The knowledge will come as gently as possible, and you will receive only as much as you can handle while staying psychologically balanced.

As the information flows through you, observe it without feeling as though you must become deeply involved. For instance, "That's interesting" might be a useful attitude.

Tomorrow we'll add the extra steps to make ghost removal complete.

276. Inner Ghost Removal – Part 2

Several steps are involved in removing an inner ghost from your past. Yesterday we focused on two. Step One was objective, where you remembered what happened. Step Two was subjective, where you added new interpretations.

Now you can completely remove the ghost from your aura. Ask a Divine Being what this will take. At the longest, your answer will come within three days. Sometimes an energy worker or healer can help, and there's no shame in paying for a little assistance; we all need that sometimes. Other times you'll immediately figure out a splendid do-it-yourself which takes very little time or effort. (Our previous technique for removing an outdated vow, for instance, might do the trick.)

All that remains is restitution. If you're the *perpetrator*, do it to the best of your ability. What if the person you hurt isn't alive or won't cooperate? Create your own Ceremony of Restitution, like the one that follows.

But what if you were the *victim?* Don't sit around waiting. This would give too much power to someone who has already hurt you. Again, take the initiative to create your own Ceremony, like the one that follows, only for you it may be about Releasing Victimhood as much as receiving restitution.

Call on a Divine Being to bring a blessing. Then speak aloud the name of your ghost. This will bring a portion of his or her energy into the room with you. Speaking aloud, go into detail about your side of the story, including your perspective about how that person wronged you, or what you did that was hurtful, or both.

Say plainly what you would like to have happened then, instead. Add what you wish could happen *now*, effective immediately.

Say goodbye to the ghost in your ceremony. And ask the Divine Being with you, "Please cut all psychic ties between [the ghost] and me, then fill me with clean new light."

Then address the ghost who has been in your ceremony. Say three times, "Leave here immediately. I command you never to return."

You're nearly finished with this vestige of your past. The last part is to check if there is some material reminder that could be thrown away or donated to charity?

Could this be the perfect time to buy yourself something new? Or can you find a perfect affirmation and place it somewhere prominent so you will see it often for a few days? Follow your inner wisdom.

Now, congratulations. You're done. Next time you look in a mirror, check out your eyes. With that ghost gone, the only one looking back will be you.

277. Guilty As Charged

Could your spiritual credit card account be weighing you down with debt? Energy transactions on earth can be paid fully as you go, rather than stored as unpaid balances. But lacking a wee bit of knowledge, it's easy to go into debt.

For example, say that a neighbor of yours has a problem. You offer to help but the neighbor declines your offer. If you let that rejection take on a personal resonance, you could be paying interest. And often those energy debts take on the quality of guilt, as in "What was wrong with me that the offer wasn't accepted. Wasn't I good enough?"

Or perhaps an overly demanding neighbor asked for a favor that you declined to give. Even though you did the right thing, the wise thing, you felt badly afterwards. Ding! Another guilt charge rang on your inner cash register.

And here's a funny thing about energy transactions. Often the amount is compounded by how much intensity the *other* person puts into the situation. So even if your first reaction is to punish yourself in the amount of one dollar, the bill could ring up more like a million. Still, not a penny of this need go into today's unpaid balance on your spiritual bank account.

It helps to understand the nature of spiritual economics. Here at Earth School, opportunities for choice abound, and each choice carries potential for regret — in monetary terms, that's spiritual debt. Nonetheless, you've heard of the term "free will," right? Your choices really can be free. Here's the trick:

After you take an action of any kind, you have the right to feel good about it. If your reaction is negative instead, question what happened. Especially pay attention when some form of guilt sets in. It's human to have distinctive ways of berating yourself, whether you favor self-criticism, helplessness, grumbling and so forth. Whatever that inner currency may be, refuse to spend it.

Understand, starting right now, that guilt means a debit has registered on your spiritual bank account. But when problems are difficult to resolve, that doesn't necessarily make them your fault. Maybe you've just taken on an ambitious assignment here on The Learning Planet. Likewise, it isn't your fault if another person does something unanticipated, ignorant or purposely hurtful. You are responsible only for doing the best you can.

So when guilt rings up, don't accept the charge. Do what it takes to clear the emotion: Take new action. Revisit the memory and change your interpretation. Or ask God to bring you extra light, love and power. Use that today to pay off past debt. Then you can enjoy the rest of today by spending some of your birthright, an inexhaustible supply of spiritual joy.

278. Breathe Peace

At work today, please give yourself a break.

You may already be given an official coffee break. If so, use it for something unusual. Close your eyes for a short visualization, where you imagine that God is giving you something surprising and wonderful. Then breathe some peace.

If your usual routine doesn't include coffee breaks, grab enough time to breathe peace secretly. Make it like a surprise birthday party that you give to yourself. (Even the stingiest boss can afford your private, two-minute celebration.)

So there you are, officially or not, on break. Breaks come in handy since one way to breathe peace is — you guessed it — to break something up.

Divide your usual breathing cycle into four segments. Be graceful about it, since it is never wise to force your breathing. Be graceful and, even, creative.

To measure each of the four breathing segments, I hope you realize that you can do something far more interesting than simply counting. Choose a phrase with special meaning for you, like "I remember that my nature is peace."

Think it on your *in-breath*, "I remember that my nature is peace."

Hold the in-breath, savoring it, and think, "I remember that my nature is peace."

Breathing out, think, "I remember that my nature is peace."

Then *hold* the out-breath, as you say to yourself, "I remember that my nature is peace."

Returning from this breathing "break," you'll find that nothing important was broken at all. Instead, you'll feel more whole.

279. More Than You Know

Today you'll work hard, doing your best,
and succeed in your goals (or maybe not)
but in God's terms, your very striving matters
more than you know.

Inevitably nighttime shadows come.
Even successes pale, their luster gone.
Yet in things big and small, your life succeeds
far better, bigger, more…than you can know.

The golden power of choice carries you forward,
that hero's sword you bring to conquer fears.
When fighting dulls your sword, leaves you exhausted,
at your side God counts up the victories
a world of them, and more than you can know.

Seek understanding and you'll start to notice:
What is your job? God wants just *that* from you?
Worry will turn to peace, delight be found
in more ways than (so far) you could possibly know.

280. Family Gems

To be understood straight to your soul, even for a few hours, is like having some-one give you a special jewel. So many relationships are more like pebbles.

Take one of the jewels from your family memory box now. Shine it up with gratitude.

- Remember that special walk with your father? Let it gleam like an emerald.
- How about that time your mother helped with homework? Her confidence in you was like a gift of pearls.
- Farther back, a loving grandmother pushed you on a swing, tossing out the equivalent of rubies for you to keep for the rest of your life. Maybe she was intimidated by you in later years, and she felt embarrassed that her English wasn't so good, but before then what enchantments you shared.

How can we repay those who gave us their very greatest gems, soul to soul? Trea-sured moments don't come labeled, neatly packaged like jewelry for sale in a store, where a set value has been written on a price tag. Often it's only in retrospect that we discern which were the real treasures, our spiritual heirlooms.

Sheer comfort can keep the best memories hidden. A perfect link between someone else's soul and yours can be overlooked just because it fits so snugly. Besides, a heavenly wisdom causes us to *expect* all family relationships to be per-fect. Therefore, we're more apt to remember the contrasts — the unpleasant jolts, the pebbles and rocks.

But today you can sort that out beautifully. Inwardly summon up your family treasures. Then pick up the phone to say thanks. Or send a prayer. Alternatively you might resolve to pay each favor *forward;* connect to someone in your life now and bring your best gifts, soul to soul.

In material life, wealth is limited. A diamond can be worn on one ring only. Spiritually, however, gems multiply. That relative who taught you how to do dia-monds will be blessed whenever you pass along the legacy. Through generosity, you can honor all those who taught you the meaning of spiritual treasure.

281. Why That Family?

"Genius" refers to your destiny as a world server, your spiritual mission. Being at Earth School, however, a person's genius usually develops the hard way, unannounced by choir music or obvious angels, and often in response to problems with family life. Looking back on your childhood, you may see problems but do you recognize how they helped to bring out your *genius*?

- Did your family neglect you? Maybe it was important for you to learn independence.
- Was your family psychologically unbalanced? Maybe you were apprenticing to serve humanity as a psychological healer.
- Were you forced to grow up too fast? By taking time as an adult to consciously nurture your Inner Child, you can become an expert at helping others to reclaim their innocence.

Nobody ever said — then or now — that worthwhile service to the world could come without struggle. If some childhood joys were missing, consider that you were pushed to supply them for yourself in order to make them extra memorable. Precisely this hard-won knowledge has helped you serve others.

No mere twists of fate, any major hideous happenings in your past were probably chosen by you. You may have felt joyful when you wrote them into your Life Contract.

Skeptical? Then think about one major childhood problem. How did you overcome it? Didn't that experience teach you something marvelous that you've used ever since to help others?

Skills that you developed for self-preservation may not feel noble but, of course, they still count. Genius is expressed by your way of being who you are. And this is exactly what your family — whether good, bad or a mixture of both — instilled into your character.

You began this lifetime as a graced child of God. However terrible any past suffering, know that it was an apprenticeship, never intended to harm you long-term.

Now the challenge is yours. Work your genius. Through inner experience, outer skills, what will you give the world today?

282. Argumentative Relatives

When you think about relatives who don't appreciate you, do many faces come to mind? Maybe it's only one distant cousin. Or, alas, it could be most of your family.

Relatives could object to your job, your marital status, your religion, your car, your parenting, your diet, your clothes. Whatever the problem, it can haunt your visits, and not like some wispy ghost but more like the unacknowledged elephant in the room.

Having big integrity, you may torment yourself about disclosure. How damaging is it to hide things from relatives? Dare you express your opinions? What will happen if relatives insist on fighting with you one more time "for your own good"?

Fortunately, you can avoid most arguments. Assess the players *objectively*. How much truth about you can each difficult relative stomach?

In some cases, it may be wise to tell them your ideas…once. Then leave them to the polite family dinner, augmented by a good stew in their own juices. Be secure in the knowledge that you've added the flavoring packet.

Will an argumentative family member ever admit that you could be right about something? Don't hold your breath, chum. Just swallow the words trying to fly out along with the carbon dioxide.

You can be remarkably effective as a long-distance relative. Try being long-distance even if in the same room! Not expecting approval, you can love relatives, hold them in the Light, do your duty by them.

But you can do all this beautifully on your own time. While you're cooped up with them, sometimes the best strategy is keeping up appearances. Go through the motions of having a polite visit. Expecting your communication to feel great on the *inside* is unrealistic. Fred Astaire could dance with a coat rack and make it look good; few of us are willing to practice that hard, and why bother? For every person who doesn't like you, there are so many more who will (if only you get to know them).

Most difficult relatives will never notice when, inwardly, you're disengaged. If anything, *the less you show up, the more they'll like you.*

So count this as doing your duty.

Furthermore, know that your job was never to give any difficult relative a perfect life, either by his standard or yours. Each man is his own responsibility. Each woman is here to live her own life. That's plenty.

So you can afford to let all your difficult relatives be. May any lack of appreciation from them motivate you all the more…to co-create a magnificent life with God and your family of choice.

283. Inconvenient Relatives

Even after you're a teenager, some relatives are just plain embarrassing. Show me a man who doesn't think his family is, in some way, weird and I'll show you an orphan.

Each of us must cope with quirks and crotchets. Many of us have to deal with tragedies in the making or tragedies overcome: Alcoholism, drug addiction, mental illness, physical illness, sexual problems. Afflictions like these are the rule in human life, not the rare exception. And, unlike what Job had to deal with, the worst grief in modern life is often hidden.

You can be sure that every family keeps secrets that are, to put it politely, inconvenient. What's astonishing is how well most of us hide them. Somehow we manage to make our lives good anyway. Even fervent atheists strive for happiness, creatively reinventing their circumstances, insisting on hope.

What counts is the striving, not the failures. In a world where fear and pain are as prevalent as gravity, all that matters is how and when we choose to lift ourselves up.

Notice it today, if you like — not necessarily with your family, but among people where you work, in your neighborhood or at the supermarket. Look carefully and you'll find someone who forces herself to lighten up with a laugh. Somebody else hides a grimace of pain beneath the armor of physical courage. Yet another brave soul struggles to solve an old problem in a new way or shows kindness when none was required.

In fact, the unsung hero who transcends life's inconveniences could be you.

284. Hurtful Relatives

Has someone in your family hurt you at one time or another? Hey, are tears wet? Earth School supplies fear and pain galore. But the good part is that no relative can damage you permanently. God has made you enormously resilient.

Old experiences have a way of replaying themselves inwardly. To change the tune, remember that your healing resources go beyond psychology. Co-create a spiritual change with God at the level of your aura and results will move outward to improve your whole life.

Read your aura for inspiration, also. You were born with at least one distinctive gift at every chakra. To start exploring, sit quietly, eyes closed, and take a few breaths. Think the name of a Divine Being. Prepare to research one chakra at a time. For instance, read your heart chakra, positioned at your breastbone.

To connect, close your eyes and lightly pay attention to that part of your physical body. Look there in the mirror. Or place one of your hands, palm toward you, several inches in front of your body at heart-chakra level.

Next, ask inside, "Emotionally, what is a gift of my soul?" An answer will come from within, perhaps staunch loyalty or a particular kind of gentleness.

Each strength can help you to deal with a hurtful relative. Besides that, each gift has a flip-side, a potential challenge. Understand it to keep people from taking advantage. For instance, if you're loyal *don't* keep giving relatives "one more chance." But *do* ask for help from old friends. With that gift of loyalty, you're sure to have long-time friends you can trust.

Another example: Should gentleness be your gift, *do* acknowledge how you've shown it. You could be the most refined person in your family. (There's a thought!) But *don't* be victimized by gentleness. Tell that family bully who's been trying to toughen you up, "No thanks." Explain that, from now on, once she starts screaming, you'll leave. Then do it, if you have to.

Every gift of your soul enables you to plant seeds of grace. Whether or not it results in a plant you can see, each good seed will flower eventually.

Meanwhile, self-knowledge will strengthen you. And what if, along with gifts, your aura shows problems? Pain caused by family members can be hard to dislodge. Ask God to help, removing one stored-up hurt at a time. After each removal, ask for your aura to be given a bandage made of light.

Sometimes healing your aura, even with God's assistance, is too tough to do alone. Then ask for human help. When the patient is ready, the doctor comes. So demand that God make you ready and then deliver the perfect healer for you.

285. The Right to Your Pain

"Oh, things haven't been that bad." It may seem to you that you've never suffered, not when compared to people you know whose lives have really been hell.

Now hear this. *You still have the right to your pain.*

Dramas recounted by people you know, or blown up extra-big on TV, can distort self-assessment. Back in childhood, what if your neighbor was raped, whereas you only had to wait many years too long to receive your first kiss? What if last year your best friend had a breakdown, whereas you just went through a tough couple of months, supposedly no big deal?

Well, you still have the right to acknowledge your pain. Thoroughly perfect lives seldom happen. If you feel that you've suffered, you're not making it up, nor are you necessarily whining.

Before you came into this life, you had attained a certain vibration of consciousness. All your suffering has been exquisitely calibrated to match this vibration. Picture this as a car driving down life's highway at a certain speed. At a lower speed (corresponding to a lower spiritual vibration), it would take a big pothole to jolt that car. But at a faster pace (corresponding to a very high spiritual vibration), even one tiny bump could set off a huge reaction.

Somebody else might call that bump a nothing, but what matters is the impact it had upon *you*. Comparing yourself to others is never a good idea, spiritually. Let assessing your life become a case in point. Minimizing your pain will only slow down your healing.

Whatever your life is like now, whatever happened to you earlier, you can count plenty of blessings. Gratitude moments, taken each day, can help you to find yet more good things. And you can ask God for even more of them, heaping blessing upon blessing.

But you also have a right to your pain. Acknowledge it honestly and you won't feel foolish asking for help with that, too.

286. Early or Late, Still Lucky

Fortunate are those whose worst suffering happens while they're still in childhood. If this is your story, you know how the pain helped you to grow up extra strong. Ever since, you've been especially grateful for blessings like good health, material comforts, every nurturing love relationship.

Yet equally lucky are those whose great trials come in early adulthood or later. If this is your story, you know that before the pain struck, you learned life is good. This sense of security has helped you to move through the rest.

Problems are inevitable. Only the timing varies. When setting up your Life Contract, you requested some big challenges. Otherwise, how could you receive a full education here at Earth School?

All the people you meet struggles in private, be it before or after you've met them. The fact that these struggles are generally kept secret only adds to their poignancy.

Wasn't your own compassion also developed in secret? That strength helps you to soothe others who need it, even when their problems aren't discussed directly.

When you're the one who needs help, don't feel shy about asking assistance from friends. That includes God, whose answers can fit your pain like a key sliding into a lock. So long as you've signed up for a tough class at Earth School, you may as well ask your Tutor to help you earn an A.

Today, observe the *hidden* process of learning that goes on all around you. Just beneath the surface of life, all of Earth School's students swap survival secrets. They're encoded into our very being.

Whether your toughest courses come early or late, you're lucky. The curriculum will challenge you to develop your highest wisdom. Then your example can help all the rest of humanity to graduate with honors.

287. Family Prayer

When you love 'em, give thanks for them. When they're hard to love, or even to like, that's all the more reason to pray for each person in your family.

Complicated though it can be to deal with relatives, at least this part can be simple. Connect to God in your favorite way. Then think of each person in turn, surrounded by white light.

Or stand facing the sun and hold out your palms. Say the person's name out loud. Imagine white light pouring through your hands, streaming like snow. The blessing will reach the recipient. When you feel the flow stop, it's complete, so say "Thank You." You're done.

Amazing things can happen when you pray for your family. Besides sending a powerful blessing to each individual, you may be offered something precious in return: An entirely different perspective.

Family portraits don't only hang on walls, you know. They lodge deep inside us. It's human to develop set ways of seeing people at their worst. And, perhaps, they wish they had been more kind or generous toward you.

Yet seen in the light of prayer, each relative's struggle may seem different to you. Remember how frail this one has been for years? Can you feel the pride of that one, pushing against obstacles? Emotionally crippled in some ways, he's still valiantly trying to do the best he can.

Sometimes the easiest way to forgive a person's imperfections isn't to dwell on problems at all. Denial won't help, either. But grace? It can add the very bit that was lacking, easing both your feelings and spilling over to help with your relative's problem.

So why not volunteer to send out a bit of grace? Unconditional love can be given in many ways beside prayer: Generous actions, a friendly postcard or phone call, any unexpected kindness.

What happens as a result? By giving, you transcend petty worries over what has or hasn't been done for you lately. Offer any simple blessing and the one that spiritual law sends you back will be even bigger.

288. Family Secrets

When you were young
they told you *what*?
That you were *who*?
That they were *that*?

But the best parts
remained untold.
Such as?
Your energy, your soul.

There's greatness in your heritage
and in yourself. Discover which
amazing folks live in your midst.
Each one is more than a mere *who*.

You are — and always were — a *wow*!

289. Your Family of Choice

As a child, you tried so hard to perfect all your family relationships. Now you can make a more mature assessment. What is reasonable to expect from any of these people?

Parents made Life Contracts to give you a body, genes and all. Any closeness beyond that is wonderful...but optional.

It takes great spiritual maturity to love and honor family members without expecting more closeness than they can give.

Especially, don't waste your time trying to convert family members into fans. If their curiosity about your life is minimal, maybe you're better off not telling them. Sure, it's human to seek approval. But get it from friends who are capable of giving it to you, none of whom must necessarily be a blood relation.

Kindred spirits are the ones to confide in. Think about how you act in some of your strongest relationships. Do these special people in your life show qualities of mother, father, sister, brother or child? That's Family of Choice.

Ask God to help you find yours, also to keep you balanced while dealing with your blood relatives.

Yes, both requests are equally appropriate. You have no right to pray that God will change relatives — just as, thank goodness, none of them has the right or power to force God to change *you*.

290. *Your Extra Mom*

Your mother did the best she could, but that's no reason you can't have an extra one or two, filling up any empty Mom-places in your soul.

Even if your original mother-figure did an excellent job, she specialized because all people must.

Was she socially adept? Then maybe you'd benefit from a homebody who wants nothing more than to be with you.

Did she make you the center of her life? Sometimes that could have felt like a burden. Now that you're grown, what's to stop you from shrugging it off? Give your shoulders a much needed ripple, then indulge in an extra, flaw-free and self-sufficient Mother with a capital M?

By now you know the spiritual principle of attraction. Intend to attract Her and, immediately, you'll start to make friends with women (and men) who embody the very qualities of motherhood you need most.

Supplementary mothers who have just these desirable qualities will show up in your life when least expected. Why, she could be on TV tonight! Or maybe you can rent her tearjerker movie or the brilliant comedy where she is the star.

What, nobody has made a movie yet about your ideal mother? And no astonishingly perfect neighbor-Mom has materialized yet? Then it's time to bring out a pillow. Play dolls in a way that you couldn't while growing up. Let Mother Doll tell you what you've been longing to hear.

Ideally, a mother doesn't give life to you only once. She does it repeatedly, nurturing the best in you. A completely satisfying mother accepts you, understanding you at every stage in your development. With her love, she draws close, yet she also provides the distance you need.

Besides this, an ideal mother can model a purposeful life. She will show tolerance for her own limitations, so you can forgive them in her... and later, with practice, accept your own.

Does your birth mother happen to fall short of this ideal in any respect? Might she have bad habits, worries or sorrows? Surely she carries at least one nasty scar someplace. Hey, she's entitled; nobody gets through this world alive. What a welcome relief, then, that you can bring on the Extras!

Ever dream about what you might be when you grow up? Your Extra Mom can help you to make it real.

291. The Dad of Your Dreams

Being a father is no easy job except, perhaps, for conception. If your father was perfect, congratulations are due — both to him and to you. Otherwise, you may wish to supplement the man who raised you with a Dad of Your Dreams.

No disrespect is meant by doing this, any more than you're scoffing at the chef who cooked your four-star dinner if, after dessert, you pop a few vitamins.

Here is your chance to make sure that you've received your total supply of father love, plus wise man-style guidance.

Did your father protect you, provide for you, give to you generously? Was he both tough and tender? Could he model the perfect combination of success at work, happiness at home?

Many a grown woman bides her time, awaiting a "Perfect Mate" who will exemplify these qualities and also be hot. Many a grown man struggles, despairing that he can't develop fatherly attributes since he couldn't apprentice them from his own parent.

Yet every good quality you seek lies within you. Ask God to show it to you. Within your deep memory of lifetimes past, *you* may have been such a father. Certainly you have known one.

In this lifetime you can know one now, too, even if you must piece him together from an assortment of human heroes. Of course you can put together this jigsaw puzzle, although it doesn't come pre-packaged in a nice box with the completed picture on the cover. You can find him and even enjoy the game. It is part puzzle solving, part scavenger hunt, part sacred mystery.

Just for today, think of one fatherly quality you're still seeking in order to complete him, this Dad of your Dreams. Feel it. Draw it. Or write it down in words: "Today I attract the quality of ___."

Then let it go.

Now you've done the "hard" part. God will hear your call. For the rest of today, you'll attract experiences that are rich in this very quality. Like a lucky detective, you will stumble upon one clue after another. Or maybe you'll find *yourself* spontaneously displaying the very quality you desire. Amazingly, yes, you may find that it already lies within you.

However it happens, give thanks when that empty Father space within is filled, once and for starters.

292. The Blessing of Divorce

"When I grow up, could I please get a divorce?"

What kid in his or her right mind would request such a thing? Yet many of us did, when making Life Contracts. The most unlikely couples get together just long enough to birth someone. Precisely that set of genes and circumstances is required, and who are we to say that God isn't, ultimately, a wise matchmaker?

A broken relationship doesn't mean either partner is guilty. Yet guilt over divorce is common, and for many of us the worst part is fear that divorce means we somehow have disrespected God. Divorce feels like a failure, even if you had good reason to do it yourself, even if during childhood you would have done anything to keep your parents together.

The fact that divorce is more common today doesn't mean that people are more unhappy, nor that we marry for sillier reasons than those property deals which used to be made via wedlock. For many of your ancestors, physical survival was sufficient. Today, people have the luxury of demanding more.

What about children caught in the middle? Some of us are learning what to avoid when we grow up. Others discover strengths we wouldn't have developed otherwise.

All of us live at a time of accelerated human evolution. Even if you don't believe in reincarnation, you're sure seeing it now. Within this one lifetime, most people are going through multiple incarnations. Aren't you? Multiple residences, jobs, love relationships — you may even be changing your religion and other deep ways of defining your identity.

In such a whirl of a world, you may need new questioning of old assumptions.

Do you believe you signed up for this contract? Then turn it into a story of triumph.

Do you believe that God is really Perfection Everywhere Now or merely some bored administrator? If parts of your story feel incomplete, ask God to help fill in the blanks. Keep asking until the whole thing makes sense to you.

Don't allow any part of your story — past, present, or future — to be diminished by divorce.

And know that you are linked to your Divine Love with bonds that can never be broken. *One day at a time, marry your good.* This is how to live happily ever after.

293. Peacemaking

Ever wish you had a knack for peacemaking? Don't judge your abilities by whether, in childhood, you could quell quarrelsome multitudes with a mere wave of your hand. Peacemaking is a *skill* that can be acquired, comparable to kneading dough.

No step of bread baking requires extraordinary talent. But it does take a combination of practice and faith. You push around a paste of flour, yeast and water, trying to make it amount to something. At first, you may be too gentle or too rough. But after a few tussles, you'll find exactly the right touch.

Dough, you'll discover, has innate resilience. So do you. It becomes fun, making that dough rock 'n roll to its own perfect rhythm.

Outside the kitchen, in life's living room (along with your challenging relationships), guess what? You can develop a similar skill at kneading people into peace. Free will being what it is, you won't be able to force everyone to like everyone else. But you can encourage a group's vibrations to take the best possible shape. To do this, calm down. Take a deep breath. Then ask inside to connect to God. Quick as thought, it's done. Now:

- Confirm Divine presence by listening for an underlying silence. Hear that? It's there, right by you, regardless of nasty vibes or hideous dialogue.
- What if you're more visual than auditory? Then notice God's presence by looking for physical light in the room. Where does that light come from, and which lovely patterns does it make?
- If you're kinesthetic more than visual or auditory, find peace within your own body. How does the God presence show up? Maybe it's the smooth flow of your breathing or the soothing drum of your heart. Maybe you'll coax in more peace by the way you plant your feet on the floor.
- You definitely have at least one good way to establish an inner connection. Do it. Then be with the *energy* of the group you are in. Set the intention to hold a space for peace.

Afterwards, here's what you *don't* have to do: Say a lot. Peacemaking doesn't depend on words. It happens when you accept the group, feel its rhythm and let things take shape in their own way. (Actually, if you allow this to happen before expressing your opinion, you're more likely to be heard.)

Will all group members feel peaceful once your meeting has ended? There's no guarantee, not for them anyway. You, however, are under Divine warranty. So breathe peace, feel peace, eat it up.

294. In My Own Way

If I have come here as a teacher of love, let me do it in my own way. Whatever else I've been taught doesn't count.

Parents, religious leaders and other role models are fine for inspiration. But nobody else can teach me *my* way to express love. It's unique.

Today I resolve to be honest with myself. When there's choice, sure, I'll take the higher road. Yet I can only choose in my own way.

Have I valued enough what I've given others? Just because I once gave without struggling doesn't mean that I must keep on giving forever until it hurts.

Have I acknowledged how tough it has been, sometimes, giving love? Maybe the person I cared about most never noticed, didn't thank me, *couldn't* thank me. But that doesn't mean my love was wasted. Each time I've felt love or shown love to someone, that person was God in disguise. On the spiritual level, at least, my love reached its destination perfectly.

What about that old trap, comparing myself to a spiritual hero and coming up short? NEVER AGAIN.

In human life no matter how noble or clever or kind I am at anything, certain people won't be as good while certain others will be better. How lucky then, that I don't have to keep score. All I need do is remember: *My own way is the right way.*

Back when I was a baby, I cooed at the world. And people cooed back, loving me just for being here, fresh from heaven.

Since then, I've learned a great deal about love. My skin may be battered, not smooth like a baby's. This change symbolizes how hard it can be to keep caring and coping. If I were baby-sized now, I'd be funny looking but — to a discerning eye — perhaps even more adorable.

It is wonderful, actually, how today I am willing to keep on loving, no matter what.

I resolve to give however I can, with enthusiasm or steadiness, strength or gentleness, keeping the personal boundaries that will help me to give more love tomorrow.

May today's love flow wherever most needed, far and wide, near and dear. Let today be a holiday of love where, without holding back, I will offer what I've always offered when at my best. I will offer my love.

295. Part CEO, Part Movie Star

Not to make you feel self-conscious about getting dressed, but do you realize that you're never alone?

A company of angels is with you. For starters, you have a guardian angel who signed up to help you 24/7 for this entire incarnation. His or her presence is so familiar, it may feel like your own inner voice, yet it's different.

Call it conscience, if you feel shy about admitting you're angel-worthy. Or think of it as a third shadow made of light (supplementing both your physical shadow and the psychological one in your subconscious mind).

Just find *some* comfortable way to think about your Family of Choice in the celestial realms, because your guardian angel is only the beginning.

Things you do in your spiritual life will add more angels to the committee, e.g., baptism, initiation into meditation, learning a healing art like Reiki.

Depending upon what you choose to learn, other angelic guides will come by to assist you temporarily. Some psychics have the ability to tell you about them in great detail. Regardless of whether or not you become conscious that these angels are present, they are whispering into your ears right now. Angels may automatically become part of your thinking process.

Yet usually these unselfish volunteers will show themselves clearly only if you ask to know more about them. The exception is the rare instance where one must intervene to save your life, like one of those mysterious near-wrecks on the highway. And fortunately most of us are spared this scary kind of drama.

Extra angels join with you whenever you assume greater responsibilities, whether receiving a big job promotion, becoming a parent or serving others through volunteer work. And have you ever done one of those *screaming prayers?* "God, how am I ever going to get through this? Help me." Enter another angel or two.

So there you are, CEO of an ever-growing company.

Don't worry. You're still in charge. You're the face out front, like a movie star who looks great because of all the makeup artists, script writers, press agents, working behind the scenes — hundreds of names that appear in the final screen credits.

All this adds to your personal power. So choose boldly what you want for your human life. And think big as you contribute to life in your spiritual role as world server.

Whatever you do today, however you decide to co-create with God, the "you" part of co-creation includes a whole company of angels.

296. Be Fruitful, Multiply

Having children is only the obvious way to reproduce. It can also be done through problem solving, cooking or conversation, making art or making love. Even dressing yourself in a new outfit counts as a bit of reproduction.

Why? Look back over any of your creative achievements. It left a fingerprint at the soul level, a memory for everyone and everything you touched. Creativity reproduces your soul's distinctive vibration, which blesses people in ways that only *they* can reckon.

Physically, you were made with a reproductive system that has amazing fecundity. Whether male or female, you've produced more sperm or eggs than could ever be brought to maturity. Even a fraction of that potential would birth a huge number of progeny.

Well, that reproductive richness symbolizes the innumerable *spiritual* ways that a person can be fruitful.

Childlessness is possible only biologically. Those who don't birth children physically receive a subtle, non-physical invitation to serve as a parent to all. Beyond that, everyone is charged to be fertile some way or other. When you find your favorite ways to be fruitful, you'll be on your way to fulfillment in life.

And, speaking of fulfillment, have you ever noticed the distinctive creativity typical of women who've gone through menopause? These crones are some of life's boldest creators. That's because each crone has learned:

- Whatever she creates will take on an uncontrollable life of its own and, therefore, bring surprising results.
- Whatever transpires, she can handle it.

In the words of one of my crone-friends, "I've seen it all. I've been through it all. I can fix it all." Regardless of your sex or age — and even within the context of a single day — you can create with chutzpah. Actually, you owe it to yourself. Your fruitfulness isn't merely potential. It's a longing.

The only way to satisfy your urge to create is to let yourself do it, preferably with exuberance. Of course you can create. You were born to be fruitful.

Another gift of yours is managerial; you will always find a way to cope with problems resulting from your creations. You'll be able to deal with all consequences, one by one.

So be fruitful and multiply, confident that you also are good at the other necessary job: Be resourceful and divide.

297. Family Hunger

God, can't you satisfy this appetite?
Please help me feel I never am alone,
a stranger amid strangers. Make me known
and loved so thoroughly that even when
discouraged or depressed, I've company.

Then send me out to gather up more kin
discerning out of all humanity
which people can be the best friends to me
and, more than friends, be like divinity
made human. Bring me new ones every day.

Then we can share new childhoods through our eyes.
No petty fights for us, just love and help.
Rebelling, we'll explore life. Growing up,
we'll share achievements, our pride running deep
and wide, until we find full family.
For our shared world aren't you, too, hungry, God?

298. Trumpets of Masculine Energy

Announcing…the force that helps you to make a name for yourself, move forward and accomplish great things. Hail masculine energy, your can-do courage!

Regardless of your gender and sexual orientation, masculine energy lives within you. It must. Otherwise you'd be a pathetic, helpless puddle of a person. Today, you're invited to savor this can-do power. Show your leadership.

Why wait for anybody else to provide that for you? With resolve, you can defend yourself from danger. With dignity, you can ignore false alarms. And conquering all challenges, you can show a kingly mercy to others when using your masculine energy. Forcefulness at its best is kind.

And by all means, notice the superb role models who come before you today. These people are magnificently aligned with their Inner Warrior. Notice how they walk, how they talk.

Learn about power from those you meet who do masculine energy beautifully. Whatever you admire in someone else will be strengthened within your own soul.

Of course, when you need extra strength, you can always call on God.

But with all the combined resources of heaven and earth, you'll still need to do your human part. So open to the mighty power of masculine energy, as expressed humanly, and discover what you can accomplish.

299. Echoes of Feminine Energy

In one respect your life today is identical to your life 10 years ago: There's plenty to do.

Yet doing — the principle of masculine energy — is only half of the equation. In your life, there is, was, and always will be plenty of ways to *be*, not just do.

Whether you're physically male or female, straight or gay or bi, sexually hot as a volcano or as chaste as new snow, God has created you with a combination of masculine and feminine energy. Masculine energy is obvious. But how can you enjoy the benefits of that more mysterious feminine side? Simply be.

Why bother just to *be* when there are so many things to *do*? Action-less action helps to manifest your heart's desire, enlisting the support of God in ways that complement human effort (and may even surpass it).

Besides, being holds bliss, the most delectable fruit of any action you might take. Deep silence wraps around it, like the peel of an orange. Even the act of releasing that fruit will entice you with the most delectable, delicate perfume.

What will you need to become more aware of your capacity to be? Time helps. And for that, a good night's sleep adds clarity. Easing a few minutes of relaxation into your packed schedule would provide extra space to breathe and be.

Yet, ultimately, you can access your feminine energy no matter what. Regardless of having an overstuffed scheduled or stressed-out physical body, your choice can be made right in the moment. Automatically space-time will open… just like a large picture window that lifts with the gentlest touch.

By your own choice, take a deep breath and enjoy the moment. Just. Being. You. In. The. Moment. Now.

After any action you take, it will strengthen your feminine energy if you'll pause to notice the reaction to what you've done. Whenever you speak or sing, with other people or alone, echoes reverberate. Explore them. Discover what happens right after you eat or drink, listen or look at, enter or exit, wake or sleep.

Always there will be gaps between any two actions. Explore these gaps, and you'll awaken your feminine energy. You may also discover another face of God, silent and loving.

300. Reclaim Sexual Power

Who controls your sexuality? Is it you? Sure hope so! Officially or not, often another person entirely has been put in charge.

For instance, your parent or lover could hold scolding rights. In some marriages, a power freak has been given permission to dole out all the orgasms for your entire life. How much sense does that make?

Sometimes religious or spiritual authorities dictate sexual choices, setting a person up for a lifetime of shoulds. Whether or not you obey, in the back of your mind, the authority figure could be scolding you every time. Shared love with a consenting partner is your right. (So is having a good time all by yourself.) And religious coercion can be released permanently, even if stuck in your aura for decades.

Just like religious bullies, some therapists can take away one's sexual power. Fear or self-doubt can make a person vulnerable when an expert holds out hope of being "normal," whatever that is.

Even pleasure vendors can temporarily wreck a person's sexuality. Pornography starts as escapist pleasure, then can turn into a frightening obsession.

Whoever, whatever, you have put in charge of your sex life…can easily control the rest of you, including your creativity, your joy, your peace of mind, your health. Why not make sure that this super-influential person is you?

If there's a problem, ask God to help you co-create a solution. (And one of the great things about going directly to God is that here, at last, is someone guaranteed to be free of sexual hang-ups.)

Sometimes prayer will lift a problem completely. Yet spiritual exercise alone won't necessarily take care of a sexual problem, no more than your car would be fixed by parking it inside a confessional. If necessary, you and God can go together for help from a non-coercive expert, like an energy healer, past-life regression therapist, spiritual counselor, psychologist or sex therapist.

Sex is a complex flow of energy. It can tangle so easily, causing guilt or shame. Did you ever appear too interested or not interested enough? As a teen, did you worry about your sexual orientation? As a child, were you caught playing "doctor"? You and almost everyone else! Why keep that old stuff stuck in you now?

Let sexual energy take its rightful role in your life as a huge energy resource. Remove extra influences until the truth is clear: *Sexually you are perfect.* May sexual wholeness make life extra-enjoyable for you — today and every day.

301. Creative You!

Ever feel stuck creatively? Maybe the problem is that you've never met Mr. Right or Ms. Right. Golly, this should only be your worst problem! Believe it or not, you can solve this problem within 24 hours, and without paying a cent to a dating service.

Allow me to introduce two kinds of Right who are already within you. Ms. Right is the feminine form of your creative energy. In the words of a rock 'n roll classic, that means "Wishing and hoping and thinking and praying," also fantasizing…with some daydreaming thrown in for good measure.

Here's how to take advantage of this lavishly liberating aspect of your creativity. Ask inside: If you were going to pick a form of creativity to awaken within you, what would it be? Take some deep breaths and fantasize away. Your answer could be photography, drawing, acting, singing, writing, dance or some obscure art form with great spiritual potential.

What if you draw a blank? Think of *helping* someone through your creativity. Fame fantasies shine with a phony luster; they're all about ego. But a daydream about touching someone's heart will move you precisely in the Right direction.

Now that you're femininely inspired, it's time to bring on Mr. Right. That's the structured, masculine side of your creative energy, remember? He will bring you discipline and action, form and technique, and the courage to move forward regardless of whether, inwardly, you feel 100% ready.

Yes sir, he is a powerful force. And enlisting his help can be way easier than taking yourself to a singles event or signing up for Internet dating. Simply schedule him in. When you list your goals each day, write in a five-minute time slot for Creative Expression.

Surely you can spare 5 minutes out of your precious day's allotment of 1,440. You could sing in the bathtub, write for an Internet blog, draw the first panel of your first cartoon. If nothing else comes to mind, blow soap bubbles--a form of performance art just loaded with potential for Divine communication.

Of course, to get results, you'll have to follow through. But with such huge potential benefits, why not? Taking action will strengthen your conscious connection to the creative power within. And if you're so bold as to assign yourself five minutes a day for the next week or longer, you'll see your relationship with Mr. and Ms. Right quickly progress from first-date flirtation to a deeper kind of love. Eventually you'll engage full expression of (and support for) your creativity.

Mr. and Ms. Right together add up to one huge creator within you. When you can bring your full human, creative self to God's altar, watch co-creation take off as never before.

302. Find Your Muse

Do you ever receive offers for credit cards in the mail? Imagine opening up one of those unsolicited envelopes to read, "You have been pre-qualified for a Greek Muse."

Ancient Greek civilization gave us excellent names for nine muses, goddesses who inspire excellence:

- Calliope for epic poetry
- Erato for love poetry
- Clio for history
- Polyhymnia for geometry
- Melpomene for tragedy
- Thalia for comedy
- Euterpe for music
- Terpsichore for dance and
- Urania for astrology

What, you find these names hard to pronounce? Then choose any name you like for a muse. Make it female or male, as you wish.

How many of the performers on "American Idol" would sing alone, just for the joy of it? The best ones would. The best artists and scientists are likewise well motivated. Whether or not they'll ever tell you so, each one has found a muse.

In physical form, a muse could be anyone who really appreciates you. That could be someone from your present or past, someone whose eyes sparkle as soon as you enter the room, someone who makes you feel wise, someone you love.

Dogs can be muses, as can cats (although they can be harder to hire).

Or you could ask a Divine Being to become your muse. Invite Him or Her right into the room and let the show begin. Make up a song. Lift weights. Cook. Change the oil in your car. Garden. Creating just about anything will thrill your muse.

To find the most inspired creativity of all, give yourself both a muse and someone to create for. Hold a space for them both, then watch the joy flow.

303. The Riddle of Kundalini

What does a shiver of excitement have in common with a yawn? Both can express movement of *Kundalini,* your life force energy. In fact, the answer to many a riddle is "Kundalini."

Commonly people equate it only with sex. But energy builds and releases in other ways, too. Right now, you're capable of a coltish scampering, like what happens inside your nose when you smell daffodils. Yet Kundalini could also give you the strength of an elephant…should you really need it.

Even without jungle-survival-type drama, Kundalini patterns can change. That energy can turn up or down, and you always can be the one in charge.

Sometimes it feels as though life brings too much, too fast. You're growing, which should be good, yet you feel terrible. Coincidences, experiences, the whole flow of life becomes overwhelming, speeding you into an uncomfortable too-fast-forward. Well, tell God, "Whoa."

Kundalini can calm down for as long as you'd like. Just don't expect the Almighty One to relate to human feelings of overwhelm. Come on, you're the one in the mud body! So make your request known. And don't worry. When you're good and ready, you can ask God to increase the energy once more.

What wakes up Kundalini? Start with intention but don't end there. Meditate. Or use energy work, exercise, yoga. A love affair might do wonders, but so might a shift in your diet.

Sometimes we spiritual seekers care so passionately about a food philosophy, alas, we omit common sense. *The purpose of food is to feed your body, not your ideology.* Why not ask your body what it wants? Appropriate diet could instantly upgrade your minimum daily supply of glee.

But no matter how wise your lifestyle choices, sometimes a person feels like a dried-up husk. Then ask God to (gently) remove blockages to your flow of Kundalini. Prince or Princess Charming is unlikely to appear in order to request this on your behalf. Besides, God is co-creating this lifetime with you, not some mystery guest who you hope will appear before the final curtain.

Many riddles of Kundalini could be answered with two simple words: You decide.

304. Five Minutes to a Better Flow

The life force energy of Kundalini flows through you right now. Mysterious though it is, you can get a working knowledge pretty easily. To begin, find a moment of undivided attention. Then close your eyes, bring attention to your body and ask, "Where is most of my energy?"

Trust your first thought.

Kundalini tends to puddle in one place or another within your body. With eyes closed, you might feel this as pressure or pain, movement or silence or, even, an inner highlighter pen. Feel free to be like the amateur art critic who says, "I may not have the ultimate education about great art but I know what I like." You are hereby declared THE world-class authority about the presence or absence of life force energy in you.

Depending on where you notice the most energy, that's the basis for improving your energy flow, which will result in a zestier life.

Does awareness shoot out your *third eye* or the top of your head? Then you can improve Kundalini flow by doing this for a total of five minutes today, off and on: Pay attention where your legs come together. Imagine a grounding cord that brings you to earth.

What if awareness mostly centers at your *belly or below*? Then invite Kundalini to rise. Here's *your* five-minute assignment: With eyes open, look up toward your hairline. Then close your eyes and pray. While doing this, occasionally look out through your forehead as though it contains a cute little window into the sunlight.

Should you notice lights or colors, fine. Should you notice a blank screen, fine. Your inner window need not be defined by anyone's shoulds. By analogy, awareness of Kundalini could be compared to looking up at the sky. Although the weather may change, cloudy or sunny, you're still viewing sky. Similarly, despite transient experience, your five-minute exercise will nudge your Kundalini upwards toward your third eye. Provided that you let it flow easily, rather than trying to push it along, you'll automatically improve Kundalini circulation.

What if your energy centers at *heart level*? Close your eyes and look out through your solar plexus. An engine of power is there. Rev it up until you feel it purr. Five minutes of that, off and on, during your day can move Kundalini nicely.

Re-routing your Kundalini flow can help you to co-create a more powerful life. Still, you may have a different experience once that energy flows through you briskly. It may seem to you then that all along — surprise! — you have been mostly Kundalini, with just enough body to keep you on-planet. Or maybe your body will always seem more important. Either way, God still is dancing with you.

305. Spiritually Sexy Sleep Ritual

The last time you upgraded your sleep ritual was…when? I'll bet your computer software is more current than how you hit that pillow.

Don't tell me that you find the topic a snoozer. Bedtime routines matter enormously. So plan yours as wisely as good parents set up bedtime routines for their children. You'll establish the tone for tomorrow's waking hours, not just how you sing tonight's z's.

Specifically, an adult's bedtime ritual can re-balance masculine and feminine energy. The *masculine* side relates to how you take action in life. Before sleep, admit that you've done enough for one day, then let the Official Sleep Ritual commence. Perhaps you'd like to invite God or a Divine Being to be part of the festivities. Your Inner Guy (a.k.a. Masculine Energy) loves an appreciative audience.

Include him in your bedtime ritual by proclaiming your achievements. State future goals and ask for help. Pin medals to your pajamas…or at least congratulate yourself lavishly. You know how work-hungry entrepreneurs advertise, "No job is too small"? Well, spiritually that happens to be true. Anything you achieved today, here on tough Planet Earth, deserves recognition.

Now on to the *feminine* energy portion of your bedtime ritual, where you get rewarded just for being yourself. Feeling, wishing, trusting, sensing spiritual truth — all these are gifts of your Inner Gal.

How much insomnia is due to discomfort over letting go of the masculine? Sleep and dreams flow best when guided mainly by feminine energy. So let it wash away the day's cares. One way to do this is to purposely use it when you wash your face: As you look in the mirror, recognize yourself, your deep self, hidden within your eyes. Reconnect to this as your feminine energy. She was born immensely lovable. What extra thing would make her more loveable? Nothing!

Finish your sleep ritual in bed. After you lie down, spend a few minutes feeling grateful for both sides of life, masculine and feminine: Your proud accomplishments plus all the good things you received today. Ask for God's blessing. Then make at least one wish for tomorrow's achievements. Who won't sleep better with a wish to dream on?

As you rest, your very breath will change its tune. Daytime breathing marches to 4/4 time, disciplined as a soldier. Sleep shifts you into breathing in 3/4 time, a swirl of feminine energy. Even the most macho guy's breath will soften when he enters God's spacious ballroom and begins to waltz.

306. Completely Yours

God, make me a much stronger man
(even if I'm a female, technically).
Shine up my mind like noonday sun,
and turn my voice bright with command.

Make me a stronger woman, too
(even if I'm male, usually).
Uncannily perceptive I'll see
beyond all obstacles, fresh and true.

All men and women whom I meet
are here to teach me sexually.
And right or wrongly, strangely or sweetly
Roughly, toughly, they complete me.

Or is the truth more, actually,
that they *erase* me, day by day,
'til wholly unexpectedly
I can be sexy in Your way.

307. Just Be Nice

Isn't it a relief when people are nice to you? Finally, someone who'll cut you some slack! When nice guys go out of their way to be helpful, you feel important. When nice gals laugh off annoyances, they make it seem easy. So, of course, you want to be around them. Maybe ease will rub off on you, like oily fingers from deliciously greasy French fries.

Except someone who's authentically nice isn't greasy, neither around the throat chakra nor any other part of her aura. A nice person is simply someone like you…who has *chosen* to be nice.

Make no mistake, it's a choice (and a wise one). Long after a man has forgotten how he met you, how talented you were or how fashionable your clothes, he will remember the answer to this one question: Were you nice or not?

If the answer is "Yes," you'll attract friends, favors, business, the best behavior of which others are capable. Nice attracts nice.

Although being nice is a simple choice, that doesn't make it easy. Depending on the situation, niceness may demand that you be kind, thoughtful, humble, patient, firm, whatever is needed, all the while insisting inwardly that you will open your heart again and again.

Nobody was born nice. It takes effort, and if this shows, your attempt at niceness is disqualified. Ironically, when you start the day with the best intentions, you will probably be rewarded by having life test you extra hard. Momentarily you'll forget all you knew about niceness and have to start learning all over again.

You can succeed, though. And God can help. Fill up with God's love in the morning, through your spiritual practice. When that inner peace feels used up, dunk yourself in God again. One quick prayer might do it. So might the sight of beauty or the photo of a loved one. Otherwise, carry a reminder that has meaning for you, like a wedding ring, and you can use it as a touchstone.

Can you commit to being nice to everyone you meet? Can you keep it up all day long?

Set that intention and you'll be given enough inner oomph to keep going.

God's loving presence is hidden, too. Yet each day that you persist, you'll learn more about that, too. Consider your search for God as practice for seeking the nice person within yourself…and within others.

308. Honor

Honor is nobility in action. It is the priceless virtue anyone can purchase because it is bought only through action. Always and everywhere, you can choose to act honorably.

What if multitudes around you make mistakes? What if their degree of ignorance is matched only by their arrogance? Don't despair. A lesson in humility won't harm you, and eventually some proud hearts may pay attention to your quiet confidence.

Regardless of whether anyone else ever notices, God will be watching. Besides, you'll learn most from each situation by making one honorable choice at a time. You don't have to know the whole outcome. Just look within your soul to make that one choice at a time.

God can be your resource for honor, as well as your witness. When you're unsure what to do, ask for help. That soft voice within is always available.

Regardless of your circumstances today, let your honor be impeccable.

Follow up on every commitment, no matter how small. And take the high road. No matter if you must walk through some slums along the way. You'll like where that high road leads you.

309. Prayers for Difficult People

Yes, it's possible that today I may have to deal with at least one difficult person. I trust that God's grace will flow through me then, supplying all the help I need to walk the tightrope.

Dealing with difficult people is, after all, a balancing act.

It's wise (not selfish) to advocate for myself. I must be the one who sets limits, choosing how much to give, why and to whom.

In a difficult situation, could I be the one at fault? Although willing to explore that possibility, I won't be too modest to recognize if most of the problem *doesn't* belong to me. Handling the situation with honor, I will move through it as gracefully as possible. I'll strive to be kind while I'm at it.

If, beyond that noble attempt, I can come from a place of peace, I will ask God to bless everyone concerned (myself included).

What if I feel emotions like anger or fear? Then I'll just ask God to bless me! Prayers involving other people may seem virtuous, but if made in anger — well, they won't be my best co-creations. Better to focus the first frantic prayer requests on myself and trust that God will extend help to everyone who asks for it.

Before this day ends, I can sweeten my way into sleep by asking for a loving perspective on today's events. Maybe, by then, I'll be able to include difficult people in my prayers.

Still, it's optional. Being honest with myself, I'll know when I feel a pull to help difficult people, with prayers or otherwise. Why force things? How much good does it really do to send the Universe a mixed message?

God's helpers are everywhere. So I'm hardly the only one who can send a blessing. And, in the long run, each person is responsible for her own life.

310. Softly

Life is better than you thought. Softer, too.

God has tucked such tenderness into this world. Whenever you find yourself in need of inspiration today, seek out something soft.

Will it be a texture? Touch a few things with your eyes (even better, your fingertips). When's the last time you explored the softness of your own cheek? Which is the softest garment you're wearing? Among all the things within easy reach, surely you can find something delightfully soft.

Colors have softness, too. Scan the vista before you to find an especially delicate hue. Let it lift your heart or change your expectations.

Extra joy can be wrung out of your workplace or home, just like squeezing a wet sponge. Even the process of wringing can reveal new qualities of softness.

Beauty beyond what you'd normally see? Of course, it's available. Just make the effortless effort to find it.

Sounds can bring different variations on the theme of softness. What's the sweetest, subtlest melody you can hear right now?

Softness can also be found as flavors. When you eat or drink, let your first taste seek out the softest flavor. There always will be one. Deep within the reality of each sense you can keep traveling, falling, exploring, releasing into new softness.

Finally, don't forget the best part. Listen to the voices of people today, or look at their faces, and ask inside, "Who speaks with a soft heart?"

Will it be you?

311. Courage Implants

What, you think you're the only one who ever needed courage? Using the language of a humorous sign I saw on somebody's desk back in the 1950's:

Thimk

Start by thinking about your parents. They needed plenty of courage to bring you into this world, and even more to raise you.

Who else in your personal history has shown at least as much courage as you need right now? God.

Almighty or not, what an act of courage it was to create people like us. All the human students at Earth School have been given enormous free will. Admittedly, it's not enough to destroy our Creator but we can cause plenty of other wreckage.

Imagine going to all the trouble of making this beautiful planet, down to the frills on the ferns and the whorls on human fingertips…imagine taking the extreme care that went into designing every bit of creation…and then making it a world where sillies like you and I could have such freedom.

Think about the big picture or just what's before you in the next few hours. Either way, you may have a sickening realization of your potential to make a real mess of things. Will you risk taking action in a world of problems? Will you dare to help, even if you're not as perfect as you might like to be?

Shakespeare had Hamlet ask himself if he dared to "take arms against a sea of troubles." Thus, even the greatest writer in the English language had the chutzpah to mix metaphors and, frankly, do some pretty bad writing.

Ralph Dehner is a highly responsible man who, during his professional training as a healer, agonized over courage.

Finally, he got to the toughest part: "Who am I to think myself worthy?" He demanded that God give him an answer.

Then Ralph heard these words from deep within:

What matters is not that you are worthy.
What matters is that you are willing.

312. Which Truth?

Today, as always, I seek the truth. But which one? And how hard should I struggle to find it?

Truth is an aspect of God. Therefore, it can be found everywhere, in every situation. Some highly ethical people obsess over truth, determined to possess an ultimate version that can be stamped with irrevocable certainty.

Why not just chase wild geese instead? At least you'd get fresh air and exercise.

This Learning Planet is based on polarity. Truths are sketched in scant bits of black and white, plus a sickeningly vast variation on gray. For the seeker of indelible black or spotless white, good luck!

Only one absolute truth can be found about life on earth: It's *ever* changing. For everyone, yourself included, truth depends on your level of consciousness, the immediate circumstances, even your reason for seeking the truth. Except for hard science, your version of truth isn't guaranteed to match anyone else's.

Yet it's tempting to be a *truth bully,* pushing your version of reality onto somebody else. What if, today, you were to give everyone you encounter the right to her own truth? Not that you'd have to agree, but you'd have to respect it. Could that bring you a new kind of freedom? Get your nose out of all the realities where it doesn't belong and the air around you will smell sweeter.

Another truth problem arises when a person cares too much, constantly agonizing, "I think xyz is true, *but am I sure?*" If that sounds familiar, remember that truth is situational. Like a letter, it is delivered to one person, date-stamped, and addressed to just one place.

What if you still yearn for rock-solid truth? Then seek the experience of God. It's omnipresent, eternal, unchanging, and will deliver the only kind of experience that can satisfy a person completely. To seek it, close your eyes, open your heart and go within. With the grace of God (and, sometimes, the help of a teacher) you'll bring awareness to That.

In the human realm, don't expect ever-changing life to contain permanent truth. Trying to find a lost wristwatch, you're unlikely to dig up a wad of eternity. Maybe your biggest discovery will be, "Be more mindful about here and now so that you'll stop losing things."

Use deeper perception to find the deepest possible truth for you, then trust it. The answers you find now may not last forever. But they will lead you to your next, bigger truth. So never stop seeking.

313. Gratitude Movie

You've heard of horror movies. How about taking yourself to a gratitude movie?

Imagine. A stranger comes into your workplace. Instead of being some monster with a hatchet, he's a darling ray of sunlight. No pool of blood results from his visit, only smiles. For the "grisly" aftermath, everyone has a perfectly sincere, even wholesome, conversation about how much fun all of you had that day.

Right!

And it gets better. This movie has no problems. Where's the suspense in the plot? Nowhere! The story recounts how, most of the time, some people get along pretty well with each other. Sometimes they like each other a whole lot.

Well, the star, at least, is exciting. It's you!

Would people pay to see your non-drama? Maybe not. But gratitude movies work best as Indie flicks, anyway. Yours doesn't have to please millions of viewers, only an audience of one.

To be really ambitious about it, you could write a script for your feature-length gratitude movie. You could adapt this screenplay from real life — in fact, sometimes you might superimpose this film over actual life events.

For "The Gratitude Movie" you get to choose all the makeup and camera angles. You adjust the lighting. Direct it. Feel free to re-do a scene if it doesn't come out right the first time. Bring in cartoon characters to guest star. Actually, you have complete creative license.

So what will you make today's movie, a love story or a mystery? Both combined? Dante wrote *The Divine Comedy.* Personally, I favor "The Divine Musical."

As for "Reality" TV shows, you could consider make your movie in that style, too. But why not aim higher? A regular TV talk show might have more class.

The funny thing is that network talks shows can be as heavily scripted as reality shows, complete with script writers and segment producers. Once I was a guest for a popular show where I was taken through the "spontaneous" interview four different times in advance of physically arriving at the studio.

Even when everything has been planned meticulously, the well scripted chatter goes smoothly and everyone grins on cue, even then, a big-time talk show host can be worried sick about ratings.

You don't have to be. Your gratitude movie will be highly watchable. It could go into re-runs.

314. We Have Come Through

Finally it happened. You knew soon as you woke up this morning. Finally, you have broken through the fog into the light.

Sometimes life grows murky by degrees, with change so imperceptible that you never feel the fog start. You only know that, increasingly, your journey has become difficult. Maybe there's a specific problem with a relationship, a job or a deadline. There can be any kind of nuisance: Repairs to your home, the illness of a loved one, your own physical worries. Newspaper headlines could match your inner doom and gloom, or set it off.

Or maybe there's no outer reason, and you know full well the problem lies within. Somehow you just don't feel like yourself. And you wonder, will you ever? You fear growing old or losing someone dear to you. At such times, getting through even one day demands so much, nearly more than you have. Still, you hold tight to your faith and keep doing the best you can.

As for those great things that you co-create…it could be all you can manage just to cry out to God, "Don't leave me."

Then one day, you simply find that the fog has blown away. Anything seems possible. Life is good, and not just because you demand that it must be so. Goodness, ease, confidence, clarity and the silence within — they're simply back. It's like going outside and, for the first time in ages, you look up to find the surprise of a big, blue sky.

Why does human life make us go through those fogs? If only there were some easier way to evolve.

Well, when the day comes that God gives you a planet to create, see if you can do any better.

Meanwhile, keep this song in the back of your mind. Keep it ready for times when you need consolation. And be prepared to sing it for the people you love.

It is the song of human triumph, God's victory march through the ages. In heaven, you may hear *all* the words but here on earth it's enough that you recognize the first line:

"We have come through."

315. Crumbs

To the Shibuya Station come 3,000 faces.
Tokyo natives are used to this. You're not.
If a cracker were crushed into pieces
and each one could walk — wait,
make that an entire warehouse-style,
humongous boxful of cracker crumbs — surely
this has got to be way, way more crumbs
than are needed — Great Baker,
here are so many
crumbs with hairstyles and cell-phones, with laughter and problems.
Well, assuming that there were this strange
(and, frankly, unappetizing) experiment,
here, at the subway, this is precisely
how all of us crumb folks would look.

We, in this multitude, think we know just
where we're going. We'd *better* think so
as we fill up the station. Heads bob up and down on each stair.
Lining up, we parade into each open door.
The train glides past Shibuya, past Ebisu,
people stuck, gliding together, and you're seeing
reflected from every glass window,
front, sideways, back — all the crumbs
just like you.

Know that this is not some mere theoretical journey
watched on TV from your favorite armchair
where you think, "My, how interesting. So many people."
They're here. They're now. Fortunately,
with great deftness and mercy
they manage to not trample you.

Yet they're breathing relentlessly next to your nose.
In your tribal, animal body
you are both alarmed and joyful.

"Where are You, God?" Questions like that
scream from your soul, including
that personal favorite, "And where am I?"

One answer is clear. God's not stingy. He has
made this weekday "Rush hour" last for at least 300 minutes.
Also, God has ticketed each thumbprint with a free pass
to travel, by most ingenious routing, home
in consciousness. You will have many stops, never fear,
and just exactly enough.

316. Bedtime Story

At a certain age, you loved a good story. For many kids, it's the best consolation for being forced to go to bed.

And should that bedtime story repeat itself, all the better. Adults find this puzzling unless they understand a little-known fact of depth psychology. People never outgrow bedtime stories at all, only most adults have the story go underground, to the *subconscious* mind. Afterwards, it will keep playing over and over again. Tomorrow you will live out last night's bedtime story.

What story exactly? It's a pattern that ties together the major themes of your life. Are you a hero? Are you a victim? There's an undertone, like when you go to a movie and you know early on whether this will be a comedy or a drama.

Anyone can become conscious of her story. It can be changed, too, by doing some *conscious myth making*. (Didn't you ever dream of growing up to be a mythtic?)

Just make up a story that centers around the purpose of your life or your search for that purpose. This need not be the complete and final version of your story. Make up something for today and, if you like, make it short. Try it out aloud.

Like it? Maybe a new touch could make it even better.

Dislike it? Add at least one new piece to your story. Or rewrite it entirely.

If nothing comes to mind, that unconscious story must be pretty boring, even to you. So give yourself the benefit of a new one. How? Make it up, of course. Choose a theme with meaning for you, like empowerment, faith, forgiveness, love, creativity or genius.

You'll be inviting some related events of synchronicity. Automatically, something good will happen by chance — all connected with the theme of your personal story. Reality *does* cluster around a person's deep expectations. It's like how learning a new word can cause it to suddenly pop up all around you. Well, your story shapes reality, too. Only you may not have noticed before because your story was operating subconsciously.

Can you control everything that will happen today? Co-creation with God won't take you that far. But you do have complete control over your story.

Ultimately that story will shape your reality, so add to your tale at will. Then before sleep, write today's perfect ending. It will shape your tomorrow.

317. Where Is My Invitation?

"Whatever doesn't kill me makes me stronger." Although a powerful spiritual truth, this saying can also be used to tell the Universe "Nyah, nyah," as if reminding an obnoxious friend, "Don't think you can get *me* riled. I'm way to cool for that."

Sure, if you manage to survive a difficult situation, on some level, you'll be tougher. In the version of your life story that you tell yourself, merely staying alive on The Learning Planet can count for a great deal. But, really, is that enough when circumstances make a person howl with pain or gulp with fear? For consolation in difficult times, remember to ask this question, to both God and yourself:

"Where is my spiritual invitation?"

Spiritual invitation? That means a highly specific opportunity to accomplish something worthwhile. Is it a lesson about learning to love yourself no matter what? Are you being invited to take more responsibility for your actions? Tucked within each difficulty, God has inserted a calling card, your spiritual invitation.

You have every right to ask God to help you figure out what it means. If only you taste that sweet spoonful of spiritual truth, it could get you through a whole cup of bitterness. Even when the answer doesn't come right away, God hears every question. Know that you will be given an answer... within three days at the most. How will you know you've received it? You'll feel spiritual sweetness, a subtle (or not so subtle) kind of peace.

Either before or after receiving your Big Answer, do your part. In a loving way, find the little answer, your human responsibility in this situation. Specifically, use deeper perception to investigate your aura, chakra by chakra.

- Remind yourself of strengths — gifts of your soul.
- Notice any negative stuff in the way, whether temporary or chronic.
- Consider how all this connects with your difficult situation.
- Which of your gifts can help you to triumph (or, at least, cope)?
- Could your problem-in-the-world be related to problems-in-your-aura? Then consider that you have uncommon incentive to heal the latter. Ask a Divine Being to help. And if more help is needed, find someone who can facilitate spiritual healing.

That oucher situation really could be a spiritual invitation. Let it help you become stronger, and not just in some abstract feel-good way but directly at the level of your aura. God can't force anyone to accept a spiritual invitation. But after you've taken the opportunity, you'll know why it was a form of grace.

318. Ouch, But in a Good Way

Whatever you love helps you to discover more truth about life. Ironically, though, you'll never evolve if stuck in one same love.

That person you trust most, be she a lover, a parent or child, a friend, a teacher…that hero still is not quite God. Your highest desires and beliefs bring inspiration…but they still aren't quite God. Any human tower of strength you adore has some aspect that can crumble. All of these are *attachments*, something depended upon or even (to some degree) worshipped as if it were God.

Whether quickly or gradually, hurtfully or gently, every single attachment of yours will be ripped away.

Why would a merciful God do such things? In the context of your soul's growth, it's a blessing.

No, I'm not suggesting that you ever try to renounce attachments prematurely. This leads to a divided consciousness in life which can actually slow down spiritual evolution.

Believe in your relationships as long and as hard as you can. Even better, be God's spoiled brat and keep asking for more fulfillment in them, enjoying whatever you've been given and coming back for more, until you're fully satisfied.

Just keep this one thought tucked away somewhere, like a small spiritual first aid kit: Whenever an attachment is destroyed, God has actually helped you.

Knowing this can help you to cope better with every experience of loss. Spiritual evolution is about far more than knowing that you can survive. When you cry out into the silence for God, an answer will come. And it will be the most loving answer, whether you hear a voice speaking comfort or you are left (seemingly alone) in the silence.

Sometimes the only thing you can know for sure is that you've had one more attachment ripped away.

And if you don't yet prefer enlightenment to a static happiness…eventually you will. Let that be incentive enough to live one more day.

You never know when you'll be surprised by joy. Nor can you predict the relief you'll feel when an inconsolable hole deep within you fills with peace.

319. Graceful Release

Always the dumpee, never the dumper — is that your complaint? Sometimes it's hard letting go of attachments. You may almost wish your lover would cheat on you or a so-called "friend" would start a fight. One way or another, you'd appreciate having a graceful way out when a relationship has become burdensome.

Objectively, there are things you can do. Tell the person that you are ready to move on. If it's true, you have the right to say so. Actually, it's much kinder to admit the truth than to hide it. On some level, the dumpee always knows.

Subjectively, though, you may first need to release an undue attachment. Only then can you find the courage to do the objective side of releasing. Our *subconscious* minds (where guilt often festers) really do love ceremonies. Here is one kind of ceremony you can stage that can satisfy your subconscious and, simultaneously, loosen the *spiritual* component of attachment.

If you're feeling unnecessarily bound to a relationship, a situation, or a cause, you have the right to release the psychic tie. Each one merits its own ceremony.

For this ceremony of Releasing Undue Attachment, you will need a string or a scarf. Tie a knot in it, symbolizing the particular attachment. Say, as you tie it, "This knot symbolizes my undue attachment to [speak the appropriate name]."

Now you're ready. Call on Almighty God, then on a Divine Being. Create a sacred space. At a minimum, light a candle. As always, add anything more elaborate that you would like to include. And be sure to subtract all distractions; for this ceremony to be effective, you'll need undivided attention.

- Say out loud, "I now release my undue attachment to [say the appropriate name]."
- Untie the knot. Know that the Divine Being is, simultaneously, smoothing out places in your aura where you have been unnecessarily connected.
- Clasp the string or scarf between your hands and visualize what you would like in your life to take the place of what has been released.
- Bring your hands up to your heart, and feel compassion for yourself. Let your heart be whole.

Your ceremony is done. Once is enough, so trust the process. Occasionally an attachment will be way stronger than a mere filament on the psychic level, so professional help will be required to release it. Usually, though, the kind of ceremony you've just done will do the job. Gracefuly releasing attachments from your aura could be one of the most useful skills you ever learn.

320. Manna on the Way

Call me a food freak if you must, but the thing that fascinates me most about the Old Testament is the manna.

Imagine what it was like to have all the food you needed, easy to gather and dependably there, day after day. Talk about miracles! It's almost enough to make someone willing to trudge through a desert for 40 years.

You can enjoy a present-day version of manna in the comfort of your own home. Or at a convenient restaurant…or in the thick of things at work…or even while forced to spend time with someone who's way too easy to dislike.

Sometimes your situation may feel as dry as a desert. Granted, you may not see actual sand. But you may hear it trickling down from the hourglass of your life. That's your very existence, being used up. "Killing time" is a way to let moments of your own life become dead.

But you can turn any desert-dry moment into a decent meal, maybe even a spiritual banquet. Three different strategies can make you an expert manna collector.

For the first method, ask inside what it would take for this situation to *fulfill* you. Then take action. Actively participate, saying or doing the best that is humanly possible. Delicious manna will arrive, faster than a singing telegram.

Now, what if you're in a bad situation that you *cannot change*? Use your wisdom to know the difference. And don't expect manna to be delivered on the same level as your problem. Instead, pursue it by this second method: Go deeper than the problem. Switch on deeper perception about other people, plants or animals, even about gifts within your own soul. Sumptuous manna is there for the taking.

And what if you're *too soul-weary* to work even that hard? Then take a rest. Really, rest. That's the third method. Surrender your expectations, just for a moment and simply be. You can find the silent presence of God, surrounding everyone and hugely abundant. It's slathered in and around you, heaped into all life's interstices as generously as frosting in a good seven-layer cake.

You see, for a spiritual seeker, manna is everywhere. And there's plenty to go around, so don't be shy. Help yourself.

321. Early Retirement

Job hunting can inspire you — at least the metaphysical version can.

We're used to thinking we choose our jobs. But what if our jobs choose *us* as part of the original Life Contract? Remember, these contracts script our early years quite thoroughly. So no guilt allowed over the work you did in your twenties! You were meant to be exactly what you became. But that was only the start.

Through this book, you've learned to distinguish two wildly different forms of employment: What you do in your human life versus your spiritual role as a world server. An ache to find your job often relates to that world server part. Co-create spiritually each day and it will help you to satisfy this need.

As for your human job, Life Contracts have never been more flexible. Nowadays who stays at one job long enough to collect a gold watch on retirement? Maybe it is time to make a career move, to change the emphasis within a career you already love, or to develop a promising new hobby.

Here's an assignment that can help you decide. Imagine that you're free to choose a new career. *Assume you've been given early retirement,* enough to provide for necessities plus a generous amount of severance pay. Though you'll need to supplement income eventually, you're freer than ever to take a job that you'd really enjoy.

Sometimes a job seeker is encouraged to imagine that he has only six months to live. Am I the only one who finds that notion depressing? This alternative version is designed to set you thinking without a morgue in the background. Let your bouquet of ideas be joyful as daffodils in the spring.

After brainstorming, you can make practical plans. Besides doing the *objective* commonsense steps, remember to include the *subjective* spiritual side:

- Hold each plan in the Light to evaluate its level of spiritual support.
- Use Creative Imagination to empower you as you take action steps.
- Express gratitude for every success along the way.
- Affirm success through your speech.
- On the appointed day, make your career move with full commitment, aligning your love, light and power.

Playing "Early Retirement" could save your life spiritually. Remember, you have the right to retire *any* notions that cramp the truth of your soul, whether socially, sexually, financially, physically or religiously. Give those limiting habits early retirement, too, and build yourself a big-enough future.

322. Volunteer Work

So you don't have time to sign up for every worthy cause you hear about. Don't feel guilty. But don't give up on helping strangers, either.

Here's one solution, suggested by Winn Claybaugh, author of *Be Nice—Or Else*. Consider this volunteer job: Be nice to the people who cross your path.

For instance, you can volunteer kindness toward the "little people" who are unloading lettuce at your supermarket or mopping the floor in your office building.

Stop to thank them. Look them in the eye and say how much you appreciate their work. Watch the lights switch on.

These days, people are more likely to talk to their mobile phones than the anonymous minimum-wagers who help them. I remember how shocked I was the first time I stood in the checkout line behind a customer who completely ignored the clerk, she was so busy chatting to the "important person" at the other end of her cell.

Even without a technology assist, it's too easy to treat strangers as though they're invisible. It hurts. Besides, is anyone or anything on our planet truly dispensable? Even a Kleenex, manufactured to be used just once, is a tiny sliver of tree.

And even tissues may have feelings, should you have the consciousness to appreciate them. People certainly do. Few things hurt a person's feelings more than being ignored. You can volunteer to change that, one person at a time. Today, become somebody else's serendipity.

323. Illusions

Co-creating with God can change your life. But how about all the times it doesn't? What about times when God seems no more than your companion in failure?

Let's say you just staged your first concert. You aimed to fill the hall, win rave reviews, become a star overnight. You invited a Divine Being to co-create with you every step of the way, using guidance, prayer and creative imagination, lavishly sprinkling on the affirmations. Surely you did an impeccable job spiritually!

You did the human work, too, honoring every commitment, always acting in an ethical manner. You practiced that music and did the practical work as well, meticulously doing everything possible to make that concert the best it could be.

Yet what happened when the concert took place? Suppose that just 12 people attended, none of them music critics. Nobody special "discovered you." After expenses, you barely broke even. Golly, after all that co-creation, you didn't even make money.

Does that make your concert a failure? No. Could you have changed 12 lives? Perhaps.

To add to the threat of failure, say that one audience member e-mails you after the concert. "For your own good" (supposedly) she criticizes your performance, accusing you of not giving enough.

What was she expecting, blood or free money? Disappointments can make you wonder if you have believed in illusions. What, exactly, was gained by your exercise in co-creation?

Don't assume the worst. Ask inside and, please, ask gently: What did you really want from what you created? How do you count your success? Even if you didn't receive what you hoped for, why might you still thank God?

No quick, one-size-fits-all answers, please.

Sometimes you won't need to search for an answer. You might love what you're doing so much that you can easily find new strength to organize the next concert. Or maybe, as a result of what happened, you will re-shape your goals. Were you really doing that first concert for the money or the fame or for something else?

One co-creator's secret is to keep asking until you find peace with simple goals like these:

God, help me reach those I can reach. Help me teach those I can teach and, along the way, learn all I can.

324. God's Song to You

I believe in you
and the things that you do.
I'm so charmed by how
your bright light shines through.

I believe in you.
All the things that you say —
I'm here every day
listening all the way.

Trust that you're headed for a happy ending
especially when things seem unclear.
Grab the power ring that I'll keep sending
until you reach for it right here.

I believe in you
and I trust you to choose.
Even behind your flaws
don't you hear my applause?

It's fascinating to me
how your soul shines through
all the great things you do.
Surprise me! And don't, too.

Remember this 'til you can feel it:
I made this world for your delight.
Life's your ripe mango, so go peel it.
You're way much more than just all right.

325. Smartie, Why Ain't You Rich?

Disregard the fashionable shoes. More important is *who* walks in them and *where* she chooses to go. Even a savvy spiritual seeker can be tripped up by appearances.

You know better than to assume that money (or its lack) equates with virtue. Still, the question may nag at the edges of your mind, especially if it could be asked of you. *"If you're so smart, why ain't you rich?"*

Until you develop a hefty share of prosperity consciousness, you're unlikely to hold onto riches, even if they are handed to you. Lottery winners prove this on a regular basis. All too often, years after winning, the windfall has gone with the wind.

Yet prosperity consciousness alone won't suffice to manifest money. Are you prepared to focus realistically on generating income? Lasting success demands that you use marketable skills backed up by ethical behavior. Cultivate good manners, honesty, service, following through on commitments. Give fair value and then some.

Even when you do all this, wealth remains part of an unfathomable game. Karma often comes back to a person financially. Therefore, a wise person will ask a more interesting question than *"If you're so smart, why ain't you rich?"* You'll ask, *"If you're so smart, why care about money that much?"*

You might be better off laughing at it. Notice especially how, if people aren't careful, they can mistake material success for the purpose of living. Just how ridiculous can that become? Here's my favorite story:

Once I was a guest in an exquisite, old-money home. Excusing myself, I entered the bathroom. Everything there was magnificent (just like the rest of the mansion). The bathroom's rich marble floor was polished to a mirror-like gloss. Walls held perfect gilt-framed paintings. The toilet fixture itself was a gleaming sculpture of chocolate brown. If Heaven had Western-style bathroom facilities, they might look like this.

As I started to flush, I took one last look and was utterly captivated. My perfect contribution floated like a great work of art in a three-dimensional frame. Mesmerizing beauty, it fascinated me for longer than I care to admit.

Suddenly reality dawned. There is such a thing as too beautiful! I laughed and flushed this "great art" away.

Wealth, and its upkeep, can become a full-time job. Don't make it yours.

326. What's Wrong with Prosperity?

Have you been resisting loss and lack? Maybe it's time to give up the fight.

When you repeatedly ask for something that never comes, God may be giving you this hint: *Your wish will be granted once you can make it from a position of balance. If I gave your wish to you now, you'd go even more out of balance.*

With finances, many of us do the equivalent of bending over backwards. We demand prosperity to help us overcome tendencies toward poverty.

But on this polarity planet, asking for one side of an equation automatically brings up the other. Straining to be good will lock you into a struggle with bad. (Think of all those outrageous ministers' children.) Financially, some of the most conscientious people you'll ever meet are driven to the verge of bankruptcy and beyond.

So the first step in overcoming financial problems can be this: Stop making money a heavily-charged metaphysical passion play. See if you could take that huge emotional energy and invest it somewhere more worthwhile. It might be helping people, gaining enlightenment, choosing one talent or skill that you develop to the fullest.

Return to the topic of money once your sense of proportion is back, and do the practical things: Live responsibly, set commonsense goals and expect abundance.

Of course it helps to include a budget as part of these goals. One couple I know is crazy about prosperity slogans. Both Mr. and Ms. Smith would literally plaster these sayings all over the walls except that, as renters rather than owners, they know the landlord wouldn't approve. So they make do with Scotch-taping their abundance affirmations onto the walls in the living room, the kitchen, even the bathroom mirror. What they never post anywhere is a budget.

Subjective-objective balance — how easy it is to forget. Affirming won't keep money in the bank if you ignore debt and buy every toy you fancy.

For prosperity isn't some capricious, mystical creature who must be tempted to step across your threshold. Not a unicorn, prosperity is more akin to how your shoelaces stay tied, a consequence. Choices and actions add up to dollars and cents. If you'll live responsibly today and fix the ordinary things in your life that are broken, tomorrow you're likely to get your fair share of money, plus interest.

327. Have a Ball with Money

Auras aren't just some metaphysical fashion show. Yours tells the story of how you relate to money, including how you balance money with other aspects of life.

Many spiritual seekers project enormous energy through the third eye. Yet their groundedness, at the root chakra, remains teensy. This is comparable to a skinny little clown wearing ridiculously large shoes, only upside down.

When it comes to the relative proportion of energy in chakras, I'm not among the aura readers who advocate rigid balance. This concept reminds me of farmers who breed tomatoes to be small, square and hard, just so they ship better. If one part of a person's aura is way bigger or smaller than other parts, there is good reason. May it continue as long as that particular set of proportions is needed!

However, a person can change the balance of chakras in a gentle way, and the desire to attract money brings great incentive to do so. Fact is, a huge third eye paired with a tiny root chakra almost guarantees financial problems.

As you may know, the size of your root chakra is directly proportional to how much people respect you, which in our society translates into your ability to make money. Maybe that seems unfair. Shouldn't your spiritual development matter more? Sure it does, for *spiritual* life. Root chakras matter more for *material* life because so many people value security over spirituality.

Supplement a strong root chakra with a vibrant third eye and wow! You're more apt to create a fulfilled life where you can buy whatever you need without thinking of cost, yet spontaneously live within your means. So instead of just visualizing plenty of green in your bank account, deposit this into your aura:

- With eyes closed, imagine a big, beautiful red ball of light at the base of your spine. Let it expand throughout your lower torso, filling it up.
- Lovingly dwell on the color, the temperature, the degree of solidity. At will, you can make that ball expand or contract.
- Open your eyes and feel the presence of your red energy ball.
- Walk around the room for a couple of minutes. Emphasize paying attention to the ball, as if the red light were in color, the rest of your body a scene in black and white.

Bring up this image several times a day and you'll strengthen your root chakra. May this visualization start the ball rolling — a great big ball of prosperity, starting with a healthy wad of it right in your aura.

328. Large Coins

You've heard of tithing, that time-tested, bank-tested tool for abundance. By giving 10% of your income back to a spiritual source, you can move your abundance forward.

Tithing is a bargain for many reasons. It helps religious communities and charities stay solvent, so they'll be there when you need them. Simultaneously, tithing helps you inwardly because you're spending out of joy, not fear. This can dispel a dismal kind of enchantment, according to which money is scary and scarce, so you had better hoard as much as possible. Giving freely can improve your relationship to money.

Yes, you and money are married, for better or worse. And tithing brings back that honeymoon feeling. Tithing means slipping money directly into God's pocket — or the closest human equivalent.

Sometimes you'll be tempted to tithe unofficially. This kind of "temptation" is really inspiration. Of course, it counts whenever you give to a source of spiritual strength, like a worthy cause or a person who has moved you ahead on your path.

One easy way to spread wealth around is to start paying with *large coins*. Here's what I mean. When paying for something well done, tip or not as is appropriate, and then add one cent to your check. Or present a shiny coin with a flourish.

Explain, "I wish I could pay you an extra million dollars for that great job you've done. At least I can give you this symbol." Ta da!

Yes, you'll see a response. Not as great, admittedly, as if you'd delivered a check for $1,000,000....

Still, you'll likely see a fair-sized twinkle received along with your payment, a reminder that ultimately money is just a symbol. Pocketing riches that endure will always be a do-it-yourself job.

329. Inner Feng Shui

Physically, my home may not have changed, but today I'll redecorate it energetically. I'll paint my walls with colors like hope, enthusiasm and security. Quick as thought, and vivid as yellow or green, these new thought patterns will stay wherever I put them. Like walls that have never been smudged with fingerprints, this new version of my home's energy is perfect.

At the entrance, I'll make room for God. And what else? And what *not*?

Where do I envision the hearth, the nourishing core of my home? (Doesn't have to be the TV!)

At my own pace, in my own way, I'll set up a living room for friendship and a kitchen for nurturing. Then I'll add as many other rooms as I desire: A meditation room, a study, a financial planning area, a guest room, and my entertainment center. Space is abundant here since, transforming my home with consciousness, I can make a "room" from a corner or even a paper clip.

And how could I forget to bless the toilet, the garbage disposal, the drains? They are such lovelies, considering that each one's job is to remove what no longer belongs.

As for my bedroom, that sanctuary of rest and rejuvenation, what can I add imaginatively to make it a special delight?

Attached to my "keeper" furniture and appliances are happy memories. The rest I'll rehabilitate, redecorate, re-associate…with sparkling new energy.

Now that the basics of my new home are in place, it's time for a housewarming party. With family and friends, or maybe just my own joyful presence, I will walk through room after room. More than a simple tour, let this be a consecration.

My home's lavish gifts from the Universe symbolize my ever-improving status. As inwardly I grow more affluent, I do better at manifesting my desires physically. And as my heart opens, I notice blessings that, previously, I might have overlooked.

Gratitude has taken up residence. Looking down, I see a magic carpet, wall-to-wall, where I can walk each day.

330. Fair Payment

Render unto Caesar that which belongs to Caesar — doing that math is simple enough. But how much is appropriate to pay someone who has served as God's mouthpiece, hands or heart or compass? That accounting can be trickier.

Some spiritual workers believe that accepting money will cheapen their Divine connection. This noble intent pleases clients enormously, and why wouldn't it? Even multi-millionaires salivate at the word "free." Yet spiritual workers deserve to charge money, not for the grace which flows through them but to recompense their human time and energy. No matter how pure anyone's heart, it beats only so many times.

Beyond that comes the question of skill. A healer or minister, teacher or psychic has worked hard to become a pure channel for grace. Even if the requisite sacrifices were made without counting cost, that background should still be honored through payment.

Whether you're the consumer or the spiritual worker, include money in your transaction. You can do better than an Oscar-winning actress I once heard interviewed about how she researched a film role as a psychic. Sounding surprised, she said that she actually found many "good, genuine psychics who never charge for their services." Evidently, she took this willingness to work for free as proof positive of purity. What a lofty view of labor, especially from someone who charges millions just to walk onto a movie set!

Many people feel that spiritual service is sullied by payment. Yet they'll cheerfully pay performers big bucks to do work that is, fundamentally, intuitive.

To right the balance, you can set an example for others by paying those who help you spiritually. When your life has improved because of someone else's time and skill, express appreciation with the coin of the realm.

And if you borrowed a book or tape that inspired you, here's a radical thought: Voluntarily send a check. Even if the author's brilliance seemed to flow easily, it takes years of work and thousands of dollars to bring a new concept to market. Inwardly, the cost may have been far greater than you imagine.

Pay your spiritual helpers in human form. It will benefit you, the giver. You'll link your own spiritual service with prosperity. And your generosity now will make it easier for the world to reward you later.

331. The First Prayer

Who should get your first prayer? Many of us have been told that we'd better pray for others first, never ourselves. Otherwise we're being selfish.

Talk about being cheap with yourself! Think you only deserve God's leftovers? Only if you believe *that* does it make sense to perpetually place yourself last, holding off until everyone else's prayer needs have been met.

Otherwise, fill up yourself first. You have figured out your best ways to do that by now. Once you feel Divine juice flowing within you, let the surplus spill over into helping the rest of the known universe.

Nobody else on earth is here to be your advocate. That's your job.

Of course you have an obligation to connect first to your Source. If you don't, no matter how generous, your prayers will be tainted with resentment, martyrdom or some other negative emotion. Even for the sake of others, put your own God connection first.

I am reminded of this principle whenever I fly in a plane. Safety demonstrations make a fascinating point. If breathing equipment drops down, you must start using yours first. Even if your helpless child sits right next to you, make sure you can breathe first. Then help the child. This increases the odds that both of you will survive.

So spend the first chunk of prayer time on yourself. Afterwards you'll have so much more to give. There's just one more safety rule to consider: Respect the other person's free will.

For yourself, it's completely appropriate to list your desires and ask to receive that or better (something God is fully capable of figuring out). Sure, demand that job, that physical healing, that loving relationship — any desire of your heart. When praying for *others*, however, your desires are gloriously irrelevant. Ideas that sound great to you may clash horribly with the prayer recipient's free will.

Even the desire to help a person recover from life-threatening illness is questionable. You don't know the number of life breaths in anybody's contract. Your insisting that someone be "blessed" with a longer life could be more like a curse.

But what if you were to modify your request, asking that someone regain health "If it is Your will, God"?

Should the answer be "No," that prayer hasn't done much, has it? But, guaranteed, there will be no waste if instead you send pure light, love and power. Spiritually, that is like giving money. Each person will know how to use it, spending God's wealth in a truly sacred manner…as defined by that person, not you.

332. Shockingly Colorful Wardrobe

How did you accessorize your aura today? The color of your clothes can vibe you up even brighter, helping you to co-create at your best.

To wear the best colors for your aura, you *don't* have to see it in color, then pick out the clothes to match. Simply wear colors which would thrill your soul.

Soul, remember, expresses your *human* self. Soul has strong likes and dislikes. And soul yearns to be recognized through your clothing choices. Early in your day, *ask yourself which colors would feel good to wear.* Such a simple way to honor your soul! Doing this will, in turn, strengthen the spiritual expression known as your aura.

But could there be practical difficulties? Worldly responsibilities may disallow your dressing like some three-year-old, where any color of the rainbow would be appropriate. Gone are the bold choices, the perpetual pink and purple for girls, or the boys' earnestly worn cartoon figures. To the degree that you dress like a responsible adult, the clothes you wear to work may be shockingly tasteful.

If female, you probably wear more black than is good for you. If male, you may stick with what's safe. However gendered, a fashionable person is at the mercy of clothing designers who choose the shades for each season. Beyond that, maybe you've had image consulting, so you always dress for success by wearing your best colors. All the more reason to do an inner makeover!

You still can express your soul through a rainbow of hues. You can do this without losing face…or your job. Just make *secret* color statements:

- Buy underwear in every color of the rainbow
- Collect wildly colorful socks
- Or go to a rock shop and purchase seven tumbled stones, ranging from red to violet. You'll be able to stash your day's choices in pocket or purse.

Now that you have *real* wardrobe potential, each morning before you get dressed, ask inside which colors best express your soul today. If time permits, also ask why.

Every color offers a huge range of healing powers for body, mind and spirit. Only a complete beginner would parrot clichés like "Turquoise is for my throat chakra" or "Red helps my root chakra." Not necessarily, not for your aura today. An actual parrot would, at least, be less boringly *dressed.* (Not original thinkers, they compensate with feathers.)

Be a bold bird, yourself. Whether secretly worn or displayed outrageously clear across your chest, today's soulful colors will add life to your life.

333. Lace

Hold me all in softness.
Let Your breath be close to me,
oh, Folder of rose petals.

When will I be beauty filled, with Your sumptuous delicacy?

Let me, so I may
unbind the veil that now covers my eyes.

Confused, I cower, shy
to gaze upon Your face that looks at me.

How You, who have crocheted me to be lace,
must laugh to watch the untangling of this knot.

334. The Luxury of a Small Room

Have you ever lived in a tiny room? When the walls around you don't have much give, you must stretch your imagination.

Then you can turn even the humblest dwelling into a mansion. Say that you own just one small table, a solitary chair. Move that chair to Position A and you're in the banquet hall. With a simple turn of your chair to Position B, you have an elegant desk. Round the table you go, a new position for every use that your heart desires.

What, you lack even a table? Then give a stretch of floor that job and, again, I do mean stretch. Children aren't the only ones with the right to play house.

Poverty can never be imposed upon you. Real treasures come from within. And the rest of your circumstances obey the same inner power. Use it to make your relationship or job the very best it can be.

How hard can it be to find extra time within everyday time? If scientists can split an atom, surely you can open up an hour. Chop up your routine, set new priorities and reassemble the package. Even if feeling discouraged, you can insert the luxury of a breath, a sigh, a wish, a prayer.

Imagination works best when you feel clear and awake. Nonetheless, your creations can accompany you during the duller times, too, if only strengthened by custom. Your positions around the table, for instance, require imagination only the first few times around. By then, you have constructed thought forms, quite solid in their way.

What if dark moods come? Your lot in life can seem so small. Well, if this happens, determine to better things objectively. Make practical plans and use your will to make them come true. Surely you can devote at least five minutes each day to improving your circumstances. The results may not be immediate, but with perseverance and creativity, your success will come. And nothing in life is sweeter than overcoming obstacles by co-creating with God.

Either way, whether being content with your lot or bettering it, you can make this a day of luxury.

335. Singing Daisies

When life brings you long-stemmed roses and rainbows, it's easy to recognize your good fortune. But what are you to make of life when all you're given is a mere handful of daisies or an on-and-off rainstorm?

Today, for instance, you may receive far less than you thought was your due. To the degree that you set lofty goals, you had all the more distance to fall. Making the best of things sounds sensible but sometimes this can be a grim slog.

Next time, do something different instead. At that very moment when you feel discouraged, make it an opportunity to co-create something new with God.

Truth is, rainbows don't need much embellishment from the likes of us. They look as if God has personally painted the sky.

Similarly, remembering to smell the roses takes no imagination. How much more interesting to boldly open up your umbrella and go forth to smell the raindrops! Puddles may leave more room for *you* to contribute some artistry.

Some homemakers have a spectacular knack for turning mundane comforts into sacred ceremonies. One Cincinnati housewife was given a handful of very ordinary daisies. Into a round glass bowl they went, each flower carefully placed as if part of a unique, improvised ritual. When she finally put the last daisy into the center of that arrangement…Wow! The perfection was startling. You could almost hear each flower sing.

Better than heavenly choirs is the singing we do here on earth. Today, in at least one situation, you'll undoubtedly be invited to play music director, artistic director and more. So let God inspire you. Then, together, bring on the singing daisies.

336. Ask for Love

Who knows best what you need? Usually it isn't a parent, child, friend or spouse. It's you. Even Almighty God can't be expected to perpetually monitor your desires. For one thing, God won't read your mind without invitation. So take the initiative and ask for love.

Specifically, let people know what you'd like from them. What's the worst that can happen, that they'll say "No"? Some of us were raised to hint. Supposedly, if the hint recipient "really loved you," he would already know.

Well, hello! Not usually, which is why you'll find plenty of unhappy and unrequited hinters. A marriage counselor named Joe told me this story. A couple he worked with for years finally chose to divorce. Joe accompanied them to the courthouse and stayed to talk with the husband, Benny. After the divorce became legal, Benny said, "I'm so glad that's over. She never really loved me."

"Come on," Joe said. "That's not necessarily true."

"Sure is," Benny insisted. "She never even tucked in my covers at night."

Now here was a new concept in marital obligation! Joe asked for further details.

Benny explained, "Everyone knows about covers. When you really love someone, you don't just say goodnight. You go over to the bed, pull the covers tight around the person's toes and finish with a hug. My mother used to do it every night."

"Did you ever *ask* your wife to tuck you in?"

"Of course not. If she really cared, she'd have known to do it."

Fathomless and innumerable, sometimes downright ridiculous are the assumptions people make about what loved ones would do if they cared enough. The antidote is simple. Ask.

Instinctively you know who is capable of responding to a particular request. You also know whether you'd prefer for the love to be shown in a specific way or if you'd rather be surprised. Well, tell that part, too.

Did you ever ask God to give you more love? Sometimes it will be downloaded straight into your heart. You'll sit in meditation or lie in your bed and good stuff will seep right into you, in God's own perfect way. Drama usually isn't part of this process. Instead you'll receive a gentle awakening, filling you with as much love as you can hold.

Usually it happens this way, but next time you ask, who knows what will happen? There's the beauty of it.

337. Outdo the Starfish

Spiritually, you have a lot in common with the starfish. Its ability to regenerate outwardly allows for some amazing self-repair. Your comparable talent is on the inner.

Depending on how you use free will, you may even go beyond regeneration, achieving a glorious kind of mutation. Have you done this yet? Under duress you develop a strength that didn't exist before. Nobody else in your family evolves this way. Were this to show physically, spronging out like a curlicue limb on a starfish, even strangers would gawk at you. But only those who love you will notice, plus celestial observers.

Thanks to the most famous prayer of modern times, most of us have learned important wisdom about serenity. To gain it, you must change what you can, accept what you can't, and develop the wisdom to know the difference. Sounds like a good start. But don't forget that you can go way beyond serenity to co-create miracles. Let the symbolism of your body inspire you. Stand with your legs spread, arms extended, head held high. Then take inventory:

- Your right leg symbolizes moving forward in *work*, even when the way is unknown or you feel discouraged.
- Your left leg symbolizes moving forward in personal *relationships*, showing courage when you need it most. Will you dare to move closer? Give sensibly? The greatest courage of all may be needed to leave, should someone you love demand too much.
- Next come the talents that show in your arms. That left arm symbolizes taking *action* in your personal life. Will you sit passively, waiting for others to help? How about showing some muscle!
- Your right arm symbolizes taking action in the *world*. How will you use your strengths? Don't wait for some fancy Joan-of-Arc-like mission to announce itself. Serve others, in moderation, and you'll feel a power surge at your mighty right arm.
- Finally, celebrate the top of the star. Awesome, such a magnificent head! God made it and it is good. When you actually use it, the *think-thing* works even better.

Close your eyes for a moment and give thanks for the five-pointed star you are. Not merely able to regenerate, you can actively co-create. So, in times of trouble, remember this. Outdo the starfish.

338. Life Awareness Day

The best-worded death announcement I've ever received began this way: "It is with great joy and sadness that I have the honor to announce our Beverly was *healed* today at 6:50 p.m. when she passed into the spiritual realm."

After a loved one has suffered a long time, it's not uncommon to feel relief when the lifetime ends. However successful that life seems to us, we sense that death brings a new start.

Often we pray for the dearly departed without considering the other side of the energy equation. A great soul, liberated from the confinement of an earth life, has reconnected with God. Gone are fear, pain and all other illusions of a life separate from Source. Therefore, the person who you thought needed *your* help is able to send bright blessings your way.

When someone you love is gone, how can you not feel the human loss? A unique personality and physical form will never return. Yet as the clear image fades from view, so much shows more clearly than ever. Whatever good that person has done can't be contained by the usual thinking, any more than the presence of a great painting stays within its frame. As for the person's shortcomings, how much easier it is now to view them with compassion.

Guilt can bring bittersweet flavors to memories of the departed. Yet we'll also remember any kindness we managed to give. Thus, death can inspire us to give more generously to loved ones who remain.

It wouldn't hurt, actually, to celebrate an annual Life Awareness Day. Any time you see a friend may be the last. Likewise, it may be the last time others will see you. Speak the kind word now, while you have a chance.

If you have good health, loving family and friends, prosperity and other blessings, all the more reason to feel gratitude! And regardless of anything currently lacking, today's a great day to be alive.

339. I Can Make This Work

You have come into this life with certain areas of mastery over earth experience. Granted, "mastery" may seem like a lofty word for these everyday areas of flow and confidence.

- Maybe it's a magical talent for cooking meals that are delicious, even when you have precious little food in the house.
- Maybe you have the perfect combination of patience and stubbornness to work out problems in any love relationship.
- Maybe you can find lost objects — not just for yourself but for others. Even in an unfamiliar house, you'll suggest the very place to look.
- Maybe you instinctively live within your means, rich or poor.
- Maybe you're a master of the road, someone who can always find a perfect parking space.

Whatever your areas of mastery, they are like sneak previews of the movie in which you star as the invincible superhero. That movie has a theme song:

With God's help, I can make this work.

If today you should find yourself in a challenging situation, hum a few bars. Then proceed, using your best judgment. Proceed as if you have all the time and resources needed to flow with the situation and create the best possible outcome. You do.

340. Human-Sized Action

"The Co-Creation Reality Show" has just come on TV. What a relief! In 30 minutes of entertainment, your every wish will be granted.

Sure. Ever wonder why life doesn't happen like that? Say that you have put in your request for a bunch of very specific desires. Here on The Learning Planet, things take their own time to manifest. Sometimes miracles happen instantly, which is when the *God-side* of co-creation dominates. But generally the *you-side* dominates, producing slow (and-not-necessarily-steady) results.

Which kind of timing will it be for you today? You never know in advance, so one of my mottoes is: *Co-create fussy, accept graciously.* Here's how it works.

- Say that you have asked to own your favorite model of Lexus, earn a law degree from Harvard, and marry that gorgeous stranger you wish wouldn't be such a stranger. God will co-create the fulfillment of each desire by opening up the possibilities that can make it happen, as appropriate for you and all others concerned. Working from infinite intelligence, The Big Wise Guy can shift all time and space to eventually bring all the *specifics* you requested, or the nearest possible equivalent.

- Now all you must do is take the action steps humanly, one foot in front of the other. As you act, you may get a feeling about being on the right track. Meeting no resistance is one sign. Joy is another. Inspiration, increased rate of synchronicity, flow — as with every other aspect of deeper perception, you have very distinctive inner signals. Accept them *graciously* as validation that you have support for your desires. Yes, results are on the way but you still must continue doing your human best.

Don't let TV train you to expect dramatic and instant results every time or you'll miss the point of the show. Snappy timing is *not* the main entertainment. Unless you keep the faith, you might only see a mess. So keep your eye on whatever you requested in the first place. Don't act in a way that contradicts it, whether speaking doubts aloud or unnecessarily investing precious resources in a Plan B.

Eventually you'll arrive at sweet victory. No doubt you'll remember your role in a job well done. If wise, you'll also remember that God played a part. There really is a "Co-Creation Reality Show," and most episodes have an identical plot: *Co-creation involves human sweat as well as God's (seemingly) more magnificent contribution.*

341. Coffee for the Soul

Chicken Soup for the Soul can work wonders, but sometimes a person needs more than comfort. A person needs oomph. When you must heal a discouraging, bewildering, or otherwise painful relationship, sorry, but it can't be done with soup. You need a good stiff drink…at a minimum, coffee.

Here's my bracing beverage for your soul, a thought to drink:

Every relationship in your life is a co-creation with God. Pleasant or unpleasant, on some level you chose it. How awake were you at the time when you started this current piece of nonsense? That's another story.

Even a small, groggy input from you counted as co-creation. But you've been evolving since then, which makes the present your time of maximum power *ever*.

With the consciousness you have now, you can co-create far more powerfully than ever before. Think about it: You're more awake within your human self. Your wisdom has increased because of all you've done spiritually, as a world server. And you have learned spiritual techniques for manifesting results, including the basic steps used for effective co-creation:

1. Think the name of a Divine Being.
2. Set an intention.
3. Do the *subjective* part. Ask one question at a time.
4. Accept the answers that come to you.
5. Follow up with the *objective* part. In each situation, do your best as a human being.
6. Pay attention to what happens.
7. Value the part you *can* use, whether lessons, inspiration, small stuff or big outrageous miracles.
8. Let go whatever you *can't* use, even if that requires you to start this same co-creation cycle all over again.

Whatever bad things have happened so far, don't lounge around in misery, sipping up pain. Brew up some fresh coffee. Actively co-create.

342. Silently

Free and clear under me, every-directional
spin with me, whirl me. Once
breathless, I'll know I can
never outrace it. Ah!
God's freshest air.

Bring me such stillness, immense, growing fatter
until I inflate with it
like a balloon, and then
slather still more of it
onto my food. Let us
picnic today on Your joy.

I'll be Your busy bee, doing good deeds
only let's have me inwardly
tucked deep inside Your heart,
synchronized with Your beat,
Our sacred background noise
Your song of peace.

343. Heal Psychic Coercion

Psychic coercion happens when people try to play God. It's the most prevalent form of subconscious debris on the planet. Ironically, the worst offenders are clueless that they have hurt anyone. More likely, they think they're helping.

Coercers dictate how you should dress. Or they've figured out how you should earn your money, also exactly how to spend it. What about your food, your hobbies, your sex life? Hey, nothing in your life is too personal for a coercer to try and "fix." Supposedly, this person has brilliant insights about everything that you *should* be doing.

That funny word "should" often gives it away. However, you won't necessarily hear any words at all. Most coercion isn't spoken directly to your face. The nagging happens behind your back or it's given the sanctimonious gloss of prayer. Right now, somewhere, someone is "praying" by asking God to inflict on others something that the coercer thinks would be good…even invading free will areas as intimate as religion, sexual orientation and political choice.

Even the nicest-sounding requests can mess up people's auras. If you're on the *sending* end, stop. If on the *receiving* end, here's how to clear that garbage out of your aura:

For this method to be effective, speak words like these out loud: "God, surround me with light. Give me a shield of protection so that, from now on, only energies of the highest vibrations may enter my aura and my home. Next, please bring in a violet flame to transmute all stale or negative energy."

Now comes the flashy part. Think the name of a Divine Being like Archangel Michael, St. Germain or Babaji. Ask him to remove all psychic coercion from your subconscious mind, flinging the unwanted stuff out of your aura and into the violet flame. ("Imagine" means that you may not necessarily see. You may feel it, hear thoughts or otherwise sense what's happening. Any of this works just fine.) When the garbage removal is complete, you'll know it. To finish, ask the Divine Being to fill you with light.

How vividly must you experience all this in order for the healing to work? Not vividly at all! Clearer experiences will come as you develop deeper perception. Ironically, garbage like psychic coercion may be what's blocking that perception. To break out of this cycle, just do the healing.

Of course you can know what *you* think, what *you* feel, what *you* desire! Pay attention. And if, in future, you hear the word "Should"…. Well, I won't order you. But I do *invite* you to question what's going on. Almighty God doesn't "should" us. Why let mere mortals?

344. Protect Yourself From Bullies

How best can you protect yourself from zealots who insist on making your religious life *their* business? Many a glorious spiritual seeker has been told that he's going to Hell. Bossy!

Remember, nobody at Earth School has the right to interfere in the life of anyone else. (Exceptions are raising a child to maturity or if you find somebody breaking the law.) When someone you know is making what seems like a mistake, it's fine to speak your opinion directly, once. Advice turns coercive when repeated, whether to a person's face or behind his back or, even worse, as a so-called "prayer."

Never let religious bullies victimize you. Yesterday you learned how to remove psychic coercion from your aura. Here are additional ways to protect yourself:

Ask God to transform *subconscious patterns* that weaken you. For instance, what if you've been made to fear that you're bad, stupid or crazy? Ask God to take negative programming away, then fill you with the opposite (usually some form of believing in yourself).

Next, ask God to alert you to anyone sending you coercion, whether an individual or a group. Have a conversation, if you can, where you tell that person in no uncertain terms, "Stop bossing me around."

Meanwhile, call on a Divine Being to break the *psychic ties* between you and that person so that you can go free. And don't worry. There's more to a close relationship than psychic ties. After they're gone, the healthy part of your relationship will remain. Most coercers aren't close to you, anyway.

Negative patterns can also be healed from your *cellular memory*. Ask God to remove the debris stuck in your cells, working out any karmic debts in the mildest possible way, like your dreams. Ask to learn the details consciously only if necessary.

Finally, ask a Divine Being to help you release "The Big One." Commonly, a person subconsciously carries one major vulnerability pattern, like "If I'm not good enough, nobody will love me," or "Worrying means that I'm responsible."

Subconscious goals like these are exhausting to strive for, and when a person feels discouraged temporarily, psychic coercion can sneak in… by the truckload.

So question inside until you find your *vulnerability pattern*. Acknowledge yourself for caring that much. Then ask God's help to throw off the inappropriate load, once and for all, and then fill you with light. No bully deserves to intrude on the big sacred space that you share with God.

345. Bring on the Violet Flame

What, your home doesn't have a violet flame yet? How come? It's the ultimate recycling gadget, super-efficient at transforming stale and negative energy. In a jiffy, psychic-level junk will be zapped away. And, did I mention? The flame is free. Just ask God to place one wherever you'd like — by every window, dangling off your eyelashes, just name it. Request it and, faster than an Internet click, you'll get it.

Violet flames remove debris from your aura. On a physical level, you might use cleanser and a mop. Well, for your aura, bring on the flame.

One of its many uses is to deflect psychic coercion. You've already learned to release pushy messages from busybodies (well meaning or otherwise). Another common source of coercion is advertising. Messages can be informative, clever and entertaining; still they have been crafted to lodge in your subconscious mind.

Like affirmations, advertising slogans gain power through repetition. To counter this, talk back to every unwanted message you hear or read. Your subconscious mind will record that you told yourself, "No, I don't believe I must buy xyz."

But what about messages that come through when you're not paying attention? Right now, you can ask for *a special violet flame to counter propaganda and subliminal messages.* Ask God for it once and instantly it will be installed into your aura, bringing lifelong protection that works like a bullet-proof vest for your subconscious mind.

Here's an example of how mine helped me. After taking my son to the orthodontist, I sat in the waiting room. A radio played in the background. Engrossed in a magazine, I suddenly sat bolt upright in my chair and shouted, "No way!"

Other parents in the waiting room stared at me. Actually, I was just as shocked. But after I asked inside what was going on, here's what was replayed from my subconscious mind. Before my outburst, the smooth-voiced radio announcer had crooned, "Ladies, I know that all of you have been considering liposuction...."

"Did you hear that ad?" I asked my companions in the waiting room. Soon we were all discussing this sneaky advertising. That's the good thing about violet flames. You get to have interesting conversations with total strangers....

Seriously, the good part is that your subconscious mind is protected even when you're not aware of the need for protection.

You have every right to go through life without being coerced. So bring on the light of a violet flame. It will help your aura and the rest of you to look gorgeous. I'd say, even better than after liposuction.

346. *Peripheral Vision*

Deeper perception can start with *peripheral vision*. Mostly you're seeing reality as usual. Then, past the corner of one eye… unsought… a subtle light flickers. Energy moves or you feel/see/know that something different is happening.

Will you let that gentle knowing count as something, even if you don't yet know what?

Or maybe you'll have a moment of *peripheral hearing*. Within a voice, you'll hear something new, something more. Will you dismiss this as a fluke?

Instead you could welcome such experiences, letting them accumulate until you get it. Aha! You've been initiated into deeper perception.

Spiritually, this takes maturity, welcoming tender new insights. Beyond that, here's something you *can* actively do. Just for today, seek a perception upgrade with an indirect approach.

- In each new situation where you find yourself, ask God to help you be of service.
- Let go any need for flash.
- Notice how you feel after helping.

A nun prayed for years but found no God presence at all. When she made it her business to simply help people, she found her God.

And a monk advised his followers to be like a car. "Don't worry about being filled up," he said, "Just help people."

Ever see a car begging for gas? Of course not. Even if it could, it wouldn't need to. Because a car makes itself available for transportation, its tank will always be filled. For you, too, giving to others will bring celestial largesse.

What a paradox! If you tend to seek God first on the inside, go out. But if you usually seek outward, go in.

Wherever the light is unaccustomed and you lack your usual words, *there* could be your best place for spiritual seeking. Either peripherally or with one big noisy chuckle, God could be just around the corner.

347. Orange Juice?

"A day without orange juice is like a day without sunshine." Sure, the words come from a silly old TV commercial, but they make the basis of a very effective spiritual exercise. A day without *what* makes your life empty? Give your first thought after each of the following questions:

- What gave me a reason to wake up today?
- What would make life smell, taste or feel good to me?
- What could I do today that would really nourish me?
- If I had to choose one great indispensable ingredient to be sure to include in my day, what would it be?

Whether the answers seem silly or sensible, they're important. To honor your own soul, pay attention. Do what you can to give this day *your* indispensables.

Ever take an orange apart, one section at a time? You find tiny globes of juice, each one shaped like a teardrop. Each morsel is shaped like an orange *seed*, only not bitter.

Interesting similarity, isn't it? That bitter seed is what grows the whole tree. But the sweet juice has its uses, too, as you well know.

Could your best "orange juice" be your connection to God? You can decide to reach for that connection in every important thing that you do, reaching out for just a few seconds. One way is to ask, "What about this activity or relationship brings me the most joy?" Listen for the answer. Or see it. Or feel it.

Joy matters. During any experience of joy, quick as thought, your consciousness will reach deep within to the feet of God. Then you'll bounce back out, first to the deepest level of perception, then out toward more surface levels of reality. Usually this sacred journey goes by so fast, a person doesn't notice it. But anyone can. Make the trip consciously often enough and, eventually, you'll be able to linger at any level of perception you like.

The sunshine of deeper perception is yours for the taking, effortless as reaching out to a ripe orange on a branch right in front of you. Hold the warm fruit in your hand, give a quick tug, and it's yours.

348. Reprogram Yourself

Change your mind and you can change your life. That's especially true if you can change your *subconscious* mind. Over this year, you've learned or refined powerful techniques for change: Affirmations, self-hypnosis and creative imagination. But I've saved the best for last: *Reprogramming ceremonies.*

What makes them so effective? The reason involves a distinction you're already familiar with, spiritual healing versus psychological healing. When you do the former, you permanently move old patterns out of your aura. Immediately afterwards, you become deeply responsive to psychological healing designed to reprogram your subconscious.

It's a highly teachable moment. For decades, I've helped clients this way, first facilitating spiritual healing, then asking them to do a five-minute reprogramming ceremony, custom designed. A sequence like this can speed you forward along your chosen path in life, helping you to release unproductive patterns and substitute something new and improved. Plus, this technique is so efficient that, by doing it only once, you'll produce significant results. Think of it as an uncannily potent TV commercial for personal growth where *you* are in charge of the message.

Remember what has happened to you so far with spiritual healing techniques from this book, like removing psychic coercion, giving yourself new family of choice or pulling an amulet out of the ethers. Immediately after receiving the healing, didn't you feel that something changed? It's common to feel gratitude, then get on with your life. Doing this, it can take months to *integrate* what has changed spiritually. Sometimes gracefully, often stumblingly, a person gradually develops behavior without the old limitations.

Any major aura cleanup must out-picture through behavior. Well, a reprogramming ceremony helps you to consciously direct this change. Reprogramming ceremonies are also useful after any experience that *shakes up* your aura without rearranging it: A fight with a loved one, illness in your family, losing a job, going back to school, marriage, divorce, becoming a parent. Within six weeks, you'll adjust somehow. But a reprogramming ceremony helps you to use the energy of disruption, direct it in a positive way and co-create a better life.

We're going to take three days to teach you this life-changing technique, not long to develop such a useful skill. Here's your assignment for today: Choose one old behavior pattern that you would like to change. Consider what would be the ideal replacement. Gather several ideas as you go through this day, and before the day's end, *write down one pair,* old pattern plus new substitute. Yes, don't just think about the pattern. Write it down. Soon you will turn your words into reality.

349. Stage It

Step right up, ladies and gentlemen. Your *reprogramming ceremony* will begin tomorrow. No rehearsals are needed. But hmmm.... Might you take the precaution of designing the show?

Yesterday you were invited to think about a *pattern*, something you would like to change. For instance, let's say that you have just ended a toxic love relationship and would like to free yourself up to attract a better one in the future. Today you will to translate a pattern into its underlying subconscious *programming*, then decide *how to replace it*.

For instance, with this same example, what programming could have caused you to shape that toxic relationship? Several ideas may cross your mind. When you find the one that matters most, plus its desired replacement, you may feel a shudder of recognition. Excellent!

Now, you've ready for the next step, which is to *stage* your reprogramming. Get Big and set the intention to design a simple ceremony that you will soon use to reprogram your subconscious mind in the direction you've chosen; the effects will be all and only good. Then start sketching out a little play that includes the following components:

1. An *Announcement*. Inform your subconscious mind that something important is about to happen. One sentence will suffice. (Use the language of affirmations to express yourself with maximum power.) For example, "Subconscious mind, I am changing how I balance giving and receiving."
2. *The Old Program*. Summarize your old program. Stage it creatively, using any props or symbols you like, from puppets to pillows to punching bags.
3. *The New Program*. Describe how, from now on, you'll deal with that same aspect of life. Again, stage it. Use the same props, only differently. Your subconscious mind loves show-and-tell.

Now, some folks love to ham things up by designing a ceremony. But if you need a nudge, revisit childhood, where you could pretend anything. Back then you could turn a table top into a piano and make up a song, moving your fingers to "play." Well, you still can do that sort of thing. And your subconscious will love it.

What if your adult, conscious self is critical? Tough! Your only *official* audience is your subconscious plus any Divine Beings you invite. On Broadway, your improvised staging might not get stellar reviews. But here all you need do is interest your own subconscious mind. Piece of cake!

350. A Cosmic Show-and-Tell

The past two days you have prepared for a potentially life-changing reprogramming ceremony. You've chosen what you would like to reprogram and how, then sketched out your Show-and-Tell. Well, today you'll get to do it.

Using a book like this on your own has many advantages over being with a seminar full of people, but one disadvantage is that you don't have group momentum to energize you. Possibly the enthusiasm of your fellow participants would be contagious here, helping your ceremony to become extra-effective.

Here's the best substitute I can muster. Imagine, if you like, that you're at a Co-Create with God Seminar and we've arrived at the part where participants stage their Show-and-Tell in front of the whole group. You feel really comfortable with everyone. People in the group like you, too, and a great deal of positive momentum is being generated. Watch the ceremony right before yours. Here goes Jen.

Reprogramming Dance with Fruit

Props: One orange, one apple and one banana, all in a nearby bowl.

Stage set: A wall mirror in one part of the room.

Announcement: "Archangel Michael, help me to reprogram my subconscious patterns with love relationships. Subconscious mind, pay attention."

The Old Program: "In the old way, I always tried hard to please my lover, constantly seeking approval. I'm going to show this pattern through Dance #1."

Jen dances across the room. Reaching toward the fruit bowl, she comes up empty. She backs away. She tries again. And a third time. Finally, she moves in front of the mirror. Slumping over, she takes a good look at herself.

The New Program: "From now on, my lover and I balance our giving and receiving. I'm confident that I am loved. I'll show this pattern through Dance #2."

Jen dances across the room, reaches out, grabs an orange and holds it. She dances around more, adds the apple. Dancing around more, she adds the banana. In front of the mirror, she sees herself holding all three "fruits of her actions" and says out loud (for the benefit of her subconscious mind):

"From now on, whenever I'm in a love relationship, I expect to receive wonderful fruits of understanding, appreciation and love. It is easy for me to accept and enjoy them. I am REALLY GOOD at being in a love relationship."

Applause builds. Now your loyal fans await *your* turn. So perform away.

Trust this: You may not literally have a room filled with people applauding you, but your whole angel committee is witnessing this, as are God and all the Divine Beings you choose. The guest of honor is your own subconscious mind. So know that your success is guaranteed. Wonderful results are on the way.

351. In a World with Terrorism, Grace

The grace of God is unexpected, too.
You will be working, trying, worrying.
Then the packed train just stops,
the usual lights go out,
irrevocably, a new time has come.

But unlike terror, grace does not bring death.
Nor need it bring a change of any kind
for someone else to see,
no shouting louder than your usual voice.

Grace will not strike with a cruel, random force.
You must rise up, requesting in your way, then wait.
Prayer's only victim is
the one who won't sing out, too proud for love.
That is not you.

Active though your call is,
you afterwards may still be made to wait
in line, or wade through doubts, or else
encounter who knows what? Such wondering,
nothing doing, makes a map for grace.
When the miraculous path peeks its way in
a different kind of wonder can find *you*.

May a stealth peace delight you every time
change you, change me, sun breaking through a cloud
when least expected. Come rewire each brain,
electrify our blood, beat in our hearts
until un-shockable, in God's deep trust
wherever we may go we know our own.

352. Who

You know so much now about how to co-create with God. Even before beginning this book, you had huge wisdom. With this book, you've added more skill. To help you move forward still further, I have eight final secrets of co-creation to share with you, concerning *who, what, where,* and so forth. Today, let's begin with *who*.

What do all your co-creative actions have in common? Whether you're making requests or prayerfully listening for answers, whether you need healing or you're volunteering to help others, two major creators will be involved. God will, clearly, show up as God. What about you?

Here's a funny thing I've learned from teaching spiritual seekers over the last 35 years. Sometimes when the topic is elevated a person tries *too high.* Not too hard — well, that's possible, too. But what's unique to spiritual endeavors is trying too high. Sometimes the student's voice literally rises in pitch or his breathing half stops, as if the seeker is trying to raise himself up by the very hairs of his head, an attempt not just doomed to failure but downright painful.

However well intended, showing up as your *partial* self will bring only partial results. If you offer God just one perfect thin slice of who you are, you limit your blessings.

Back when you were a teenager, did you ever try really hard to impress The Crush? Striving to seem ultra-cool, a love-smitten teen may succeed in grabbing attention. But any victory will be, at best, short-lived. Eventually, the aspirant will be found out and discarded. Ironically, if she had dared to be authentic, a love-me-or-leave-me type, her romance had at least a smidge of hope.

By adulthood, most of us have learned to stop playing games in relationships. Yet spiritually we wish that someone would teach us how to act, who to be.

But co-creation requires no special pious personality — fortunate, because acting holier-than-self might not fool God anyway. Besides, without my personally knowing every crush from your past, I'm pretty sure that God is even smarter and nicer and (spiritually) better looking. Actually, you could come across as the biggest phony in all the world and, unlike The Crush, God would still love you for it.

To save yourself unnecessary agony, once and for all, stop worrying about the WHO side of co-creation. Connect with God whether you're happy or sad. Sure, co-create when you feel wonderful. But on those days when you bumble around, glaringly imperfect, don't wait until you feel better before you phone Home.

Life offers opportunities galore to feel ashamed. How you relate to God need never be one of them. Nothing about you, good or bad, can scare off That love. So whenever you wish to co-create with God, don't be shy. Just be you.

353. Who NOT

Co-creation is NOT just for you.

Even for purely selfish reasons, you'd want to co-create altruistically sometimes. By helping someone else overcome an obstacle, you can repay a karmic debt and not have to go through a similar problem yourself.

Now, sometimes you may feel way too worthless to co-create for anyone else. My technical term for this is feeling like "a splot." If you feel like a splot, must you wait until you feel back to normal before you help anyone?

You might be waiting a very long time. Helping people can put your own troubles in perspective. Of course, it's wise to fill yourself up before attempting volunteer work. But, after asking God to help you, there are powerful ways that even a splot can co-create for others:

- You could pray for your family and friends, sending each one a glow of pure white light.
- Or try an anonymous act of kindness, like blessing a dollar which you then drop on the street for someone to find.
- Or you could co-create help for someone you barely know, like drivers stopped by the side of the road. Ask Zeus to help you hurl a thunderbolt of peace before you drive on.

Actually, you can take a hint from good drivers. They don't merely look a car-length ahead; they scan the road in every direction. This perspective makes a drive safer. Similarly, when problems get you down, open up your perspective. Especially when your progress seems thwarted, see farther by volunteering to help someone else. *Who is involved in co-creation?* Not just you, Buddy!

For a completely different shift in perspective, you can learn about co-creation by standing quite still. Difficult yoga postures often begin with this instruction: Choose a point in the distance. Watch that point while you do the difficult stretch. Automatically, you'll find a place of balance within you.

Who is involved in co-creation? No matter how many others you benefit, the process is going to help you.

Co-creation is the most exquisite combination of balancing in one spot yet traveling, helping others yet also remembering to help yourself. Even if you feel like a splot, affirm:

I am ready and worthy to co-create with God.

354. What

What are you going to co-create? Unless you know, begin by asking questions. Even if you already have a vague goal in mind, you can ask to receive your next set of instructions.

Assembling your set of questions can be a relief in itself. You'll need 10 minutes of time and your favorite recording device, be it old-fashioned pen and paper or some high-tech recording gizmo.

For best results, assume that gathering questions does *not* count as co-creating with God. Focus this set of questions on your completely human problems and needs. Especially if you spend much of your life being "The Strong One" for others, know that it's impossible to be too needy or vulnerable when listing questions here. Your upcoming conversation will be utterly private; no other person on earth ever needs to be told a word about it.

To gather these very personal questions, I recommend that you do NOT use the Get Big technique. Instead, imagine that you are going to have a private audience with the wisest human being you can think of. This could be a spiritual advisor, a trusted relative or friend, a world-class psychic. You can afford any fee. And even if that person is normally hard to reach, a special exception has been made in your case. Step up to the head of the line!

Since your confidential appointment is coming up soon, you'd better list all your important questions right now.

Setting the stage in this way brings out your most practical self, your highly savvy Inner Consumer. Write down more than you would need to fill your hour with this world-class expert. Write everything. Let the questions flow.

After your 10-minute brainstorm, go back over your list and edit. Put your questions in order. Co-creation is a duet between your human self and Divine inspiration, but choosing good questions must be your solo. Once you've done this, the tough human part, you'll have done your full share for receiving God's answers.

355. What NOT

Doubts about your skill at contacting God can tie a person up in knots, but why lead such a twisted life? Stop giving attention — and power — to the knots. Bigger than any NOT, Almighty God isn't going away any time soon, certainly not just because a person feels a bit insecure.

Know that you have the chops to call on God effectively, regardless of whether or not you're fully convinced of your huge self-worth. Use techniques like those in this book, and just go step by step. Results over time will prove to you that something real has happened. And aren't genuine results more important than mere theoretical certitude? As soon as you've found a spiritual practice that interests you, doubts will seem less important anyway.

So how will you co-create? *Just choose something.* You might enjoy thoughtful prayer, an unscripted eyes-closed conversation with God, deep meditation, contemplating a phrase from scripture, even simple body awareness. Choose something and then, should doubts come up, doubt your doubts.

If you still need reassurance, remember that you're not cold-calling some stranger here. This is neither some vengeful ex-lover nor a rigid authority figure nor some sadist who wishes to torture you by playing hard to get. This is God.

You've always been connected really. So please don't expect that the point of your spiritual exercise is something flashy. Stunning contrast occurs only if you were never much connected in the first place. (Give yourself and God, both, some credit.)

Go ahead with whatever method you're using to strengthen your conscious connection with Source. Your intent will be honored; the technique you used will even be upgraded, if necessary.

God and you have a relationship, and neither side needs to be passive.

That's why, whenever you try making God "It," this loving companion of yours can find the perfect way to tag you back.

What NOT to do in order to co-create with God? The only NOT to do is nothing at all.

356. How

How can you co-create most successfully? *Act appropriately, then let go.*

Consciously or unconsciously, people constantly co-create with God. We send out one desire after another. But unless we engage purposefully in the process, we miss much of the fun and most of the spiritual learning.

So be specific as a co-creator. Say what you want and life will shift to support you. It's like the great proverb, "For a web begun, God sends the thread."

We might add, "And for each new work begun, an angel arrives." Because it does.

Ever study Reiki? At each attunement, an angel is added to your personal entourage. Every new subject you study, each new group of people you decide to serve, each vacation or sport begun…Boing! Up pops a new Light Being, willing to help you as long as the two of you get along. You know, you're not so much one person as the CEO of a large company of angels. So yes, angels will be part of any co-creation, and it's only fair to thank them.

But angels will help you regardless of whether or not you focus on them. By contrast, Divine Beings usually help only when you ask. For that reason, I recommend that whenever you have a desire to fulfill, often your first step will be to Get Big. Then you'd be wise to set an intention, which will be heard by that Divine Being as well as your whole company of angels. After that, just get out of the way.

What if you need help afterward? Repeat the cycle. Get Big by thinking the name of the Divine Being. Put in a new request for help and again let go and let God.

It's like pumping on a swing. Bend forward as far as you can, then lie back and relax. Just keep holding onto the swing and repeating the process. You'll go higher and higher.

I've had the privilege of watching the auras of world-class healers, counselors, teachers, writers and entertainers. Sure they show skill but, more fascinating to me, is their trust about letting go. Before they move into co-creation, what typically shows in their auras? Gifts of the soul display at each chakra. Along with this you'll usually find plenty of human stuff — temporary worries, old stuff in the way, personal growth in progress — just like anyone else.

What's remarkable is how the great ones change when they co-create. Consciously or not, they get completely out of the way. Huge light pours through the person's crown chakra and splashes outward in her distinctive auric display. You, too, can flow with Divine inspiration. Set up your co-creation consciously, Get Big and trust.

357. How NOT

In a life of regular collaboration with God, you'll constantly find things you don't know and seek new answers. But here's one trap to avoid, The Naughty Affirmation. This is an enormously popular set of words. You'll hear it everywhere — except that after reading what follows, you may stop hearing it from your own lips.

The Naughty Affirmation is simply this: "I don't know." Three simple words add up to one rotten and futile method of self-sabotage.

Usually, as you know, affirmations are spoken for self-improvement. This one isn't. People aren't even conscious of saying it, half the time. Unfortunately, subconscious minds are notoriously literal. Repeatedly used, any well-constructed affirmation will stick to your subconscious mind where it will harden like cement.

Except for being undesirable, "I don't know" follows every rule for a well-constructed affirmation. It's personal, simple and present-tense. In its vague way, it's highly specific. And it's definitely believable. So, what does The Naughty Affirmation do for you? Insidiously, it persuades your subconscious mind that you're ignorant.

Co-creation with God will bring up all possible insecurity, worthiness issues, doubts about your sanity. This is normal. Self-doubt needn't be a permanent affliction...unless you keep using The Naughty Affirmation. Why volunteer it?

- Probably you say The Naughty Affirmation out of modesty. But did dumbing yourself down ever help anyone else become smarter?
- Sometimes the ominous words are uttered as a misplaced kind of truthfulness. Instead, say something context-related like, *"I don't know the answer to 'How much is the square root of 3,962,088?'"*
- Most insidiously, The Naughty Affirmation is used as a kind of spiritual reaching. "I want to experience God more clearly but (Sigh!) I don't know." In a dreamy kind of way, this is charming. But so is a soused alcoholic pondering the meaning of life. Snap out of it, darling! You have a good brain.
- Why wait for someone else to tell you the answers to your own life? When you don't know something, don't whine about it. Go find out.

It's easy to break the habit of using The Naughty Affirmation. When you find yourself starting to say, "I don't know," take a few breaths. Ask God for help. Then gently ask about whatever is puzzling you. If nothing comes, say nothing. But often you will find an answer, energizing as a breath of fresh air. *Spiritually, you can always know the truth.*

358. Where

Everything's almost ready. Equipped with your list of questions, you're prepared to Get Big, state an intention, and let go. Just find a suitable environment and you'll have ideal conditions to co-create.

Whenever you aim to upgrade your skill at co-creating with God, it helps to be in a sanctuary. Some folks have the luxury of a separate meditation room or chapel. But you can consecrate any room to this purpose. Just bring in a crystal or candle or other sacred object. And resolve to keep that part of your home clean, even if you're too busy to tidy up the rest.

Make that place as quiet as it can be, and forestall interruptions by welcoming pets and children *out* of your room. Ask any human roommates to give you privacy. A simple sign on the door can do the trick.

Next, freshen up your physical temple. Some people even like to wear a special outfit, reserved for spiritual exercise. For your sanctuary at home, "Sunday best" means comfortable and clean.

It's time to take out your list of questions. And speaking of equipment, please don't put yourself in the awkward position of trying to remember what happened while it is happening. Bring in a recording device or simple pen and paper, etc. Please reserve any fancy journal book for later, so that now you can be utterly spontaneous, even messy. Making your notes pretty is a separate and optional task.

What else will help you to receive your good with undivided attention? One good stretch could do it, or you might prefer to do a few yoga postures. Must you remove every extraneous thought from your mind? Only if you wish to co-create as a dead person! Relax. However you think is fine.

Take a deep breath or two. Ask one question. Release it by taking a few deep breaths. Then start speaking or writing. No censoring, please. Ask follow-up questions galore (but one at a time) and, again, record whatever you receive.

Don't wait for an inner voice that sounds different from your own. Information could come as images, physical sensations, emotions, tastes, smells. Whatever comes to you, it has arrived in a sacred context, so let it count. After you're done, give thanks. Look over what you received. Now's the time to write the highlights in a journal if you have one or to put action steps on your calendar.

Confidence as a co-creator is cumulative. Eventually, you will need no special sanctuary, no props, not even any official technique. Where did you learn reading and writing, mostly in school? But once literate, you could read everywhere, easily. As a co-creator, your destination — and destiny — is Perfection Everywhere Now.

359. When

When is the best time to co-create with God? Considering that He/She is available 24/7 and beyond, any time would appear to be good. Yet some times could actually be better than others. It's very personal and, of course, you'll be the best judge:

- *Early* in the morning is excellent because the rest of your day will structure around it.
- *Middle* of the day can be superb. If you've come to the end of your rope, a second rope will be provided. And, if needed, additional ropes will appear in sequence.
- *Late* at night is magnificent because your dreams tonight, plus the start of tomorrow, will be structured around your co-creation. (For added benefit from late-night co-creation, be sure to journal your dreams first thing the next day.)

Another way to think about timing takes biorhythms into account. Whenever in your day's cycle do you feel clearest? Co-create then. You'll feel most powerful.

Or, hey, create whenever you feel dull or discouraged. That can work!

Whenever you're willing, God is, too. Whether crammed into a second of free will or keeping you company throughout long stretches of discontent, God will most certainly show up.

When *isn't* a good time? Constantly.

To create effectively as a human, you need to get a life and be completely involved in it. Otherwise, you risk becoming spiritually self-conscious and could wind up like an affected performer who is always being "AN ACTOR."

Better to leave your major co-creating for one or two periods each day, when you can give it full attention. This would be dedicated time, not stolen minutes while you're driving. During your spiritual exercise, be 100 percent committed to it. Afterwards take action in the world.

You'll be on your own, improvising your share of co-creation (except for the occasional, and always honored, yelp for help).

Pacing yourself spiritually, you may find that a time will come when God sticks to you so thoroughly that you feel strongly connected constantly. Spiritual victory! But that will happen sooner if, most of the time, you act as though what matters most is your human life.

360. When the Time Comes

Welcome to My world of miracles.
It was not time before. It is time now.
Always your prayers were heard. Know they were held
in trust by Me until the perfect hour.

Know, too, how I have loved you. I'm so proud
that this idea of mine, the soul you are
evolved until it could stand on its own.

Now co-create with me, Beloved One.
You cleaned your glasses. I will wipe your tears.
Breathe with me. Heal with me. Most of all, play,
and let your heart keep opening in wonder.
Mine does that, too, you know.

361. Emmanuel

Imagine if you could have studied with one of the world's great gurus, like Jesus or Buddha. "Guru" means an enlightened teacher whom you commit to and follow the rest of your life. Your goal will be to gain that caliber of perfection.

Alas, if you're like most people, you don't have even the luxury of a third-rate personal guru. Sure, you've had a teacher here or there. But you remain in charge of your spiritual journey. Well, what if this isn't such a bad thing? What if you're fulfilling prophesies like that of the Second Coming of Christ? You know: Emmanuel, God within each of us, very much alive in consciousness.

Is humanity ready to make such a huge collective step forward? You are, which is all you can be responsible for. Regardless of your religious affiliation, you have chosen to become an awakening being. Day by day, you've been enlivening your connection to God. Co-creating takes you beyond sweet mysteries of theology and the beauty of time-hallowed rituals. You have been drawing That huge, ingenious presence into the world.

Will your full awakening be flashy? Don't expect that. Or you could miss the quietly beautiful show. They say a watched pot never boils. Actually, that's true only if you're oblivious to the heating-up process. Should you care exclusively about one big, boiling climax, sure you'll be bored while you wait.

Otherwise, it can be great fun to watch a pot of water heat up. Slowly, the subtle currents gather intensity. You can reach out safely to put your hand just close enough to feel warmth above the surface. What a choreography when the first, pioneering bubbles start to dance! Then a different kind of delight ensues, as the rest of the water joins up and the whole pot of water is, finally, boiling.

This can be your process of finding Emmanuel. Awakening grows within you, first slowly, then faster…one achievement at a time, one moment of ecstasy, one inner Aha! Each bubble is glorious. First just a few come. Then so many swirl around, you can't count them all. For you and maybe for the whole human race, too….

Did you decide to co-create with God for personal reasons? Hope so! You'd be a fool not to. Nonetheless, your personal spiritual quest couldn't be a bigger gift to the world. All people are spiritually interconnected. So don't be dismayed by the polarization of current events. World consciousness is heating up, causing people to follow their truth to the utmost. Each of us moves through our passions, releasing what we must so that we can awaken together. One human soul at a time, spiritual light is glowing up all over the globe. Be one of the first bubbles in the saucepan of the world. More and more of us, awakening, create a global Emmanuel.

362. How Would Jesus Drive?

In any given situation you can ask, "What would Jesus do?" But wouldn't it be more interesting, as well as realistic, to ask, "How would I do [whatever I'm doing] if Jesus were there along with me?

After all, your goal isn't to *become* Jesus — or Buddha or Muhammad, Archangel Ezekiel or any other chosen ideal. Question any spiritual teacher who demands that you become someone other than yourself. Jesus didn't require this.

Who knows how Jesus would drive your car? But you can definitely figure out if you would drive differently *having Him as your passenger.* Imagine Him or another Divine Being with you today, sitting right next to you.

In His company, will you tailgate or be overly cautious? Will you follow the rules of the road, like remembering to turn on the headlights when it rains? In my neighborhood, turn signals have become optional in the minds of many. One otherwise intelligent woman explained it to me this way:

"Why don't I signal? Guess I just don't feel the need."

Would she drive differently if a police officer were in the car? I'd especially love to watch from the back seat if she had a policeman plus Jesus.

Truth is, we drive according to our level of consciousness. Rules of the road, common sense or even common courtesy — none of this matters much when the driver's consciousness is half asleep. Even with all good intentions, even if you were carrying the finest passenger in all the world, with sleepy consciousness you wouldn't drive well.

But anyone's consciousness can wake up. It just takes some time each day where you have the intent to give God your undivided attention. Then use some technique of your choice to connect with the Divine presence.

Once awake, consciousness can *move.* Another name for moving spiritual consciousness is...*co-creating with God.*

Who gives you license to be so ambitious? Trust the only human being with the appropriate credentials to decide: Yourself.

Eventually it seems superfluous to figure out answers to questions like, "What would Jesus do?" Ask Him yourself. Or do something even better. Co-create with a Divine Being and express the inspiration as *you*.

363. Day of Completion

Today is a day of completion. However long a project has been hanging, eventually all missing details will be set right and your project will land safely on solid ground. Finally you can collect the reward for all you have done.

Full results can't reach a person until a project has been completed. It's like the sense of accomplishment when you've put money in the bank. That messy wad of cash, that pile of loose checks, coins and bills on your desk, seems to gain substance only after being deposited. Literally as well as figuratively, it adds up.

Many of us have struggled for years with completion...and the story is not over yet. Even the most organized person goes through circumstances where nothing can be finished. You're stuck, awaiting a missing piece of paper or the cooperation of people who can't be reached. Sometimes you're simply ahead of your time; you must wait for the consciousness of this slow planet to catch up with you.

But sometimes completion *does* arrive on demand. You summon up the force of your will, choose one project and decree, "Today I will pull this together."

It happens, too.

Once I heard a crossword puzzle expert answer the question, "What's the best way to get good at those tough puzzles in the newspaper?"

He answered, "Train yourself to finish." He explained that, even if you have to look up answers while developing your skill with the puzzles, what matters most is that your mind and body can register the sense of completion.

He claimed, this habit will carry you forward until you can come up with answers on your own.

So let today be a day when you complete *something*. It could be a mere puzzle in today's newspaper or a project that matters more deeply to you.

Afterward, take a moment to savor the most delicious part. Finishing has an echo: Peace.

Once you have finished something, pause before you tune into the next project. Listen for that echo or feel it reverberate within your body. Take a moment to see perfection where you are right now. Deep within you, in your own way, feel the peace.

It is a wonderful quality of God's presence, available always. But before you can relish it, sometimes you must earn a rest.

364. Finished at Last!

So many things in life end before we'd like them to, causing even a delicious outcome to leave a bitter aftertaste. In retrospect, the loss of a job can be seen as a blessing. The death of one friendship can make room for the birth of another. Yet only a hardened bliss maniac would relish this kind of consolation.

From a spiritual perspective, nobody on earth has the power to cut you off from your good, be it love or prosperity or doing the work that thrills your soul. And ultimately every friend or boss is an expression of God who will be replaced in your life by another expression at least as good. To realize this is to find consolation. Still it takes a heaping portion of consolation to cancel out human regret.

And it is very human to want to say the last word, to choose your own ending…or, at the very least, to foresee it.

Some of the outcomes we envision never even happen. How annoying when you can't have closure because some clueless person refuses your offer to clear the air! And sometimes you come so tantalizingly close to getting what you want, it's like licking your ice cream cone only to have that precious scoop of chocolate fall right to the floor.

So thank goodness for what we *can* finish. That used-up tube of toothpaste, for instance, can become a treasure. Before you pitch it into the trash, give yourself credit for finishing something. Making the bed, checking off an item from your to-do list — value all your completions today.

Unless you seize these moment of triumph, you can miss so much satisfaction. Before you rush on to your next chore, please take a moment to acknowledge that you just kicked in a goal. Hear the cheering crowds and watch your efforts light up the scoreboard.

Whether you praise the good job you've done or you search for lessons to apply in future, even if you simply say "Good riddance," every ending is potentially a sacrament.

You are hereby authorized to celebrate the rites.

365. Traveling Song

Let's put on the traveling music.
It's my time to go again.
That relentlessly restless soul of mine
has sent me moving on.

Although I'll miss forever
the friendship we had here,
the yearning of my soul to grow
outweighs the loss, the fear.

Please, don't think that I'm ungrateful
or worry that I won't return.
I'll be listening for your story
and, daily, cheer you on.

Then, once we have our reunion
It will be as if we'd just said,
"Excuse me,"
disappeared for two minutes
and raced right back, renewed.

Meanwhile, accept this music
with its sacred power to heal.
Under this song's rhythms and silences
hear the love in my farewell.

Acknowledgments and Blibliography

Before the Internet age, it didn't make sense to combine acknowledgments with bibliography, but these days you (or your librarian) can easily google your way to any book. Rather than supplying the standard details about publishers and so forth, I'll refer to authors, titles and websites as applicable, and then use the extra space to add juicy details about acknowledgment. Sometimes I'll simply cite people instead.

As I give credit where credit is due, perhaps you will make a connection with one of my favorite resources. When you read, if any of the following people should light up for you inside, seek away! I can promise you this: If you get to know any one of these spiritual luminaries, you are fortunate indeed.

Bill Bauman, Ph.D., taught me to stop begging God and start co-creating. His influence is the strongest of anyone's for helping me to write this book, and I thank him particularly for the sections about "How Big," "Attributes," "Trinity" and "Four Worlds of Healing." Meet the personification of *Oz Power* at www.billbauman.net.

Teaching of the Inner Christ (TIC), an organization devoted to interdenominational spiritual experience, has been a huge resource for me, including this book's sections on "Thought Form Alert," "Protect Yourself from Bullies," "Speaking of Balance" and "Bring on the Violet Flame." Learn more from AlixSandra Parness, DD at www.innerfocus.org and the TIC website, www.teachingoftheinnerchrist.com.

For 16 years, I taught for Maharishi Mahesh Yogi, Mr. "Gradual Click." His teachings have greatly influenced all I have done since, including this book.

More gratitude goes to Mary McColl Mock, both her talent and her example, including "Thank That Third Teacher" and those pennies I wear in my shoes.

Despite being willing to be polite to God, I haven't always been thoughtful about how I treated mere people. Thanks for reminding me, Winn Claybaugh, with *Be Nice (Or Else!)*— in my book, your influence shows in "Just Be Nice" and "Volunteer Work." See more at www.BeNiceOrElse.com.

The concepts presented in "Elusive Genius" and "Why Bad Families Happen to Good People" came via *The Soul's Code* by the brilliant James Hillman.

Without Shakti Gawain's teachings about *Creative Visualization* and *Living in the Light*, I couldn't have written the section on "Your Power to Manifest." Find Shakti's books, classic and recent, at www.shaktigawain.com.

Thanks, Sri Harrison Snow, for teaching me about Comfort, Learning and Panic Zones. (His website is www.teambuildingassociates.com.)

British healer Mhairi Kent introduced me to techniques that I adapted for "Beats Gardol" and "Colorful Resolutions." Learn more at www.hartlands.co.uk.

Emmet Fox wrote the daybook I love most, *Around the Year with Emmet Fox.* If he hadn't made writing this sort of thing seem easy, I never would have dared to begin.

Pitch-perfect columnist Marguerite Kelly is another role model for literary tone and spiritual clarity. (She has, incidentally, written my favorite parenting books, such as *The Mother's Almanac.*)

To jump-start my experience of Divine Beings, I have found these books particularly helpful:

- *Goddesses in Everywoman* by Jean Shinoda Bolen. Explore her magnificent body of work at www.JeanBolen.com.
- *Care of the Soul* by Thomas Moore. Meet him via www.careofthesoul.net.
- *Till We Have Faces* and *Surprised by Joy* by C.S. Lewis.
- *The Glass Bead Game:(Magister Ludi)* and *Siddhartha* by Hermann Hesse.

Scriptures of many religious traditions have inspired me, as have hymnals and sacred music. But the ultimate spiritual reference books are the Divine Beings themselves. Remember, *never be afraid to make an ask of yourself!*

Friends, students and workshop sponsors, you know who you are and how much you have helped me to refine the techniques and words in this book. Space doesn't permit me to name all of you, but here are some especially honorable mentions:

- "Inner Feng Shui" was written for traffic-stoppingly lovely Molly Blayney.
- J.P. Fernow's visit in Tokyo inspired " Friendship Song."
- "Who Is This Child of Wonder?" arrived for Esmeralda Corbett.
- My wonderful volunteer Gail Glassmoyer brought out "Co-Create or Pray?"
- For the handy technique in "Family Prayer," credit goes to Chrissie Blaze of www.chrissieblaze.com.
- Lisa Paradis inspired me with her Wishing Box.
- Dr. Gary Kaplan once prescribed the technique I adapted as "Divine Temper Tantrum."
- My talented friends Marilyn Cooley and David Ginder have fine-tuned my ears.
- Susan Kingsley-Rowe connected me to my best past and my sweetest future.

Finally, gratitude goes to my family, especially my two favorite people on earth: My husband, Mitch Weber, who has taught me more about love than anyone, and my son, Matt "Webster," now 14 and smartening me up on a daily basis.

How to Order Rose's Books

It's easy to order these life-changing books.
Within the U.S., call tollfree: 800-345-6665.
Online, secure ordering is available, including international orders.
Just click on www.Rose-Rosetree.com.

- **Let Today Be a Holiday** $18.95

- **Aura Reading Through All Your Senses** $14.95

- **The Power of Face Reading** $18.95

- **Wrinkles Are God's Makeup** $19.95

- **Empowered by Empathy** $18.95

- **The Roar of the Huntids (Novel for empaths)** $22.95

- **Thrill Your Soul (Video)** $24.95

Note: Prices listed here are subject to change without notice.

Also Available Now

Rose Rosetree's monthly E-zine (Internet magazine) gives you face readings and aura readings of people in the news. It's fun and it's free. To subscribe, sign on at www.rose-rosetree.com. And click onto co-createwithGod.com for a brand new website.

You can work directly with America's leading expert at deeper perception. Choose from telephone sessions of aura transformation and face readings. Find details at www.rose-rosetree.com or send a stamped self-addressed envelope to WIW, 116 Hillsdale Dr., Sterling, VA 20164.

If you like what you've found here, please tell your friends.
Help Rose to reach kindred spirits like you
and teach all those who would enjoy what she has to teach.

Three Wishes

What are three ways that you wish this book could help you?

Write and date your wishes below.

Note, too, when those wishes come true.